Anatomy
of an
Execution

Todd C. Peppers and
Laura Trevvett Anderson

ANATOMY
OF AN
EXECUTION

The Life and Death of
Douglas Christopher Thomas

NORTHEASTERN UNIVERSITY PRESS | Boston
Published by University Press of New England
Hanover and London

Northeastern University Press
Published by University Press of New England
One Court Street, Lebanon NH 03766
www.upne.com
© 2009 by Northeastern University Press
Printed in the United States of America
5 4 3 2 1

Library of Congress Cataloging-in-Publication Data
Peppers, Todd C.
Anatomy of an execution: the life and death of Douglas Christopher
Thomas / Todd C. Peppers and Laura Trevvett Anderson
    p. cm.
Includes bibliographical references and index.
ISBN 978-1-55553-713-5 (cloth: alk. paper)
1. Thomas, Douglas Christopher, 1973–2000. 2. Death row inmates —
Virginia — Biography. 3. Juvenile homicide — Virginia. 4. Capital
punishment — Virginia. I. Anderson, Laura Trevvett. II. Title.
HV8701.T56P47   2009
364.66092 — dc22   2009026950
[B]

University Press of New England is a member of the
Green Press Initiative. The paper used in this book meets
their minimum requirement for recycled paper.

To my children, Gabrielle Sofia and Samuel Joseph — may you someday live in a country that has recognized the folly of the death penalty.

TODD C. PEPPERS

This book, nine long years in the making, is dedicated to my husband Ross, who has stood beside me throughout; to Chris, for teaching me about life and love; and to Todd, for being there to tell this story.

LAURA TREVVETT ANDERSON

Contents

Foreword

In November 1991, I was the executive director of the Virginia Coalition on Jails and Prisons, a project I had founded in January 1983. The coalition provided pro bono legal assistance for the defense in capital cases from pretrial through clemency or execution. I also was the coalition's mitigation specialist.

Most experts agree that in a capital trial, the mitigation specialist is the first person the defendant's lawyer brings onto the defense team. The mitigation specialist interviews family, friends, neighbors, teachers, coaches, clergy, counselors, doctors, and others who have knowledge of the defendant. We dig up every record ever made on the defendant and his parents, siblings, and sometimes grandparents, including medical, psychological, institutional, educational, employment, social services, police, court, and military. We look for evidence of mental illness, retardation or low I.Q., learning disabilities, brain damage, neurological problems, physical or psychological abuse, and a wide range of other problems in the defendant's life. We are not looking for excuses but for anything in the life history that might explain the defendant or take the death penalty out of the legal equation. We conduct hundreds of hours of interviews, and gather and assess the life records; if necessary, we then motion the court to appoint an expert, such as a neuropsychologist, to explain to the jury how the defendant's brain damage affects his judgment. Mitigation must be integrated into the entire trial, so the mitigation specialist works closely with the defense lawyers from voir dire through the entire trial.

Such a trial is a defendant's right according to our Constitution. I also see it as a jury's right. How can we ask twelve of our neighbors to decide whether a human being should live or die, if the only thing they know about him is his crime? But that is exactly what we demanded of Chris Thomas's jury.

Chris's arrival on death row was sad, frustrating, and maddening. Sad, because I was raising my second son, who was five months older than Chris. Frustrating, because Chris's original appointed lawyer had refused the offer of free assistance from the Virginia Coalition on Jails and Prisons. Maddening, because I knew the procedures and rules in Virginia meant that once a defendant was sent to death row his chances of not being executed were all but nil.

My son, Robert, and his best friend, Hashim (who spent more time at my house than he did his own) were very intelligent, loving, and good kids. Yet they bungled into messes on a routine basis. Even actions they undertook with the best of intentions would nearly give me a heart attack. They were both intent on not getting into or allowing their friends to get into drugs; after becoming aware of a drug dealer hanging around their school, they took it upon themselves to confront and threaten him. No matter how many times I explained consequences to them, they seemed incapable of thinking beyond the immediate moment. I did my best to balance giving them enough freedom to learn how to deal with the world and enough supervision to keep them out of serious trouble. Part of that supervision was spending a great deal of time listening to and talking to them. There were times when I verbally threw up my hands, asking, "What were you thinking?" But I knew from my training as a mitigation specialist that what develops last in the human brain is judgment, and the teenage brain has not yet fully developed.

Had Chris's trial lawyers accepted the assistance of the Virginia Coalition, the lag in brain development is just one of the things I would have had presented to the jury. The red flags that he needed help — which he constantly threw up after his uncle's and grandparents' deaths and which were ignored by his family — were others.

By the time Chris came to death row, the coalition had assisted in more than two hundred capital trials. Only two of those defendants had received the death penalty. But every year a number of lawyers with capital defendants refused our assistance, and Virginia's death row continued to fill and men continued to be executed. I know I am a very good mitigation specialist, but I also know these results were not simply because I was good. What they proved to me was that Virginia juries were not so gung ho to execute people as they were to follow the law. They were not simply willing to consider evidence that supported a life sentence; they expected such evidence. When none came, or when "evidence" was really lame, they assumed there was none. The response of many jurors when they heard about evidence of compelling mitigation produced at habeas or clemency was anger at the trial lawyers, who they felt had forced them to make a terrible decision without all the information they deserved to have.

Sometimes those jurors tried to help the defendant at habeas or clemency, but by the time a defendant came to death row in Virginia the legal avenues were closed—and unless that defendant had strong evidence of innocence, so were the political avenues. In Virginia, procedure was elevated over substance. A combination of procedural rules prevented habeas courts from considering any evidence that was not presented at trial and any errors that were not rigorously preserved and appealed to the Virginia Supreme Court. The most draconian of these rules was the "21 Day Rule," which prevented any evidence, even concrete evidence of innocence, from being considered more than twenty-one days after the sentencing.

Nonetheless, the coalition and lawyers kept trying, and in Chris's case I held out the hope that if all else failed, surely whatever governor was in office when Chris faced execution would not allow a child to be killed by the state on his or her watch. I was grateful and relieved when Laura Anderson called. I knew from our first conversation that this boy had an advocate who would go the distance for him, including talking to the press and pleading with a governor. Governors and the press expected family members to plead for clemency. They did not expect teachers to come forward, and I was sure Laura would make them look at Chris and question whether we really were a people who killed our own children.

I was wrong. Those in authority only saw Chris's crime. No one looked at Chris. And if the question about us was asked, the answer they gave was the exact opposite of the one I would have believed. They decided Chris was no more than his crime, and we were a people who killed our own children.

Through my work with and for Chris, I had come to know and care about him. I'd watched him grow and mature into a young man who grieved for the Wisemans and their family and would have done anything to take back the harm he had caused. When Chris committed what I believe was one murder, he simply did not have the ability to imagine the Wisemans' mortality, his own mortality, or the pain he would cause those who loved the Wisemans and Chris. He truly was still a child.

We were not children when Chris was put on death row and eventually executed, yet we lacked the imagination to see him as a child and to believe in the potential of any child, as Justice Anthony Kennedy wrote in *Roper v. Simmons*, "to attain a mature understanding of his own humanity." This book is important because it *does* look at Chris, and it asks us to answer the question about killing our children.

Virginia also executed a retarded man who had been diagnosed by the state with paranoid schizophrenia. A reporter who had not decided where he stood on the death penalty told me that the day after this execution, he went canoeing in Dismal Swamp, something he did regularly. As he rounded a curve, he saw that someone had hacked down a huge tree that must have been hundreds of years old. Shocked, he got out and sat beside the tree, running his fingers over the raw circles of time it had endured. He realized that this tree was unique. No other tree in the swamp or anywhere was like this one, and he thought about the man we had just executed and began to cry. When he got back to Richmond he called to tell me about his trip and coming to understand my passion for stopping the death penalty. Each of these people is unique, he said, and we simply erase them.

Each is unique. Each is part of the creation of life. One day the United States will join most of the rest of the world and rid itself of the death penalty. When we do, a new generation will ask why we were a people who killed our own and who were the people we killed. This is not an anti–death penalty book, but a book that examines one case and lets us know one person — one boy — we executed. It will help answer those questions and keep that generation and those to follow from repeating what we have done.

MARIE DEANS
Charlottesville, Virginia
August 2009

Preface

On a chilly afternoon on Saturday, January 15, 2000, Laura Anderson stood with a group of mourners in the Harmony Grove Baptist Church Cemetery in Topping, Virginia. She felt completely numb — not from the wind that blew across the cemetery, but from the events that had consumed her over the last five days. On January 10, 2000, Laura had gently kissed the cheek of a young man named Douglas Christopher Thomas and then watched as her former high school student was quickly and efficiently executed in the death house at the Greensville Correctional Center in Jarratt, Virginia. Less than a week later, Laura presided over Chris's funeral and now mentally prepared herself for the final task of the graveside service.

As the mourners joined hands, circled the casket, and sang "Amazing Grace," Laura was flooded with memories of the last nine years. Although she did not know it at the time, her journey to this small graveyard had begun in 1989, when she worked as a special education teacher at Clover Hill High School in Richmond, Virginia. In January of that year, Laura met the young, introverted Chris Thomas. Chris was a fifteen-year-old whose life had been in a tailspin since the deaths of his beloved grandparents in 1985. Chris had lived with his maternal grandparents since the age of two, growing up in rural Middlesex County, Virginia. In the five years since his grandparents' deaths, Chris had begun a slow descent into alcohol and drug abuse as well as petty crime and truancy.

Laura's daily contact with Chris ended in January 1990, when Chris announced his fateful decision to leave Clover Hill High School and return to live with relatives in Middlesex County. Although Laura attempted to stay in touch with her former student, their lives momentarily separated until the evening of November 10, 1990, when Laura learned that Chris had been arrested and charged with the murders of his girlfriend's parents. For the next nine years, Laura's and Chris's lives became intertwined as Laura became his friend and struggled to understand the enormity of Chris's crimes. Ultimately, Laura would serve as his spiritual advisor during his final days in the Commonwealth of Virginia's death house. The frantic efforts of Laura, a team of appellate lawyers, and members of Chris's immediate family to save his life had fallen short; as Laura stood at the gravesite her grief was magnified by anger, exhaustion, and a nagging sense of failure.

I did not know Chris Thomas. I first met Laura Anderson in the spring of 2003, when she spoke to the students enrolled in a death penalty seminar I was teaching at Roanoke College. I found myself moved by the passion and conviction that Laura invested in her one-woman crusade against the death penalty, and we became friends and, subsequently, coauthors. While Laura and I come from different educational and professional backgrounds, and I have not had the horrific experience of witnessing an execution, we both share the conviction that any benefit gained from the execution of even the most hardened criminal is far outweighed by its moral, social, religious, and economic costs. And we both share the belief that Chris's death can bring a fresh perspective to a debate filled with misinformation and political rhetoric.

This book is first and foremost the story of the life and death of Chris Thomas, a young man whose life — to paraphrase Sister Helen Prejean — was worth much more than his worst act, and of Laura Anderson, a former high school teacher who found herself unwillingly thrust into the grimmest corners of our criminal justice system. This book, however, also contains a critical examination of the larger issues that underlie the modern death penalty in America. We utilize Chris's story as a case study by which to highlight and explore such timely social and political questions as the execution of minors, the quality of legal defense provided by court-appointed counsel, the trial and appeals process of capital cases, the prison conditions on death row, the methods of execution, and the role of spiritual advisors.

Although the United States Supreme Court recently decided that the Eighth Amendment of the Constitution prohibits the execution of offenders who committed their crimes as minors,[1] the Supreme Court was sharply divided over the issue. In the last several years alone, the Supreme Court has moved back and forth on the death penalty: for example, holding that lethal injection for those convicted of capital murder does not violate the Eighth Amendment prohibition against cruel and unusual punishment,[2] but that the Bill of Rights forbids the execution of those who rape (but do not kill) children.[3] Moreover, public support for the death penalty — which had been slowly eroding in the last decade — appears to be inching upward again.

Given the changing composition of the Court, the ephemeral nature of legal precedent, and the evolving standards of decency of our society, the subject of the death penalty will continue to be debated by the federal judiciary, politicians, and the American public.

In his final conversation with Laura, Chris expressed the hope that his tragic story could illuminate and bring perspective to the debate over the modern death penalty in America as well as warn juveniles against the folly of violence. Chris repeated that hope in a 1999 interview with an Amnesty International reporter; when asked how he might give back to society if his death sentence was commuted, Chris stated:

> Maybe a chance to just tell someone else who has maybe struggled or is struggling with the same decisions I had . . . Maybe if they hear my story it may persuade them not to make that decision. Even . . . with a life sentence, a life behind bars, you can still make a positive difference. . . . Just trying to help other kids not make the same mistake. Someone who has been there and walked that walk. If I can help one person, then I have accomplished a goal.

Chris didn't get a chance to tell his story, but we will tell it for him. Whether you, the reader, are for or against the death penalty, we hope that this book will cause you to reflect carefully on our nation's long practice of executing individuals. Even if the constitutional ban against the execution of minors remains in place, Chris's story warrants our attention: it raises additional, important questions about how smoothly, justly, and accurately the "machinery of death" functions. If Chris's story can deepen the public debate over the death penalty, or deter a single teenager from making a terrible life choice, then Chris's death will not have been in vain.

TODD C. PEPPERS
Salem, Virginia
August 2009

Acknowledgments

In the five years that it took to research and write this book, Laura and I have been the grateful beneficiaries of assistance from many individuals. At the top of that list must come Beth See, a Roanoke College student who spent four years working as our research assistant. Over the course of her college career, Beth helped find, copy, catalogue, review, and analyze thousands of documents; in addition, she interviewed witnesses, conducted factual and legal research, proofread endless drafts of the manuscript, and calmly fielded an endless stream of seemingly random research questions. We are so thankful for the invaluable work of this outstanding young woman. Additional research assistance was provided by a number of former and current students, including Bridget Tainer-Parkins, Nerissa Rouzer, Sarah Seufer, and Andrew Staub.

Second on our "thank-you list" is Marie Deans. A native of South Carolina, Marie became involved in death penalty work after the murder of her mother-in-law by an escaped convict. Many would have reacted to such a brutal crime by becoming supporters of the death penalty, but Marie responded by forming a murder victims' reconciliation group. When she moved to Virginia in early 1983, Marie founded a nonprofit organization— the Virginia Coalition on Jails and Prisons—dedicated to securing the rights of death row inmates and attacking their convictions. Specifically, the coalition helped lawyers and inmates with a number of different aspects of capital defense work, including investigations in capital murder cases, the gathering of mitigation evidence for trials and appeals, obtaining appellate lawyers for inmates, and pursuing clemency. Marie, arguably the nation's leading death penalty mitigation specialist, possesses unique and penetrating insights on the death penalty. Her knowledge of the death penalty comes in part from her work in the shadow of death: Marie witnessed thirty-four executions in Virginia and South Carolina.

For decades, Marie was a familiar and comforting presence to the men on Virginia's death row—and a thorn in the side of the Virginia Department of

Corrections, which resisted her public calls for prison reform. It was on death row that Marie first met Chris Thomas, when in June 1993 she travelled to the Mecklenburg Correctional Center to interview Chris and begin gathering mitigation evidence for his appeals. During the next two years, Marie spent many hours in a small, cramped conference room with Chris, getting to know the young man and carefully collecting information that might help save his life. Additionally, Marie and her small team of investigators descended on Middlesex County and conducted exhaustive interviews of Chris Thomas's friends, family members, former teachers, and neighbors.

The data gathered by Marie—including typed interview notes, Chris's school records, psychological examinations, juvenile court records, prison documents, and the hundreds of letters sent to Chris by Jessica Wiseman—were carefully organized into an extensive mitigation report and preserved by the attorneys at the Virginia Capital Representation Resource Center in Charlottesville, Virginia. Thanks to the permission of Marie Deans and Margaret Thomas, Chris Thomas's mother, we were able to obtain and review the extensive information contained in Marie's mitigation files. Moreover, Marie read multiple drafts of the book manuscript and patiently spent hours explaining to us the hidden world of death row and the subtle nuances of death penalty litigation. Marie is an unsung hero in the battle to bring an end to the death penalty in America, and we could not have asked for a better guide and teacher. She is a dear friend, and to her we owe a debt of gratitude.

As Laura and I researched the history of Virginia and the death penalty, we relied heavily on the staff of the Fintel Library at Roanoke College. We owe a special thanks to Roanoke College reference librarian Rebecca Heller and interlibrary loan coordinator Jeffrey Martin. All matter of clerical requests large and small were efficiently fielded by Roanoke College Department of Public Affairs administrative assistant Judi Pinckney, who also graciously volunteered to proof multiple iterations of this manuscript. Additional legal questions were expertly answered by former federal and state prosecutor Morgan Scott, now a teaching associate at Roanoke College and a valued colleague and friend. Needed research funds were provided through grants from the Faculty Development Committee at Roanoke College and the Lucas Hathaway Charitable Trust; the last burst of work on this project was facilitated by a one-semester sabbatical granted by the college. After it appeared that we had exhausted our research funds, Roanoke College benefactors Robert and Christine Staub came riding to our rescue with two generous annual fund gifts that allowed us to travel back to Middlesex County and complete our data collection.

Laura and I thank all the people who shared their memories of Douglas Christopher Thomas and his death penalty case with us, including Barbara Ann Williams, Wanda Martin, Alan W. Clarke, Rob Lee, Benton Pollok, Damian Horne, Glenda Corbin Thomas Kennedy, Marie Deans, and Robert Deans. Special thanks go to Margaret Thomas, who allowed us access to Chris's personal pictures, records, and letters. Our understanding of the operations of Virginia's death row in the 1990s was enriched by the contributions of former death row inmate Joseph Giarratano, and we are grateful for his help. Finally, we thank Sister Helen Prejean for her repeated encouragement to write Chris's story.

I must also thank my family for their love and patience. Simply put, I could not have been part of this fascinating project without the support of my wife, Michele, who read endless versions of the manuscript, served as an invaluable sounding board, offered encouragement when my spirits and energy lagged, and cheerfully assumed more of her fair share of parenting responsibilities when I asked to stay "just one more hour" at the office. As for my children, Gabby and Sam, I shall try to follow their sage advice, namely, "finish writing your book and come play!" The extent of my children's angst about Daddy's preoccupation with this project was revealed in December 2008, when Sam announced that he hoped Santa would bring me a present that would magically complete this book! I did not know whether to laugh or cry. I also thank my parents for all the weekends that they babysat the grandkids so their son could write, and my sister, who sacrificed several days of "beach time" at the Outer Banks of North Carolina in order to read my book manuscript.

Finally, I thank my friend and coauthor, Laura Anderson, for generously asking me to join her on this fascinating project and for trusting me to tell Chris's story, and the editors and staff members at University Press of New England, who gave us the opportunity to tell this story. Special thanks go to Richard Pult and Ann Brash.

The Major Figures

The Thomas and Marshall Family

Douglas Christopher Thomas	*Defendant*
Margaret Marshall Thomas	*Mother*
Robert Christopher Thomas	*Father*
Virginia Elizabeth Marshall	*Grandmother*
Herbert Benjamin Marshall, Sr.	*Grandfather*
Barbara Ann Childress Williams	*Aunt*
Winfrey Childress	*Uncle*
Brenda Marshall	*Aunt*
Herbert Marshall, Jr.	*Uncle*
Lainie Marie Creech	*Cousin*
Glenda Corbin Thomas	*Wife*

The Wiseman Family

Jessica Lynn Wiseman	*Defendant*
Kathy J. Thomas Wiseman	*Mother*
James Baxter Wiseman II	*Father*
Arvazine Thomas	*Grandmother*
Denby Thomas	*Grandfather*
Edmonia Eastman	*Great-grandmother*
Ernest Eastman	*Great-grandfather*

Legal Figures

James H. Ward, Jr.	*Middlesex Commonwealth Attorney*
Judge John M. Folkes	*Ninth Circuit Court Judge*
Roger G. Hopper	*Jessica's attorney*
Benton H. Pollok	*First attorney assigned to Chris*
Dawne I. Alexander	*Pollok's first trial co-counsel*
Damian T. Horne	*Pollok's second trial co-counsel*
Sydney K. L. West	*Horne's trial co-counsel*

James C. Breeden   *Chris's state habeas attorney*
Alan W. Clarke   *Chris's state habeas attorney*
Lisa Palmer O'Donnell   *Chris's federal habeas attorney*
Lawrence Hunter Woodward, Jr.   *Chris's federal habeas attorney*
Robert Lee   *Capital Representation Resource Center*
Marie Deans   *Mitigation specialist*
Laura Anderson   *Spiritual advisor*

Anatomy
of an
Execution

1

The Seeds Are Sown

Abandonment, which caused an ever growing need to be in an intensely close relationship, has been the primary theme in Chris Thomas' short life.

MARIE DEANS

In order to trace the path of Chris Thomas's journey to the cold steel gurney that sits in Virginia's death chamber, we must first travel to the rural back roads of Chris's boyhood home outside the small town of Saluda, Virginia. After exploring the rivers and woods of Chris's youth, we shall turn our attention northward to Chesterfield County, Virginia — where a grieving twelve-year-old, effectively orphaned after a trio of sudden deaths, found himself living with a mother who he believed neither loved nor wanted him. We start with Chris's childhood and adolescence because it is there that we find the early social, cultural, and economic forces that would transform a plump and giggly little boy into an angry, confused seventeen-year-old who was willing to kill to prevent two adults from denying him access to the love of his life — a fourteen-year-old girl named Jessica Lynn Wiseman.

Sociologists and criminologists who study the causes of juvenile delinquency have generated a host of different theories to explain why adolescents

FIGURE 1. *Undated elementary school photograph of Chris Thomas. Photograph courtesy of the Thomas family.*

commit crimes. Criminologists Siegel, Welsh, and Senna write that there are three fundamental theoretical approaches to the study of juvenile delinquency: the individual, sociological and development views of delinquency.[1] The *individual* view of delinquency argues that the explanation for criminal behavior is internal, not external to the individual. Two competing individual-view theories are rational choice theory and trait theory, both of which focus on the choices individuals make. Rational choice theory argues that juvenile offenders "choose to engage in antisocial activity because they believe that their actions will be beneficial and profitable . . . [and] their delinquent acts are motivated by the reasoned belief that crime can be a relatively risk-free way to better their personal situation."[2] In sum, juvenile defendants engage in a rational, cost-benefit analysis of whether the risks of getting caught and punished outweigh the rewards attendant with the spoils of their crimes. Alternatively, trait theory points out that some criminal activity is too impulsive, self-destructive, and illogical to be explained as rational choice. Instead, trait theory argues that some physical or psychological flaw unique to the individual explains deviant behavior.[3]

The second general theoretic framework, the *sociological*, suggests that delinquent behavior is best explained by the socioeconomic environment in which children are raised. Consider the young child growing up in the inner city, deprived of a stable family environment and positive adult role models, exposed to a daily diet of drugs and violence, denied access to proper medical care, good nutrition, or a functioning educational system, and unlikely to find employment opportunities. Is it any surprise that children raised in this environment will turn to criminal activity more often than their more affluent, well-educated counterparts?

In accordance with this framework, criminologists and sociologists have proposed a host of different theories that look to socioeconomic and cultural factors to explain juvenile delinquency. Siegel, Welsh, and Senna write that these theories can be broadly categorized as: (1) social structure theories (juvenile delinquency is a product of an adolescent's place in our socioeconomic hierarchy, including the adolescent's struggle to pursue material goals and/or conform to values common to all of society); (2) social process theories (delinquency is a function of an inadequate or incomplete socialization process); (3) social reaction theories (children labeled as delinquents are stigmatized by label and act accordingly); and (4) social conflict theories (social and political elites use the legal system to maintain control and those who struggle against such laws are deemed criminals).[4]

The third major theoretical framework, the *developmental*, is a blend of the aforementioned internal and external factors. Siegel, Welsh, and Senna write that development theory is divided into two different subtheories or categories. First, the "life course theory" argues that "delinquent behavior is a dynamic process, influenced by individual characteristics as well as social experiences, and that the factors that cause anti-social behavior change dramatically over a person's life span." Second, a variant of that theory argues that some people have a trait for criminal behavior that remains constant over time, while what changes is the social environment and/or opportunity for the expression of that trait.[5]

The authors of this book believe that social process theory provides the best explanation as to the causal forces that shaped Chris's behavior. As we explore Chris's childhood, keep in mind the basic axioms that undergird this theory. First, family is one of the most important factors to a normal socialization process, and there is a reduced likelihood of delinquent behavior if a child is raised in a stable, supportive family environment that fosters self-esteem, security, and healthy independence.[6] Second, other important causal factors for positive socialization include a strong school environment in which a student is helped to achieve his or her potential, a peer group that promotes (rather than undermines) the adoption of good values, and exposure to religious beliefs and the moral principles they espouse.[7]

Chris was born at Chippenham Hospital in Chesterfield County, Virginia, on May 29, 1973, at seven o'clock in the morning. His biological parents were Margaret Lois Marshall Thomas and Robert Christopher Thomas; on his birth certificate, however, his parents were listed as Herbert Benjamin Marshall and Virginia Elizabeth Marshall—Margaret Thomas's parents. Margaret Thomas later explained that she listed her parents' names in hopes of making Chris eligible to receive Social Security benefits through his grandfather.[8]

Bobby and Margaret met in the spring of 1972 at Donk's, a shabby pool hall in Mathews County, Virginia. At the time of their meeting, Margaret was twenty-one, while Bobby was twenty-three and working for a construction contractor as a rigger. Margaret was undeterred by the rumors that the young man she met had a serious criminal record, and they were soon married in the Mathews Baptist Church, directly across the street from the pool hall in which they first met. The marriage was rocky from the start, and economic

FIGURE 2.
Undated photograph of Virginia Elizabeth Marshall, grandmother of Chris Thomas. Photograph courtesy of the Thomas family.

pressures forced the couple to live in a modest trailer on land owned by, and located adjacent to, the home of Margaret's parents. Herbert and Virginia Marshall had lived in the small community of Christchurch, Virginia, all their lives, raising a family of three children on Herbert's modest salary as a worker for the Virginia Department of Transportation. Herbert and Virginia purchased the trailer for Margaret and her new husband, hoping that it would help them start a new life together.

In divorce papers filed before Chris's birth, Margaret stated that shortly after their marriage her husband "became increasing harsh, cruel and unkind" and had "cursed and abused her." At some point Bobby tried to prevent Margaret from seeing her parents, which resulted in an armed confrontation between Bobby and Herbert Marshall, Sr.. Relatives believed that Herbert would have killed Bobby if the young man had not backed down, and the dispute furthered the split in Bobby and Margaret's marriage. Bobby and Margaret separated for several weeks in November 1972, but briefly reconciled after Bobby promised to treat his pregnant wife better.

Despite the reconciliation, tensions in the marriage continued to grow and Bobby allegedly became physically and verbally abusive—even telling Margaret's parents at one point that she was "not worth a damn." On February 6, 1973, the abuse grew too much for Margaret to bear, and she fled from the trailer to the safety of her parents' home. Margaret claimed that the

FIGURE 3.
Undated photograph of Chris Thomas with his grandfather, Herbert Benjamin Marshall, Sr. Photograph courtesy of the Thomas family.

harassment and abuse by Bobby continued during the separation, including Bobby's successful efforts to get his wife fired from her job at Rich's Market, a local grocery store. Bobby did not contest the divorce, and the couple was officially divorced in February 1974. Chris never received any financial support from his father, and in fact, would not meet his father until shortly before Chris's first execution date in June 1999.

After Chris's birth in May 1973, Margaret and Chris continued to live with Herbert and Virginia Marshall in their two-story, white frame house on a small acreage in Middlesex County, Virginia. The county was established by English settlers in 1673 and lies at the tip of eastern Virginia's middle peninsula. The county's northern border is formed by the waters of the wide Rappahannock River, while the Chesapeake Bay serves as the county's eastern border. To the south and west of Middlesex County lie the meandering Piankatank River and Dragon Run Swamp. All in all, the county boasts more than two hundred miles of shoreline dotted with marinas and villages; at one time countless watermen plied the waters for the bountiful oysters and crabs that lay where the Rappahannock River and the Chesapeake Bay met. While disease and overharvesting led to a dramatic decline in the number of commercial oyster-shucking houses that once employed Middlesex County residents, each year the small town of Urbanna still proudly holds its annual Oyster Festival.

For approximately the first two years of Chris's life, Margaret worked to earn a degree at Rappahannock Community College and subsequently took a position as a deputy sheriff at the Middlesex County Jail in nearby Saluda, Virginia (the same facility that would someday hold her son). At the jail, Margaret fell in love with a female inmate. Upon the inmate's release Margaret announced that she was moving to Richmond, Virginia, to be with her girlfriend. According to family members, Herbert and Virginia Marshall refused to let Chris move to Richmond—resulting in Margaret leaving without him. Margaret would eventually find work as a correctional officer at the State Penitentiary in Richmond, then the site of both death row and the electric chair.

Margaret's departure from Saluda led to her parents legally adopting Chris. At first Margaret only returned home during holidays, but family members recall that in later years she made monthly visits to see her parents and Chris. Despite giving up her parental rights, there is evidence that Margaret wanted to have a formal role in raising her son. In the consent form to Chris's adoption, Margaret wrote in the following language: "Also, I would like to know by signing this paper will Douglas C. Thomas at [my parents'] death come back to me is why I gave consent for them to have custody of my son is because [his grandfather] wanted to put him on his social security & his insurance papers." Years later, Margaret's words would be scrutinized by the Virginia Supreme Court as it deliberated whether Chris Thomas deserved a new trial.

By all accounts, Chris led a happy childhood. He once commented to his appellate lawyers that his first memory was of his grandparents. To the outside world, Chris seemed untroubled by the fact that his mother was, at best, an infrequent visitor, and he would later remark that it never occurred to him to ask his grandparents why he was not living with her. His teachers at Rappahannock Central Elementary School stated that Chris was an average student; a quiet, friendly boy whose giggling sometimes got in the way of his work, and they were struck by the love and attention given to Chris by his grandparents. Years later the teachers recalled that his grandparents attended all of Chris's after-school activities, and they also remembered receiving handwritten thank-you notes from Chris's grandmother at the end of the school year.

Chris was drawn to the woods, streams, and rivers that made up Middlesex County. His free time was spent exploring his surroundings, first on a bike, and later on a moped. Chris's out-of-school activities included hunting and fishing with his grandfather, Cub Scouts, and Little League baseball. Like many who lived in the county, Chris became an avid hunter and fisherman at a young age. By the age of six he proudly reported to his mother that he had not only killed his first wild turkey, but—with some hesitation—assisted his grandmother in cleaning and cooking the bird for a celebratory dinner.

The attention that Chris received from his grandparents was supplemented by weekend visits by his uncle and aunt, Winfrey and Barbara Ann Childress. Chris considered Uncle Winfrey, who played baseball with him and took him to the local stock car races, to be a "second father." A petite, attractive woman with a soft southern accent and an innate air of graciousness, Barbara Ann—the older sister of Margaret Thomas—also formed a strong bond with the blue-eyed, sandy-haired boy that she nicknamed "D.C." In return, Chris affectionately called her "Cox" (a nickname from her childhood). Looking back, Chris himself described his childhood as one of love and security with family members who spoiled him. When asked during a death row interview to share a specific childhood memory of Christmas, Chris instead spoke generally of the love and warmth he felt: "[I remember] a sense of family. You have to understand that everyone came to my grandparents' house. I can still remember everyone sitting around eating dinner, laughing, [and then] opening presents. Just everyone being there. Just a sense of family, a sense of love."

In looking over interviews of family members conducted by Chris's appellate lawyers, however, one finds tensions running under this idyllic image. Six-year-old Chris was afraid of the dark, and he would not venture outside at night unless accompanied by an adult. A fear of separation often led to Chris sleeping with his grandmother. Years later Chris recalled that he tried sleeping in his own room, but the old home would start to creak and settle, strange shadows would appear outside his window, and "I'd hardly get the covers up before I'd be heading for her [his grandmother's] room."[9] When visits with friends or relatives ended, Chris often sobbed uncontrollably.

While to the outside world Chris appeared indifferent to his living arrangement, he later confessed to his lawyers and a probation officer that he thought that his mother couldn't afford to raise him and didn't want him. In fact, Margaret herself wondered if her son resented her decision to give him up for adoption. In a psychological evaluation prepared after Chris's conviction, a psychologist concluded that Chris's behavior was suggestive of a "separation anxiety possibly linked to abandonment by his mother as a toddler."

Moreover, at least one family observer thought that Margaret was jealous of the attention that her parents lavished on Chris.

Chris was a rambunctious, sometimes hyperactive young boy from whom neighbors hid their candy out of fear that it would send Chris into greater waves of animation. And he had a stubborn streak. "Chris always seemed to be a happy little fella," recalls his aunt, "but when it came to discipline, that was another story. He always wanted his own way." Chris often pushed his grandfather into threatening to use a belt on him, and on at least three occasions Chris's misbehavior resulted in whippings that drew blood. Chris remembered that additional punishment was meted out by his Uncle Herbert. "Chris said Herbert came to his grandparent's house nearly every day, that Herbert knocked him around, taunted him, and stole his candy. He remembered . . . one time Herbert grabbed him, dragged him down the concrete stairs and bodily threw him on a pile of wood, because Chris said he wasn't going to chop wood."[10] When Chris's grandparents died, Chris recalled that Herbert told him: "You're the reason they died."[11]

Chris's grandfather sometimes drank to excess, which not only introduced stress into the household but also let the young boy push rules and boundaries. A relative recalled that Herbert Marshall, Sr., "loved having a drink," and as a youngster Chris emulated his grandfather by sneaking sips of wine and beer. His grandmother struggled to stop Chris's behavior, eventually giving up and letting an eleven-year-old Chris sit at the table with her and have a "pony" of Miller beer. Chris later reported to a probation officer that "alcohol did play a big part in my life when I was with my grandparents."[12]

In 1985, eleven-year-old Chris's happy and secure world came crashing down around him. In a span of six months, he lost three of the most important people in his life. His Uncle Winfrey was killed in a gruesome workplace accident, crushed to death when a concrete highway embankment fell on him. Years later, Chris keenly recalled jumping on his moped and wildly riding through the back roads of Saluda for hours while crying uncontrollably. Winfrey's death was quickly followed by his grandfather's death from a malignant brain tumor in August 1985 and his grandmother's slow and painful death from breast and colon cancer in December 1985. During the final weeks of his grandmother's life, Chris cooked meals for his grandmother and struggled to keep up with household chores.

Within that six-month span, Chris was effectively orphaned. "Chris couldn't understand why his uncle and grandparents had died," observed

Marie Deans in a mitigation report. "He felt deserted, abandoned and he desperately missed them and his life. For a long time after their deaths he cried often and a lot, especially in bed at night." The crushing grief associated with the deaths of his grandparents remained with Chris for the rest of his life. In an interview given shortly before his death, Chris remarked that "until this day I don't think I have completely gotten over their death. Not a day goes by that I don't think about them."

The shock waves from these three deaths overwhelmed the entire Marshall family; in later years a close relative of Chris's remarked that "nobody really had time to be close to Chris." Chris begged members of his extended family to let him live with them and stay in Middlesex County, but, in the grip of their own grief and loss, they turned down his repeated pleas. Chris decided that he was a child that nobody wanted. His childhood destroyed, Chris prepared for the first time to live with his mother.

In January 1986, Chris Thomas moved to Chesterfield County, just south of Richmond, Virginia. He moved into a small ranch home that included his mother, her lesbian partner Joan,[13] and Joan's teenage son and daughter. While Chris did not initially know of the romantic relationship between his mother and Joan, he immediately resented the intrusion of Joan and her family. He saw them as strangers who thwarted his efforts to bond with his mother. It was especially galling to Chris that his mother, who gave her own son up for adoption, was helping to raise Joan's son and daughter. A psychologist later described Chris during this time as a "needy and clingy" adolescent, a teenager struggling with his unresolved grief who soon became "confused and conflicted by his gradual realization of the nature of his mother's personal life."

While Margaret struggled to become a parent for Chris, her efforts were undercut by her refusal to discuss the true nature of the relationship between herself and her "roommate" Joan. When Chris was thirteen years old, Joan's son told Chris that Margaret was gay. At first, Chris didn't know what the term meant. After the boy explained it to Chris, he confronted his mother — who denied it. A family member recalled that the same boy later showed Chris their mothers in bed together having sex, and later that night Chris was picked up on the side of the road drunk. In fact, it would not be until the sentencing phase of his capital murder trial that Chris would hear his mother state that she was gay. As a result of the deception and confusion in the household, the same psychologist concluded that "Chris came to feel unloved and rejected by his mother despite her efforts to be a parent." Chris announced to a school counselor that his mother and her subsequent partner (Margaret had broken up with Joan) were "stuck together like glue," and he told his friends that his mother did not care about him.

At times, Chris's efforts to become close to his mother took on a frantic air. A former girlfriend recalls that "Chris was obsessed with his mother. He always wanted to be near her. He also wanted to be near her belongings. When some of her things were locked in a cedar chest he'd break into it to get her things. . . . He would always be right up under her." The former girlfriend hypothesized that Chris's behavior stemmed from the fear that his mother would be the next adult to abandon him, but his obsessive behavior often had the contradictory result of pushing his mother away. Moreover, Margaret herself may have been ambivalent about developing a close relationship with her son. "Margaret also reports that she still holds a grudge against her parents for giving Chris more attention and things than they ever gave her," later wrote Chris's appellate lawyers. "The anger may have influenced her reactions to Chris's needs as well. In addition, Margaret had no real knowledge or understanding of Chris or how any adolescent deals with trauma." [14]

Adding to Chris's adjustment was the simple fact that he was no longer the doted-upon child of elderly caregivers. "Chris also had the shock of adjusting to no longer getting anything he wanted," recalled a family friend. "With his grandparents he would puff his cheeks and get red, and he got anything he wanted. He tried tantrums with Margaret . . . but they didn't work. Margaret did not have the money to get Chris what he wanted, such as certain jeans or shoes."

Chris's attitude toward his mother is perhaps best summarized in a "sentence completion exercise" that he took in December 1988, as he underwent a psychological evaluation at his high school. The pain, confusion, and hostility that Chris felt toward her, himself, and his life virtually leaps off the page:

The happiest time:	"is when my mom is not there"
I want to know:	"how to get rid of my roommate"
At home:	"my mom really doesn't care what I do"
I regret:	"having to live with a roommate"
People:	"have a great influence on me"
A mother:	"should care what there [sic] son does"
I feel:	"like killing myself sometime"

My greatest fear:	"is to talk back to my mom"
I can't:	"talk to my mom alone"
When I was younger:	"I did well in school"
My mind:	"Always now thinking about my girlfriend"
What pains me:	"is my mom"
My father:	no response
My greatest worry is:	"my mom hitting me"

To be fair, one must remember that the above responses were written down by a confused and angry adolescent and do not necessarily reflect the reality of his home life. Regardless of Chris's perceptions, the fact remains that Margaret was learning how to be a full-time mother while simultaneously working diligently with teachers and school administrators to try to formulate a plan to combat Chris's failing grades and truancy.

Chris's struggle to adapt to the dramatic changes in his life was made more difficult by his immediate dislike of his new urban surroundings. Marie Deans reported that Chris "hated" the heavily populated and developed Chesterfield County. "He said there were too many people and no privacy," wrote Marie. "[Chris complained that] 'you couldn't take a walk or play basketball without having fifty people around you.' He missed his life in Middlesex [County] with his uncle and his grandparents. He hated school and being confined."

While at first Chris struggled to integrate himself into his mother's life, Chris subsequently pulled away from her, and mother and son stopped communicating. Instead, Chris decided that he would both get his mother's attention, and punish her for what he perceived to be her failings as a mother, by getting into trouble. In Chris's own words, he was "trying to find every way to throw back at her." Chris's grades began to drop sharply, going from As and Bs in the seventh grade at Swift Creek Middle School to Ds and Fs in the eighth grade. In the fall of 1987, Chris enrolled at Clover Hill High School in Midlothian, Virginia, but he failed ninth grade. Chris started drinking alcohol and using marijuana on a daily basis, while occasionally using harder drugs like cocaine and LSD or over-the-counter medication like Robitussen cough syrup. Mixing together beer, liquor, and pot each day gave Chris a "light and giggly" feeling that he liked, a sensation that dulled the pain and depression. "I just didn't care," recalled Chris. "Before [I started using drugs] I did have a little sense, but when I did [drugs], I lost all reality."

By late fall 1988, Chris's truancy, dismal grades, and general lack of interest in school triggered a review by the Clover Hill High School child study team to decide if Chris suffered from a disability. Based upon the study team's recommendation, a full battery of tests was ordered, including psychological, sociological, educational, and medical evaluations. After administering a battery of tests, Bonnie Reid, a school psychologist, drafted a psychological evaluation that foreshadowed later reports: Chris was an angry and depressed young man who was estranged from his mother and who required a great deal of structure and counseling—both with a school psychologist as well as a grief-counseling group—in order to recover. Based upon the tests, it was concluded that Chris's failure in school was a result of his emotional problems; therefore, he would be classified as " seriously emotionally disturbed" and be given assistance through an individualized education program. In the "Eligibility Committee Summary Report" that was prepared at the time of Chris's diagnosis, the record observed that while Chris had "average intellectual ability" and "no developmental problems," he "does not appear to have worked through his feelings about the deaths of his grandparents" and had suffered "significant trauma" from their deaths. In retrospect, the next fifteen months at the high school represented the best, and last, chance Chris had to pull out of his downward spiral and stop his journey toward the death house. It would be an opportunity squandered.

Laura Trevvett Anderson first met Chris in late fall 1988, after he had begun his psychological and educational evaluations. Laura was in her second year as a special education teacher at Clover Hill High School, teaching students who had been diagnosed as learning disabled or severely emotionally disturbed. Invited by Bonnie Reid to meet with Chris in the cafeteria, Laura vividly recalls her first encounter with the young man who changed the course of her life:

Across the rows of tables sat a young man. Sitting alone and motionless, his head hanging low. With his fingers inter-twined and resting on the table, he looked like he didn't have a friend in the world. He was smaller in size than I expected. Looked to be about 5'6" or 5'7". Small in build. Mrs. Reid called him by name: "Chris." He turned his head slightly in the direction of her voice, not completely lifting his head. I guessed he must have recognized the voice since he didn't look up to see her face. "Chris, I wanted you to meet Miss Trevvett. She is one of the teachers you will have with your new schedule." Chris didn't really lift his head now either, just mumbled a greeting—"hey"—with a slight nod of his head. That was it. "Hello Chris, nice to meet you." I said, not really knowing what else to say at this point.

"Miss Trevvett's classroom is around the corner. I saw you sitting here, so I thought you two might like to meet." Mrs. Reid attempts to engage him in conversation, but there is no response from Chris. It wasn't that he was rude, more that he was in deep thought or preoccupied. He really had nothing to say to us. Chris continued to stare into space, looking very lost. "Yes, Mrs. Reid, I did want to meet Chris." I added. I felt like we were intruding into HIS world. Sitting all alone, not having any demands on him. No chance for failure. No one to answer to. No one telling him what to do. "What class are you suppose to be in, Chris?" Mrs. Reid asks. "I don't know, English maybe." "Well, you better get going then." "Right," Chris responds. We say our good-byes and head back down the hall towards my classroom. I turn to see him leaving through the side door towards the parking lot. He's not going to English class that way. . . .

By early spring 1989, Chris became one of Laura's special education students. This meant that Chris would spend the entire day in her "self-contained" classroom as Laura taught her students a variety of different topics, including algebra, coping skills, English, and world geography. Only if Chris's grades improved, and he demonstrated that he could act responsibly, would he also start attending regular education classes in other parts of the school.

From the beginning, Chris proved to be a difficult student to handle. In the first weeks of his studies with Laura, Chris would stay in class for only a few minutes each morning before abruptly walking out of the room. Often, Chris's sudden departures were triggered by the sight of his girlfriend Dawn[15] in the hallway. A petite fourteen-year-old whose dark black hair bore witness to her Native American heritage, Dawn was seemingly the only person about whom Chris appeared to care. In subsequent weeks Chris was less likely to suddenly bolt from Laura's classroom; nonetheless, she thought that Chris was just "humoring" the teachers and counseling staff that were struggling to connect with him. Laura tried strategy after strategy to engage Chris—from arranging for in-school interventions with his mother to distracting Chris with video games—and she commented to others that she "felt like a magician, trying to find something in my magic bag to interest Chris and keep him at school."

For Laura, the turning point in her struggle with Chris came on a winter's morning when she literally threw her body in front of Chris to prevent him from leaving.

I decided I would do anything I could to keep Chris in school. I had two exit ways out of my room. One exit led to the main hallway on the lower level of the school. The other exit led to an adjoining classroom. My students had learned not to use the doorway to the second classroom as an exit. We had progressed to the point that Chris usually did not leave until his girlfriend came to the classroom door. This particular day I was ready. I had locked my classroom door and closed it—something I rarely did—and when I saw her come to the window, I attempted to distract Chris by offering him a computer game. Chris looked over at the door, and not seeing his girlfriend, said he would play the game. I thought I had him.

But Chris became suspicious and started for the door. I moved quickly and blocked the door. He told me to get out of his way, but I did not move. He looked over at the other door and contemplated moving in that direction. I moved quicker than he did and blocked that door. The other students in the class thought this was great fun. I, on the other hand, did not. Chris became agitated and was huffing and puffing a bit. "You better get out of my way, or else," Chris threatened. But, since I was not intimidated by him, I just shrugged my shoulders and smiled. Chris said "I AM going to get out of this classroom!" And for a few minutes we ran back and forth between the two doors. I finally gave up and said, "Go ahead Chris, you can leave. I want you both to stay in school, but I give up." Chris left the room with hesitation, but I felt as if I had gotten through to him a little that day.

In the weeks that followed, Chris did not seem so anxious in the classroom environment and gave the new educational program a chance. Laura watched as Chris made friends with the other students in her classroom, and she held her breath as his grades started to slowly rise. Moreover, in Laura's eyes a different side of Chris's personality began to emerge. Flashes of humor started to appear. The sullen demeanor was replaced with a smile. Chris and a fellow classmate plotted ways to make Laura fuss at them, including serenading the class with "Love Shack" by the B-52's. After getting a good laugh from the rest of the class, and Laura's gentle redirection, Chris's attention to his studies returned.

While Laura occasionally heard Chris and a male classmate discussing weekend antics, including jokes about drinking cold medicine, she was not aware that, outside school, Chris was shoplifting and using drugs. As early as 1987 Chris was routinely shoplifting cigarettes and other items from stores; a successful string of robberies came to a crashing halt, however, when Chris was charged and convicted of petit larceny for stealing cassette tapes from a local department store in August of that year. At the time, Chris assured a social worker involved in the case that the arrest had so frightened him that he would no longer shoplift.

His promises of reform may have been sincere, but, by the summer of 1988, fifteen-year-old Chris resumed stealing cigarettes and other small items from local stores. In March 1989, Chris was convicted in the Chesterfield County Juvenile and Domestic Court of breaking into the house of a school friend to steal alcohol, a handgun, and a hunting rifle. Chris's explanation for the crime reflected his immaturity. He told a social worker that "since he could not have unlimited access to his hunting rifle at his aunt's, he decided to steal two guns, one to use for hunting and the other to sell for pin money." Chris told the same social worker that he was initially scared by the idea of breaking into a home, but he found courage by smoking a marijuana joint laced with PCP. Chris's conviction of grand larceny was quickly followed by subsequent convictions for stealing cigarettes and trespassing at his high school (Chris had been suspended from school for cursing at a teacher and was charged with trespassing when he returned to school and attempted to talk to a principal about his suspension). In the spring of 1989, Chris found himself facing a three-month sentence at the Hanover Learning Center, a detention center for male juvenile offenders run by the Department of Juvenile Justice. At the age of sixteen, Chris Thomas was spiraling out of control.

On April 25, 1989, a call was placed to a local 911 center in Chesterfield County. The caller was Chris Thomas, and he reported to the dispatcher that he had taken an overdose of medication. Chris was rushed from his home to the same medical center where he had been born almost sixteen years earlier. Upon his admission to the emergency room, Chris told an ER doctor that, faced with incarceration in a juvenile detention center, he swallowed thirty penicillin tablets in hopes of killing himself. In the days following his admission, Chris downplayed the suicide attempt. Whether or not Chris truly tried to commit suicide, the hospital records reveal a young, confused teenager in pain. Notes taken on the day of Chris's admission record that Chris told the doctors that "he wanted help . . . [but] was reluctant to discuss the help that he needed because he was concerned it might get him into some type of trouble." The next day Chris again talked to the admitting physician, this time stating that he sought hospitalization because "I wanted to get like a psychiatrist—somebody to listen. I mean just nobody listens, they contradict me like I'm lying. Just listen to my feelings 'cause nobody else will." By the time a formal psychiatric evaluation was conducted on April 29, Chris strenuously disavowed the suicide attempt—but repeated his plea for help. "I got scared and thought they would send me back to the detention home [Chris had been briefly sent to a detention home for an earlier crime] so I took some penicillin," a psychiatrist's notes record. "I didn't really want to die. That's about it. No other problems." Yet although Chris stated that he faced no other problems except the detention center, the notes add: "Douglas [Chris] expressed a desire to be involved in outpatient psychotherapy indicating a need to discuss his behavioral problems of late. 'I don't know why I do it.'"

A formal written psychiatric evaluation was generated after Chris's hospitalization, based upon interviews Chris gave to his doctors. The report stated that Chris "harbors suicidal thoughts, has problems in family relationships, and exhibits antisocial behavior" and was depressed. Moreover, the report noted that "additional procedures reflected his anger at his mother who he views as irresponsible and failing to care for him properly. He feels ignored by others and acts out his aggression in a manner such as to promote negative personal consequences." Interestingly, the consulting psychiatrist observed that Chris originally failed to tell his doctors about his mother's homosexuality. "Douglas denied that this was of any concern to him when confronted with this omission. There is much dynamic material which needs to be addressed and this will be difficult as he seems to have essentially no insight into the influential dynamics in his life." Unfortunately, Chris would not gain this critical insight in the coming months.

After recovering from his hospitalization, Chris was placed in the Hanover Learning Center, a juvenile detention facility due north of Richmond, Virginia. He stayed at the Learning Center from May 15 to September 1. Chris's stay at the detention center was initially rocky. Assigned to live in a cottage of young offenders of similar backgrounds and offenses, Chris's efforts at good behavior quickly evaporated. A "cottage performance report" written after his first week at the center stated that Chris became "hard headed and at times a smart alec" once he became oriented to his new environment, and that his "overall adjustment went from one that was very good to unsatisfactory. Chris was often involved in arguments with his peers for one reason or another. He feels things should go his way or done the way he wants them." The report concluded that Chris was "very immature, very impulsive, verbally aggressive, can be physically aggressive, very temperamental." Subsequent reports, however, reported that Chris's impulse control, judgment, and ability to withstand negative peer pressure had all dramatically improved and he earned the privilege of placement in an honors cottage program.

While at the Hanover Learning Center, additional psychological evaluations uncovered the same symptoms and warning signs documented during Chris's hospitalization. A staff report noted that "this youngster has suffered some severe psychological traumas, first in abandonment by his natural parents, then by loss through the death of three persons particularly close to him. He was returned to his natural mother who is essentially a stranger." It further observed that Chris is "obnoxious and resistant toward adult authority," but speculated that "his behavior at home was most likely acceptable because of the reality that his mother had once abandoned him and would do so again should he give her sufficient cause . . . if my speculations are correct, this will probably be a core issue that needs to be addressed in therapy." The report concluded: "Douglas [Chris] is in need of therapy." Although Chris indicated to the staff that he wanted to continue therapy after his return home, he did not do so.

As Chris descended into drug use and shoplifting, he also became sexually active. With a series of young girlfriends, Chris entered into a pattern of behavior that would repeat itself so tragically in the future: obsession and hypersexual behavior, as the girlfriends provided the love and companionship that Chris so desperately sought. "Chris's relationships with girl friends tended to be intense," remembered a friend from that time period. "He'd get real close to them real quick." Chris himself did not understand the source of these extreme feelings. "He believes he was more active sexually than most kids but has no insight into why," wrote Marie Deans in a mitigation report. "He denied any concern that his mother's sexual preference could affect him, but thinks he might have wanted to just get close to someone." A psychiatrist who was later involved in Chris's capital appeals mused whether Chris's excessive sexual activity was an attempt to reassure himself that he, unlike his mother, was not gay.

Unaware of Chris's convictions and his suicide attempt, or his incarceration in a juvenile detention facility, during summer vacation Laura worried whether the long break would undo the work that she had accomplished with Chris. While the in-class antics continued, especially when Chris and his friends vied for the attention of a young and attractive new teacher, in the fall of 1989 Chris's academic turnaround continued. By late fall, Chris began attending some regular classes, that is, courses in which he was "mainstreamed" with regular students. The first class that he earned the privilege of attending outside of his self-contained classroom was biology. Based on Chris's past tendency to abuse the less restrictive atmosphere of regular classes, it was decided that each day Laura would escort Chris to his biology class and intercept any distractions that might tempt Chris along the way. Embarrassed by the fact that he required an adult to monitor him, Chris started announcing to his friends that Laura was his "escort service." To Laura, the slightly off-color joke was further evidence that Chris was emerging from his shell. Just as important, Chris's pattern of petty crime and juvenile delinquency seemed to have stopped that fall, although he continued to abuse alcohol and marijuana.

In November 1989, Chris travelled back to Middlesex County for the Thanksgiving holiday. When he returned to school the following week, he excitedly announced that he would complete the semester before moving back to Saluda to live with his maternal uncle, Herbert Marshall, Jr., and his wife, Brenda. To Laura, Chris explained that he wanted to return to Saluda because he had "such a good time" during his Thanksgiving visit and he missed the fishing and hunting of his childhood home. Chris later told Marie Deans: "I was a troublemaker, and everywhere I went there was a cop. My heart was in Middlesex. I didn't want to accept the city. I had more freedom in the country. I could pee out the back door in the country and nobody would call the cops. When I got out of Hanover—I'd been in trouble for two years. I needed to change."[16] Although Chris did not say so, his spontaneous decision may have also been triggered by the fact that Middlesex County provided an escape from the taunts of "jailbird" hurled at him by classmates as well as the tightening web of rules that bound Chris's daily life.

To Laura, it seemed as if a rug had been pulled out from under her. After all the struggles over the last fifteen months, Chris had unilaterally decided to remove himself from the structure and support that he so clearly needed. Hurt and upset, Laura called Margaret Thomas and voiced her concerns.

FIGURE 4. *Chris Thomas and Jessica Wiseman in the summer or fall of 1990. Photograph courtesy of the Thomas family.*

"Margaret stated that Chris had told her the same, and she couldn't prevent him from going," recalls Laura. "She did not convince me that she wanted Chris to stay, even though she stated that she wanted him to stay." Margaret had diligently worked with Laura over the last year to turn Chris's behavior around, and one wonders if her decision not to oppose Chris's return to Middlesex County stemmed from fatigue and frustration with her son. On death row, Chris would summarize his decision to return to Middlesex County as "the worst mistake of his life."

In January 1990, sixteen-year-old Chris Thomas returned to Middlesex County. While the rural surroundings that drew him home remained unchanged in their beauty, Chris himself was a different person. Gone was the slightly pudgy, grief-stricken boy of his youth. In his place was an angry, confused, and impulsive teenager who routinely turned to drugs and alcohol to deaden a pain that he did not understand and who compulsively sought female companionship and sex to fill a loneliness he could not face. In the modest housing division in which his aunt and uncle lived, additional forces

FIGURE 5.
James Baxter "J. B."
Wiseman, father of
Jessica Wiseman.
Photograph courtesy
of the Daily Press
(Newport News,
Virginia).

would swirl around Chris and hasten his march to the death house. In that vacuum of parental supervision and academic structure, Chris would meet and fall in love with Jessica Wiseman. And when faced with the perceived loss of that love, he sealed his fate.

We do not argue that Chris Thomas was so overcome with forces beyond his control that he was not morally responsible for the terrible criminal acts in which he participated. At a basic level, Chris's choice to partake in a plot to kill Jessica Wiseman's parents was the product of free will and self-interest. Chris and Jessica wanted to be together, unfettered by the rules of their caregivers, and they deliberately and knowingly selected a course of action designed to achieve that goal. While the plan they devised was ill-conceived, poorly planned, clumsily executed, and painfully naïve, it was the product of rational choice.

We do believe, however, that rational-choice theory only helps us begin to understand a young teenager's path to murder. In our opinion, a true and complete appreciation of Chris's path to the death house must involve a thorough examination of the life events and environmental forces that buffeted and shaped Chris. While Chris enjoyed a secure and relatively happy childhood, by the age of sixteen he had been scarred by the abandonment of his biological father, the estrangement of his biological mother, the death of the grandparents who raised him, and the stigma of being categorized as an emotionally disturbed student and "jailbird." Removed from his rural surroundings and thrust into the urban setting of Chesterfield County, Virginia,

FIGURE 6.
*Kathy Wiseman, mother
of Jessica Wiseman.
Photograph courtesy of the
Daily Press (Newport News,
Virginia).*

Chris reacted by escaping into a haze of alcohol and drugs and engaging in a pattern of petty crime, all the time desperately searching for love and companionship from a string of younger girlfriends. Finally, when Chris was faced with losing Jessica, he passively submitted to a string of events that ended in the deaths of two innocent people.

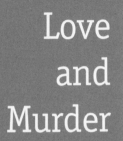

Love and Murder

You can't play Romeo and Juliet with a script written for Bonnie and Clyde.

JIM SPENCER

In January 1990, Chris Thomas moved from the hectic and unpredictable living arrangement with his mother in Chesterfield County into a small, red-brick ranch home located in a sprawling subdivision known as Piankatank Shores. The home was owned by Chris's uncle and aunt, Herbert and Brenda Marshall. Herbert worked as a machine operator in the bleach plant at a local paper mill, while Brenda was a registered nurse who was on medical disability. As a child Chris had feared his Uncle Herbert; years later Chris still vividly recalled the physical punishment and taunting that his uncle directed his way. Chris later told a probation officer that on "several occasions I didn't do things he asked and he slapped me for no apparent reason,"[1] and that Herbert would threaten to send him back to Chesterfield County if he didn't behave. While physical violence is never justified, we should take Chris's claims that he never provoked his uncle with an appropriate amount of skepticism. Nevertheless, the fact that Chris decided to live with his uncle is proof of the lengths to which Chris would go to return to the place he considered home. Later that year Brenda Marshall's twelve-year-old niece, Lainie Marie Creech, would come to live with the Marshalls. Young Lainie moved in with the Marshalls in July 1990, and she would play a pivotal role in the future murder trials of both Chris and Jessica Wiseman.

After the urban sprawl of Chesterfield County, the Piankatank Shores subdivision was a welcome change for Chris. The development took its name from the nearby Piankatank River, which ran along the southern edge of the subdivision. Four recreational areas dotted the subdivision's shoreline (all aptly found on "Shore Drive"), and the children and teenagers who lived in Piankatank Shores congregated among the wooden picnic tables, concrete basketball courts, rusty playground equipment, and sagging marinas that constituted each recreational area. The development itself consisted of modest ranch homes and bungalows built in the 1970s and 1980s, with many of the houses dwarfed in size by fishing boats resting on trailers in their side yards. Neatly painted homes decorated with cheerful wooden signs and nautical gear were interspersed with poorly maintained houses in which rusting cars and washing machines served as lawn art. The subdivision itself was heavily wooded and crisscrossed with meandering gravel roads bearing the names of native trees, and the preferred mode of transportation for many of its residents were aging, slow-moving golf carts.

To those who had known Chris before his move to Chesterfield County, he now seemed a very different young man. Brenda Marshall herself later reported to Marie Deans that "she had never seen anyone change as much as Chris did between the time his grandparents died and he came back to Middlesex." A childhood friend of Chris's remarked that the funny young boy had been replaced with a quiet teenager who "acted bad," chased girls, was "mess[ed] up with drugs," and hung around "trashy and sleazy" friends. Even Chris's name had changed. The little boy once called "Douglas" or "D.C." by friends and family now insisted on being referred to as "Chris."

While Chris hoped that his return to Middlesex County would signal a new start, he could not outrun his demons and familiar problems soon resurfaced. Chris later explained to a probation officer that "things were going pretty good until they started to enforce rules and let my cousin move in." His aunt and uncle established rules for Chris, including a weeknight curfew of 10:00 P.M. and a weekend curfew of 11:00 P.M., but the rules were seldom enforced.

While Brenda sincerely tried to provide structure and discipline for Chris, her health problems — including hip problems, epileptic seizures, and an alleged overdependence on pain medication — undercut her ability to enforce the rules; she often spent her days in her bedroom or watching television. Herbert Marshall worked the night shift at the local paper mill, and Chris quickly perfected the practice of sneaking out his bedroom window after his aunt went to bed and his uncle worked. Chris was soon telling his friends that his aunt and uncle "did not care what he did," and the tensions between Chris and his uncle quickly resurfaced. According to Chris's appellate lawyers, Brenda Marshall herself believed that "Herbert may be jealous of Chris and the attention his grandparents gave him, while Margaret Thomas's former lover, Joan, told the lawyers that "Herbert would hit Chris. On one occasion, Chris was chewing on a pork bone after everyone had finished eating and Herbert ripped it out of Chris's mouth, hurting Chris's mouth and face."[2]

In January 1990, Chris enrolled in the tenth grade at Middlesex High School. A review of his school records show that the academic strides Chris had made at Clover Hill High School quickly unraveled, as Chris's grades again sank and his penchant for cutting classes returned. At night Brenda Marshall worked with Chris on his homework, but told Marie Deans that "he would get very frustrated. He had no concentration, and he couldn't remember anything." By the end of the school year, Chris was missing at least one day of school each week. In May 1990, he underwent another round of testing to see if he should be classified as a disabled student. The educational evaluation confirmed the academic advances Chris had made at Clover Hill High School, finding that Chris was functioning at a higher grade level in his reading and writing skills (but with a slight weakness in math). Based on classroom observation, the report noted that Chris "does a lot of daydreaming instead of listening" and "gets easily upset." The educational evaluation report concluded: "His weakness is his emotional behavior. He easily gets upset and can't separate what he is doing with the feelings."

As with his Clover Hill High School assessment tests, a psychological evaluation was prepared by Middlesex County High School psychologist Beverley Parker. The report noted that Chris initially resisted taking the tests associated with the psychological evaluation, complaining that he had been repeatedly tested in Chesterfield County. Chris eventually capitulated, although he refused to complete a few examinations. Ms. Parker's report echoes the findings of the Clover Hill School psychologist Bonnie Reid: "Chris is an anxious, somewhat guarded adolescent who has trouble controlling his impulses. . . . His retreat into drug abuse and antisocial behavior were ways he chose to avoid a loss of control over hostile, aggressive impulses. His tendency to think about self destructive behavior were additional ways to avoid looking at his unsupportive, somewhat disorganized environment." While the report observed that Chris was depressed, Ms. Parker did not find evidence of suicidal thoughts. The report ended with a hauntingly familiar conclusion: Chris needed to be in therapy. In a subsequent interview conducted by Marie Deans's mitigation team, Ms. Parker stated that Chris's family never came to school to discuss the report or the recommendation of private counseling. Concludes the mitigation report: "Ms. Parker felt that if someone would take an interest in Chris it would have helped."

The summer of 1990 represented a "perfect" storm for Chris's downward spiral: the lack of structure that school provided, lax rules at home, escalating drug and alcohol abuse, and a series of younger girlfriends — usually fourteen or fifteen years old — with whom Chris was sexually intimate. A good-looking teenage boy, Chris had no trouble finding female companionship. "Chris was obsessed with girls," Brenda Marshall recalled during a meeting with Marie Deans. "They were his. He was no longer alone. They adored him and didn't want to leave him." A fourteen-year-old friend of Chris and Jessica's echoed Brenda's comments in a newspaper interview. "[B]ecause of his friendly attitude and looks, 'every girl around here fell in love with him,' she said. 'At the time this [the murders] happened, I was still in love with him.'"[3] The young woman interviewed by the newspaper reporter was Glenda Corbin, and in February 1999 she would ultimately marry Chris Thomas in a small ceremony on death row.

While several of Chris's relationships were short-term liaisons involving causal sex, in the early summer of 1990 Chris met and fell in love with a young girl named Tracy. The relationship would follow a pattern established in Chesterfield County, as the emotionally needy Chris became obsessed with spending every waking moment with her. When not chasing girls, Chris could be found at one of the four recreational areas that lined the Piankatank Shores subdivision and provided access to the winding Piankatank River — often partying with other teenagers from the subdivision or fishing for bluefish, stripers, and spotted trout. Weather-beaten signs posted in the recreation areas reminded the teenagers of a midnight curfew, but they were usually ignored.

At some point in the summer of 1990, Chris became romantically and physically involved with Jessica Wiseman. While it is difficult to pinpoint the exact date when Chris and Jessica considered themselves a couple, a reasonable guess is that the relationship did not become serious until Tracy's family — alarmed by Chris's brushes with the law — ordered her to stop seeing Chris in late July 1990. Perhaps it was inevitable that Chris's roving eye would have eventually landed on Jessica, a fourteen-year-old brunette whose great-grandparents lived within fifty yards of the Marshalls' home. Jessica's parents had recently reconciled after a series of separations, and during the spring and summer of 1990 they were living in a neighboring county as they tried to rebuild their marriage. Both maternal grandparents and her great-grandparents lived within ten miles of each other, and Jessica had bedrooms in each home. Jessica spent most of her time with her great-grandparents. Some neighbors believed that Jessica preferred her great-grandparents because age and infirmity rendered them unable to monitor her activities as closely as her parents could, although her stepgrandfather, Denby Thomas, claimed that the arrangement was selected so Jessica could help the elderly couple.

A newspaper article written immediately after the murders provided the following description of Jessica Wiseman:

> Although Jessica was described by neighbors and relatives as a reliable babysitter and a pleasant and responsible girl, she appears to have easily gotten her way with her grandparents and great-grandparents. Her parents bought her a golf cart to get around the neighborhood when she complained of pains in her legs. When that broke, they got her another one, Mrs. Eastman said. Her parents bought her an all-terrain vehicle for a recent birthday. Her great-grandparents kept frozen pizza in their refrigerator because they knew she liked it, and Jessica had friends sleep over "almost every night" during the summer and on weekends after school started, Mrs. Eastman said. In her room, Jessica had her own videocassette recorder and stereo. Also in Jessica's room is a key chain that reads "Waiting for the right man, meanwhile having a great time with the wrong ones."[4]

While after the murders some of Jessica's peers waxed poetic about her kind nature and good looks, other youngsters in the community took a more jaundiced view, describing Jessica as a "hellion" and a spoiled and manipulative teenager who usually got what she wanted — and pouted if she didn't. One former childhood friend of Jessica's recalled a vacation that Jessica and her grandparents took to Tennessee, a trip that was cut short when Jessica demanded to go home early and see her beloved puppy dog.

Like Chris, Jessica had never known a stable home life. Her father, James "J. B." Wiseman, was a waterman who had most recently worked for the Ward Oyster Company in neighboring Gloucester County. Described as a friendly and hardworking man, a local newspaper reported that J. B. "had a weakness for marijuana and alcohol" and had been arrested for drunk driving.[5] At least one of Jessica's childhood friends was afraid of J. B., asserting that he had a mean streak, drank to excess, and grew his own marijuana in pots in his family's home.[6] Her mother, Kathy Wiseman, worked as a bookkeeper and office manager for her stepfather's heating and air conditioning business and was employed by a local hair salon. Relatives claimed that Kathy Wiseman tried to protect her daughter from J. B.'s addictions; the result was that Jessica spent most of her childhood in the care of her grandparents and great-grandparents. "Her [Kathy's] way of shielding Jessica from it was to keep Jessica from home. And in turn it made Jessica feel like she wasn't wanted," explained Kathy's stepfather, Denby Thomas.

Jessica did not attend school — she claimed that migraines, leg pains, and taunting by schoolmates made school unbearable — and she was enrolled in a correspondence school to which Chris subsequently applied. Thus in the summer of 1990 two immature teenagers who both had experienced unstable family life and the bitter sting of parental rejection, and who both were essentially unsupervised, undisciplined, and isolated from their peers, began an intense romantic and sexual relationship.

Looking back from death row nine years later, Chris Thomas described the origins of his relationship with Jessica:

> How it all started . . . she was living with her great-grandparents and I was living with my aunt and uncle. And her parents didn't live in the area, they lived in a neighboring county. And everything was going pretty smooth without her parents because she could do whatever she wanted to. She could stay out all night. She didn't have to go to school, she went to school at home. And I was the same way, I pretty much stayed out all night. I had a curfew, which was ten-thirty or eleven, but I could sneak back out. We were pretty much together every minute of the day.

In the beginning, the relationship was not without its rocky spots. Friends recalled that Chris would goad Jessica into temper tantrums, and in the early months of their relationship Chris was sleeping with other girls while denying to Jessica that he was doing so. Chris and Jessica quickly began having sex, and throughout their relationship Jessica repeatedly thought that she was pregnant.

During the summer, Chris again began committing petty juvenile crimes. On July 13, 1990, Chris was arrested for stealing a tire for his Camaro. It was hardly an act of a master criminal: Chris drove his car—with the mismatched tires—past the very sheriff's deputy who was investigating the crime. Charged with grand larceny and the destruction of property, Chris was told by his aunt and uncle that he had crossed the line and would be sent back to his mother. Before Margaret could drive down to Middlesex County to get her son, Chris, his girlfriend Tracy (Chris was not yet dating Jessica), and a male cousin went on a mini-crime spree. The decision to flee was triggered by Chris's fear that he would be returned to Chesterfield County as well as by the efforts of Tracy's parents to end the relationship because of Chris's arrest. After stealing a 42-foot boat from a local marina and taking it on a spin around the harbor, the three came across a Cadillac—keys inside—at the same marina. Knowing that witnesses had spotted their unauthorized boat ride, the three stole the Cadillac and drove it to the Outer Banks of North Carolina. They returned back to Middlesex County and tried to convince another female companion to join them; when she wisely declined their offer, the three teenagers stole some gas and returned to the Outer Banks. Friends later alleged that Chris was "engaged" to Tracy during the trip to North Carolina, and while at the beach Chris talked about committing suicide. Chris himself claimed that after returning home from North Carolina, "I asked several times to see a psychiatrist but Brenda [Marshall] ignored my request."[7]

The adventure ended when the three were spotted in the stolen car and reported to the police. Chris was arrested, charged with possession of stolen property (Chris took a camcorder from the car's trunk), and spent four days in a county jail in Currituck, North Carolina. On October 8, 1990, Chris returned to North Carolina for sentencing. The judge imposed a two-year suspended jail term and four years of supervised probation. The conditions of probation required Chris to stay in school, have a part-time job or participate in a school athletic program, and follow a curfew from 8:00 P.M. to 6:00 A.M. for forty-five days. Seventeen-year-old Chris was considered an adult by the North Carolina court, but none of his prior juvenile records were deemed relevant and he was treated as a first-time offender for purposes of sentencing.

On October 9, 1990, Chris and his aunt Brenda briefly met with a North Carolina probation officer in Currituck. Chris was instructed as to the conditions of probation, issued travel papers, and told to meet with George Drummond in the Middlesex County Probation Office by October 12, 1990. It is not unusual for a probation officer from one state to supervise an individual placed on probation by a court in another state. Under a formal agreement between states, the state in which a court sentences an individual to probation can formally request that the individual's home state supervise the probation. This paperwork, however, takes time to process and can produce a gap in the supervision of an individual's probation. Some states avoid the gap in coverage by refusing to permit a probationer to enter the state until an investigation has been conducted and the state has formally agreed to supervise probation. In October 1990, however, Virginia did not stop probationers from other states from entering Virginia prior to accepting the supervision of their probation.

Chris and his aunt met with Drummond on October 11, who instructed them that Chris would be formally assigned to the then-vacationing probation officer Deborah McLeod. At this time, Virginia had not even received the paperwork from North Carolina requesting that Virginia assign a probation officer to decide whether Chris should be on probation and, if so, to supervise compliance with the conditions of probation. On October 31, 1990, the Middlesex County probation office finally received the North Carolina paperwork and began an investigation to determine whether the office would accept the transfer of probation. The Middlesex County probation office had forty-five days in which to conduct the investigation and make its determination. On the same day that he received the paperwork, Drummond called Chris and told him to contact McLeod and schedule a meeting time. Chris called the Middlesex County probation office on November 2 and scheduled a meeting with McLeod for Friday, November 9. Chris never showed up for the appointment. While standard operating procedure would have been for the probation officer to notify her supervisors of the missed appointment, that notification did not occur until Monday, November 12 — two days after the murders of Kathy and J. B. Wiseman.[8] When the Middlesex County Probation Office learned of Chris's role in the murders, they called their regional office and recommended that Chris's request to be on supervised probation for the North Carolina offense be denied.

Would proper vigilance by probation officers in North Carolina or Virginia have prevented the murders? Clearly, Chris did not meet any of the specified conditions of probation: upon his return to Virginia, Chris worked for only one day in a grocery store before quitting; he dropped out of school; and he repeatedly violated curfew. Unfortunately, there was no probation officer to whom to report the multiple infractions. The case had not been formally assigned to a Virginia probation officer, and the supervisor of the North Carolina probation office that processed Chris's case claimed that— despite Chris's probation violations—she would not have required Chris to return to North Carolina for a probation revocation hearing. "Terminating probation in the first month because of such infractions would have been giving up too soon," stated North Carolina probation officer Mary Lou Sutton in an interview with a local newspaper. "That's the purpose of probation, turn people around."

One person, however, voiced his outrage of the perceived failure of the system: Kathy Wiseman's stepfather, Denby Thomas. "Kathy and J.B.'d be living, Jessica'd be at home," angrily remarked Thomas to a newspaper reporter. "It kind of makes you feel like, who's responsible for people like these? They just let 'em roam around pretty much as they damn please."[9] Of course, the same question could be asked of the adults charged with supervising Chris and Jessica.

More troubling is the fact that the Marshall family did not punish Chris for his joyride. While Chris returned with his mother to Chesterfield County for two days, his uncle and aunt gave him permission to return to Middlesex County. "I told him after he stole the car that if there were any more shenanigans, he would have to go back and live with his mother," Herbert Marshall later told a newspaper reporter. "He promised me he would get his act straight."[10] To compound the mixed messages he was receiving, Chris was given a new car—he had totaled his old Camaro after falling asleep at the wheel while driving back from his sentencing hearing in North Carolina, and it was replaced with a 1987 burgundy Camaro. To say that Chris was receiving contradictory signals from the adults in his life would be an understatement.

Chris's car theft caught Kathy Wiseman's attention, however, and she forced her daughter to briefly stop seeing Chris. In a letter written to Chris after the murders, Jessica writes that she became suicidal during the short separation." "I don't know what it did to you, but I really and truthfully didn't want to live anymore. I took a whole bottle of real strong pain pills. I was determined that if I couldn't live with you then I wouldn't live at all."[11] If Jessica's mother discovered the alleged suicide attempt, Jessica doesn't mention it.

The forced separation was short-lived. Chris stole the car on July 17, yet Jessica's grandmother reported that Jessica "didn't consider herself liking Chris until her birthday, July 22. They got to the point where they rambled around more together."[12] When Kathy caught Chris and Jessica together at a local marina, she relented and permitted her daughter to resume dating, but allegedly put some modest restrictions on the young couple—such as forbidding Jessica to take long rides with Chris in his Camaro. Moreover, there is evidence that Kathy Wiseman made other efforts to place some rules on her daughter. In an interview given after the murders, a local Hollywood Video clerk recounted that Kathy tried to rent movies that were not violent or overly sexual. "I remember she decided not to take home [the movie] *Roadhouse* because sex scene was too extreme," recalled the clerk. "In the end, she took it home but said she was going to fast forward through the steamy scenes."[13]

In general, Jessica seemed to clash less with her mother than her father. "Her mom was easygoing and fun when she was separated from her husband, but when they got back together she changed," stated a childhood friend. She pointed to such examples as Kathy driving Jessica to restaurants to meet boys, adding that Kathy also encouraged Jessica to have male friends over for dinner. When Kathy and J. B. Wiseman reconciled and Jessica returned home, however, the childhood friend claimed that Jessica was permitted neither to socialize with males nor to have them over to the house.

If Kathy Wiseman's new rules were designed to slow down the relationship, they didn't work. By the beginning of August, Chris and Jessica were exclusively dating, spending days and nights together, and were completely free of parental supervision. Chris flirted with the idea of employment that summer, but managed to work a grand total of four days at two different local grocery stores and a local construction company. Chris later told a probation officer that he quit the jobs because he hated to work inside; more likely, employment was incompatible with his carefree lifestyle and obsessive relationships with girls. Frankly, Chris had little incentive to work: if he needed money for clothes or gas, he could turn to a modest trust fund established by his grandparents or his grandfather's social security benefits.

In September 1990, Chris and Jessica found their perfect arrangement threatened not by parents, but by the institutional rules of government: Chris had to return to the Middlesex County High School to start eleventh grade. The problem, however, was easily solved. From the very start of the school year, Chris was missing more classes than he was attending, and he managed to get himself suspended for three days in late September for bringing a vibrator onto a school bus. Moreover, Chris complained of respiratory problems—despite the fact that he smoked cigarettes and pot—as well as teasing from other students regarding the car theft. After a meeting with school administrators in late October, Brenda and Herbert Marshall decided to allow Chris to drop out of school and take correspondence school classes from the same program in which Jessica was enrolled. At the point he left Middlesex County High School, Chris had completed 9.5 academic credits and his cumulative grade point average was a 1.1. In later years a psychologist familiar with Chris's educational record commented that the Marshalls' decision was "very bad" because the correspondence school provided neither the structure nor attention that Chris required.

After the murders, Jessica Wiseman's great-grandmother, Edmonia "Tootie" Eastman, tried to paint a positive picture of the two teenagers' activities in the late fall of 1990. Mrs. Eastman described a typical fall day as Jessica dutifully doing her schoolwork in the morning, often joined by Chris, with afternoon outings in the Camaro or Jessica's ATV or golf cart. She stated that Jessica spent the evenings with her girlfriends, ordering in pizza or making her favorite meal (instant mashed potatoes and corn), listening to music, or watching videos. In fact, Chris had no homework to do because he had not received his first assignments from the correspondence school. Instead the two young people were spending day and night together, creating an elaborate fantasy world in which they would soon be married and free from any parental restrictions. They remained sexually active, even though Jessica continued to worry about becoming pregnant. Friends observed that Jessica began to mimic Chris's tastes and interest, with Jessica adopting Chris's practice of wearing the "Quicksilver" brand of clothes, a clothing line marketed to teenagers interested in surfing and skateboarding.

In the fall of 1990, another, more serious threat emerged to the teenagers' relationship: the reconciliation of Kathy and J. B. Wiseman and their return to the Piankatank Shores subdivision. The Wisemans worked quickly to create a home for themselves and Jessica in their small bungalow-style home, building a new deck in their yard around a small swimming pool, hanging a porch swing, and placing a wooden sign on the front porch which proclaimed in carved letters "Wiseman's View" on one side and "J.B., Jessica, Kathy" on the other. More changes were in store, however, as Jessica soon learned that her parents did not approve of Chris and intended to restrict her activities. Many of her parent's concerns were legitimate: they thought that Chris was too old for Jessica (Chris was now seventeen years old, Jessica was fourteen), a reckless driver, an underage drinker, and prone to violent outbursts. Lainie Creech testified at trial that Jessica "wished that they [her parents] weren't there and wished to get rid of them," and Jessica complained to Chris that her parents were too strict and that they wanted to break them up. Jessica started talking about marriage, arguing that if they got married her parents could no longer control her.

After catching Chris and Jessica in several compromising situations, including finding Jessica naked in Chris's room, Brenda Marshall sat down with the two teenagers to have a serious discussion about sex. Jessica was in the midst of another pregnancy scare, and the conversation revolved around pregnancy tests. Despite the importance of the discussion, Brenda admitted that she ended the conversation abruptly: "I told her we'd talk more when we got back home because we were in a hurry and had to leave."[14] Herbert and Brenda then left for a trip to Roanoke County, where they planned on spending the next five days hunting on land owned by an uncle. For Chris Thomas, who in the last six months had dropped out of high school, continued to abuse drugs and alcohol, and been convicted of his first criminal offense as an adult, being left alone and utterly unsupervised with his fourteen-year-old girlfriend was the worst possible scenario. What makes the situation more tragically absurd is that Chris, who couldn't keep himself out of trouble, was asked to take care of his twelve-year-old cousin Lainie.

On Saturday, November 3, 1990, the small riverfront city of Urbanna celebrated its annual Oyster Festival. A two-day affair, the festival featured an art show, a carnival, such musical groups as the Christchurch Boys Chorus and Harmony International Sweet Adelines, clogging, a parade of tall ships, loads of fried seafood, the Virginia Oyster Shucking Championship (featuring a $500 first prize), two parades, and a pageant to select an Urbanna Oyster Queen from a field of fourteen lucky young ladies. More than fifty thousand people attended the annual event, pumping much-needed dollars into the local economy.

For Chris and Jessica, the big event was the festival's parade on Saturday afternoon. Including clowns, ten marching bands, antique cars, a replica of the U.S.S. *Alabama*, show horses, and the antics of local Shriners, the parade also featured special floats sponsored by area businesses and organizations.

On one of those floats would be Jessica Wiseman, serving as the "Poppy Queen" and representing a local branch of the Veterans of Foreign Wars. As Jessica rode in the parade on that mild and sunny November afternoon, waving to the crowd assembled along the parade route and carrying a bouquet of flowers, she wore a rhinestone tiara made by her mother and a white gown purchased at a Richmond bridal boutique. She sat on the back of Chris's new Camaro. Directly behind Chris came J. B. Wiseman, driving a car that carried Lydia Gilbert, Jessica's friend and the VFW's "Loyalty Queen." Frying oyster fritters in a local Lions Club tent, Henry O. Gwaltney watched the young people drive by. A state psychologist, Gwaltney would become involved in Chris's and Jessica's murder trials; years later he remained haunted by the case.[15] Kathy Wiseman videotaped the parade as it passed, recording her daughter waving from the Camaro as well as Chris and Jessica kissing. For Jessica's great-grandmother, the lasting memory of that day was that the Wiseman family was "so happy."[16]

A precise narrative of the next couple of days is impossible to re-create, and a "true" account of the events leading up to the murders of Kathy and J. B. Wiseman often turns on which witness one believes. Little evidence remains as to Chris and Jessica's activities on the Sunday or Monday after the Oyster Festival, although a newspaper account written shortly after the murders claims that Chris and Jessica's life "appeared to return to normal." At some point on Monday, November 5, or Tuesday, November 6, Chris and Jessica began talking about getting married. The discussions may have been triggered by Jessica's continued belief that she was pregnant, although her great-grandmother later reported that she was "certain" that pregnancy was impossible, given that Jessica had had her period the week before these conversations.[17] Whatever triggered talk of marriage, Chris and Jessica spoke about their plans with her great-grandparents, who allegedly told Chris and Jessica that they "ought" to get married.[18] Brenda Marshall later stated that "Chris and Jessica used her phone [the week before the murders] to call states all over the country looking for a place where they could be legally married."[19]

On Wednesday morning, November 7, Chris and Jessica unsuccessfully tried to get a marriage license at the Middlesex County courthouse. Given Jessica's age, they were undoubtedly told that Virginia law mandated that her parents consent to the marriage. Chris never testified at either murder trial, but nine years later he discussed the sequence of events on Wednesday during a telephone interview from death row:

And we tried, calling places but they wouldn't marry a fourteen-year-old. But we tried, we tried a lot. This was like a Wednesday morning. She called me and was crying and said we would never be together like we were. And trying to be macho to comfort her I said that if you think they are going to interfere with our relationship just get rid of them. And when I made that statement, I wasn't being serious, I was in a sick sense trying to comfort her. Try to make her feel like she was loved. I didn't have any intentions on what happened. Initially I was just trying to comfort her. And this was Wednesday morning and then we thought about it. And they say that the premeditation was planned a week in advance but that isn't true. Wednesday, that morning we talked about it after I said, "get rid of them." And she said, "would you do that for me?" and I said, "well, yeah." And she asked how I would do it and I said, "the only way I know how to do it is to shoot them." And she got to smiling, well I can't say smile, but she got to laughing. So, I mean that is kind of how this whole thing got started. So later on that day we were talking and I told her, "well, are you serious about doing it?" and she was like, "yeah." And I said "ok, I will just come over there." It was going to be on a Thursday.[20]

There is a troubling inconsistency, however, that has never been resolved. During both Chris's and Jessica's murder trials, Lainie Creech testified that she overheard Chris and Jessica plotting the murder of Kathy and J. B. Wiseman on Tuesday, November 6—the day *before* Chris claims that he first raised the idea of murder. Specifically, Lainie testified that on Tuesday she overheard Jessica ask Chris if he "had enough bullets" and then map out how the murders would take place. It is possible that Lainie Creech overheard the Wednesday morning telephone call, and then either accidentally or deliberately claimed that (1) the conversation took place in person, not over the telephone, and (2) the conversation took place on Tuesday, not Wednesday. The twelve-year-old may have further confused this conversation with events she witnessed in the early evening of Friday, November 9. As for why Creech didn't call the police after overhearing these plans, she claimed that Chris and Jessica often teased her, and she apparently did not take their discussions seriously.

After the phone call, and their futile efforts to get a marriage license, Chris and Jessica announced to her great-grandparents that they needed to drive to Roanoke and take clothing to Brenda and Herbert Marshall, who were still on their hunting trip. The two teenagers left at approximately 1:00 P.M., driving four hours to the southwestern Virginia city of Roanoke. While it is uncertain whether Chris and Jessica subsequently tried to get a marriage license in Roanoke—contemporary reports stated that they did—it is undisputed that Chris and Jessica drove to the home of Herbert's uncle and located Herbert's pickup truck. Chris then cut the truck's brake line and put gravel and dirt in its gas tank. Chris would later claim that he never wanted to kill Herbert and Brenda Marshall, but that he simply wanted to delay their return to Middlesex County. Herbert and Brenda discovered the vandalism the next day, as they drove down a steep mountain road and the brakes failed. Herbert was able to avoid a tragic accident by using the truck's emergency brake and turning the truck into a field.

Assuming that Chris meant to merely disable the vehicle, an unanswered question still remains: why? Driving to Roanoke and damaging Herbert's truck in order to delay Herbert and Brenda's return simply to get some more unsupervised time with Jessica seems like an extreme solution to a nonexistent problem; in point of fact, Jessica and Chris enjoyed almost unlimited free time together. If, however, Chris disabled the truck in order to prevent Herbert and Brenda from returning home in time to stop the murders of Kathy and J. B. Wiseman, then the trip to Roanoke and the vandalism of Herbert Marshall's truck contradicts Chris's assertion that he was not serious when he talked about murdering the Wisemans during his Wednesday morning telephone conversation with Jessica.

Moreover, why is the question of Chris's intent so important? Chris's explanation for cutting the brake line and polluting the gas tank is relevant because the vandalism would be described by prosecutors at Chris's capital murder trial as an attempt to kill Herbert and Brenda Marshall. Through the testimony of Herbert Marshall himself, the jurors learned of the vandalism. And they heard Herbert opine that the brake line was cut in a clumsy effort to kill him and Brenda. Undoubtedly in their deliberations, the sabotage of the truck impacted the jury as they decided not only whether the murders of the Wisemans was premeditated, but also whether Chris was a violent individual who would pose a future danger to society if not executed.

As Chris and Jessica pulled into the driveway of her great-grandparent's home on early Thursday morning, they were confronted by a furious J. B. and Kathy Wiseman. Earlier in the evening Kathy Wiseman had learned of Chris and Jessica's trip, and she called the Middlesex County's sheriff's office to report the missing teenagers. By the time Chris and Jessica returned from their illicit trip to Roanoke, J. B. and Kathy Wiseman were enraged and tempers quickly exploded. In a shouting match in the great-grandparents' backyard, J. B. Wiseman demanded that Chris and Jessica end their relationship and threatened to kill Chris if he tried to see Jessica again. Relatives of J. B. and Kathy Wiseman later downplayed the early Thursday morning confrontation, claiming that the parents merely wanted to slow down the relationship. "They weren't broken up on Thursday," later claimed Jessica's grandmother, Arvazine Thomas. "Kathy (Jessica's mother) told Jessica she couldn't see Chris for a couple days, but they talked on the phone on Friday and Kathy told her to invite him to dinner Sunday."[21] Some familiar with the case have suggested that it was the Thursday morning confrontation between Chris and J. B. Wiseman that panicked the two young teenagers and set into motion their murderous plans. While this is a plausible argument, it cannot be reconciled with either Lainie Creech's testimony that Chris and Jessica discussed the murders on Tuesday morning or the fact that Chris disabled Herbert Marshall's truck on Wednesday afternoon—events that occurred before the emotional clash between the young lovers and the Wisemans.

Chris and Jessica remained separated for no more than twelve hours. After J. B. and Kathy Wiseman left for work, Chris slipped into the Wisemans' residence. In an Amnesty International interview given on death row, Chris recalls what he discussed with Jessica:

> Thursday morning I went over there and we were talking, not really about planning it, any murders or anything like that, but like boyfriend and girlfriend. That was when we were planning how to get married and I said I would come over that night, which would have been Thursday night and the whole time I wasn't serious. And the day passed and I went about doing what I normally did, driving around, talking to everybody and Thursday night came and I went to sleep. I wasn't serious about doing it, I just went to sleep and Friday morning she called me and asked why I didn't come over and I said I had fallen asleep.[22]

Chris may have been initially more serious about the plan to kill the Wisemans than he subsequently claimed. At his trial, Lainie Creech testified that Chris announced on Thursday night that Brenda and Herbert's return home would be delayed due to "truck problems." Lainie recalled that later the same night Chris was visibly startled when a refrigerator door suddenly opened.

When Creech asked Chris why he was so jumpy, she claimed that he replied "he has got to kill two people, and that he was real nervous." In short, Chris's behavior does not comport with his death row claim that he was merely humoring Jessica. If Chris had planned on murdering the Wisemans that night, his plans were abruptly thwarted by the return of Herbert and Brenda Marshall from Roanoke, Virginia. Their truck repaired, the Marshalls pulled into their driveway at 9:00 p.m. A surprised Chris Thomas listened to their story of vandalism and then went to bed.

On Friday morning, an angry Jessica Wiseman called Chris and demanded to know why he had not come to her home as promised. After mollifying her, Chris took Jessica on a ride to a local store. When they returned to the Wisemans' house, however, Jessica again raised the topic of murder. Recalls Chris:

> We were sitting around and it came up and she said "how are we going to do this?" And I was thinking that we could make it look like a drug ripoff because her parents had cocaine and marijuana in the house. My first thought was to make it look like a drug ripoff. And that is when, I guess, the planning of the crime actually transpired. She asked, "what type of gun are you going to use?" and "what are you going to wear?" and stuff like that. And I told her I was going to use my gun, which was a 12-gauge shotgun, and I was going to wear camouflage because I didn't want anyone to see me. And then we talked about that we would do it at night time because no one would see us, it wouldn't be as obvious trying to get away. And that is about as much planning as we did.[23]

At around dinner time on Friday, Chris and Lainie drove to a local grocery store to get a loaf of bread. As they returned to the subdivision, Chris had his young cousin deliver a handwritten note to Jessica. On the note, Chris wrote: "Do you still want me to come over there tonight?" He "put a yes and no with little boxes and put 'check one.'" If the note had not involved the murder of two innocent people, the entire situation would seem sophomoric. When Lainie returned with the note, Jessica instructed Chris "that if her bedroom window was up to come in and if it was down that the plan was off." Despite Jessica's response and detailed directions, Chris claimed that "I still wasn't taking any of it seriously" until he received a phone call from Jessica, asking Chris if he was still coming. "The conversation was about, you know, how much she disliked her parents, how much she hated them, how she wanted

FIGURE 7. *Chris Thomas with what appears to be his grandfather's shotgun, Christmas 1989. Photograph courtesy of the Thomas family.*

to be with me, her love was eternal. That no one could separate them [Chris and Jessica]." It was that phone call that convinced Chris how deadly serious Jessica was. Chris and Lainie subsequently took a second drive around 7:00 P.M. — ostensibly to look for a missing cat — and during the drive Chris remarked to Lainie, "I hope I don't get in trouble for going up to Roanoke," adding that "he didn't travel 500 miles for nothing." Chris stopped several blocks from Jessica's house, scribbled a note in an *Auto Trader* magazine, and asked Lainie to deliver the magazine to Jessica. Inside the magazine was a second handwritten note, announcing that Chris would be coming to the house later that night.

When Chris and Lainie returned to the Marshall home, they decided to watch television. Herbert Marshall was leaving to work the night shift at the paper mill, but Brenda Marshall joined Chris and Lainie. According to court testimony, the three watched the movie *Firebirds*, a forgettable 1990 film that starred Nicholas Cage and Tommy Lee Jones as brave American helicopter pilots who heroically battle overseas drug cartels. When the movie ended at approximately midnight, Brenda Marshall claimed in a self-serving newspaper interview that she told Lainie and Chris she loved them, went to bed, but then checked on both children at approximately 1:00 A.M. to make sure they were in their bedrooms. Whether the bed check occurred or not, at some point after midnight Chris asked Lainie if she wanted to walk with him to the Wiseman residence. There is no doubt that Lainie knew the purported goal of the visit, but she did not hesitate to accompany Chris (she later claimed she didn't believe that Chris was serious). Chris donned camouflage boots, a camouflage hunting suit, camouflage hunting gloves, and a stocking cap, and got the Browning Model 85, 2¾-inch automatic shotgun willed to him by his grandfather. He had no problem gaining access to the gun; the home's gun safe was full, so the shotgun was kept in a closet next to the safe.

The sky was overcast and gray, and a steady rain fell as Chris and Lainie walked through the dark night. There were no streetlights to illuminate the deep shadows, and they walked undetected down the subdivision's narrow gravel roads. His resolve failing, Chris stopped at a one of the recreation areas near the Piankatank River, handed the shotgun to Lainie, and lit a joint. Perhaps delaying, perhaps waiting to feel the effects of the drug, Chris sat for almost fifteen minutes. As the rain increased in intensity, the two young people resumed their journey through the darkness—with twelve-year-old Lainie carrying the shotgun. Lainie later recalled that Chris was "laughing and acting strange," telling her, "It isn't bad when you shoot game, but it's a different story when you shoot a human . . . it's even worse that I know these people and it's even worse it's not one, but two."[24] As Chris and Lainie approached the road that ran along the side of the Wisemans' home, Chris stopped, motioned for the gun, and remarked, "I guess this is our final departure."[25] Lainie watched Chris disappear in the darkness before trudging back through the night to the Marshalls' home, where she crawled through a window and fell asleep. While we shall never know what was running through her mind as she walked back to the Marshalls' home, we do know that Lainie Creech never warned a soul of the tragedy that was about to unfold.

All was quiet and still at the Wisemans' home. A lone porch light burned, a pumpkin decorated the small front porch, and the Wisemans' two cars were parked in their driveway: a white Chrysler LeBaron convertible bearing the personalized license plates "KJW II" and a GMC truck with plates

"JBW II." There could be no doubt that Kathy and J. B. were home. If Chris had peered in the kitchen window, he would have seen flowers on the kitchen table—a gift from J. B. to Kathy Wiseman to celebrate their fifteenth wedding anniversary.

Jessica's bedroom occupied the front right corner of the house, with bedroom windows in the front and side of the structure. As Chris carefully approached the front of the home, he saw the agreed-upon sign: Jessica's front bedroom window was open. "I came to her window and she was laying on the bed waiting for me," recounted Chris. "I was at the window talking to her and I was hoping in the back of my mind that she would see me with the gun, dressed like a combat soldier, that she would say 'go home, I was only playing, go home, I was testing you to see if you really loved me and I know that you do, so go home.'" Jessica did not. When Chris tried to hoist himself through Jessica's bedroom window, he failed—prompting either Jessica or Chris to go to the garage, get a bucket, and use it as a step to get through the bedroom window (in his confession Chris stated that he got the bucket, but in subsequent interviews he claimed that Jessica did). The idea of simply using a door to enter the house didn't appeal to Chris: "I wasn't too familiar with what door to use and I didn't want to make a lot of noise to wake anyone up."

Chris unloaded the shotgun to prevent it from accidentally discharging, hoisted himself into the bedroom, and sat down on Jessica's bed. Having prudently lubricated the bedroom window with Vaseline to prevent squeaks, Jessica silently shut and locked the window. Her screen and storm window remained open, which later caught the attention of the crime scene investigators. Once in the room, Chris reloaded the shotgun, "just in case they were to catch me." The automatic shotgun could be loaded with five shells and therefore could be fired five times without reloading.

As Chris reloaded, Jessica crossed to her parents' bedroom—located immediately across the hallway from her own room—and retrieved a box from their headboard. Inside the box were roach clips and other drug paraphernalia. Jessica carefully placed the contents of the box on her parents' floor, and then laid the box itself on the floor. The intent, according to Chris, was "to make it look like a drug ripoff." Even inside the Wiseman home, armed with a shotgun, dressed in hunting gear, and watching Jessica prepare the crime scene, the reality of the situation did not dawn on Chris. For the next two hours, Chris and Jessica lay on her bed and Jessica rubbed the back of Chris's head as they talked, listened to the stereo, and drank alcohol taken from the

Wisemans' liquor cabinet. "We laid [sic] there and talked, not really about [our plan], we still weren't talking about committing a crime," recalled Chris. "I was laughing because I was high and everything was funny. In the back of my mind, I knew I wasn't going to do it."

According to Chris, it was Jessica who ended their snuggling. "She got up and said they [Kathy and J. B.] would be waking up, so if we were going to do this we needed to do it." Leaving the gun in Jessica's room, Chris got up and looked into Kathy and J. B. Wiseman's bedroom. As Chris peered into the dark bedroom, he could barely see how the Wisemans were positioned in their bed. Crossing back to Jessica's bedroom, he told her in a hushed voice that he "couldn't see them very well." Jessica quickly walked to a small bathroom that was located next to her bedroom and across the hall from the parents' bedroom and turned on the bathroom light, which helped illuminate her sleeping parents. Jessica also turned on a small floor heater in the bedroom to mask the noise of their preparations and put the family dog outside.

Chris again crossed the hallway to the Wisemans' bedroom, peered in, and raised the shotgun. The sight of the parents spooked him. He lowered the gun, walked back to the bedroom, and told Jessica "I am getting the fuck out of here." Jessica quickly responded, "you can't," reminding Chris that the drug paraphernalia already lay on the bedroom floor and that her parents "would kill us both" if they awoke and saw the drugs:

> And that kind of struck a chord because he had told me that if he caught me around his daughter again he was going to kill me. So, I raised the gun back up but I still couldn't pull the trigger. I was looking down the barrel, looking down the sights. I held the gun on my shoulder and I said, "here, you do it. If you don't do it, it won't get done." And she said she couldn't. She was standing beside me so all she had to do was just put her hand up. And she didn't. She said she couldn't do it. And then I was sitting there for a few minutes and I thought about [it]. Well, I guess it wasn't a few minutes, it was a few seconds. And I thought about what she had just said. That if her parents wake up they are going to kill us both. And then she said, "if you really love me you will do it." That is when I raised the gun and it was kind of like an impulse. I just shot once and then shot again.

J. B. Wiseman was instantly killed with a shotgun blast that entered above his upper lip, blowing a 1½-inch hole in his face and destroying his brain. At first Chris believed that Kathy Wiseman was also dead, but then he watched, horrified, as she began to slowly move. The second shot had struck her left cheek, with the pellets shredding the tissue on the left side of her face and neck, but had not immediately caused her death. "Then her mother kind of rose up, I guess, the only way, like you are laying [sic] in a bed and just kind of sit up. And then, she started shaking her husband and screaming his name. I was kind of freaking out, I didn't know what to do."

Chris stood in the bedroom door, frozen, until he saw Kathy Wiseman, dressed only in a long red T-shirt, struggle and rise from the bed. Chris turned, ran into Jessica's bedroom, and dropped the shotgun on the mattress as he dove behind the bed frame. As Chris recounted years later, what happened next spelled the difference between his own life and death:

> I dropped the gun on the bed as I was diving over it. After the first two shots, I mean, she [Jessica] stood there and watched the whole thing, but when I moved she moved and she went to the back of the room. And then, her mom came into the bedroom and that is when it kind of. . . . There are two sides of the story being told. One is that I fired the shot and the other is that she [Jessica] fired the shot.[26]

When asked which version of the story was true, Chris flatly replied. "She fired the shot."

The third, and fatal, gunshot blast caught Kathy Wiseman full in the right eye and blew out the back of her skull, spraying blood, bone, and brain matter onto the walls. Some of the birdshot passed through Kathy's body and continued traveling down the hallway (later found on top of the kitchen cabinets by crime scene investigators). Kathy crumpled and fell where she stood in the hallway outside her daughter's bedroom, with her foot and right leg across the threshold of Jessica's bedroom. Years later, Chris described the third and final shot as follows: "It is kind of hard to put into words what I saw. I guess if you have seen a movie of someone's head that is being, for a lack of a better word, you know, exploded like a pumpkin. It was just all down the hallway. The smell and all that."

Jessica took Chris's hand, helped him step over the body of her dead mother, and crossed to the kitchen door. A family member later claimed she was told that Jessica paused, reached down, removed her mother's ring, and told Chris that "now we can be married."[27] How the two walked down the hallway without getting blood on their shoes or clothes is unknown, but the subsequent police investigation did not record the discovery of any such trace evidence. The two exited the house, quickly walking back through the rain and wind to the Marshall residence. In the home they left behind, shotgun shell casings littered the floor and the acrid smell of cordite hung in the air. Water gushed out of the jagged holes made in the waterbed from the first two shotgun blasts and mingled with J. B. and Kathy Wiseman's blood, creating the illusion that the master bedroom was flooded with blood and leading some television journalists to refer to the Wisemans' home as the "house of blood."

We do not know what Chris and Jessica discussed on their half-mile walk back to the Marshall residence, or whether the enormity of their actions had begun to register. Perhaps conversation was precluded by the sounds of the gunshots still ringing in their ears. Chris entered the Marshall home at approximately 4:00 A.M., stripped off his camouflage clothing, returned the shotgun to the closet, and climbed back into his bed. He must have signaled to Jessica that he was ready, for she immediately started pounding on the front door. Awakened from sleep, a frightened Lainie Creech opened the front door and found Jessica Wiseman. Brenda Marshall was woken up by the noise, and came out of her bedroom. "She was screaming, 'My mama's dead! Oh, her eyes! She's dead,'" Brenda later told a newspaper reporter. "I said, 'Where's your daddy?' And she said, 'He's dead, he's dead, he's dead.'" At 4:08 A.M., Brenda Marshall called the Middlesex County sheriff's office to report that something terrible had happened in the Wiseman home. She then called Jessica's grandparents and told them that there had been some gunfire around the Wiseman's home. As she made the calls, Chris Thomas held Jessica in his arms.

After notifying the police, Brenda loaded Chris and Jessica into her car, and quickly raced to the Wisemans'. "She [Brenda] had the idea that maybe they were still alive," explained Chris. "So we got in the car, all got into the car, and we went back to the house . . . for my aunt to see if they were still alive. And, I already knew in the back of my mind that they weren't alive. It was a strange feeling having to go back to the house."[28] One can only imagine the surreal scene of Jessica and Chris sitting in the backseat of Brenda's car, racing through the predawn darkness to the crime scene they just created.

When they reached the house, however, Brenda could not make herself go in. The first law enforcement officer to arrive on the scene was Middlesex County Deputy Sheriff Donald Rhea. Pulling up to the residence at 4:27 A.M., Rhea quickly walked over to Jessica Wiseman and asked her what had happened. This was Jessica's first opportunity to test her rehearsed story on a law enforcement officer. Rhea later reported: "I questioned Jessica who stated that she heard an argument between J. B. (victim above), her mother, and an unknown third party. Jessica stated that then she heard a shot, then she heard another shot while her mother was screaming. Jessica stated she saw her mother lying in the hall as she ran out of her bedroom."[29] After searching outside the house and the surrounding property for either a gunman or any sign of forced entry, Rhea approached the dark home and shined his flashlight into a window. What he saw were the lifeless bodies of J. B. and Kathy Wiseman.

After learning from the paramedics that the Wisemans were dead, Brenda drove Chris and Jessica back to her house. Brenda later described Chris Thomas as frightened and ghostly white. "He leaned over to me at one point and whispered, 'Do you think [Jessica] did it?' And I said, 'Chris, I don't want to think that.'"[30] Given Chris's involvement in the murders, and his vow to protect Jessica, it was a bizarre question to ask. Brenda gave each of them a Valium, and sat them on the living room couch. Chris had not slept in two days, and the Valium, combined with the lingering effects of the alcohol and marijuana, caused him to quickly fall asleep. In the coming months, the story of the two teenagers, sleeping in each other's arms after committing cold-blooded murder, would be recounted in gossipy meetings in coffeeshops and gas stations around Middlesex County. That image would also be burned into a future jury's mind as proof that Chris Thomas was an unremorseful killer.

Chris and Jessica's hours of freedom were ticking down. Faced with a grisly crime scene with multiple victims, the Middlesex County Sheriff's Office immediately requested the assistance of the Virginia State Police. Jessica was questioned first, and a state police report provides the following summary of Jessica's first interview:

> She tells a story of an unknown man coming to her parent's house earlier in the evening and arguing with her father about drugs. She claims later in the evening/morning she was awaken [sic] by two gun shots. She could hear her mother calling her father, saying "wake up." Her mother was hitting on her father and was telling him to wake up. She was saying "J.B." wake up. The only light on was the hall bathroom light. She was in her bedroom by herself and her bedroom door was half open. She got off her bed and got down behind it. While she was behind her bed she saw a large man move down the hall from her parent's bedroom towards the kitchen.

He had on dark clothes and had something covering his face. He had something in his left hand and he did not say anything. . . . She heard her mother moving and she was coming to her bedroom. She saw her mother's hand on the bedroom door frame. She knew it was her mother because she could see her fingernails. She heard a third shot which came from down the hall toward the kitchen. Before the third shot her mother was crying and was saying "help me, help me." She did not see a flash from the gun. Every shot from the gun numbed her ears. The shots were very loud and sounded like a long gun. After the third shot she saw her mother fall in the hallway. She then heard the person she had seen run out the front door of the house. She did not hear any car in front of their house. She put on her shoes and had to jump over her mother to get to the living room. She ran out the front door and ran to the home of Brenda Marshall.

The report adds: "It should be noted that during this entire interview Wiseman appeared to be crying but there were no tears coming from her eyes." In short, the investigators were immediately suspicious of Jessica's story.

Chris was interviewed by the state police at approximately 2:00 P.M. on Saturday, November 10. The interview took place in the Marshall home, and both his mother and aunt were present during the questioning. Chris told the investigators that Jessica had been grounded after she and Chris took a ride to Richmond, Virginia, and Newport News, Virginia, on Wednesday (he made no mention of the trip to Roanoke), and that Chris had not seen Jessica again until she banged on the door on early Saturday morning and announced her parents' murders. Chris confirmed for the investigators that he and Jessica were sexually active, and he denied any involvement in the murders. To the investigators, Chris appeared "very calm" and "well within himself," but Margaret Thomas recalled that during that afternoon Chris was nervous and crying.

After the interview concluded, the state police returned to the Wiseman residence. Chris walked through his backyard to Jessica's great-grandparent's house, which was located approximately fifty yards from the Marshalls' home. He found the house filled with family and friends, all milling around in shock. Chris wanted to talk with Jessica, but he was unnerved by the crush of people and "didn't want to seem obvious whispering questions to her." Deciding to leave, Chris stopped briefly to hug Jessica's grandmother, Arvazine Thomas. As he murmured his sympathies to her, Chris's eyes were drawn to another person in the room. "I remember as if it happened a second ago, there was a woman in the house who lived beside her mother and father's house that was there and when I hugged her grandmother I kind of stared at her and her eyes were like piercing into my soul like she knew that I was involved. I still remember that feeling because it is a very weird feeling to have someone stare at you like that and I already had a guilty conscience and I was trying to act as normal as I could."[31] At least one person at the gathering would also have her suspicions about Jessica's behavior as well. "I saw her at her grandmother's house. I hugged her and she hugged me and we both cried," a neighbor recalled. "But I thought it was odd when she said, 'It couldn't be helped.'"[32]

In fact, Chris had more than a guilty conscience; he was panicking and ready to run. Sensing that Chris was preparing to bolt, Brenda Marshall gave Margaret Thomas the keys to Chris's car. "I wanted the keys so me and Jessica . . . could leave and just try to run away from it," recalls Chris, but his mother wouldn't hand over the keys. While this parental concern was appropriate and probably saved Chris from a deadly, high-speed police chase, the attention was too little and too late.

At 7:00 P.M., the state police returned to Jessica's great-grandparents' house for a second interview. Sitting in his kitchen, Chris turned off the kitchen light and stood at a large sliding glass door to watch the investigators pull into the driveway. The sight must have filled him with dread. Curiously, Jessica's grandfather, Denby Thomas, requested that the second interview be conducted in Special Agent Johnson's car. Perhaps he did not want to subject his in-laws to further stress from a police interrogation. At first Jessica maintained her story of a mysterious stranger in the house and shots coming from the master bedroom (the first two shots) and the kitchen (the third shot), but Special Agent Johnson interrupted and told her that the third shot must have come from her bedroom because a spent shell was found in the room. "At first, she was very adamant that it wasn't, couldn't have. Then she finally admitted there was a man in her bedroom, that this man was crouched down by her bed opposite the door. He told her if she didn't keep quiet and if she told anyone, he would kill her."

Johnson asked Jessica if the man she described was Chris Thomas. "She very emotionally said no!" the report observes. When Johnson asked Jessica if she were the killer, "she shouted, 'no, how could you say something like that?'" The report notes that Jessica left the vehicle, went over to her grandfather, and then disappeared into her great-grandparents' home. After Johnson advised Denby Thomas that he "was of the opinion that JESSICA was lying and did know who killed her parents and could very well be involved herself," Johnson asked Denby Thomas for permission to resume the conversation "and see if he could get her to tell the truth." Denby Thomas went into his in-laws' home, and in a few minutes returned with Jessica. Grandfather and granddaughter got into the back of the squad car, Jessica was read her Miranda rights, and she executed the form acknowledging that she received her rights. At that point, the following exchange took place between Jessica and Special Agent Johnson:

Q: Did "CHRIS" come to your house this morning?
A: Yes, to see me because he loves me.
Q: How did he get in?
A: Through my front bedroom window.
Q: When?
A: After my parents went to bed.
Q: How did he get over?
A: He walked.
Q: Did he have his shotgun when he came in?
A: I don't want to answer that.
Q: Did "CHRIS" shoot your parents?
A: He was scared of mommy and daddy. I guess "CHRIS" was afraid of daddy. Daddy said he would kill him if he caught him around the house.
Q: Did you leave the house with "CHRIS"?
A: (Nodded) Yes.
Q: Where did you and "CHRIS" go?
A: Walked to BRENDA's.
Q: Did "CHRIS" go in first?
A: Yeah, and I knocked on the door.
Q: (From Mr. Thomas): Did "CHRIS" shoot your mommy and daddy?
A: I don't know.
Q: Did he, "CHRIS" kill your mommy and daddy?
A: He didn't mean to, he didn't mean to.
Q: What about the shotgun?
A: He brought the shotgun because he was afraid of daddy.

Q: Where did he put the shotgun?

A: (*No answer*).

The report concludes as follows: "JESSICA WISEMAN began demanding that she be able to see 'CHRIS' before she would answer any further questions, so the interview was terminated.[33]

As Jessica crumbled and pointed to Chris as the killer, Chris turned from the kitchen door and called his mother. Margaret had driven back to Chesterfield County—apparently seeing no need to stay with her son—and now Chris called and asked permission to come to her home. When he returned to the sliding glass door, Chris was greeted by the sight of a Virginia State Police car slowly pulling away from the house at approximately 9:00 P.M. "I stayed at the patio and I watched them pull out but I didn't see Jessica get out of the car. When I saw the car moving I kind of knew that she had told, that she had broke."[34]

Chris did not have long to wait. Within minutes, two Virginia State Police cars pulled in front of the Marshalls' home, while a third, unmarked police car moved into the backyard. Chris was trapped. Virginia State Police investigators Larry A. Johnson, Sr., and Robert W. Stanek approached the front door and were ushered into the living room by Brenda Marshall. There they found Chris, sitting in the dark and watching television. Lainie Creech hovered in the shadows nearby. Johnson later described Chris's demeanor to be "alert to me when I told him what I was there for."[35] Johnson informed Chris that new evidence had been discovered that implicated Chris in the murders of Kathy and J. B. Wiseman; he told Chris he wanted to question him about the new information. Johnson subsequently read Chris his Miranda rights, and at 9:23 P.M. Chris executed a document indicating that he had been read, and understood, his constitutional rights to remain silent and to have access to a lawyer, but that he wished to waive those rights. That document would subsequently be entered into evidence at Chris's trial, with the Advice of Rights form signed in Chris's neat handwriting and each page of the confession—written in Special Agent Johnson's hand—initialed by Chris.

Margaret Thomas was not in the house when her son waived his Miranda rights, and there is no evidence that Brenda Marshall tried to dissuade Chris from talking to the state police as she watched him silently sign the waiver. In fact, Brenda Marshall signed the document as a witness. Why an adult did not step in and protect Chris is a mystery. After questioning Chris and eliciting a confession, Mr. Johnson drafted up a handwritten confession that Chris reviewed and initialed. In the rambling and disjointed document, Chris stated the following:

> We got in a little "spat" that I wasn't going to do it [shoot her parents]. I told her to do it. They [her parents] wouldn't going [sic] to let us see each other permanently. She said if he [Daddy] gets up he will kill us. For about 10 or 15 min. we sat talking about killing them. I fired the gun into their bedroom, twice — I couldn't see them. After that I really don't remember . . . her mom was coming in there. Jessica said "Oh God, shoot her again [her mother]." I was laying on the floor on the opposite side of bed when her mother came in. Jessica was standing in front of the window when I shot her mother in the doorway. I at first didn't think either one was dead after hearing Jessica's mother. Jessica had closed the window and I couldn't get out. I was pretending I was going to shoot them. She said she wanted it done. At the very end I didn't want to do it. . . . I told her to do it. I didn't [shoot] want too. She wouldn't. . . . At first I asked Jessica if she regretted it. She said no, only hurting a lot of people. I guess her grandparents.

It took less than one hour for Chris to give his full confession and sign the four-page document.

One of the Virginia State Police investigators later testified that Chris was "very calm," "very deliberate" and "immensely cool" during the questioning, adding that "it was one of the easiest confessions I have ever had. It just seemed like to me he was ready to get it off his conscience." Chris's lawyers, however, would strenuously object to the admissibility of the confession, arguing that an exhausted, drugged, and immature teenager was coerced into involuntarily waiving his Miranda rights. Regardless of Chris's emotional and mental state on that Saturday evening, one thing is undeniably true: if an attorney had been present to defend Chris, he or she would not have allowed him to answer any questions.

In the years following his conviction, both his defense team and his family skeptically challenged Chris's assertion that he fired the third shot. Chris steadfastly stuck to his story, but in the final years of his life he finally publicly claimed that he did not shoot Kathy Wiseman as she stood in the doorway of Jessica's bedroom. When asked why he lied in his confession, Chris explained simply: "I didn't implicate her [Jessica] as doing anything because like I said, I promised her I would protect her. And I thought I would only get a little bit of time and she could come see me and then I would get out and everything would be over with."[36] In short, Chris was so utterly naïve that he did not understand the legal consequences of confessing to the premeditated murder of two individuals. "I didn't think about a life sentence. . . . I only thought you could get the death penalty for killing a police officer," claimed Chris. "I didn't know all the factors that, or the list of factors that warranted the death sentence." Indeed, Chris later asked his interrogators if he could avoid being charged with murder if he enlisted in the army.[37]

After giving his confession, Chris was escorted into his bedroom and told to pack up some clothes. As Special Agent Johnson entered the bedroom, he noticed some camouflage clothing in the room. Turning to Chris, Johnson asked if these were the clothes that he had worn to the Wisemans' home. Chris indicated that they were.

Chris was handcuffed and escorted out of the Marshalls' home. As he left the house, he turned to his aunt and told her, "I really didn't want to do this." Outside sat several state police cars, including one holding Jessica. As Chris passed by her open passenger window, Jessica called out that she was sorry. Chris was placed in the back of the police car, and neighbors stood in their yards and watched as it slowly pulled out of the Piankatank Shores subdivision. Within weeks, Chris would be indicted for capital murder and face the specter of the electric chair.

3

The Death Penalty in Virginia

No state [other than Virginia] has a lengthier, more intimate relationship with executions. That is in part a matter of historical coincidence, in part a product of temperament and philosophy.

MARGARET EDDS

After his arrest on the evening of November 10, 1990, Chris was transported to the Chesterfield Juvenile Detention Home in Chesterfield, Virginia. Despite the fact that he would soon be charged as an adult, state law prevented officials from housing seventeen-year-old Chris with adult offenders. Chris's world collapsed in upon itself in the days after the murders, and the detention facility records graphically recorded the teenager's struggle to comprehend what he had done. While Chris "exhibited no aggressive behavior towards peers or staff," a counselor observed that he "appears to be chronically depressed, suffers from nightmares regarding the instant offenses, and 'certainly would not turn down an opportunity to committ [sic] suicide if it were offered to him.'"[1] Chris remained at the Chesterfield Juvenile Detention Home until late January 1991.

In the eight weeks following the murders of Kathy and J. B. Wiseman, events moved at a rapid pace. A local attorney named Benton H. Pollok was assigned to represent Chris in juvenile court. A graduate of William and Mary

Law School, Pollok had previously defended Chris in a petty larceny case. Pollok's appointment was arguably a lucky break—in an era where many indigent defendants in capital murder cases were assigned counsel with little criminal defense experience, Pollok had already defended five capital murder cases and saved all five clients from the electric chair.

The competency of court-appointed counsel in death penalty cases is one of the most criticized aspects of the modern capital punishment regime. The Sixth Amendment of the United States Constitution mandates that the state must provide an indigent defendant with legal counsel in felony cases.[2] The state is not, however, required to hire the best attorney available, just one that is minimally competent[3]—and minimal competence does not cost much to buy. As succinctly summarized by Columbia Law School professor James S. Liebman, "capital defense all too often falls to the worst lawyers the bar has to offer—frequently lawyers who can find no other work—while placing the highest demands upon them."[4] The inevitable product of mediocre representation, of course, is a greater likelihood of conviction. Stephen B. Bright, director of the Southern Center for Human Rights, explains: "Arbitrary results, which are all too common in death penalty cases, frequently stem from inadequacy of counsel. The process of sorting out who is most deserving of society's ultimate punishment does not work when the most fundamental component of the adversary system, competent representation by counsel, is missing."[5]

Bright adds, moreover, that the adversary system cannot function as designed when the two state governmental bodies charged with litigating death penalty cases, the prosecutor's office (which handles the original case) and the attorney general's office (which handles appeals), are given greater financial resources than counsel assigned to represent the indigent defendant. Finally, the judicial system itself does nothing to rectify this imbalance in talent and resources. "Many state court judges," writes Bright, "instead of correcting this imbalance, foster it by intentionally appointing inexperienced and incapable lawyers to defendant capital case, and denying funding for essential expert and investigative needs of the defense."[6]

In short, a capital defendant's right to a fair trial and effective assistance of counsel disappears in a sea of incompetence, disinterest, and unfairly allocated resources.

Death sentences have been imposed in cases in which defense lawyers had not even read the state's death penalty statute or did not know that a capital trial is bifurcated into separate determinations of guilt and punishment. State trial judges and prosecutors — who have taken oaths to uphold the law, including the Sixth Amendment — have allowed capital trials to proceed and death sentences to be imposed even when defense counsel fought among themselves or presented conflicting defenses for the same client, referred to their clients by a racial slur, cross-examined a witness whose direct testimony counsel missed because he was parking his car, slept through part of the trial, or was intoxicated during trial. Appellate courts often review and decide capital cases on the basis of appellate briefs that would be rejected in a first-year legal writing course in law school.[7]

In the era of the modern death penalty, the poor quality of defense counsel is most prevalent in the states that can least afford mediocre attorneys, namely, the handful of states that lead the country in executions. "The problem of bad lawyering is especially acute in the 'death belt' — the nine states in the South [Alabama, Florida, Georgia, Louisiana, Mississippi, North Carolina, South Carolina, Texas, Virginia] that have accounted for 90% of the nation's executions since capital punishment was reinstated in 1976. For example, a recent study of capital trials in the death belt revealed that lawyers who represented death row inmates at trial were subsequently disbarred, suspended, or otherwise disciplined at a rate three to forty-six times the average for those states."[8]

In the early 1990s the Commonwealth of Virginia lagged behind most states in both the quality of the legal representation provided to indigent defendants as well as the level of compensation paid to its court-appointed lawyers. The problem was simple to diagnose: Virginia paid a mere pittance to lawyers who handled death penalty cases, and the state had no established guidelines as to the professional training required of attorneys who sought appointment in capital cases. Therefore, some of the attorneys willing to take on indigent clients were lawyers with mediocre professional records whose practice depended on taking a high volume of court-appointed cases. During the 1970s, Virginia capped compensation for attorneys who represented indigent defendants in death penalty cases at a mere $400 per case. The salary cap was raised to $600 in the early 1980s. Given the complexity of capital murder cases, and the enormous amount of time needed to prepare for trial (typically between 300 to 500 hours), attorneys who diligently worked on behalf of their clients were making less than minimum wage. While the Virginia

General Assembly subsequently removed the salary cap in 1984 and authorized trial court judges to set limits on fees, a study conducted in 1988 found that the average compensation for attorneys in death eligible cases only rose by an average of $200.00. "In comparison, it was noted that the customary fee for privatively retained counsel in cases involving the possible loss of a driver's license is in the range of $500 to $700."[9]

In the fall of 1987, the Virginia State Bar hired an outside research organization to take a close look at Virginia's indigent capital defense system. In preparing its report, the think tank looked at existing state laws and informal norms regarding attorney compensation; it also surveyed judges and lawyers involved in death penalty cases. The report concluded that in Virginia's criminal justice system, the best and brightest criminal defense attorneys simply could not afford to accept appointments to capital murder cases. Those attorneys who did accept cases found that the representation took hundreds of hours of preparation, forced them to ignore their other clients (a violation of the ethical canons governing the profession), and produced woefully inadequate compensation.

A second major problem with Virginia's indigent defense system was the lack of training or standards for attorneys appointed to capital cases. Simply put, "there were no formal standards or specific qualifications for counsel to be eligible to represent indigent defendants in capital cases at trial in Virginia . . . the appointing judge generally has discretion in making the choice of counsel."[10] In the early 1990s, the Virginia General Assembly took a few modest steps toward addressing these problems. The state legislature passed new legislation requiring a public defender commission to promulgate standards that lawyers should meet in order to defend death penalty cases and to maintain a list of attorneys meeting said standards. Even so the qualifications were arguably minimal and more "concerned with past experience rather than past competence."[11] Subsequent changes have been instituted in the last five years, including the creation of capital defense teams staffed by experienced public defenders. Chris Thomas, however, did not benefit from these reforms; at the time of his trial there were no standards for court-appointed counsel and no attempts to fairly compensate attorneys who represented indigent defendants.

Given the state of the indigent defense system in Virginia in the early 1990s, having appointed counsel with Benton Pollok's experience was rare. Pollok was fond of Chris, whom he referred to as "my lad," and he traveled to the Chesterfield County Juvenile Detention Home "every chance I could get." From the start, however, Pollok struggled to break through the walls that Chris had erected:

He was . . . in such a protective mode [of Jessica] that he was not respond-ing as well as he could. He wasn't forthcoming with the information that I needed to defend him. We never had a cross word. And I kept pleading. I actually pleaded with him. "Chris, this is a serious, serious case, lad . . . they could take your life from you." But he was in a state of confusion about things at this particular time and trying to remain loyal to Jessica. He was, I mean, that lad was so defensive about her, extremely so. She was an obsession to him.[12]

While frustrated, Pollok understood his client's motivation. "He found some-one he thought really loved him, and he was going to protect her in spite of everything." At times, however, even the gregarious Pollok struggled to engage the increasingly despondent teenager. "A lot of times when I would go talk to him he'd just stare off into space. And I'd ask him, I'd say 'Chris, don't you realize how serious this situation is? They could take your life.' He'd just continue to stare off out there somewhere."[13]

As Benton Pollok met with Chris, the Virginia State Police collected evi-dence in their case against Chris and Jessica. The state police were forced to interview and reinterview the young girl who would prove to be their key witness: Lainie Creech. The repeated interviews were required because Lainie was not completely forthcoming with the investigators. In her first interview (conducted on the day of the murders), Lainie recounted nothing unusual in the weeks or days leading to the murders of the Wisemans. She did, however, state that at 8:00 P.M. on the evening before the murders, she and Chris saw "two (2) guys in long 'trench coats' [in the neighborhood]. When these sub-jects saw them they would run into the woods. They appeared to be 15 to 20 years old. Both white. One was skinny and the other 'tubby.'" We don't know whether Lainie actually saw two such individuals, or if she was protecting Chris by feeding false information to the police.[14]

After Brenda Marshall informed the Virginia State Police that Jessica told Lainie Creech confidential information about her parents' murders, Special Agent Larry A. Johnson, Jr., returned to Middlesex County to reinterview her. Brenda Marshall and Creech's parents were present at the second meet-ing. Lainie told the investigator that approximately three months earlier she had overheard Jessica and Chris discussing "getting rid" of Jessica's parents. The conversation took place shortly after J. B. and Kathy Wiseman had reconciled, and Jessica was chafing under the new disciplinary rules imposed by her parents. Lainie added, however, that she interpreted "getting rid" of the Wisemans as "just scaring them away."[15]

During her second interview, Creech recalled a second conversation that she overheard in the Marshall residence on the Tuesday before the murders. The report states:

> While they [Chris and Jessica] sat on the sofa, she [Creech] overheard them talking about getting rid of JESSICA's parents Thursday night (11–8). She heard JESSICA ask CHRIS if he had enough bullets? CHRIS told her he did. CHRIS asked JESSICA what time she wanted him to come over. They were mumbling something about the time when LAINIE said she got up [from the kitchen table] and went to the kitchen sink. She thought they knew she was there and was just trying to scare her. When CHRIS saw her, she knew he and JESSICA wasn't aware she had been in the kitchen. She said CHRIS asked her if she had heard what they had been talking about. She told him she didn't know what they were talking about. CHRIS started telling her, "If you tell, I'll . . ." JESSICA sorta grabbed his leg and squeezed it to keep him from finishing, but CREECH said she heard him mumble, "You going to get it or you're gone or something like that." CREECH said that in her mind, she thought they were discussing killing someone and it frightened her, but it wasn't until she heard them talking about JESSICA's parents that she suspected it was them they were talking about. After going to her room, she thought about it and assumed it was just a joke.[16]

Lainie volunteered a slew of additional new facts: Chris announcing on Thursday night that Herbert and Brenda had "a little truck problem" and wouldn't be coming home that night. Chris's fear that he would be punished for going to Roanoke and polluting the gas tank of Herbert Marshall's new truck with oil, gravel, and water and cutting the brake line. Lainie's delivery of *Auto Trader* magazine to Jessica's bedroom window. The most dramatic, however, was saved for last. Lainie now claimed that while the Virginia State Police conducted their first, posthomicide interview with Chris, Jessica confessed all the details of the murder plot to Lainie. "'Oh, Lainie,' she reported Jessica as saying. 'If you could have seen mommy [wounded and crawling into the hallway] you would have started crying.'"[17]

Lainie's memory continued to improve. The Virginia State Police received a second telephone call from Brenda Marshall, announcing that Lainie had left the Marshall's home with Chris on the morning of the murders. On November 26, 1990, Special Agent Johnson returned to Middlesex County for a third interview. This time, Lainie talked about Chris's anxiety on the Thursday night before the murders, when he told Lainie he was jumpy because "'I'm killing two people tonight'" and later expressed shock at the early return of Brenda and Herbert Marshall. Lainie admitted that she accompanied Chris on his fateful walk through the early morning darkness to the Wisemans' home, even carrying the shotgun for Chris during a portion of the journey. Finally, Lainie disclosed to Special Agent Johnson that Chris had confided the postmurder plan to her: Chris returning home and feigning sleep; Jessica pounding on the front door, screaming of murders and drug conspiracies.[18]

What should we make of Lainie Creech and her evolving story? Was she a frightened twelve-year-old, clumsily protecting a cousin for whom some claimed she had her own romantic feelings? Was she holding back information to hide her own complicity in the murder plot? Or was she embellishing the facts, adding false information to curry favor with law enforcement officers? The answer may never be known, but the information provided in the second and third interviews provided the evidence of premeditation critical to a capital murder case.

In the days following the murders, the local newspapers published story after story on the young teenagers and their tale of love and murder.[19] Often the characterizations of the major players in the tragedy varied wildly, as reporters embellished the crime and painted barely recognizable caricatures of the major players. Some articles described Chris as an ordinary teenager, who loved cars, skateboarding, and hunting. He was "a surfer who wanted to practice law," explained one reporter.[20] Other accounts pointed to Chris's previous brushes with the police, his stint in juvenile hall, and his confrontations with the Wisemans over dating their young daughter. Jessica Wiseman was either "'a normal child, as sweet as she could be'"[21] who fell hard for a good-looking older teenager and "dreamed of becoming a housewife and mother,"[22] or a spoiled and manipulative brat who drove around her housing development in her own golf cart and whose temper tantrums bent adults to her will. As for the Wisemans, some stories described them as good parents and a loving couple. "They didn't raise some kind of wild child," protested one neighbor. "'They weren't a heathen family.'"[23] Other accounts, however, spoke of marital problems, drinking problems, and halfhearted attempts to discipline a headstrong daughter.

Brenda Marshall seemingly gave interviews to every journalist that wandered into Middlesex County. Despite professing her love for both Chris and Jessica, in interview after interview Brenda single-handedly made a first-degree murder case against the teenagers. Brenda announced to the media that both Chris and Jessica confessed to the murders after police interrogation, relaying to reporters that after the arrests a handcuffed Chris Thomas had told her "he wished he hadn't have done it, he just wished he hadn't have done it," while Jessica had sadly confided to Brenda from the back of a patrol car that "they just thought the only way they could ever be together was if they killed her parents."[24] For good measure, Brenda provided a motive for the murders, telling reporters that Jessica was pregnant and fearful of her father's reaction. "'It's just something they couldn't get out of,' she [Brenda] said. 'She was expecting. Her parents didn't want them to see each other any more, and they didn't see a way out.'"[25]

In fact, Brenda suggested that the two youngsters were so desperate to be together that they tried to kill her and her husband, Herbert, by polluting their truck's gas tank and cutting a brake line. "'We think they were trying to do us in so we couldn't get back here and find out what was going on,'" Brenda explained.[26] In the very same interview, however, Brenda tried to rationalize their behavior. "'I think they just panicked,' Marshall said. 'I don't even want to think that they would want us dead because this kid lived right here at my house.'"[27] Perhaps aware that the lax supervision of her young wards might be criticized, Brenda explained that the shotgun used in the murders was the only gun that could not be locked in the Marshalls' gun safe because "its barrel was too long." No newspaper reporter asked Brenda why she left twelve-year-old Lainie Creech and seventeen-year-old Chris Thomas alone while she and her husband went on an out-of-town hunting trip or whether she considered canceling the vacation after learning of Jessica's pregnancy fears.

On Tuesday morning, November 13, Kathy and J. B. Wiseman were laid to rest in matching blue caskets in the cemetery behind the Lower United Methodist Church in Hartfield, Virginia. Their only child was conspicuously absent from the proceedings. As the funeral service took place, Middlesex County Sheriff Lewis Jones III was driving to the juvenile detention centers in Chesterfield and Richmond, Virginia, to pick up Jessica and Chris. Jones later recalled a conversation that he had with Jessica: "She casually remarked,

'When are my parents' funerals?' And I remember, I looked at my watch, I said, 'right now.' She said, 'Oh.' No remorse," said Jones, who now works for the Virginia Marine Resources Commission. "It wasn't until many years later," he said, "she actually had an interest and did come down and view the grave site under the security of the juvenile system. I guess they considered it part of her rehabilitation."[28]

Unbelievably, the two co-conspirators were permitted to sit in the back of the patrol car and talk on the way to their first juvenile court hearing. "He [Jones] said he told them they could talk to one another, and what they said to one another would not be used against them. During the ride, Jones said he turned the radio up. The teen-agers whispered together, and the only thing the sheriff heard them discuss were conditions in their detention centers."[29] The ride also afforded at least a moment of physical intimacy. "[A] fter seeing you and kissing you Tuesday it kills me knowing I can't [kiss] you all the time like before," wrote Jessica to Chris two days after the detention hearing."[30]

In the afternoon of November 13, Chris and Jessica appeared before Juvenile and Domestic Relations Court Judge Herbert I. L. Feild at the Gloucester County Courthouse, a distinguished older man and a longtime juvenile court judge. Chris was served with petitions for capital murder, first-degree murder, and two counts of the illegal use of a firearm. Jessica Wiseman was not served with the petitions for two counts of murder, but soon would be. As Commonwealth Attorney James H. "Jimmy" Ward, Jr., stood before Judge Feild and summarized the petitions, Margaret Thomas, sitting next to her son, struggled to make eye contact with him and silently wept. Jessica sat slumped in a nearby chair, holding a red rose from her parents' graves (neighbors who attended the funeral had brought the rose to Jessica) and occasionally leaning over to ask her attorney a question. At the close of the hearing, lawyers for both Jessica and Chris asked Judge Feild to order psychological testing for the two teenagers.

On Wednesday, November 28, Judge Feild announced that Jessica Wiseman's murder trial would be scheduled for January 23, 1991. Under Virginia law at the time, juveniles under the age of fifteen could not be tried as adults. Thus, at most Jessica faced confinement to a juvenile facility until the age of twenty-one. Apparently believing that the bench trial would be quick, Judge Feild further announced that he would hold a hearing on the same day as the trial to decide whether to try Chris as a juvenile or an adult. Faced with almost daily news stories on his client, defense attorney Benton Pollok requested that Chris's transfer hearing be closed to the public. The intent of Pollok's request — the minimization of pretrial publicity — was undercut by Judge Feild's decision to have an open hearing on the request to have a closed hearing, a proceeding held in open court on December 12.[31]

At the December 12 hearing, Benton Pollok vigorously argued for closing the transfer hearing. "[H]e waved clippings from the *Daily Press*, the *Richmond Times-Dispatch* and the weekly *Southside Sentinel* of Urbanna in the air and called coverage of the case 'irresponsible reporting'" noted the Newport News *Daily Press*, one of the newspapers pilloried by Pollok.[32] In "dramatic, impassioned tones," Pollok argued that "it would be impossible to find a juror in the county who had not read or heard about the case. An open hearing, he said, 'will do nothing more than fan the flames and kill any chance for an impartial trial.'"[33] After allowing attorneys for the news media to argue in favor of a public transfer hearing, Judge Feild turned Pollok's argument on its head and concluded that open and unfettered media coverage could actually prevent the dissemination of inaccurate and damaging stories as well as assist in public understanding of the murders. The motion for a closed transfer hearing was summarily denied.

Sitting at counsel table and wearing a dark blue windbreaker, jeans, and white Nike tennis shoes, Chris half-heartedly followed the back-and-forth jousting of the lawyers. During a pause in the proceedings, he leaned over the railing that separated the well of the courtroom from the gallery, talked with his mother (who passed Chris some cigarettes), and even hugged Brenda Marshall. Either Chris did not know that Brenda was giving incredibly damaging interviews to the media, or he needed the emotional support of *any* friendly face, even that of a relative whose news conferences were fueling the very media firestorm that his own attorney was fighting to stamp out. In the coming months, Chris would take a less forgiving view of Brenda Marshall's behavior.

At the transfer hearing, Judge Feild would decide whether Chris should be transferred to circuit court (the state's trial court for all felony cases) and be tried as an adult. In making this determination, Virginia law required the judge to answer the following questions: (1) whether probable cause existed that the juvenile committed the act or acts charged; (2) whether the juvenile was "amenable to treatment or rehabilitation as a juvenile through available facilities, considering the nature of the present offense or such factors as the nature of the child's prior delinquency record, the nature of past treatment efforts and the nature of the child's response to past treatment efforts"; (3) whether the juvenile was either insane or mentally retarded, and (4) whether "the interests of the community require that the child be placed under legal restraint or discipline." Regarding the second question, namely, whether the juvenile was amenable to treatment, Virginia law stated that if a juvenile was charged with armed robbery, rape, or murder, the juvenile court judge did not have to determine the willingness of the juvenile to undergo treatment before transferring the case to circuit court.[34]

The transfer hearing, however, was never held. On January 23, 1991, Benton Pollok announced that his client would waive the transfer hearing and agree to be tried as an adult in circuit court.[35] In court, Pollok explained to Judge Feild that it was "in the best interests of his client not to hold the hearings" as "'no meaningful purpose could be served' by the hearings . . . and that news media coverage of them could have an impact on future proceedings."[36] In short, Pollok believed that it was inevitable that Chris would be tried as an adult and didn't want to waste the time and energy on a pointless transferring hearing that would only further feed the hungry media.

It was a risky gamble. The waiver of the transfer hearing would be revisited in the weeks leading up to Chris's capital murder trial, with a new set of defense attorneys arguing that the waiver was improper and ill-advised. As Chris Thomas left the courthouse after his aborted transfer hearing, nearly a dozen photographers and journalists jostled to get a picture of the young man. Watching from a distance, Commonwealth Attorney Ward loudly observed that the crowd was "'[l]ike vultures on a dead animal.'"[37]

In Virginia the decision whether to seek an indictment for capital murder from a grand jury is made by the commonwealth attorney who represents the county or city in which the murder occurred. The commonwealth attorney presents a "bill of indictment" for capital murder to the grand jury, and, based on the evidence presented by the prosecutor, the grand jury decides whether there is probable cause that a crime occurred. Only the commonwealth attorney presents evidence. If the grand jury answers in the affirmative, then a "true bill" is returned by the grand jury.

The commonwealth attorney has the sole discretion to decide how to charge a suspect. This unfettered power has concerned those who study the Virginia judicial system, including the Virginia Chapter of the ACLU. In a 2003 report entitled *Broken Justice: The Death Penalty in Virginia*, the report's authors conclude that whether an individual is charged with a capital crime in Virginia turns on such arbitrary, extralegal factors as the geographic location of the crime (the less populated the county, the more likely the commonwealth attorney will seek the death sentence) and race (the probability of being charged with capital murder increases if the victim is white and/or the perpetrator is black).[38] In other words, the ACLU report argues that some (not all) prosecutors seek the death penalty not for the most hardened criminals and for the most vile crimes, but to placate a conservative and/or racist constituency.

It was Commonwealth Attorney Jimmy Ward who sought a capital murder indictment against Chris Thomas. A native of Middlesex County and the son and grandson of "watermen" (a term used to describe men who fished the Chesapeake Bay for oysters and blue crabs), Ward graduated from Middlesex High School before earning his undergraduate and law degrees from the University of Richmond. After working as in-house counsel for a mortgage company, Ward returned to Middlesex County and went into private practice. He was first elected Middlesex County Commonwealth Attorney in November 1979, at the relatively young age of thirty. Besides serving as commonwealth attorney and (briefly) as the county attorney, Ward was a deacon in a local Baptist church and coached in a youth basketball league. Ward was widely considered to be a competent, professional, and fair attorney—not only by his clients and friends, but by the judges he appeared before and the defense attorneys with whom he battled.

Ward faced reelection in the fall of 1991, and he told voters that he wanted to return as commonwealth attorney because of his "desire to utilize my legal education to give back something to the citizens of this county in return for what they gave me when I was young. If re-elected, I intend to continue my committment [sic] of the last 12 years of diligent prosecution and the protection of the rights of the individual."[39] Whether he desired it or not, Ward's prosecution of Chris Thomas and Jessica Wiseman earned him valuable political support from both the local community and the media. "We see no compelling reason to unseat 12-year incumbent James H. Ward Jr.," opined the Newport News *Daily Press*. "[A]nd in fact his re-election would be a vote of appreciation for his professional prosecution of the touchiest county case in years, the double murder of Jessica Wiseman's parents at the hands of their teen-age daughter and her boyfriend."[40] Running as an Independent, Ward easily won reelection. Certainly a gruesome double murder provided sufficient reason to contemplate bringing charges of capital murder against Chris Thomas. But were other, extralegal factors at play? Did a pending election in a conservative county play any part in Ward's decision to charge Chris with capital murder?[41] In correspondence with these authors, former Thomas defense attorney Damian Horne believes that there were, voicing his belief that Ward did not lower the charges to first-degree murder in exchange for a plea agreement because it was an election year.[42]

On January 28, 1991, Chris Thomas was indicted by a Middlesex County grand jury for the murders of Kathy and J. B. Wiseman. Specifically, he was indicted on one count of first-degree murder (the killing of J. B. Wiseman), one count of capital murder (the killing of Kathy Wiseman), and two counts of the illegal use of a firearm. In keeping with his poor education and utter naïveté, Chris never contemplated the possibility that he might be executed for his crimes. From the perspective of a criminal defendant, he could not have picked a worse state in which to participate in a double homicide.

Since the founding of the first colonial settlement in 1607, more than thirteen hundred men, women, and children have died in Virginia's gallows, electric chair, and lethal injection chamber—more than any other colony or state. In the "modern" death penalty era (commonly defined as 1976 to present), the pace has not slackened. Virginia has executed 103 inmates in the last twenty-two years and has averaged approximately nine executions a year. The only death penalty state that has executed more inmates since 1976 is Texas.[43] While it is impossible to find a precise figure of the total number of individuals executed by the American colonies and states from 1607 to present, conservative estimates place the number somewhere between 19,000 and 22,000.[44]

The first execution in American history occurred in Jamestown, taking place within the first year of the founding of the settlement by the Virginia Company. The unfortunate soul was Captain George Kendall, one of the original leaders of the Jamestown colony, who was convicted of spying for Spain. Some historians have speculated that Kendall was nothing more than a "troublemaker" who was at the losing end of a political tussle among leaders of the settlement's ruling council and was convicted on the flimsiest of evidence. "The only accuser [of Kendall] of whom we have record is James Read, the artisan who had insulted Wingfield [the council president] and who at the moment he made the accusation was standing on the gallows awaiting [his own] execution."[45] Thus Kendall has the dubious honor of not only being the first execution in what would become the Commonwealth of Virginia, but perhaps also the first innocent man executed on Virginia soil. Despite his treasonous behavior, "Kendall was a gentleman, and as such was entitled to be shot instead of hanged . . . had he been a noble he would have claimed the right to be beheaded."[46] With a cloth covering his face, Kendall was brought before a firing squad and executed in late 1607.[47] The corpse of Captain Kendall was subsequently accorded full military honors and buried in a coffin inside the settlement's walls.[48]

In 1611, Sir Thomas Dale was appointed the acting governor for the Virginia Colony. Dismayed by the abysmal conditions that he found, Dale implemented the colony's first legal code: "Articles, Lawes, and Orders Divine, Politique, and Martiall." A draconian set of laws, the code imposed the death penalty for such acts as blasphemy, the uttering of "traiterous words" or "unseemly, and unfitting speeches" against the colonial government, failing to honor the Sabbath, bartering with Indians, stealing roots, herbs, grapes, corn, or livestock, perjury, robbery, sodomy, adultery, rape, and murder. The code implemented by Dale, however, was unique in that it was designed to both create order and discipline within the tiny settlement as well as protect the shareholders' financial stake in the Virginia Company.

Dale's Laws remained in effect until 1619, when the Virginia General Assembly passed its first set of criminal laws. From 1619 to 1796, Virginia followed the English practice of (1) separating crimes into the general categories of misdemeanors and felonies, and (2) imposing the death penalty for *all* felonies.[49] It was pursuant to these laws that Daniell Frank was executed on March 1, 1622, for stealing livestock (the first recorded hanging in Virginia); in 1624, Richard Cornish, convicted of bestiality, buggery, and sodomy, became the second colonist to swing from the hangman's noose. The first execution of a woman in the new colonies also occurred in Virginia. Jane Champion was hanged in approximately 1632 in James City, Virginia, for the murder of a child born from her adulterous affair with William Gallopin; in 1633, Margaret Hatch was hanged for murder.[50] From 1619 to 1796, Virginia imposed the death penalty on her white citizens primarily for the crime of murder.

It is instructive to place Virginia's criminal laws in their proper historical and legal context. During the 1600s and early 1700s, all American colonies relied upon capital punishment, a practice they imported from the mother country. The thirteen colonies differed, however, in *which* crimes were death eligible. Author Stuart Banner writes that "the law in the southern colonies

... included capital punishment for more property offenses and fewer morality offenses than in the northern colonies. As the northern colonies gradually de-capitalized blasphemy and the like, the southern colonies were left with the greater number of capital crimes, particularly where property was concerned."[51] Faced with the necessity of controlling an expanding slave population, the South also adopted a slew of death penalty statutes that applied only to slaves and free blacks. For example, "Virginia, fearing attempts at poisoning, made it a capital offense for slaves to prepare or administer medicine.... Georgia ... made it a capital offense for slaves or free blacks to strike whites twice, or once if a bruise resulted."[52]

In the decades following the Civil War, the Virginia General Assembly passed legislation giving juries the discretion to impose the death penalty against *all* citizens (white or black) for the crimes of attempted rape, rape, robbery, and burglary. The death penalty remained mandatory for murder, arson, and treason. While the new laws seemed to abandon Virginia's practice of treating blacks and whites differently, the practical impact of the new laws was not race neutral. "The [effect of the new] legislation was once again to authorize the death penalty for these crimes. But since the legislature apparently felt it impolitic to distinguish penalties by race, they made the death penalty discretionary for these crimes, and placed their trust in the judgment of white judges and white juries."[53] While it was possible that free whites could be put to death for rape, robbery, and burglary, the combination of white judges and juries meant that the ultimate punishment was reserved for black, not white defendants.[54]

While the dramatic disparities in the application of the death penalty have faded in the last forty years, there is evidence that the Commonwealth of Virginia does not apply its capital murder statute in a racially neutral fashion. From 1982 to 2008, Virginia has executed 103 men for the crime of capital murder. Virginia has executed approximately the same number of blacks and whites during this time period,[55] giving rise to the claims that the Commonwealth had ended its racially discriminatory application of the death penalty. Yet studies have shown that racism can be found in Virginia's crime statistics, a bigotry that shows more concern with punishing those who kill white citizens.[56] Other stark patterns are found among those sentenced to live or die by Virginia juries. While quantitative statistics on the socioeconomic backgrounds of Virginia's condemned prisoners are not available, the attorneys, mitigation specialists, and spiritual advisors who work with the men of the row see damaged and broken men who came from impoverished homes; endured physical, mental, and sexual abuse as children; struggled in school; became addicted to alcohol and drugs; and disproportionately suffered from mental illness and retardation. In keeping with their backgrounds, the men could not afford to hire legal counsel when charged with crimes and were forced to rely upon the tender mercies of the Commonwealth of Virginia to provide competent legal counsel. As the old death row saying goes, "those with the capital don't get the punishment."

Children and teenagers did not escape the gallows in Virginia; between 1866 and 1962 there is documented evidence of four black minors being executed for the crime of rape. There are no records of white children facing similar punishment. The youngest person ever executed in Virginia was a twelve-year-old slave named Clem, who was tried and convicted of the two murders of his owners' juvenile sons; he was hanged outside of the Sussex County courthouse on May 11, 1787.[57]

The juvenile death penalty is not a relic of the colonial past, and the first three decades of the twentieth century witnessed the execution of thirteen juveniles in Virginia. One of those teenagers was Alfred Wright, who in 1912 was charged with the rape of a white widow named Bertha Ferguson. Wright was convicted and sentenced within two days of the purported rape. The trial court judge denied the young man's request for a trial continuance, writing that Wright's crime "is regarded as the worst . . . [n]o other crime so excites, alarms, and arouses our people. It not only violates the laws of God and Man, but owing to the peculiar conditions prevailing in this our land, it is a deadly menace to the very frame-work of society itself." Accordingly, the trial judge denied the motion based on the ground that "the highest and most sacred public interests demand a speedy trial."

The judge had cause to claim knowledge of public interest: a noisy lynch mob filled his courtroom during the trial, and the jury deliberated for a mere fifteen minutes before returning with a sentence of death. According to a newspaper account of the trial and verdict, "The community was entirely satisfied, and while the prisoner will be taken to Richmond at once, all fear of lynching is now over."[58] The Virginia Supreme Court denied Alfred Wright's appeal, and within eight weeks of his trial he was executed. All in all, between the years 1787 and 1924, Virginia executed sixteen black defendants under the age of eighteen.[59] The last male juvenile offender to be tried and executed in

Virginia prior to Chris's case was Sam Pannell, a black male who was electro-cuted on May 20, 1932, for the rape of a white female.

In the same year, Virginia executed its last female juvenile. Her name was Virginia Christian, a seventeen-year-old black servant who went to work at age thirteen to help support her seven brothers and sisters. Christian was convicted of strangling her employer, Mrs. Ida Virginia Belote, after Mrs. Belote repeatedly struck Virginia with a spittoon and accused her of steal-ing a skirt. The murder was highly publicized, with the media breathlessly reporting on the depravity of the crime.

The trial took place a mere two weeks after the murder of Mrs. Belote, and two black attorneys represented Christian at trial (it was rare for a minority to have legal representation during a felony case). During the trial, "[t]he social position and popularity of the victim [a white female] stood in stark contrast to the Christian family background and to Christian's unkempt appearance and rude manner in describing the crime."[60] Not surprisingly, Christian was summarily convicted and executed on August 16, 1912, in the penitentiary's death house. Virginia Christian does not have a final resting place; her family was too poor to pay to have her body shipped home to Hampton, Virginia, and it was donated to a local medical college.

The practice of executing children is not unique to Virginia. Law professor Victor L. Streib, an expert on juvenile executions, reports that 281 children have been executed in the United States from the years 1642 to 1986 for crimes committed while under the age of eighteen.[61] Streib suspects that the actual figure of juvenile executions is higher, but that inadequate record-keeping and the informal practice of lynchings have lowered the number of documented executions. Although the execution of juveniles slowed to a trickle in the last fifty years, states continued executing juvenile offenders. Given the long periods of appeals that follow modern death penalty convictions, however, there was one critical difference between the executions of juveniles in the eighteenth and nineteenth centuries versus those of the twentieth century: the condemned prisoners of the late twentieth century were adults when they were strapped into the electric chair or tied to the lethal injection gurney, sparing correctional officials and witnesses the sight of tiny legs dangling from the electric chair inches above the floor, gangly limbs that squirmed under the adult-sized straps that bound them, or small bodies, like that of David Owen Dodd, that "dangled writhing in the air [from the gallows] . . . so slender and light was the body that the soldiers present had to pull and jerk it in order to break his neck."[62]

This was the history that loomed over Chris Thomas as he was indicted for capital murder. The judge who would preside over Chris Thomas's capital murder case was John "Jack" Montague Folkes, a recent appointee to the Ninth Judicial Circuit Court (the state trial court with jurisdiction over serious felony cases in Middlesex County). A native of Richmond, Virginia, and a graduate of the T. C. Williams School of Law at the University of Richmond, Judge Folkes practiced law in nearby Gloucester County, Virginia, before his appointment. While Folkes earned a reputation as an eloquent and tough judge, after his death local attorneys and judges claimed that it was a facade. "'On the surface, he was brusque and acerbic, but he looked at sending someone to prison as a last resort. Jack was very forgiving of character flaws in people, but he didn't want to seem too soft,'" explained former Commonwealth Attorney Robert D. Hicks. "'Really, the courtroom demeanor was just an act.'"[63] Often in court, Judge Folkes's comments were peppered with quotations from literature, the Bible, and popular culture.

On the same day that he was indicted for capital murder, Chris was transferred to the juvenile section of the Newport News City Jail. During his stay at the facility, Chris was repeatedly beaten up and, on one occasion, forced to defend himself with a homemade knife (a "shank"). Chris later claimed that he also tried to hang himself in his cell. Because of Chris's allegations of assault, he was sent to the juvenile section of the Richmond City Jail on February 27, 1991. Both facilities, however, were plagued with unsanitary conditions, overcrowding, and violence, and those close to Chris believe that he was sexually assaulted at either the Newport News or the Richmond City facility. Chris subsequently told a counselor that on two different occasions he tried to kill himself at the Richmond City Jail, once by drinking ammonia and once by taking a combination of Tylenol and cold medication tablets. Chris remained at the Richmond City Jail until June 25, 1991.

As Chris's world crumbled around him, the one constant in his life remained Jessica. She wrote Chris almost every day, and her correspondence continued for the next two years. While we do not have copies of the letters that Chris mailed to Jessica, Chris saved most of the letters that he received from Jessica. He eventually turned them over to Marie Deans as possible mitigation evidence. Given the seriousness of the charges filed against the two teenagers, as well as the conflicting nature of their legal defenses, it is surprising that their attorneys did not take concrete steps to prevent Chris and Jessica from corresponding. While Jessica's attorney knew of the correspondence and seized some of Chris's letters, in none of the letters does Jessica indicate that she has been ordered to cease communication.[64] Jessica, however, did appreciate the dangers in writing Chris. "Something else you have to promise me you won't do and that's telling Brenda [Marshall], your mom, or your lawyer anything I say . . . cause it will just make EVERYTHING WORSE!"[65] Reading between the lines, by "worse," Jessica meant worse for herself and her legal defense.

But for the fact that both the writer and recipient of the letters were charged with murder, many of the letters seem as superficial as the love notes that high school students scrawl to each other on notebook paper during study hall. Decorated with flowers and hearts as well as proclamations of undying love, filled with spelling, grammatical, and punctuation errors, and signed "Mrs. Jessica Thomas," the letters talk of wedding plans, future names of their children, petty jealousies about imagined suitors, disappointment about not receiving more letters, demands for pictures, their physical relationship, and eternal love.

> Chris, I love you sooooooo [sic] much and its [sic] killing me not being with you. I just got your letter and it was sweet. I cried over almost everything you said not, because it upset me, but because I was so happy when you were "I think" happy about the baby and when you said you would always want me & it was like a dream come true—us being together.[66]

What is chilling about Jessica's letters is that her parents are never discussed. Evidence of guilt, remorse, or grief over their murders is absent among the hundreds of pages of letters. It is as if J. B. and Kathy Wiseman never existed. The only expression of contrition involves not the death of Jessica's parents, but that the murders led to the young lovers' physical separation. "You know we really messed up this time," Jessica concludes. "[I]t [the murders] only made us further apart."[67] In a subsequent letter, Jessica writes that "the biggest mistake in my whole life" would be damaging her relationship with Chris.[68] One wonders where murder ranks on the scale of mistakes.

For Jessica, Chris is the only person of significance in her universe—or so she claims. "[Y]ou mean everything to me," Jessica writes. "If they (court) takes [sic] you away from me, then I would have lost the most important person in my whole life, someone very special, my one and only true love."[69]

"I Love You more than anything in this whole world."[70] For Jessica, "*no* one has ever loved me and cared about me as much as you do!"[71] Curiously, Chris seeks reassurance that Jessica's immediate family members also love him. "AND NO nanny and pawpaw don't hate you. I *Promise!* Their [*sic*] upset with 'both' of us! But they told me they love 'both' of us and they still want us to get married. . . . I 'know' that your mom HATES me! I don't blaim [*sic*] her though. The only people in my family that don't hate me are nanny, pawpaw and I think tootie and Ernest [her great-grandparents]."[72]

In many of the letters, a needy Jessica demands reassurance that Chris still loves and wants her. "I'm sooooo [*sic*] 'scared' of losing you! Chris, I can't live without you and even if I could I *don't* want to not now or ever. . . . Baby your [*sic*] the only thing that's keeping me going. . . . You say I'll *never* have to worry about losing you, but I know I wouldn't be able to handle it, so I do worry 'all the time'!"[73] In another letter Jessica admits that she fears that Chris won't want her because "I've gotton [*sic*] fat,"[74] and she confesses her fear that her incarcerated lover will be untrue. "[A]ll the girls are telling me a lot of stuff like you don't love me anymore and that you are going with some girl named Joy that's [*sic*] locked up with you."[75] To guard against infidelity, Jessica warns Chris to ignore the written siren songs of former lovers. "I swear to you that if Kari, Tracy, or Shalonda writes you, I don't even want to think about what I'll do to them when or if I ever go home."[76]

In keeping with the teenagers' youth, immaturity, and lack of education, the letters evidence a fundamental misunderstanding of how the legal system operated, the legal defenses available to them, and the severity of the probable consequences. Regarding the charges filed against Chris in juvenile court, Jessica writes that Chris must "get your lawyer to try to change the capital [charge] to 1st degree or its gonna [*sic*] be bad."[77] If Chris can't get the charges reduced, then Jessica has another plan. "[R]emember when you told me to plead insanity," Jessica writes. "[A]t this point in time it won't really help me, I mean it will, but it will help you more! So promise me that's what you will do. Unless you know of something better."[78] In Jessica's eyes, an insanity defense was the proverbial "get out of jail free" card that could restore their romantic dreams for the future. "[I]f you plead insanity you can get off completely and just have counseling," Jessica later advises Chris.[79] Jessica adds, however, that there is a downside to Chris's pleading insanity. "I will be locked up til' [*sic*] god knows when. So now you have to promise me that if that does happen [and Chris is free due to an insanity plea] you *won't* cheat on me!"[80] At times,

Jessica is confused as to her own legal options. In a letter written shortly after the murders, she tells Chris that "I have to plead guilty. You have a choice [but] I don't," although she doesn't explain to Chris why a guilty plea is her only recourse.[81]

In the first month after the murders, Jessica sends mixed signals as to whether Chris should accept the full blame for the crimes. In a letter written almost three weeks after the deaths of her parents, Jessica writes:

> To answer your question about you taking the blame, its [sic] NO! Theres [sic] no way that I would do that to you. Because of me you have to get locked up, its [sic] not your fault. It is "all" my fault. I should be the one with all the blame. That was really sweet of you to offer to do that, but I Love You and if you have to be locked up so do I![82]

Should we take Jessica's statement at face value? At that point in time, did she sincerely believe that she — not Chris — was the guilty party and deserved the entire blame for her parents' death? Does Jessica mean that she merits "all the blame" because she masterminded the murders? Is this acknowledgment that Chris did not fire all three shots?

When Jessica believes, however, that Chris might actually publicly blame her for the murders, the tone of her letters shifts dramatically. Only four days after reassuring Chris that "[i]t is 'all' my fault," Jessica accuses Chris of betrayal. Announcing that she is "not doing good at all," Jessica writes:

> [M]y doctors & lawyer came and told me the reason why [she wasn't being allowed to go home]. Its [sic] because your doctors told mine that *you* "said" it was all my fault and I told you if you didn't do it that we couldn't (so to speak) make love *anymore*! So I am completely confused? Please explain to me whats [sic] going on, I mean has your lawyer turned you against me? Please say he hasn't, and be truthful! Chris, baby I Love You and I'd never do anything to hurt you . . . please promise me you won't listen to your lawyer [or] anyone about us, because baby we have something . . . special that can last forever if we let it.[83]

As Chris's defense lawyers worked to break through the unreality that their client had erected around himself, Jessica undermined their efforts by emotionally manipulating Chris and telling him to ignore his attorneys.

The mixed signals continued. After accusing Chris of being deceitful, Jessica again changes her position on the blame game. "I don't think its [sic] a very good idea for you to say its 'all' your fault because you might get a worse punishment if you do, and Chris I want you & me out of this as soon as possible so we can go home and be 'together' always and forever!"[84] In a subsequent letter, Jessica magnanimously tells Chris to accept the full blame if he so desires. "I don't want you to go as far as saying you held the gun up to my head, because it will make it much worse on you. You can get me off if you want, but that [does] *NOT* mean that you'll lose me if I go home, because as soon as they tell me I can visit you, where ever [sic] you go, I'm going to [sic]!"[85]

As Jessica and Chris prepared to face formal legal proceedings in January 1991, the mind games ended. In a letter dated January 10, 1991, Jessica starkly revealed her intentions as to whom would play the sacrificial lamb:

My lawyer told me that your gonna [sic] plea-bargain. In a way that's good, because you will get a much shorter sentence, but I hope you understand that, that means your [sic] putting *all* the blame on me and that I could be locked up longer than you. Plus in court *you* and a whole bunch of other people will testify against me. You are gonna [sic] have to say bad things about me to my face. I don't understand why, I mean are you doing this so you can get a shorter time and hoping that since I'm a juvenile that I'll get out soon anyway or are you doing it because you'll get out soon and then forget all about me. . . . Chris, baby remember how I used to tell you to be yourself and don't act how you think everybody wants you to! Well your [sic] not being yourself, because I know and hope that you do love me. . . . I don't know what else to say, because I can't make choices for you. But, baby if what their [sic] saying is true please think about it. We are so happy and sooooooooo [sic] much in love![86]

Two days later, Jessica returned to the topic of the plea bargain. Reminding Chris that he would have to testify against her, Jessica begs Chris to "think about what your [sic] gonna [sic] say before you say it, because what ever or how eve[r] much you say is gonna [sic] depend on how long I [am] locked up!! In other words, I could be locke[d] up for 7 years (til' I'm 21) and you only 5 yrs."[87]

Parties involved in the Chris Thomas case assert that a plea bargain was tentatively brokered at least once in the months prior to Chris's trial, and on several other occasions Judge Folkes signaled that a plea bargain (which meant that the judge, not a jury, would sentence Chris) would save Chris's life. Defense attorney Damian Horne recalls that Judge Folkes did more than hint that a plea bargain would save Chris:

> There were no hints. There were promises! Of all the things I recall most vividly, this one stands out the clearest . . . even above the pronouncement of the Death Sentence. Judge Folkes called me into Chambers with Jimmy Ward and said: "If either of you ever say a Circuit Court Judge participated in plea negotiations, I will call you both liars . . . but Jimmy, can't you give Damian something? If I sentence, he will spend the rest of his life in jail, but this is a case of the heart not the mind. . . . He did a horrible thing . . . but . . ." Jimmy would not consider dropping [the charges from] Capital to First Degree. It was an election year and that was the reason he gave. So then Judge Folkes turned to me and said: "Damian . . . you must know that I will not disturb a jury verdict. You've heard what I will do. You must tell your client . . ." (or words very similar to those).[88]

After the meeting, Horne went to see Chris and "virtually begged" him to plead guilty. "Unfortunately, he was very immature, I was not experienced enough and I did not FORCE him to plea guilty. I tried, but I failed. The client is always boss and that decision ultimately remains with them, but, under the circumstances, that one is on me and always will be."[89] Concludes Horne: "When we left—unsuccessfully—Sydney told me I had probably violated my duty to him [Chris] as an attorney because I had put so much pressure on him to plead. She indicated that I appeared on the verge of physical violence."[90] Based on Chris's misplaced devotion to Jessica, and his self-defined role as her protector, it's likely that Chris would never have agreed to a plea bargain after receiving such a letter from Jessica. How could Chris betray the only person in the world who loved him?

Fortunately, Jessica was not the only person writing to Chris Thomas. In the weeks following the murders, a still-shocked Laura Anderson wrote the first of a steady stream of letters to Chris.

> I hope you are holding up O.K. This is a very difficult letter to write as you can imagine. All of this is very overwhelming. I am very concerned about you. I think about you very often and wonder what I can do to help you. Chris, if you need me to do anything, just ask. I think you may request to start classes again. That might be in your best interest.
>
> Chris, please know that I put a great deal of myself in your teaching,

in helping you and I still care what happens to you. I have talked to your Mom twice because I am also concerned with how she is doing. Please try to keep your chin up. Let me know if I can do anything for you. Since you were a special education student you can probably get spec. ed. services now. Look into it — It might help.[91]

Laura did not hear from Chris until February 6, 1991, when she received a letter written in Chris's careful hand on a single yellow sheet of lined notebook paper. After thanking Laura for her letter, Chris apologized for not writing sooner. "I've had a lot of things on my mind," Chris explained. "This seems like a nightmare coming true. I never thought I would do something this dumb."[92] Heeding Laura's advice regarding his education, Chris promised her that he was going to work towards his GED. Laura's pleas for Chris to resume his education would be a constant theme in the letters that followed, as she pushed and prodded Chris to find a way to pull himself out of the emotional and spiritual abyss in which he had tumbled.

In the late winter months of 1991, defense attorney Benton Pollok prepared for trial. He faced both a trial in which the jury would decide whether Chris was guilty of capital murder, and then, if Chris were found guilty, a separate sentencing trial in which the same jury would decide whether Chris should live or die. The compressed trial scheduled adopted by Judge Folkes meant that Pollok had limited time to prepare for what some have referred to as "the most technically difficult form of litigation known to the American legal system."[93] Defending a capital murder case is especially challenging because "[t]he law that governs capital trials differs from that of ordinary criminal trials at virtually every stage — from jury selection to closing arguments to jury instructions to proportionality review."[94] He was briefly assisted by a young attorney named Dawne Alexander, and then by Damian T. Horne. A former army ranger and graduate of the William and Mary law school, Horne had practiced law in Virginia for approximately five years and had defended serious felony cases — but never a capital murder case.

Curiously, Judge Folkes aggressively pushed to schedule Chris's capital murder. During a January 28, 1991, status conference, Pollok repeatedly reminded the court of the defense's limited resources and pleaded for the court to schedule the case for a trial date later than April (the judge's preferred date). At one point in the hearing, a frustrated Pollok complained about the time and expense involved in making the 120-mile roundtrip to consult with his client at the Chesterfield Juvenile Center, travel for which Pollok was not reimbursed and, more important, which ate into his trial preparation. "Well, you know, it's all part of life's pageant," was Judge Folkes's cavalier response,[95] as he set a February 28, 1991, deadline for filing motions and a May 29, 1991, trial date (which was Chris's eighteenth birthday). "This was the first Capital Murder case Judge Folkes handled," writes Horne. "It was clear to everyone that he was very concerned on how he might appear in the newspapers, to the Supreme Court, to fellow members of the bar. Who can blame him?"[96]

Unfortunately for Chris, Judge Folkes's push to try the case speedily was combined with the judge's distain for Pollok. "Judge Folkes harbored an intense dislike of Ben Pollok," explained co-counsel Damian Horne. Horne suggested that the source of the enmity traced back to Judge Folkes's initial nomination for the circuit court bench, when Pollok supported another judicial candidate. "Judge Folkes could certainly nurse a grudge." The tension between Judge Folkes and Pollok also stemmed from the judge's pronounced suspicion that Pollok would encourage his client to take the witness stand and lie about the murders. "I remember when Judge Folkes called me in to offer me the case, he did not refrain from several unflattering remarks about Ben," writes Horne. "I seem to recall his joining with Jimmy Ward in endorsing my appointment to this case because they both thought Ben was determined to suborn perjury [namely] insist that Jessica fired either one or two shots." Of course, it is an attorney's responsibility to explore all possible defenses available to his client, and, if Horne's recollections are accurate, it is highly disturbing that a trial court judge had made up his mind about a case before the trial had started.

The second volley in Pollok's pretrial strategy came with two critical motions that the attorney filed in March 1991:[97] (1) a motion to suppress Chris's confession on the grounds that Chris did not voluntarily, knowingly, and intelligently waive his constitutional rights to remain silent and to consult with an attorney, and (2) a motion to change the venue of the trial to a neighboring county, or, alternatively, to bring in potential jurors from another county based on "contamination" of potential jurors owing to press coverage.[98] At the request of defense counsel, Judge Folkes granted the defense two weeks in which to have an expert conduct a survey of Middlesex County residents to see if pretrial publicity had rendered it impossible to seat an impartial and unbiased jury.

On March 22, 1991, the attorneys reassembled in the Middlesex County courthouse to argue the motions filed by Pollok. The motions were denied in quick order. Turning first to the admissibility of Chris Thomas's confession to the Virginia State Police, the court did not accept the conclusions made by the defense's expert witness, namely, that Chris's lack of maturity, emotional state, lack of sleep, and previous consumption of drugs and alcohol led to the teenager's making an uninformed decision to waive his Miranda rights.

The motion to move the trial to another county (change of venue) or to bring a new pool of jurors in from another county (change of venire) was argued next. In support of the motion, the defense introduced the report of Dr. Donald H. Smith, a professor in the Department of Sociology and Criminal Justice at Old Dominion University in Norfolk, Virginia. During the hearing, Dr. Smith explained that he surveyed a random sample of registered voters in Middlesex County (individuals eligible to be called for jury duty) and found that 98 percent of the respondents were familiar with the Thomas case. Of the respondents who had heard of the case, approximately 40 percent stated that they believed that Thomas was guilty. From these findings, Dr. Smith concluded, "It is an extremely high exposure rate and it is very unlikely that you will be able to find a jury panel that hasn't been exposed [to the pretrial publicity]."[99] While Dr. Smith testified that approximately 58 percent of the individuals surveyed *claimed* to have no opinion on the case, he concluded that many of these respondents were likely "contaminated" by the pretrial publicity.

In opposition to the motion to change venue, Commonwealth Attorney Ward introduced into evidence one hundred affidavits executed by Middlesex County residents. The affidavits were circulated by the Middlesex County sheriff, who testified at the hearing that he simply approached residents and asked them to sign the affidavit. All but two agreed to do so. The affidavits simply stated that the affiant knew "of no mass feelings of prejudice in the community that would prevent DOUGLAS CHRISTOPHER THOMAS from receiving a fair and impartial trial in Middlesex County by a jury drawn from the community." Unlike the survey conducted by Dr. Smith, the Middlesex County sheriff did not select a random sample of potential jurors; most likely, many individuals were approached because the sheriff knew they would sign the affidavit. Because the sample selected by the sheriff was not random (and was more likely heavily biased in favor of the prosecution), the sample did not represent a cross-section of attitudes held by potential Middlesex County jurors; therefore, generalizations to the attitudes of the entire county could not be drawn from the biased sample. This point was highlighted by Pollok during the hearing, when he pleaded with the court to understand the biased nature of the affidavits. "[I]f I had a uniform on and [was] the sheriff of the county and walk[ed] around to people and asked them to fill out an affidavit I bet you two to one I would get 102 [affidavits], too."[100] The change of venue motion was summarily denied. In ruling from the bench, Judge Folkes rejected the argument that the majority of potential jurors had been contaminated by pretrial publicity. "I think the best tool for searching for the truth is a voir dire examination conducted under oath in a judicial atmosphere in all its intended sublimity."[101]

Almost two decades later, Dr. Smith keenly recalls the small role that he played in the Thomas murder trial. "This was probably the most frightening court experience I have ever had," says Smith. "The level of incompetence demonstrated by many of the participants was bizarre." Specifically, Dr. Smith points to Judge Folkes's inability to appreciate the flawed methodology used by the prosecution to rebut the charges of potential jury contamination. "This change of venue survey [Thomas's] was conducted following then-current ABA [American Bar Association] guidelines. The Judge didn't know there were ABA guidelines and didn't understand why my survey was any better than the one the sheriff had conducted in the coffee shop the morning of the trial [hearing]." As Dr. Smith left the courthouse after the change of venue hearing, the assembled reporters asked him for his opinion of Judge Folkes. Unable to contain his disgust, Dr. Smith snapped: "The only thing that exceeds his arrogance is his ignorance." Dr. Smith later described the trial process as an "abomination."

On April 9, 1991, Benton Pollok filed a motion to continue the trial from its May setting. Pollok requested the motion because he had agreed to join the defense team in a high-profile murder trial taking place in Virginia, a trial in which Virginia's official archaeologist, Herbert G. Fisher, was accused of murdering his wife. The first murder trial against Fisher had ended in a mistrial, and Pollok subsequently agreed to represent Fisher in his second trial—a trial scheduled to begin on April 22 and expected to last several weeks. The hearing on the motion for a continuance was heard by an exasperated Judge Folkes on April 16, 1991. When Pollok announced that he had been retained by Fisher in his murder trial, Judge Folkes interrupted and commented that Pollok had taken his new client while "[k]nowing full well you had this responsibility to proceed."[102] Pollok explained that "as long as I have not been paid by the State [in the Thomas case], I have to do something to keep my office open. The State is already in my pocket for considerable money and I do not feel I should finance the State in this case and that is what I am doing."[103] In contrast to the Thomas case, Herbert Fisher had privately retained Pollok as counsel—with the presumption that he would be more prompt in paying his legal bills than the Commonwealth of Virginia. "I feel it is an injustice to my client that an attorney has to be put in this position," added Pollok.[104]

The hearing quickly turned confusing and contentious, perhaps resulting from previous tensions between Judge Folkes and Pollok. Repeatedly interrupting Pollok, Judge Folkes reminded him that during an early hearing on April 5 (a hearing at which neither a court reporter nor the defendant was present), Pollok threatened to withdraw as counsel if his motion for a continuance was not granted. Pollok challenged Judge Folkes's recollection of the April 5 hearing, but Judge Folkes continued, telling Pollok that the motion to withdrawal as counsel had been granted during the earlier hearing and, for good measure, was granted again in the present hearing. As Pollok objected, Judge Folkes made his ruling: "[I]t is obvious to me that with this other case and by his own statement, he [Pollok] is not going to be ready to try this case and I am not going to continue it. So, it is the ruling of the Court that he be allowed to withdraw. In fact, I am going to enter an order requiring him to withdraw."[105] In Pollok's place, Judge Folkes appointed Sydney West—the law partner of Damian Horne. As the hearing closed, Benton Pollok hurriedly asked a series of questions that ominously foreshadowed future events.

> MR. POLLOK: If your Honor please, I would like to get on the record, if I may. Mr. Horne, have you ever tried a capital murder case before?
> MR. HORN[E]: No, I haven't.
> MR. POLLOK: How about you, Ms. West?
> MS. WEST: No.
> THE COURT: Anything further, Mr. Pollok?
> MR. POLLOK: Nothing further.[106]

Pollok continued to battle. On April 19, 1991, Pollok wrote Judge Folkes and requested that the judge recuse himself from the case. When that tactic didn't work, Pollok followed up his letter with a petition to the Supreme

Court of Virginia. In the petition Pollok accused Judge Folkes of bias, and claimed that the judge violated procedural rules by having neither a court reporter nor the defendant present at that fateful April 5 hearing. Further, he argued that the new defense attorneys did not have sufficient time to prepare for trial, and demanded to be reinstated as Chris's attorney based upon his client's constitutional right to select his own lawyer.[107] Not only was Pollok's petition denied by the Virginia Supreme Court, but ironically in the fall of 1991 Pollok was forced to sue former client Herbert Fisher for $12,118.75 in unpaid legal fees.[108]

Thus approximately six weeks before his capital murder case, Chris Thomas found himself with a new team of lawyers. Assuming that Horne and West took a hard look at the case file, they must have concluded that they were woefully unprepared regarding the sentencing phase of Chris's upcoming trial. At sentencing, the same jury that decided a defendant's guilt or innocence is charged with determining whether the defendant will be sentenced to life in prison or be sentenced to death. The first phase of the sentencing hearing is referred to as the eligibility phase, where a jury decides whether the defendant is eligible for the death penalty. In Virginia, eligibility is established if the prosecution has established beyond a reasonable doubt one of two different aggravating circumstances: (1) "there is a probability that the defendant would commit criminal acts of violence that would constitute a continuing serious threat to society," or (2) "that his conduct in committing the offense for which he stands charged was outrageously or wantonly vile, horrible or inhuman in that it involved torture, depravity of mind or an aggravated battery to the victim."[109]

If the jury finds that the defendant is eligible for the death penalty, then it moves to the second phase of the sentencing hearing (referred to as the "selection phase") and decides whether it will, in fact, sentence the defendant to death. During this second phase of sentencing, the defense introduces mitigating evidence, namely, evidence why the death penalty should not be imposed. Regarding mitigation evidence, Virginia law states:

Facts in mitigation may include, *but shall not be limited to*, the following: (i) the defendant has no significant history of prior criminal activity, (ii) the capital felony was committed while the defendant was under the influence of extreme mental or emotional disturbance, (iii) the victim was a participant in the defendant's conduct or consented to the act, (iv) at the time of the commission of the capital felony, the capacity of the defendant to appreciate the criminality of his conduct or to conform his conduct to the requirements of law was significantly impaired, (v) the age of the defendant at the time of the commission of the capital offense, or (vi) . . . the sub average intellectual functioning of the defendant.[110]

Virginia, like other death penalty states, has fashioned aggravating and mitigating factors in order to "bridle the sentencer's [sic] discretion within constitutionally permissible bounds."[111]

Despite the critical importance of mitigation evidence, one of the most common errors made by inexperienced attorneys is the failure to collect such evidence. Law professor (and former Chris Thomas appellate lawyer) Alan W. Clarke writes: "Lawyers all too often do a competent job at investigating and trying the guilt phase of a capital trial while neglecting, failing to understand, and ultimately bungling the penalty phase."[112] Adds law professor Gary Goodpaster: "The differences [between the two stages of a death penalty trial] are so fundamental that counsel quite able to try a complex criminal case may not be competent to handle a penalty trial in a capital case." Goodpaster describes a penalty trial as "a trial *for* life" because "the defendant's life is at stake" as well as a "trial *about* life . . . because a central issue is the meaning and value of the defendant's life."[113]

Even when lawyers recognize this dilemma, they often have neither the training nor the experience to conduct a mitigation investigation. The solution is "a team approach to capital litigation, utilizing mitigation specialists who are 'investigators, paralegals, social workers, psychologists and others who have a thorough understanding of mitigation and how it works into the capital trial and who are skilled interviewers.'"[114] Unlike lawyers, mitigation specialists are trained to interview family members and friends and collect the voluminous educational, medical, psychiatric, and legal records that provide perspective, meaning, and value to a defendant's life. Once this information is amassed, a mitigation specialist can organize the data into themes or patterns that relate to relevant aspects of a capital murder defense as well as determine whether an expert, such as a psychologist, should be retained to draft a mitigation report based on the evidence and testify about his or her findings during the sentencing phase.[115]

Without a thorough and sifting mitigation review, jurors are left to consult their own values and prejudices in fashioning an appropriate sentence.

Lack of mitigation evidence means sentencing trials often take less than a day, and jurors must make life and death decision with little information about the client . . . when appellate lawyers investigate the cases and backgrounds of those sentenced to death, they frequently unearth evidence of mental retardation, brain damage, mental illness, child abuse, extreme deprivation and other forms of brutalization. But once a death sentence is imposed, this information can have little impact in Virginia.[116]

Clarke is more blunt regarding the consequences of failing to gather mitigation evidence: "The lawyer who focuses entirely on the guilty stage without attending to the sentencing stage may be consigning his client to the electric chair."[117]

By April 1991, Chris's attorneys had neither formally asked the court to appoint a new mental health expert to prepare a mitigation report nor retained a mitigation specialist to conduct a mitigation investigation—despite the fact that at the very start of the pretrial proceedings mitigation specialist Marie Deans had offered her services—for free—to defense counsel.[118] Instead, defense counsel planned on asking a psychologist who had previously examined Chris to draft a mitigation report. The prosecution had retained its own mitigation expert—Dr. Henry O. Gwaltney of Virginia's Central State Hospital—who had previously examined Chris on issues related to competency and waiver of rights.

At a meeting attended by both the prosecution and defense counsel (the meeting was likely held in late April 1991), Gwaltney felt compelled to address the quality of the defense's mitigation work. Specifically, he warned Horne and West that the previous reports submitted by the defense's psychologist were "substantially deficient" and told defense counsel that "they should get a good psychological evaluation to determine the mitigating evidence for the penalty phase."[119] Gwaltney felt so strongly about the need for a competent mitigation review that he asked the prosecution to release him as a witness and permit him to work solely with the defense attorneys. Commonwealth Attorney Ward, however, refused.

Unable to help the defense team directly, Gwaltney persisted in lending a hand. He volunteered to contact the Institute of Law, Psychiatry and Public Policy at the University of Virginia and arrange for a battery of psychological examinations and tests from which a detailed mitigation report about Chris Thomas could be prepared. Gwaltney called the institute the next day, convinced the staff to examine Chris, and immediately called defense counsel with the good news. Chris's attorneys never returned the telephone call (and claimed that they did not receive it), although Gwaltney asserted that they later acknowledged that they had received it.[120] Gwaltney would not hear from the defense team until August 25, 1991—the Sunday before Chris's sentencing hearing.

On May 21, 1991, Commonwealth Attorney Ward and defense counsel Horne and West appeared before retired Circuit Court Judge John E. De-Hardit, who was filling in for an ailing Judge Folkes. At the hearing, defense counsel admitted that they had not given Commonwealth Attorney Ward timely notification that they intended to rely upon expert testimony and reports in both phases of the upcoming trial. Specifically, Virginia law required that the defense give the prosecution twenty-one days' notice if the defense decided to present evidence of insanity[121] or the testimony of an expert witness regarding mitigation.[122] Standing before Judge DeHardit, Sydney West explained that defense counsel "have had our noses to the grindstone for the past five weeks preparing for this case"[123] and had been on track for the May 29, 1991, trial date until they suddenly realized they had not complied with the aforementioned notice requirements. Seemingly implicit in West's representations to the court was that the evaluations regarding both the insanity defense and the mitigation defense had been conducted and the reports prepared, but that the failure to provide proper notice would prevent the completed reports and attendant expert testimony from being introduced into evidence. Defense counsel thus gave the Commonwealth Attorney fourteen days' notice and "asked the commonwealth to waive any objection to the introduction of such evidence at trial,"[124] claiming that defense counsel had merely forgotten to comply with a procedural rule.

In her next breath, however, West announced that one evaluation (mitigation) was not completed and that the insanity report was not prepared (or was missing). She concedes that on February 13, 1991, Judge Folkes appointed an expert to evaluate Chris Thomas and prepare a report regarding a possible insanity defense at trial, but the court did not appoint a mental health expert to evaluate Chris and prepare a mitigation report to be used at sentencing. Having made this discovery, West admitted that "we are in the position of needing some time in order to make sure that the mitigation examination *has been properly done* so that it can be introduced."[125] Stated West:

Dr. Williams indicates to us that he has done all the testing with regard to the order that was entered [a sanity evaluation], but that does not include the mitigation side of it. However, we do not have the [insanity] report. We have some verbal statement from him as to what it will contain, but we do not have a report. I think we need to consult with him as to whether we need to have another psychologist appointed for the mitigation aspect or whether that is something he can do too.[126]

In short, one week before Chris Thomas's death penalty trial, neither a report regarding a possible insanity defense nor an investigation and report regarding mitigation had been completed. More shockingly, these oversights were discovered only two weeks prior to trial. West concludes her argument by throwing herself and co-counsel Horne at the mercy of the court: "Although we have been diligent, we do not feel at this time that we are prepared to go forward and give our client the effective assistance of counsel that he is required to have under the constitution, so we would ask you to please consider in your discretion allowing us to have a continuance in this case."[127] Ironically, what Benton Pollok tried and failed to obtain—a trial continuance—was granted by the court, and Chris Thomas's trial was rescheduled for August 1991.

On June 25, 1991, eighteen-year-old Chris Thomas was transferred to the Middle Peninsula Regional Security Center in Saluda, Virginia. Now an adult, Chris could be housed with adult offenders and his transfer was timed to coincide with Jessica Wiseman's June 26, 1991, murder trial. The next morning, Chris was taken two blocks from the Security Center to a holding cell in the Middlesex County Courthouse. Chris was sworn in as a witness, but announced that he would assert his Fifth Amendment rights against self-incrimination and refuse to testify as a prosecution witness unless Commonwealth Attorney Ward reduced the charges against him from capital to first-degree murder—a deal that Ward refused.[128]

In yet another surreal twist, before the trial started, Chris and Jessica had the chance to talk to each other briefly through the screened window of the holding cell. Overcome with emotion, Chris wept during the short meeting. Damian Horne later reported that Chris was "concerned that the stress of the trial would be difficult" for Jessica and wanted to see her: "'He looked haggard and worn. . . . He was in a great deal of mental anguish.'"[129]

FIGURE 8. *Chris Thomas leaves court, June 1991.*
Photograph courtesy of the Associated Press.

Jessica was charged with two counts of first-degree murder as a principal in the second degree. The trial was held in Middlesex County Juvenile and Domestic Relations Court. The presiding judge was Herbert I. L. Feild, the same judge that Jessica and Chris had appeared before in the weeks following the murders. In the prosecution's case-in-chief, Commonwealth Attorney Ward wove together the testimony of Lainie Creech, Brenda Marshall, and Virginia State Police investigators Robert E. Lackey, Robert Staneck, and Larry A. Johnson, Sr., to paint Jessica Wiseman as a spoiled girl who methodically planned the murder of her parents and then manipulated Chris Thomas into carrying out the killings. Jessica "pulled the strings the whole time," submitted Ward in his closing argument.[130]

Not surprisingly, the key witness for the prosecution was Lainie Creech, "a skinny, sandy-haired 13-year-old kid in bobby socks, tennis shoes, faded denim shorts and a T-shirt advertising a theme park roller coaster,"[131] who testified that she overheard Chris and Jessica making plans to murder Kathy and J. B. Wiseman. Lainie also testified about delivering the note hidden in a magazine from Chris to Jessica on the night of the murders, as well as walking to the Wisemans' house with Chris in the early morning hours of November 10. Additionally, one of the special agents for the Virginia State Police testified that Jessica Wiseman told him: " 'No one will ever understand [about the murders], but I had good reason." '[132] The only defense witness was Glenda Corbin, called by defense counsel Roger Hopper in an effort to undermine Lainie's testimony by showing minor inconsistencies in her statements to the police and her comments to friends about the night of the murders.[133]

During the trial, Jessica Wiseman wore a white dress with matching white heels and red fingernail polish. "Syd [Sydney West] and I thought she was Lady Macbeth," recalled defense attorney Horne. "I shall never forget that she wore finger nail polish that could only be described as 'Transylvania Red.' It literally looked like there was blood dripping from her hands." On her left index finger was Chris Thomas's high school ring. She sat next to her grandmother throughout the hearing, and a local newspaper reporter observed that Jessica appeared "calm" during the trial, even smiling and waving to a group of friends in the gallery.[134] Her unruffled composure cracked, however, when Judge Feild found Jessica guilty on all counts. "When Feild announced his verdict, Wiseman wiped her eyes with a tissue. But several minutes later, as lawyers conferred about a sentencing date, she banged her fist down on the arm of her chair. Leaving the courtroom, she angrily told photographers, 'Get out of my face' as her grandfather denounced Lainie Creech as a liar."[135]

Jessica's departure from the Middlesex County Courthouse neatly symbolized the paradoxical efforts of the criminal justice system to treat Jessica Wiseman as both a wayward child and a murderess. After the trial, Jessica climbed into the front seat of a squad car driven by Middlesex County Sheriff Lewis Jones: "They rode off, windows down, doors unlocked, headed to a state juvenile detention facility where Wiseman is being held until she's sentenced July 31. Only as Jones pulled past reporters did he lock the car doors."[136]

Chris was despondent after Jessica's trial, telling a counselor at the security center that the entire county hated him and that someone would likely sneak into jail and kill him before trial. "He reports his attorney has informed him that he will probably get death sentence," a preadmissions screening form reported. Within two days of the trial, Chris became suicidal and was transferred to the Central State Hospital for psychiatric evaluation. At the time of his transfer, the "Criminal Mental Temporary Detention Order" recorded that "[i]nmate is expressing suicidal ideation, is withdrawn, depressed and is

FIGURE 9. *Jessica Wiseman arriving for a hearing.*
Photograph by Tom Chillemi, Southside Sentinel.

extremely paranoid" and that "[i]nmate is dangerous to self." His probation officer later observed that Chris remarked that "'[i]f I would have had a gun I believe I would have done it [killed himself].'"

As Chris lay in the Central State Hospital, Jessica wrote him a letter decorated with hearts and proclaiming "Happy 11th [month] Anniversary." In the letter, Jessica begins by·answering several questions that Chris had apparently asked her during their brief encounter at the holding cell prior to her trial. "The reason I didn't have your rings on when I talked to you is because Nanny had them with her in the court room and I saw you before I got to see her." Jessica is referring to Chris's high school class ring and likely the mysterious wedding ring. "I did put them on as soon as I sat down." After reassuring Chris that he still looked handsome, Jessica writes that one thing has changed in the intervening months.

> Chris, theres [*sic*] something that I want to tell you. All this time that we've been together "I did believe" that you loved me, but not as much as I loved you. That was until Wed. [the trial]. This is the Gods [*sic*] honest truth. I

would have never believed that anyone could love somebody as much as you've proven that you love me! I don't know what's changed, but when I looked into your eyes it was different than before. I mean you didn't even have to say that you loved me, I could see it in your eyes. Even though you were upset, I could still tell.[137]

It is difficult to discern the exact meaning of this passage. Is Jessica telling Chris that the enormity of his sacrifice (taking the entire blame) did not register with her until she looked into his eyes on Wednesday morning? Or is she indirectly thanking him for not testifying against her at the trial? Begging for Chris to forgive her for doubting his fidelity, Jessica writes: "I will trust you for now on 'completely' and I '*do*' believe that you love me 'very much!'" She ends the letter with another promise that will not be kept. "I promise you this from the bottom of my heart I will never give up until we're back together again." Chris returned to the Middle Peninsula Regional Security Center after three days of evaluation, and he remained there until November 1991.

On July 30, 1991, Judge Feild sentenced Jessica Wiseman to a minimum of eighteen months and a maximum of six years with Virginia's Youth and Family Services Agency. His nonbinding recommendation was that Jessica remain in state custody until she turned twenty-one. In announcing his sentence, Judge Feild explained that he imposed the maximum sentence permitted under law because "'the charges are so grave that the protection of the community is the foremost consideration.'"[138] As Judge Feild announced his sentence, Jessica Wiseman — wearing the same white dress and sitting between her grandparents — started to weep.

We do not know how Chris Thomas reacted when he learned of Jessica's sentence. Perhaps he considered it a victory and fantasized that somehow he would escape the electric chair and someday join Jessica in the outside world. Maybe he realized that the sentence represented an irreconcilable divergence in their fates. Whatever Chris Thomas thought, he was a mere three weeks away from his own capital murder trial.[139]

On Trial for His Life

On the morning of August 21, 1991, jury selection began in Chris Thomas's capital murder trial. Voir dire (a French phrase that means "to speak the truth") is the term used by judges and lawyers to describe the process by which a jury is selected. In all states, jury selection takes place in two stages. Once a pool of potential jurors is selected from driver's license lists, voter registration rolls, or other government records and is assembled at the courthouse, the individuals (commonly referred to as "veniremen") are questioned by the judge and the lawyers representing the parties in the legal action to see if there is any legitimate reason why the veniremen should not be selected to serve as jurors. In this first stage of jury selection, the main question is whether there is "cause" to excuse a prospective juror due to his or her bias or prejudice (for example, a potential juror is related to one of the parties or has already formed an opinion about the case from reading the newspaper). There are no limitations on the number of veniremen who may be excused for cause.[1]

The United States Supreme Court has held that during the first phase of jury selection prospective jurors must be excused "for cause" if they would not, under any circumstance, vote to impose the death penalty in a capital case. Explains law professor Scott Sundby:

These are called *Witherspoon*[2] questions . . . [and] are intended to cull out jurors who are so opposed to the death penalty that they never would be able to impose it even where the law allowed it to be imposed; otherwise, a single person—the juror who did not believe in the death penalty—could effectively veto the legislature's intent of making the death penalty a possible punishment for those convicted of capital murder.[3]

Thus eliminating the possibility of jury nullification, that is, a juror that refuses to apply existing law because it clashes with his or her own beliefs, is the primary reason for the rule that prospective jurors must be "death qualified" before serving in a capital murder case. Because a jury verdict must be unanimous in both the guilty/innocence and sentencing phases of a death penalty trial, a single juror can result in a hung jury. Alternatively, jurors who would not consider any other penalty but the death penalty in a capital case (such as life without parole) are also excused.[4] The death qualifying process has come under withering attack by social scientists and legal scholars on multiple grounds, including claims that it produces juries that are more likely to find defendants guilty and that it eliminates a greater number of minorities and women from the jury pool.[5]

The first round of jury selection continues until the court and attorneys select a panel of qualified jurors. In Virginia, this panel must be composed of twenty potential jurors. In the second stage of jury selection, the attorneys for each party are granted a limited number of peremptory challenges (Virginia law grants each side four peremptory challenges). These are used by the attorneys "to eliminate those who they believe would be unfavorable to their side even though no overt reason for bias is apparent. . . . The use of peremptory challenges is more of an art than a science and is usually based on the hunch of the attorneys."[6] Lawyers cannot, however, strike jurors based solely on their race or gender.[7]

Once a jury of twelve men and women is empanelled in a capital murder case, the jury will effectively hear two separate trials. "Modern" death penalty trials (namely, trials after 1976) are "bifurcated" or divided into two separate trials. In the first trial, the jurors are charged with deciding whether the defendant committed a capital offense. If a jury finds a defendant guilty of capital murder, the death penalty is *not* automatically imposed.[8] Instead, a sentencing hearing is held in which the jury weighs the evidence and decides if the death penalty is warranted. The United States Supreme Court held in *Gregg v. Georgia*[9] that state law must provide standards that give guidance to juries as to when the death penalty is appropriate. Typically referred to as "guided discretion statutes," the laws provide juries with a list of aggravating and mitigating factors to consider in deciding whether to impose the ultimate punishment. Explains Sundby:

> The [Supreme] court has held that the Eighth Amendment embodies a principle of "individualized consideration," a principle that requires that before a sentence of death can be imposed, the jury must first consider a defendant's individual circumstances. The principle of individualized consideration means that a capital defendant must be allowed to present to the jury what are termed "mitigating factors," which, according to the Supreme Court, are "any" facts about the defendant or the crime that might serve "as a basis for a sentence less than death."[10]

The practical effect of a sentencing hearing in which aggravating and mitigating evidence is heard is "essentially to put the defendant's entire life on trial."[11] Professor Sundby adds that a defendant has wide latitude in presenting mitigating evidence: "It takes only a little imagination to realize that possible mitigating factors can cover a huge expanse of evidentiary territory." He continues: "A small sample of potential mitigating evidence includes psychological evidence that the defendant was mentally ill, a prison guard's observations that the defendant conforms well to the structured setting of prison, a mother's testimony that the defendant was a good son growing up, and accounts by siblings of the abuse that the defendant suffered at the hands of a parent."[12]

These are the rules and standards surrounding jury selection in the Chris Thomas case. Judge Folkes began the voir dire process by explaining the basic legal principles underlying the case and asking a battery of questions designed to ferret out any potential juror bias to groups of three veniremen. Although Virginia law expressly granted attorneys the right to ask questions during voir dire,[13] Judge Folkes refused to permit defense counsel to do so, instead telling the parties that they could submit written questions for him to ask. Although the record is ambiguous, it appears that the judge asked some, but not all, of the questions submitted by defense counsel. Besides the standard inquiries regarding bias, Judge Folkes asked one question touching upon Chris Thomas's juvenile status: "Do you believe that young people are responsible for their actions?"[14]

It does not appear from the record, however, that Chris's lawyers objected to Judge Folkes's ruling banning the lawyers from asking questions during voir dire, thus preventing Chris's appellate lawyers from later attacking the judge's decision on appeal.[15] Failing to object to the rulings of a trial court judge can be fatal to a defendant's chances of seeking review by a higher court. Federal and state trial courts are overseen by appellate courts, which review cases for legal errors made by trial court judges. If an appellate court finds that a trial court judge made an error, and the error was not harmless, an appellate court may reverse the ruling of the trial court judge and remand the case back to the trial court for further proceedings. Attorneys must, however, make a timely objection to what they believe is an erroneous ruling by a trial court judge, or that objection is deemed to be "waived" and cannot be reasserted on appeal.[16] The failure to recognize incorrect rulings by Judge Folkes and make contemporaneous objections to said rulings in order to "preserve them for appeal" is a tragic thread that runs through Chris Thomas's case.

The fact that the murders had occurred in a small, close-knit community became quickly apparent, a validation of the study submitted by Benton Pollok in support of his motion to change venue. During the first stage of voir dire, forty of the forty-eight veniremen stated that they had heard about the case through the media or other sources. When these prospective jurors professed knowledge of the case, Judge Folkes asked if that knowledge prevented them from rendering a fair and impartial verdict. In all, Judge Folkes excused nine men and seven women on the grounds that the information that they had heard from these sources prevented them from being fair and impartial. Additionally, twelve of the veniremen reported that they were either friends or clients of Commonwealth Attorney Jimmy Ward. This number included two future jurors, one of whom stated that he and the Ward "grew up together"[17] and that he knew Jessica Wiseman, Brenda Marshall, and Herbert Marshall.

Throughout the voir dire process, Judge Folkes "death qualified" the jury by asking each potential juror whether he or she could impose the death penalty. Occasionally the form of the question was inelegantly asked: "Do you have any opinion which would prevent you from convicting anyone of an offense punishable with death?"[18] "Would you have any problem in that you could never vote to impose the death penalty, or would you even refuse to consider its imposition in this case?"[19] Alternatively, Judge Folkes asked: "Do you have any philosophical, religious or moral beliefs dealing with capital punishment that would prevent you from sentencing the defendant to death, if he's convicted and the evidence so dictates?"[20] On several occasions the jurors confessed confusion with the question, and at one point Judge Folkes himself joked: "It's [the question] is confusing to the Judge, too, frankly."[21] Given the critical nature of the death qualification process, Judge Folkes's struggle to properly frame the death qualification questions is troubling. Ultimately, six veniremen (three men and three women) were struck from the jury because they stated that they could never impose a sentence of death.

At the end of voir dire, Judge Folkes had impaneled twenty-one prospective jurors. Satisfied with the pool, he discharged the remaining thirty-nine veniremen. At this point, Horne made multiple objections to the voir dire process. After objecting to the fact that Judge Folkes had not used all of the voir dire questions submitted by defense counsel (a copy of those questions does not remain in the voluminous court file), Mr. Horne asked that the pool of prospective jurors be dismissed (1) "on the basis that every single veniremen knew about this case . . . [and] were well acquainted with the coverage by the media,"[22] (2) "because at least six of the veniremen were friends, acquaintances, or business associates with Mr. Ward,"[23] and (3) "because there are two veniremen with relatives who are the very custodians of Christopher Thomas at the jail, and one who is dispatcher at the Sheriff's Department."[24] Judge Folkes denied the motions, responding, "I want the record to also show, that in each instance in which you complained, there was an unequivocal examination by me of the veniremen resulting in their stating that they knew of no reason they could not be fair and impartial jurors."[25] Do such questions, however, truly root out bias? And are jurors always the best judges of their own biases and prejudices? Critics of the modern jury selection process have argued that asking a biased person if he is unbiased and impartial is often tantamount to asking an alcoholic if he has a drinking problem.

Voir dire moved to its second phase, and the attorneys in the Chris Thomas case used their peremptory strikes to remove eight jurors. The law does not require the attorneys to state the basis of their strikes (unless the strikes are allegedly made for discriminatory reasons), and we do not know what "hunches" or strategies that Jimmy Ward or Damian Horne followed in using their peremptory challenges. With that, the Thomas jury—consisting of twelve jurors and one alternate—was selected. The jury included five house-wives, a stockbroker, two laborers from the local paper mill, a cabinetmaker and a hardware store owner. It appears that all jurors save two were Cauca-sian. After instructing the Thomas jury as to their duties (don't talk with any one about the case, don't talk with fellow jury members or your family, don't read about the case), Judge Folkes excused the Thomas jury at 6:25 P.M. that evening, charging them to return to the courtroom at 10:00 A.M. for the start of the trial.

On the night before trial, Laura Anderson—Chris's former high school teacher—received an ominous telephone call from Damian Horne. Laura had been in bed when the telephone rang, but she was unable to sleep and sat straight up in bed when Horne grimly announced: "Chris needs your help." "What is it you need," Laura replied, alarmed. "I have been with Chris most of the evening. I have been trying to convince him to take the stand," said Horne. "He is refusing. It is like he is shutting down and won't help himself." Chris's appellate lawyers later argued that Horne and West made the tragic mistake of not establishing a relationship of trust with Chris. "Trial counsel failed to establish a sufficient relationship with Chris Thomas to persuade him to act in his own best interests," wrote the appellate lawyers. "According to counsel's own time records, they spent only a few hours on three occasions actually talking to Chris Thomas. According to the defendant a significant portion of this time was spent reading law cases to him that he could not understand."[26]

To Laura, Horne sounded angry and almost insulted by his client's recal-citrance. "I don't understand," Laura admitted. "What can I do?" "Can you meet me at the Saluda Jail early tomorrow morning and try to talk sense into Chris?" Laura felt her anxiety turn to dread: "Of course, I will do what I can. But I don't know if he will listen to me." After hanging up the telephone, Laura turned to her husband, Ross, and began crying. Her fears that Chris would not try to save his own life had become reality. "How am I going to convince him to testify? They've told me all along that Chris was doing so well, that he was so involved in his defense," she said to Ross. Laura did not sleep the rest of that night.

At 7:45 A.M. the next morning, Laura arrived in downtown Saluda, Virginia. As she drove by the quaint Middlesex County courthouse where Chris's trial would be held, she was struck by the beauty of the small town. The court-house itself had been built in 1852, and the two-and-a-half-story, red-brick building is surrounded by a green lawn and marked with a tall marble monument erected by the Daughters of the Confederacy "to commemorate the valor and patriotism of the men, and devotion and sacrifice of the women of Middlesex in defense of their liberties and their homes." Other historic markers are scattered across the small green. The close-knit nature of its legal community was reflected in the fact that Commonwealth Attorney Jimmy Ward's office was in a gracious, white frame home a mere two blocks from the courthouse; across the street from the commonwealth attorney was the office of the attorney who defended Jessica Wiseman in her murder trial.

The picturesque beauty of the community ended, however, at its jail, a low-slung, utilitarian building located a block behind the courthouse. A pickup truck with the vanity license plate "BUBBA LAW" was parked in front of the jail. To her horror, Laura soon discovered that the truck belonged to Damian Horne. Laura met Horne in the lobby of the jail, and her first impression was that the young attorney seemed agitated. *"Has he handled a capital murder case before?"* she wondered. Laura's sense of dread was returning.

After going through a security checkpoint and a pat-down search, Laura was led to Chris's cell. Her heart shuddered in her chest as she entered the small room. Two years had passed since Laura had seen Chris, and the changes in her former student caused tears to well in her eyes. Chris was sitting in an orange jumpsuit, his hands cuffed and legs in shackles. His gaunt face, with its sunken eyes and pale white skin, reminded Laura of a terminally ill patient. Chris looked small and helpless, slumped over with his elbows on his knees and a blank expression etched onto his tired face.

"Chris," Laura managed to say. "Are you all right?" "Considering where I am, I guess I am okay," he replied in a hushed, flat voice. Chris did not look at Laura, and he certainly did not seem happy to see his former teacher. Laura didn't know how to broach the subject of the trial, but she knew that her time was limited and pressed on. "Do you know why I am here?" "I guess to talk me into taking the stand," Chris said in the same flat tone. He looked drugged and depressed, and Laura questioned whether he was mentally capable of even assisting in his own defense. "You have to, Chris," Laura blurted out. "It is the only way to save yourself."

Chris did not react to Laura's emotional plea. "These people have already made up their minds," he said. "I don't have a chance, and nothing you say will change my mind." Laura knelt before Chris and took his hand, trying to reestablish a connection with him. He remained motionless, as if he did not notice his crying teacher's face. "You must take the stand, Chris. You must tell them the truth. I know that you did not do this by yourself. Please tell your story." Laura could not get Chris to respond to her pleas, and it was time to go. As she walked out into the warm air of that humid August morning, Laura cried harder. Self-sacrifice seemed the only explanation for Chris's maddening refusal to help himself. He would fall on his sword for Jessica.

The opening statements in the capital murder trial of Douglas Christopher Thomas took place on the morning of August 22, 1991, in the Middlesex County courthouse. The courtroom itself was located on the second floor of the courthouse, which was reached by two narrow and twisting stairways. A long, rectangular room with wooden, theater-style seats for the gallery, the far end of the courtroom was dominated by a large wooden judge's bench that was flanked on each side by witness boxes. A jury box sat perpendicular to the bench. In keeping with the county's celebration of its Confederate past, a large marble tablet dominated one wall of the courtroom. Emblazoned with the Confederate battle flag, the tablet bore the following dedication: "To the deathless memory of the Confederate women of Middlesex County who sent their sons to the distant battlefronts of the South and defended their homes by their own invincible virtue." Below the tablet hung a faded print of Robert E. Lee and his generals; the courtroom's other walls bore oil paintings of Middlesex County natives, many of whom had fought in the Civil War. Referring to the historic trappings of the courtroom, Horne writes that "all of this ghostly entourage gazes down with almost Gothic disdain."[27]

For the attorneys, the opening statements in the Chris Thomas trial provided the first opportunity to introduce the jury to their "theory of the case" and the evidence they would rely upon in support of their respective theories. "Trial lawyers agree that opening statements often make the difference in the outcome of a case," observes law professor and trial advocacy expert Thomas A. Mauet. "Studies have shown that jury verdicts are, in the substantial majority of cases, consistent with the initial impressions made by the jury during the opening statements."[28] For Mauet, effective opening statements are simple, logically organized, efficient and "based on effective storytelling. After all, a trial is essentially a contest to see which side's version of a disputed event or events the jury will ultimately accept as true."[29]

There are limitations and pitfalls, however, to the opening statement. Observes former United States Supreme Court Chief Justice Warren Burger:

"An opening statement has a narrow purpose and scope. It is to state what evidence will be presented, to make it easier for the jurors to understand what is to follow, and to relate parts of the evidence and testimony to the whole; it is not an occasion for argument. To make statements which will not or cannot be supported by proof is, if it relates to significant elements of the case, professional misconduct."[30] Professor Mauet echoes Chief Justice Burger's warning about the dangers of overstating the evidence. "The only thing a trial lawyer has to sell to the jury is his credibility . . . nothing is more damaging than to overstate facts in your opinion statement. The jury will remember it, resent your misrepresentation, and no longer trust you."[31] Unfortunately for Chris Thomas, his attorneys would make this fundamental error during opening statement.

The theory of the case presented by Commonwealth Attorney Ward was succinct and straightforward: Chris Thomas carefully planned and executed the murders of Kathy Wiseman and J. B. Wiseman. "This is a very heinous crime," Ward informed the jury. "It's a situation where two people were asleep in their bed at night, bothering no one, and this man came over and shot them."[32] Explaining that Kathy and J. B. Wiseman "tried to do what they could do to prevent" their daughter's love affair with Chris Thomas, Ward promised the jury that the evidence would show that the killings of Kathy and J. B. Wiseman were not "just a spur of the moment situation" but the result of planning "over a long period of time, over at least a period of a week."[33] Strikingly missing from Ward's opening statement was the theory of the case that he had articulated in Jessica Wiseman's trial only weeks earlier, namely, that Jessica "pulled the strings the whole time."[34] Now the spotlight was focused squarely on Chris.

Defense counsel's opening statement was made by co-counsel Sydney West, a young woman who had never tried a capital murder case. Unlike the concise opening statement of the commonwealth attorney, West's opening statement was rambling and disjointed. After introducing herself to the jury and commenting briefly on the prosecution's opening statement, West made a rather startling concession:

> although Mr. Ward did not say so, you will find when you listen to the Commonwealth's case, that this is a case where the defendant has admitted certain things. He has made a confession to certain things, and I'm here to tell you right now that the statement that Christopher Thomas wrote in his

FIGURE 10.
Thomas defense attorneys Horne and West, leaving the Middlesex County Courthouse.
Photograph by Tom Chillemi, Southside Sentinel.

own hand to the police and which he confessed that he pulled the trigger in this case will not be disputed by the defense.[35]

Admittedly, defense counsel had fought and lost the pretrial battle to keep Chris's confession from being introduced into evidence, and arguably West was preemptively telling the jury about one of the major weaknesses in the case. This is a tactic used by defense attorneys, referred to as "drawing the sting." "There is obviously no point in volunteering a weakness that would never be raised at trial," Mauet observes. "Where, however, that weakness is apparent and known to the opponent, you should volunteer it. . . . The key is to mention the weakness without emphasis and to present it in its least damaging light, where it will blend easily into the story."[36] What is jarring, however, is that the admission comes at the start of the opening statement,

FIGURE 11.
Lainie Creech leaves Jessica Wiseman's trial, accompanied by Brenda Marshall. Creech proved to be a critical witness at the trials of both Jessica Wiseman and Chris Thomas. Photograph courtesy of the Daily Press *(Newport News, Virginia).*

before defense counsel introduces the jury to their theory of the case. Why not talk about Chris Thomas, his childhood, the tragedies in his life, and his desperation to find someone to love before telling the jury that the defendant has admitted to killing two people in their own bed? And why box yourself into a corner—admitting that your client confessed and that the confession is an accurate summary of the murders—at the start of the trial?

The fatal error in the opening statement soon followed. After reminding the jury that the prosecution had the burden of proving "to a moral certainty that the defendant's actions on the night of November 10th, 1990 were willful, deliberate, and premeditated," West rhetorically asked, "So what will the defense present in this trial? What will our evidence be?"[37] Nothing more than the testimony of the young man on trial for his life, namely, Chris Thomas.

> What we plan to do is to bring you the truth, the truth of what happened inside the doors of the Wisemans' house on that very tragic evening. The truth, through the testimony of Douglas Christopher Thomas. You ladies

and gentlemen will be the first to publicly hear each and every detail on what did go on in that house. Because you can readily see, because the only two people who can possibly tell you what really went on is Jessica Wiseman and Christopher Thomas. . . . And in the interest of allowing you as the jury to judge this case with all the evidence before you, all the evidence, Christopher Thomas will take the stand in his own behalf and testify as to what did happen on that fatal evening.[38]

West's promises to the jury continued. Not only would Chris Thomas testify to the terrible events that occurred in the predawn hours of November 10, 1990, he would tell the jury about how he met, and fell in love with, a thirteen-year-old girl named Jessica Wiseman. He would talk about that first meeting in January 1990, when "he first saw her . . . a very pretty girl driving, driving, a Chrysler LeBaron convertible."[39] He would testify as to how Chris and Jessica sneaked out of their bedrooms at night to be together, became lovers, and spent "hours together talking about everything under the sun."[40] Chris would tell the jury how Jessica "was insistent that her parents didn't love her," that "she hated them," and how she announced "that her life would be perfect if only they were gone."[41]

From the witness stand, West promised, Chris would explain to the jury how Jessica's anger and resentment flared to a boiling point in the fall of 1990, when her parents reconciled and announced that she must end her relationship with him. Faced with a distraught girlfriend, Chris would testify that "in an attempt to calm her down" he made the false promise that he would "get rid" of Kathy and J. B. Wiseman. Chris, however, would reassure the jury that he never meant it. Finally, Chris would tell the jury of the pressure that Jessica exerted on him over the final days before the murders as well as the plans that Jessica masterminded. She plied him with drugs. She greased her bedroom window so it wouldn't squeak. She locked him into her bedroom. She argued with him when he lay in her bed and begged her to let him go home. She spread the drugs on the floor of her parents' bedroom. She turned on a bathroom light so Chris could see the sleeping forms of her parents. She told him, "you have to do it now. [If] Daddy wakes up, he's going to kill us."[42] And when a bloodied and dazed Kathy Wiseman staggered out of the master bedroom, Jessica yelled at Chris to "shoot her again."

It was a powerful story that defense counsel Sydney West promised that her client would tell. A tale of a desperate young boy who never planned or intended to commit murder until he was pushed over the edge by a manipulative and immoral young girl. Testimony that would prove to the jury that Chris was not a cold-blooded killer. There was only one problem: Chris Thomas never took the witness stand. Based on Laura Anderson's conversation with Chris Thomas on the morning of his trial, it is baffling why Chris's attorneys told the jury that he would testify. In conversations with these authors, Damian Horne claims that Chris told his lawyers that he would take the stand and only later changed his mind;[43] indeed, Chris Thomas's trial files contain a partially completed direct examination script written by his attorneys. Nevertheless, should West and Horne have known that there was a substantial likelihood that—regardless of what Chris said—he was not going to testify, and should they have softened their promises to the jury? "I certainly knew enough about criminal law, capital murder sentencing and the social outlook of rural Virginia that we thought Chris should take the stand and beg for his life," explains Horne. "They wanted—NEEDED—to hear from him. And yes . . . Chris waffled . . . more than that, he kept me and Syd in the dark . . . it was like pulling teeth . . . we didn't know from one moment to the next what to expect . . . whether he would 'chicken out' or testify . . . whether he would open up, or reluctantly answer questions."[44] The unexplained failure to put Chris on the witness stand must have been, in the eyes of the jury, a crushing blow to his attorneys' credibility and to his case.

As with his opening statement, Commonwealth Attorney Jimmy Ward methodically made his case against Chris Thomas. The first witness to testify on behalf of the prosecution was Middlesex County Deputy Sheriff Don Rhea, the first law enforcement officer to arrive on the scene and enter the Wiseman home. Buttressing the deputy sheriff's testimony with photographs of the interior of the Wisemans' home and the murder victims, Ward used the witness to skillfully paint a picture of a grisly crime scene. Rhea provided the jury with the first evidence of how the murders were carried out, noting there were "no signs of forced entry" (in fact, the front door was unlocked) and that "[t]he storm window and screen and such were raised or gone, and the bedroom window was closed."[45] While Judge Folkes undoubtedly would have overruled the objection, one could question why the testimony of Deputy Sheriff Rhea was relevant, given defense counsel's concession that Chris committed the murders.

The next prosecution witness was Ellen Vest, a member of the Middlesex Lower Rescue Squad that responded to Brenda Marshall's call. Vest testified briefly, identifying the crime-scene photographs of Kathy and J. B. Wiseman as the individuals that she examined and determined to be dead. Vest was followed by Virginia State Police Special Agent Larry A. Johnson, Sr., who testified that he attended the autopsies of Kathy and J. B. Wiseman. Through Johnson, the commonwealth introduced into evidence some of the buckshot and birdshot pellets that were removed from the bodies of the Wisemans, the shotgun willed to Chris by his grandfather, and the camouflage clothing worn by Chris. Again, was this evidence relevant, given that defense counsel had told the jury that their client committed the murders?

Johnson returned to the witness stand later in the prosecution's case in chief, this time to testify regarding Chris's confession. Johnson testified regarding the two interviews he conducted with Chris, the first in which Chris confirmed that he was romantically involved with Jessica Wiseman and the second in which Chris confessed to the murders of Kathy and J. B. Wiseman. The bulk of the prosecution's questions involved the confession, with Johnson testifying that Chris was properly advised of his legal rights, waived those rights, appeared eager to talk, and provided a detailed confession of the murders. Johnson repeatedly referred to Chris's demeanor during the confession, remarking that he was "very calm" and "[v]ery deliberate in what he had to tell me."[46] Defense counsel seized on Johnson's observations during their cross-examination of the special agent, eliciting the further testimony that "it was one of the easiest confessions I have ever had. It just seemed like to me he [Chris] was ready to get it off his conscience."[47] The testimony about Chris's behavior served both sides: it allowed the prosecution to show that Chris's confession was not coerced, while the defense could point to the testimony as evidence that Chris was remorseful and relieved to own up to the terrible crime.

Prior to taking Chris's testimony, Johnson had interviewed Jessica and obtained her confession. Defense counsel tried to get Johnson to testify about the content of that confession, but Judge Folkes sustained an objection by the prosecution on the grounds that statements given by a co-conspirator were not relevant. The ruling is odd. If Jessica Wiseman had implicated herself in the murders of her parents, or told the investigating officers that the murders were not premeditated, then wouldn't that testimony be highly relevant to Chris's capital murder trial and the critical question of whether Chris killed the Wisemans with malice aforethought? Interestingly, there is no indication in the trial record that defense counsel tried to introduce the confession at the sentencing hearing, where the evidentiary rules are relaxed.

Johnson was followed by another Virginia State Police special agent, John R. Polak. Testifying that he arrived at the crime scene at approximately 7:30 on the morning of the murders, Polak, like Deputy Sheriff Rhea, noticed that there were no signs of a forced entry and that the screen and storm window in the front right bedroom (Jessica's room) were raised. Despite objections by defense counsel — arguing that "good taste and decorum" counseled against forcing the "gentle people" of the jury to review additional crime-scene photographs — Commonwealth Attorney Ward used Polak to introduce additional images of the Wiseman home, including the wooden box that contained the drug paraphernalia and "a photograph also taken from the inside of the master bedroom towards the hallway to show the extent of the biological materials and the blood on the walls and doors."[48] Polak had prepared a diagram of the crime scene, and he explained to the jury the layout of the Wiseman home and the position of the bodies.

In the afternoon, Commonwealth Attorney Ward called two expert witnesses to the stand: David K. Wiecking, Virginia chief medical examiner, and James L. Pickelman, a firearms expert at Virginia's Division of Forensic Science Laboratory. A highly respected doctor largely credited with restoring the prestige of Virginia's medical examiner system, Wiecking had conducted the autopsies of Kathy and J. B. Wiseman and prepared an autopsy report, a toxicology report, and a medical examiner's report on each victim. Wiecking testified that Kathy and J. B. Wiseman died from shotgun wounds to the head, hardly a surprising conclusion. Regarding Kathy Wiseman, Wiecking stated that the first shot caused a "wound to the left cheek, which came out behind the left ear . . . the holes were large, the size of buck shots; and it took off much of the tissue of her left side of the face going on back to the left neck." Wiecking described the second shot as going "through the right eye and through . . . the back of the head, and it fractured the skull and upper neck with great destruction to the brain."[49] When asked which shot was the fatal one, Wiecking responded that "either of them could be fatal if untreated. Certainly, the one that went in the right eye was much more serious medically."[50] When pushed on the question of the fatal shot during cross-examination, Wiecking refused to give a definitive answer. "I think either one [shot] would be lethal," he stated. "I think the one that went through her right eye would immediately put her down."[51]

Turning his attention to J. B. Wiseman, Wiecking testified that he died of a single shotgun wound to the head. Based on the powder burns on the decedent's face, Wiecking concluded that the muzzle was within "several inches or several feet" from J. B. Wiseman when fired. Despite Jessica's claims that her parents were drug users, neither toxicology report found the presence of illegal drugs. Pickelman's testimony and ballistics report were equally unsurprising. Finding that the shotgun was in working order, Pickelman concluded that the three spent shotgun shells found at the Wiseman residence were fired from Chris's shotgun.

Two family members were called as prosecution witnesses: Brenda and Herbert Marshall. Through the testimony of Herbert Marshall, the prosecution established that the shotgun linked to the spent shells found at the murder scene was owned by Chris Thomas. "It was normally kept in my closet just to the right of my gun safe," stated Marshall. "The reason it wasn't kept in the gun safe is because it's pretty well filled up."[52] Marshall added that on the afternoon of November 10, 1990, he removed the gun from the closet at the behest of Special Agent Johnson and noticed that "it smelled like it had been fired very recently."[53] Marshall also testified about the cut brake line. Marshall did not witness the cutting of the brake line and, therefore, he was not directly asked the identity of the perpetrator. When asked to describe what had happened to the brake line, Marshall stated, "[t]he one he cut was for the front."[54] While Judge Folkes sustained the objection by defense counsel and instructed the jury to ignore Marshall's testimony regarding the identity of the vandal, the damage was done; Marshall had conveyed to the jury his unsubstantiated opinion that Chris cut the brake line. On cross-examination, Marshall conceded that he did not see Chris Thomas during the Roanoke hunting trip.

After Herbert Marshall completed his testimony about the cut brake line, his wife, Brenda Marshall, was called to the stand. Brenda was first asked about Chris's relationship with Jessica, describing it as "very intimate" and recalling an occasion when she found a nude Jessica Wiseman in bed with Chris. Brenda also confirmed that Kathy Wiseman was concerned about her daughter dating an older teenager. "I did talk to Kathy," Brenda testified. "And we both felt that Jessica was a little young for Chris."[55] Brenda added that Kathy insisted that Jessica give Chris back his class ring. Regarding the night that Brenda and Herbert Marshall returned from their Roanoke hunting trip, Brenda testified that Chris "sort of moped about" the house and told her that Jessica wasn't there because "she was being punished [by her mother] because she was late from coming home one night."[56] Through this line of questioning, the prosecution was establishing the motive for the murders. Motive and intent are different concepts, but are interrelated. Motive is defined as the reason why someone commits a murder, while intent relates to the state of mind regarding the act of murder. By eliciting testimony regarding Kathy Wiseman's concerns about the relationship and her grounding of Jessica, Commonwealth Attorney Ward was buttressing his theory of the case, namely, that Chris and Jessica decided to kill the Wisemans because the parents were interfering with their freedom.

From the prosecution's perspective, the critical witness for their case-in-chief was thirteen-year-old Lainie Creech. It would be through Lainie's testimony that the prosecution would establish the critical element in their capital murder case against Chris Thomas: that the murders of Kathy and J. B. Wiseman were premeditated. Now an eighth grader, Lainie was carefully examined about the events that occurred in the Marshall household in the week prior to the murders. In a soft, barely audible voice, the blonde, frail-looking girl testified that in August 1990, she had had a conversation with Jessica Wiseman regarding the reconciliation of Jessica's parents and their return to the Piankatank Shores subdivision: "[S]he said, she didn't want them, she didn't want them there. That they would just interfere with her life."[57] Prompted to further explain Jessica's comments, Lainie added that Jessica "wished to get rid of them."[58]

Jumping ahead to the days prior to the murders, Ward asked Lainie if she recalled overhearing a conversation that took place between Jessica and Chris in the Marshalls' home on Tuesday, November 6.

> Q: Now calling your attention to about right before the killings, the murders that Tuesday the 6th. Just prior to that Friday night, you were at the Marshalls' home and Chris and Jessica were there; weren't you. They were having a conversation; weren't they?
> A: Yes.
> Q: Tell us about that, if you would.
> A: Well, from what I heard, Jessica asked Chris about how many or—
> Q: What were they talking about?
> A: What I could tell was getting rid of her parents, getting rid of somebody.
> Q: Getting rid of her parents?
> A: (*The witness nods her head*).

Q: All right. What was said?

A: She asked if he had enough bullets? Or something like that. And he said, what time should I come over?

Q: What did he say in answer to the bullets?

A: He just—yeah, got enough.

Q: Then what did he say?

A: He asked her, what time should he come over.

Q: Asked her about what time to come over. What was her response?

A: She said, that if the window is down to go away or just—it's off. Or if the window is up to come on in.

Q: What time? Did they say what time?

A: Midnight.[59]

Turning his attention to the evening of Thursday, November 8, 1990, Ward asked Lainie about a conversation that she and Chris had had in the kitchen. "Well, the refrigerator door doesn't close tight," recalled Lainie. "It kind of opened up when he was making a sandwich, and he jumped. And I asked him why he was so nervous? And he said something, he has got to kill two people, and that he was real nervous."[60] Chris had told Lainie earlier in the evening that Herbert and Brenda Marshall would be delayed returning home because of "truck problems," and Lainie testified that Chris acted skeptical when she announced that someone had pulled into the driveway. "Then I said, it's Brenda and Herbert, and he said, Wow, and went to check at the window."[61]

In a final series of questions, Ward asked Lainie about the evening of November 9, 1991. Lainie testified that at approximately 7:00 P.M., she and Chris left the Marshall residence to get a key made and to search for a cat. Lainie recalled that during the drive Chris remarked, "I hope I don't get in trouble for going up to Roanoke for cutting the brake line." Lainie told Chris that she didn't believe him, to which he responded that he "didn't travel 500 miles for nothing." Lainie added that Jessica had accompanied Chris to Roanoke.[62] Before returning home to the Marshalls', Lainie stated: "We stopped a couple blocks away from Jessica's house and he wrote something down in the *Auto Trade* magazine, and he told me to take it to Jessica, and I went and took it to Jessica."[63]

Lainie testified that she entered Chris's room at approximately midnight and found him "putting on a hunting outfit." Continuing to build the case that the murders were premeditated and carefully planned, Ward asked if Chris had mentioned what would happen immediately after the murders. "Jessica was suppose to come and bang on the [Marshalls'] front door and that he was going to go in through his window and act like he was sleeping."[64] While Lainie later wavered in her testimony, evidencing some confusion as to whether she learned all the specific details of Chris's alibi before or after the murders, she emphatically maintained that Chris divulged some of the postmurder plan in advance.

Lainie's testimony raises a number of puzzling questions. Why did Chris Thomas share so many of the details of the murder plot with her? And why did Chris invite Lainie to witness his walk to the Wisemans' home? Some have suggested that Lainie exaggerated the extent of information that she learned prior to the murders, but there is another possibility—maybe Chris was desperately hoping that Lainie would stop him.

Moreover, why didn't Lainie tell someone, anyone, about the plan? Lainie testified that she walked with Chris to Jessica's house, and that Chris continued to discuss the killings as they trudged through the darkness. Lainie even conceded that she carried the shotgun for part of the journey. Did Lainie truly believe that Chris and Jessica were playing a practical joke on her, as they sometimes had in the past? On cross-examination, Lainie testified that she did not really believe that Chris was going to shoot two innocent people—but was she agreeing to defense counsel's question because it was a true statement or because it minimized her own moral culpability?

All in all, Commonwealth Attorney James Ward called nine witnesses and introduced more than thirty exhibits. Including the opening statement, the prosecution's case-in-chief lasted approximately six hours. It was a thorough and methodical presentation of the evidence in support of the charge of capital murder, and the strength of the prosecution's case made defense counsel's decision to go to trial all the more bewildering.

Defense counsel's cross-examination of the prosecution's witnesses was largely perfunctory and ineffective. For reasons relating to the upcoming sentencing hearing and whether the murders of the Wisemans constituted "aggravated assault," defense attorney Horne questioned Special Agent Johnson about the shotgun and established that it was an automatic weapon that could fire three shells in rapid succession. Horne later asked Special Agent Polak whether he could identify the types of pellets that were fired from the spent shell casings found in the bedroom and whether he knew what "double magnum four shot means?" When Horne had the opportunity to cross-examine both James Pickelman and Herbert Marshall, Horne again focused on the shotgun and asked multiple questions about how quickly one could fire three shots with the gun.

On Friday, August 23, 1991, Chris Thomas's attorneys presented their defense. It lasted five minutes and consisted of one witness and no exhibits. When Jessica Wiseman was called to the stand, a newspaper reporter present in the courtroom depicted the scene as follows: "Wiseman entered a hushed courtroom wearing the same white dress she wore when she was convicted of two counts of first-degree murder. . . . She clutched a white handkerchief in one hand and walked quickly across the courtroom without looking at Thomas, who stared down at the table in front of him."[65] The newspaper account does not record whether Wiseman still wore Chris's class ring, as she did at her own trial. Crossing to the witness stand, Damian Horne asked Jessica a single question: "Jessica, we want to ask you some questions. Will you answer them for us, only to help Chris?" In what the same newspaper reporter described as "a small and shaky voice," Jessica Wiseman turned to Judge Folkes and said: "I refuse to testify under my Fifth Amendment rights on the grounds that it might tend to incriminate me."[66]

The young girl who had promised her eternal love to Chris Thomas, who repeatedly wrote that she could not live in a world without him, left the courtroom without lifting a hand to save him. And what consequences would have Jessica faced by testifying on Chris's behalf? Jessica had already been convicted of two counts of first-degree murder as a principal in the second degree. While she was appealing the sentence at the time of Chris's trial, one nonetheless suspects that perhaps the appeal was filed so Jessica could successfully assert her Fifth Amendment rights at Chris's trial. In theory, Jessica's testimony at Chris's trial could have impacted both her appeal and the amount of time that she would be committed to a juvenile facility. Even in a worst-case scenario, however, Jessica's testimony would have cost her no more than six years in a juvenile treatment center — a small price to pay if it saved the life of the only person in the world that Jessica professed she couldn't live without.

As Jessica Wiseman left the courtroom, defense attorney Horne shocked the listeners in the courtroom by announcing "the defense rests."[67] No explanation was given to the jury as to why Chris Thomas would not take the stand. In a criminal case, a defendant does not have to testify, and Judge

Folkes instructed the jury: "The defendant does not have to testify and exercise of that right cannot be considered by you."[68] This jury, however, had been repeatedly promised by Sydney West that Chris would testify and tell them "the truth" of what happened in the Wiseman home. It would be impossible for any jury not to consider such a dramatically broken promise.

Chris's lawyers did not contemplate an "actual innocence" defense, namely, that Chris did not fire the third shot that killed Kathy Wiseman. "There was no room in Jessica's room . . . and therefore no angle that Jessica could have achieved to fire the second shot and result in what the photos showed. To have argued something different would have been patently absurd . . . AND, clearly, perjury," Horne explained later. "The picture painted by the crime scene photos . . . the blood splatters, the marks on the bodies etc are not only precisely how Chris described it, but the ONLY way it could have happened." In short, "it is an absurdity to believe anything other than what Chris said and the evidence showed. . . . The sad, sad, fact of the matter is that Chris was under the spell of Jessica . . . but he killed them both. Period."[69]

Chris's state habeas lawyers would subsequently argue, however, that physical evidence of innocence existed. "The two children were positioned in Jessica Wiseman's bedroom such that it is highly improbable that Chris could have fired the second shot at Kathy Wiseman. From all accounts Chris was behind Jessica's bed and at right angles to the door which Mrs. Wiseman walked through. Jessica, however, was at the foot of her bed facing the door and facing her mother."[70] The habeas petition further pointed out that while Jessica Wiseman had blood on her shoes, there was no blood on Chris's clothing.

In fact, Dr. Williams, the mental health expert appointed by the court to examine Chris and determine whether his confession was voluntarily, expressed skepticism about Chris's claims that he fired the third shot. "Doctor Earl Williams questioned Chris Thomas's account of the murders from the very beginning. He attempted to warn counsel that Chris Thomas was attempting to protect Jessica and that Chris had not fired the second shot at Mrs. Wiseman."[71] The failure to investigate and present evidence that Jessica Wiseman killed her mother would be cited by Chris's appellate lawyers as one example of the mistakes made by trial counsel.

Prior to closing argument by the attorneys, Judge Folkes instructed the jury as to the substantive legal provision to be applied in Chris's case. First, he instructed the jury as to the basic elements of the crime of capital murder.[72]

The defendant is charged with the crime of capital murder of Kathy J. Wiseman. The Commonwealth must prove, beyond a reasonable doubt, each of the following elements of that crime: 1. That the defendant killed Kathy J. Wiseman and James Baxter Wiseman, II; and 2. That the killings were malicious; 3. That the killings were willful, deliberate and premeditated; and 4. That the killings occurred as a part of the same act or transaction.[73]

Clearly the fundamental question in the case boiled down to whether Chris Thomas had the requisite intent to be guilty of capital murder. Judge Folkes further defined premeditation for the jury: "Willful, deliberate and premeditated means a specific intent to kill adopted at some time before the killing, but which need not exist for any particular length of time." He continued: "Where a mortal wound is given with a deadly weapon in the previous possession of the slayer, without any provocation or even with slight provocation, it may be inferred, in the absence of evidence to the contrary, that the killing is willful, deliberate and premeditated."[74] As for the element of malice, Judge Folkes instructed the jury that they "may infer malice from the deliberate use of a deadly weapon, unless from all the evidence, you have a reasonable doubt as to whether malice existed."[75]

Commonwealth Attorney Jimmy Ward gave the first closing argument: "[T]he evidence of guilt in this case is just overwhelming."[76] Not only did the two young lovers have the motive to kill the Wisemans, but the evidence introduced by the prosecution established beyond a shadow of a doubt that the murders were carefully planned. Carefully Ward walked the jurors through the days leading up to the murders, emphasizing the steps that Chris and Jessica took to prepare for the murders. The cutting of the brake lines. The plan for what Jessica would do after the murders. The camouflage clothes. The shotgun. The open storm window, signaling to Chris to come into Jessica's bedroom. Reloading the shotgun after he entered the Wisemans' home. The two-hour wait in Jessica's bedroom. Spreading the drug paraphernalia on the floor of the master bedroom. Perhaps anticipating that the defense might make a desperate, last-minute attempt to blame the third shot on Jessica, Ward directed the jury's attention to the pictures of the carnage.

You see in the pictures the people who were shot, and if you look at the blood splatters, you will see that from the angle that he was shooting from, he shot Mrs. Wiseman and the blood went up against the door. If you remember . . . there were pellets found down the hall. And the reason they were found down the hall is because when he was shooting on an angle, the pellets were out, killing Mrs. Wiseman, they ricocheted out and went down the hall. He did it, he was right beside the bed. "I was laying on the floor opposite the side of the bed where her mother came in. Jessica was standing in front of the window. I shot her mother in the doorway. I shot her mother in the doorway."[77]

Drawing to a close, Ward challenged the argument that Chris Thomas valued the sanctity of human life. "He said his girlfriend wouldn't do it, so I did it. What kind of concern does this man have for human life?"[78] And Ward reminded the jury that Chris and Jessica stepped over the dead body of Kathy Wiseman as they left the Wiseman residence. By the time Ward returned to counsel table, he had effectively hammered home his theory of the case: Chris Thomas had carefully planned and executed the murders of two innocent parents.

The closing argument by defense counsel Damian Horne was self-congratulatory, self-pitying, and disjointed. Then again, he had little with which to work. He began by thanking Judge Folkes for not only "fairly and impartially" administering justice, but also "because of the special care he has taken during this our first capital offense."[79] Mentioning that defense counsel had never before tried a capital murder case may have been a nod to the court's courtesy; it was also the first (but not last) attempt to engender sympathy from the jury. Horne next turned to Commonwealth Attorney Jimmy Ward, thanking him "not only because he has been a gentleman adversary throughout these proceedings, but because he has represented the people of this Commonwealth, you and me, with vigor and determination."[80]

Horne saved his most lavish praise for his co-counsel (and future wife), Sydney West: "I have special thanks for my lovely and beautiful partner, Ms. West, Sydney. She has spent countless hours, innumerable hours, sleepless nights preparing for our defense. She has toiled relentlessly to insure those precious rights we all enjoy, do not become tarnished. I would like to say that she has helped me, ladies and gentlemen, but that would not be true. I hope that I have helped her protect justice."[81] Bluntly put, there is no place in a capital murder trial for an attorney to praise the aesthetic beauty of his co-counsel.

Horne, however, was not done with his list of thanks. The most important group in the courtroom—the jury—had not been properly praised.

Finally, all of you sitting here deserve our special gratitude, for you must administer, you must seek justice and you must protect justice. That is what makes our system the greatest ever conceived. Sure, your system's not perfect. Sometimes the guilty escape retribution and sometimes the innocent are punished. But the ultimate issue of guilt or innocence is decided by you, not the administrator of justice, not the seeker of justice, not the protector of justice, but by you, ladies and gentlemen. You must combine all these roles and become the doers of justice."[82]

What immediately comes to mind is a quote commonly attributed to United States Supreme Court Justice Oliver Wendell Holmes, Jr. During oral argument in a case before the Supreme Court, a young attorney begged the justices to act justly. Justice Holmes purportedly shot back, "This is a court of law, young man, not a court of justice."[83] Juries are not "doers of justice." Juries are charged with determining the relevant facts of the case and applying those facts to the law (as instructed to them by the judge) to reach a verdict. To tell a jury that they are "doers of justice" and wield the power of judge, prosecutor, and defense attorney demonstrates that the speaker either fundamentally misunderstands the structure of the criminal justice system or realizes that his client's only chance is to ask the jury to ignore the facts of the case and act mercifully.

Horne finally turned his attention to the young man sitting at counsel table, making the jarring declaration that "Chris is a lucky man, not because he's on trial for his very young life, but because he has an opportunity to face a jury of his peers."[84] Horne was trying to make the point that Chris was fortunate to be facing the judgment of a jury, "a wholly and peculiar American institution," rather than the unfettered judgment of a king—but how "lucky" could Chris have felt as he listened to defense counsel? Horne's celebration of the American justice system continued: "[W]e just fought the war, completed a war with a man, one tyrant, Sadaam Hussain [sic], who made all the decisions in his country. This colossal fight resulted in the death of thousands. It is easy to see the risk of absolute power, when guilt, innocence, and punishment are decided by one man. Cast in this light, how lucky we are that the administrators of justice are not also the all-powerful doers of justice."[85] The salute to the American judicial system droned on. "For 73 years, the government in the Soviet Union has been a police state, and in all that time, the prosecution has never lost a single case, not one. Are we not happy that we have a system where the seeker of justice is not also the doer of justice."[86] Of course, a few minutes earlier Horne had told the jurors that they, as doers of justice, combined the roles of administrator, seeker, and protector of justice, but now Horne labeled such political systems totalitarian.

Changing gears, Horne lauded the ability of American courts and juries to resist the razzle-dazzle of unscrupulous defense attorneys. Admitting that "in some of our courts today, people escape justice by novel manipulations of the insanity defense, by some hidden technicality," Horne reassured the jury that "these are the rare exceptions, because our system protects — has safeguards against the protectors of justice who, in their zeal, may not protect at all, but warp and misshape."[87] Patting himself on the back, Horne reminded the assembled jurors that he had not blinded the jury with legal mumbo-jumbo and sleight of hand. "You have not heard the testimony of the psychiatrist. You have not witnessed lengthy cross-examinations, and you have not been subject to bizarre legal motions that confound and confuse."[88] Moreover, Horne tried to turn the failure of his client to testify — as promised by Sydney West repeatedly during opening statement — as further evidence of defense counsel's sincerity. "In fact, you haven't even heard a new, sanitized confession. The rehearsed version from Chris, recycled by his innumerable meetings with his lawyers. You have seen the original confession, complete, unabridged, unedited. You have heard the complete truth."[89] What should a jury conclude from this statement: that defense counsel had planned on tricking them with a "rehearsed" and "sanitized" confession that was the product of "innumerable meetings" with defense counsel, but then came to their senses, determined that such behavior was beneath them, and decided not to put their client on the stand?

At long last, Horne turned to his theory of the case. "Chris pulled the trigger. That is undisputed, but there was no premeditation. There was no intent, there was no plan and there was no malice."[90] While Chris was "the trigger man" and "the vehicle by which they [Kathy and J. B. Wiseman] died . . . he is not the agent of their death."[91] As for the agent: "That person refused to testify today. She said nothing that would shed light on these terrible events. She said nothing to the police. She said nothing at trial. She said nothing to save Chris. She said nothing to you, the doers of justice. She simply sits in silence and waits and bides her time, because there is light at the end of her tunnel, but only darkness for her father, only darkness for her mother, and only darkness for Chris."[92]

Finally seizing on the heart of his defense, Horne hammered away at Jessica Wiseman. She planned the murders. She lured Chris to her home and trapped him in her bedroom. She deliberately pushed Chris toward the crimes. She forced Chris into her parents' bedroom. She maliciously "commanded" Chris to again shoot the still living Kathy Wiseman. "Yes, ladies and gentlemen, there was malice. Such maliciousness that I quake at the thought of Jessica Wiseman."[93] Neither author was in the courtroom as Horne spoke, and a written transcript cannot convey an attorney's tone of voice or emotional state. For a newspaper reporter watching the closing statement, however, Horne "raged with anger at Jessica Wiseman for planning the murders and persuading Thomas to carry them out."[94]

Yet as soon as Horne found his rhythm, he lost it. After hammering home the argument that Chris lacked premeditation, that he was a pawn in the hands of Jessica Wiseman, Horne reassured the jury that he understood that there was no moral difference between premeditated and unplanned murder. "Paraphrasing Shakespeare, ladies and gentlemen, all the perfumes of Arabia will not sweeten these little hands. But that is not what the law commands of you. The act cannot be whitewashed, it can only be defined so justice may be done."[95] If, however, the role of "doers of justice" is to achieve a morally just result, and if Horne concedes that there is no moral difference between the acts committed by Jessica (premeditated murder) and the acts committed by Chris (non-premeditated murder), then how can Horne argue that Chris's lack of malice and premeditation deserves "something less than capital murder, because capital murder contemplates the ultimate punishment, and Douglas Christopher Thomas is not the ultimate perpetrator"?[96]

Seemingly exhausted by the inconsistencies in his own theory of the case, Horne turned back to himself. "I woke up this morning, ladies and gentlemen, exhausted, yes, and despondent. The defense has not had an easy case, but it is one in which I believe. Because if there's anything in this horrible affair, anything at all that is redeeming, it is the honesty in which the evidence was presented."[97] Announcing that he and Sydney West had been roundly and constantly criticized for defending "such a person," Horne responds that their "shield" to all the attacks was that "[w]e have allowed the truth to surface."[98] Of course, it is not the job of a defense attorney to allow the truth to surface. If so, the courts would not see involuntary confessions challenged, crime-scene photographs characterized as prejudicial, or hearsay objected to. The job of a defense attorney in a capital murder case is to save his or her client's life while operating within the rules and procedures established by the state.

Horne returned to the difficulties endured by defense counsel while representing Chris Thomas.

> Shortly after I was appointed to this case, my own precious mother, to whom I owe everything, was diagnosed with breast cancer. It is inoperable. It is in the doctor's words, incurable. I swear before you, and I swear before God, it has not—the news of that has not made this defense any easier for me. I don't mention it as any cheap attorney trick to generate sympathy and shame to anyone who thinks so. This case has been an agony and has provoked searing, soul-searching moments. The type of which only a criminal defense lawyer, and yes, a son who adores his mother, can know. I have used the same strength and conviction that will undoubtedly bear you through this ordeal, because now you suffer even a greater burden.[99]

As Horne discussed his mother, he wept. Former defense counsel Benton Pollok, watching from the gallery, left, dismayed by Horne's performance. What exactly was the message that Horne delivered to the jury? Was Chris Thomas such a terrible human being that the mere representation of him "provoked searing, soul-searching moments" tantamount to the trials and tribulations of Job? Was he asking the jury to return a verdict in favor of the defense to reward defense counsel for so bravely suffering? And what was the purpose of revealing that his mother was ill but to shamefully tug at the jury's heartstrings? Having exhausted his appeal to the jury's sympathy, Horne closed by sharing a biblical passage that once again, in the words of defense counsel, reminded the jurors that they were "doers of justice. "And what does the Lord require of you but to do justice, and to love kindness, and to walk humbly with your God?"[100]

Rising to his feet for rebuttal, Commonwealth Attorney Jimmy Ward had the difficult task of responding to Horne's closing statement without appearing unsympathetic. "I have the utmost compassion for anybody who has to go through what this man has been through," began Ward. "But we're not talking about today, his sick mother or whatever, we're talking about this man being accountable for killing those two people."[101]

Matching Horne's biblical quotes with one of his own—"thou shalt not kill"—Ward mocked defense counsel's claims that Chris Thomas lacked the requisite intent to be guilty of capital murder. "How can they come before us today, how can they come before you and say that this man didn't intend to do this? He didn't intend to get caught."[102] Reminding the jury that Chris Thomas, not Jessica Wiseman, was on trial, Ward directly attacked the claim that Chris acted without malice or premeditation. If no intent, then why did Chris come to the Wisemans' residence with a loaded shotgun? If he did not want to kill the Wisemans, then why did not Chris simply leave their home? If Chris blindly fired the shotgun with no intent to kill, then how did he hit J. B. Wiseman squarely in the face? "He, and he alone, made the final decision to pull that trigger," concluded Ward. "She [Jessica] may have said for him to do it, but he made the decision to do it, and he should be held accountable."[103]

There was nothing left to say. The jury retired to deliberate, having been previously instructed on the controlling principles of law by Judge Folkes. We have sent multiple surveys to the surviving members of the Chris Thomas jury, but none of the former jurors ever responded to our informational requests and none have ever talked publicly of their deliberations. In short, we do not know what happened in the jury room.

The jury deliberated for only three hours, yet another ominous sign for Chris Thomas. As the jury weighed the evidence, the crowd awaiting the verdict filled the courtroom to capacity and spilled out into the external hallway. A local newspaper reporter noted that defense attorneys Horne and West joined the spectators sitting on the floor of the hallway, writing, "Their blank expressions belied emotionally-drained persons."[104]

A verdict was returned in the early evening of Friday, August 23. After standing, the clerk of the court read the verdict to the assembled crowd:

We, the jury, find the defendant guilty of the capital murder of Kathy J. Wiseman, under the legal theory that the killing of Kathy J. Wiseman occurred as part of the same act or transaction as the killing of James Baxter Wiseman, II.[105]

As the jury verdict was read and the individual jurors polled, Chris Thomas remained stone-faced. Others, however, could not remain so composed, and the sounds of weeping carried through the courtroom. A newspaper reporter wrote: "The face of Middlesex County Commonwealth's Attorney James H. Ward Jr. appeared relieved . . . [and] [h]e sat back in his chair, his face looked less strained."[106] J. B. Wiseman's mother wept and rushed over to thank Ward. As she left the courthouse, Jean Wiseman told a reporter, "'to me it was black and white. . . . They took the life of my son and daughter-in-law. Now, they should take his.'"[107] Added the reporter: "As she [Jean Wiseman] came out of the courthouse into the last light of evening, she clenched both fists, pumped them in front of her and stamped her foot on the ground. 'Yes!' she exclaimed."[108]

That night, Chris Thomas sat alone in his jail cell and wrote a letter to Jessica Wiseman. For unknown reasons, it was never mailed.

> I'm not doing good at all. The jury found me guilty of Capital Murder. They didn't recommend a sentence though, but Jimmy Ward indicated that the only punishment I deserve is the electric chair. I can't believe he is doing this. I will "*never*" get out of prison. "*EVER!*" It will either be that or the other thing (E.C.). To tell you the truth I really don't care anymore. Just as long as this horrible nightmare ends.
>
> So how do you think I looked today. You looked so beautiful. If only you would smile more. Can you believe that I almost got on the stand and said Lainie shot someone. I was that desperate but like they say "I have to suffer the painful consequences of my actions." Look, I want your opinion on this. If they do something where I will never get [out] (I'm saying if) you should just go on with your life. Because the life we planned together will never come true. . . . I want you to be happy. . . . You deserve the absolute best and I feel I don't meet those standards.

We do not know what Chris meant when he wrote that he almost testified that Lainie Creech was directly involved in the murders. Whether this is a macabre joke or an actual strategy, it appears nowhere else in the volumes of records that we have reviewed from the case. What the letter does reveal, however, is the adoration that Chris Thomas felt for Jessica Wiseman on the night that he was convicted of killing her parents, and his fatal determination to protect Jessica.

With the verdict of guilty, Chris's attorneys had forty-eight hours to prepare for a sentencing hearing that would determine whether their client would live or die. We do not know when defense counsel realized the enormous task before them, but on the Sunday before the sentence hearing, Dr. Hank Gwaltney claimed that he received a telephone call from Damian Horne. Gwaltney had not talked to the defense attorney since that fateful meeting in early spring, when Gwaltney had warned Horne that a proper mitigation evaluation was needed. During the telephone call, Horne announced "something to the effect of: 'Hank, we don't know what we are doing; can you help us?'"[109] Concluded Gwaltney: "It appeared to me that the defense lawyers recognized that they had not adequately prepared their psychological mitigation defense, and that they really did not know what to do at that point."[110]

Gwaltney was scheduled to meet with the commonwealth attorney that afternoon, and he invited Horne and West to the conference. At the meeting, Gwaltney grimly declared that the report prepared by the defense's expert psychologist was, as he had predicted, "inadequate" and "that the prosecuting attorney would be able to use the report to a disastrous end for Mr. Thomas."[111] Gwaltney advised defense counsel to immediately request the court to continue the case, adding that, alternatively, they could fire their own expert and rely upon Gwaltney's testimony. The state psychologist, however, warned of the inherent risks involved in using him as both a prosecution and defense expert.

> [B]ecause I had been engaged only by the prosecution to do the penalty phase for the Commonwealth I advised them that I had not done a complete mitigation review as I would have done for the defense if I had been initially contacted for that work. I emphasized to them I was not prepared at that point to do a complete and adequate mitigation review which would have been done by the Institute. . . . I emphasized that there was a tremendous amount of mitigating evidence that could be found in a proper mitigation review and that with such a review I or the Institute could have orchestrated a good mitigation case. I pointed out that with no adequate evaluation and with literally less than 24 hours to prepare, it was impossible to do anywhere close to a decent and adequate job.[112]

There is no evidence in the record that defense counsel formally requested a continuance of the sentencing hearing, instead settling upon the dangerous strategy of using the commonwealth's expert witness.

On Monday, August 26, the sentencing hearing began at promptly 10:00 A.M. Before the jury was brought into the courtroom, defense counsel Sydney West moved the court to dismiss the jury and instead have Judge Folkes determine the sentence. The motion was swiftly denied. If Chris Thomas's attorneys had convinced their client to plead guilty to capital murder, they would have received exactly what they just requested the court to do—impose the sentence in lieu of the jury. However, under Virginia law the jury was charged with selecting a sentence for the man they had convicted.

Damian Horne also requested to put a brief statement on the record, namely, that "defense counsel would like to note that, against the advice of his attorneys, Chris Thomas has refused to take the stand and speak on his behalf. We would like for the Court to note that for the record, if it please the Court.[113] Clearly confused, Judge Folkes reminded defense counsel that "[t]he defendant, however, is not required to take the stand," to which Horne replied, "We realized that, Your Honor."[114] Defense counsel's declaration about Chris's unwillingness to testify was not made to preserve any error or objection by defense counsel; it was arguably a self-serving attempt to protect the defense attorneys against any future claims that Chris did not receive effective assistance of counsel as guaranteed by the Constitution.

As with the guilt/innocence phase of the trial, both the prosecution and defense counsel are afforded the opportunity to present an opening statement at the start of the sentencing hearing. Their opening statements, and the evidence introduced by counsel during the hearing, are shaped by the controlling legal principles regarding capital sentencing. A defendant is deemed eligible for the death penalty if the prosecution has established beyond a reasonable doubt one of two different aggravating circumstances: "there is a probability that the defendant would commit criminal acts of violence that would constitute a continuing serious threat to society," or "that his conduct in committing the offense for which he stands charged was outrageously or wantonly vile, horrible or inhuman in that it involved torture, depravity of mind or an aggravated battery to the victim."[115]

The definition of "aggravated battery" as evidence of the vileness of the crime would prove critical to the Thomas sentencing hearing. The Virginia Supreme Court has defined aggravated battery (in the context of evidence of vileness) as "a battery which, qualitatively and quantitatively, is more culpable than the minimum necessary to accomplish an act of murder."[116] The Virginia Supreme Court revisited the definition of aggravated battery seven years later in the case of *Watkins v. Commonwealth*,[117] in which the court held that "proof of infliction of multiple wounds may meet the test for an aggravated battery."[118] Specifically regarding the defendant in Watkins, the Virginia Supreme Court observed that a defendant who "exceeded the quality and quantity of force necessary to accomplish . . . murder"[119] can support a jury's finding of aggravated battery.

Prosecutors can argue both that a crime was vile and that a defendant poses a future risk of dangerousness; at the Thomas sentencing hearing Commonwealth Attorney Jimmy Ward would take just such a tack. According to the Virginia Supreme Court, "the relevant inquiry is not whether . . . [a defendant] could commit criminal acts of violence in the future but whether he would."[120] The Virginia Supreme Court has permitted a wide range of evidence to be introduced to show future dangerousness. "In addition to evidence of prior criminal convictions, the court has approved evidence of the sentences imposed, the details of prior offenses, unadjudicated misconduct occurring before and after the capital offense, *and juvenile offenses*"[121] — including evidence of such nonviolent juvenile offenses as car theft[122] and reckless driving.[123]

If the jury finds that the defendant is eligible for the death penalty, then it moves to the second phase of the sentencing hearing (referred to as the "selection phase") and decides whether it will, in fact, sentence the defendant to death. During this second phase of sentencing, the defense introduces mitigating evidence; that is, evidence why the death penalty should not be imposed. Regarding mitigation evidence, Virginia law does not provide a definite list of mitigation facts, but suggests that the facts "may include" (1) the fact that the defendant lacks a "significant history of prior criminal activities," (2) the fact that the defendant committed the criminal acts while "under the influence of extreme mental or emotional disturbance," (3) the fact of the defendant's age when the criminal acts were committed.[124] Law professor Ronald J. Bacigal adds that "[a] consistent theme in the capital jurisprudence of the United States Supreme Court has been the insistence that there be no barriers to the presentation and consideration of virtually unlimited factors proffered by capital defendant as a basis for a sentence less than death."[125]

Commonwealth Attorney Ward gave the first opening statement in the Thomas sentence hearing. Although Ward announced to the jury, "It's the Commonwealth's contention that it was a vile crime,"[126] he immediately began summarizing the evidence that would show that Chris posed a risk of future dangerousness: "[W]e will attempt to show his past record, his juvenile record . . . and [also] will attempt to prove that during his incarceration in the regional security center down here, he attempted to escape."[127] The evidence of Chris's dangerousness would also include cutting Herbert Marshall's brake line, an act that could have resulted in injury or death to Chris's "surrogate parents." Regarding the vandalism of the truck, Ward told the jury that it "shows the thought processes of this individual" and Chris's "lack of sanctity for human life."[128]

Finally, Ward stated that the evidence would show that Chris remained unrepentant for the murders of Kathy and J. B. Wiseman. "We don't believe that there's been any remorse for the dastardly deed he did. The only remorse that he has is that he's facing this jury today, and in your hands is whether to sentence him to life or to death."[129] All in all, the evidence of past criminal acts and the lack of remorse would be analyzed by the prosecution's expert witness, Dr. Henry O. Gwaltney. "I think the main thing that Gwaltney will tell you is that he can't exclude the fact that this man will do this again."[130] Chris's appellate lawyers would later argue that Ward's statement was objectionable because it inappropriately shifted the burden of showing future dangerousness from the prosecution to the defense, and that the failure to object to the mischaracterization of the law was one of many examples of the ineffectiveness of Chris's attorneys.

As with the guilt/innocence phase of the trial, Sydney West rose to give the opening statement at the sentencing hearing on behalf of Chris Thomas. "We knew that the prosecutor had an overwhelming case of evidence against our client," West stated. "The state police and the local police have done a superb job of preserving evidence from the scene of the crime. It was meticulously tested and the results were very clear and very unchallenging—our client made a full confession."[131] This, of course, begs the question of why defense counsel did not successfully negotiate a plea bargain for their client. In their habeas corpus petition, Chris's appellate lawyers claimed that an ulterior motive explained the failure to pursue a plea agreement: "Defense counsel, Sydney West, had told the prosecutor, James Ward, before trial that they could not plead Chris Thomas guilty because to do so would hurt their professional reputations."[132] While we ourselves challenge many of the decisions made by defense counsel in the Thomas case, we do not believe that the failure to secure a plea agreement was due to any concerns that defense counsel allegedly had about their professional reputations. The combination of a commonwealth attorney who was facing reelection, a revolving cast of defense lawyers, an antagonistic relationship between a mercurial trial court judge and the original team of defense attorneys, and a disengaged and uninterested defendant with whom trial counsel did not establish a relationship of trust and understanding tragically doomed the chances of the parties entering into a plea agreement that would have saved Chris's life.

West continued:

[W]e believed that the best defense was not to attempt to manipulate the evidence, but rather just to allow the facts to be put before you. We even decided, after the prosecution rested, that our client's own testimony could rise no further with regard to his guilt or innocence, than the confession that was already presented by the prosecutor. So rather than to appear to you to attempt to sanitize or fix-up the confession in some way, we decided just to let it stand. And we let you decide—we let you decide what to do with that confession.[133]

Several responses spring immediately to mind. First of all, defense counsel's theory of the case was that Chris did not murder Kathy and J. B. Wiseman with malice aforethought, but that he was the pawn of Jessica Wiseman. The confession alone, however, did not support this claim. In order to establish that Chris was the unwitting "agent" of Jessica Wiseman, the defense had to put Chris on the witness stand to refute the evidence of premeditation that was introduced through the testimony of Lainie Creech. Whether Chris refused to take the stand or whether defense counsel failed in their duty to establish a relationship of trust with Chris and convince him to take the stand, the critical point is that he did not, despite defense counsel's promises. Now to tell the jury that Chris's testimony was unnecessary—and would smack of an "attempt to sanitize or fix-up the confession"—further diminished Horne and Ward's credibility.

After telling the jury that the defense "can do nothing other than applaud and thank you"[134] for doing "exactly what the Judge told you to do,"[135] West confessed that defense counsel felt "much more confident in the evidence that we have to present [at sentencing], than we did at the guilty stage of this trial, for at this stage, it is the prosecutor who has a very difficult task."[136] That statement belies the commonwealth attorney's challenge in the guilt/innocence phase, namely, proving all elements of capital murder beyond a reasonable doubt. As the jury had already been told, West continued, the prosecutor's "astounding burden" is to prove either that Chris posed a future risk of dangerousness or that his crimes were "outrageously or wantonly vile." And, West instructed the jury, even if the prosecution proved beyond a reasonable doubt one of these aggravating factors, "you will never, never, never be in a position today where the evidence and the law will require you to impose a death sentence"[137] because of the role of mitigation evidence.

Ominously, the shortest part of the opening statement was a summary of the mitigation evidence that the defense team intended to introduce. West told the jury that they would hear the story of a young boy who effectively never knew either parent until the age of twelve, when the sudden deaths of his grandparents and his uncle triggered "the beginning of Mr. Thomas' downfall in many ways."[138] Forced to move in with his mother, and "thrust into a lifestyle which he did not really approve of,"[139] Chris's downward spiral continued. West stated that Chris's special education teacher (Laura Anderson) would testify that Chris was "an emotionally needy child, who fought very, very hard to overcome his problems in school and was making very, very good progress," but that the teacher was unable to convince Chris not to return to Middlesex County. The defense team would present testimony showing the jury that "Chris was known by his friends and his family to be gentle and caring; that he has no prior history of violence; that those who know him have never known him to be violent."[140] West concluded by asking the jury to "look into your soul, into your very morality and make your decision."[141] "I feel confident that you will find that our mitigation evidence in this case is compelling and that you will have no other choice at the end of these proceedings, than to choose a life sentence."[142] As with the first phase of the trial, however, the defense team would fail to produce sufficient evidence to support their theory of the case.

The first witness called by the prosecution was Robert J. Sowell, a Middlesex County probation officer. Sowell had collected Chris Thomas's juvenile records, and, without objection by defense counsel as to the relevance of the testimony or the admissibility of the records themselves, he testified as to Chris's history of petty, nonviolent juvenile offenses. Petty larceny. Breaking and entering. Possession of an alcoholic beverage. Grand larceny. Possession of marijuana. Trespassing on school property. Destruction of private property.

The next prosecution witness was Herbert Marshall. Having previously testified about the shotgun and the cut brake line during the prosecution's case-in-chief, Marshall testified that on the morning of the murders he returned home at approximately 7:30 A.M. There he found Chris and Jessica, sleeping (close enough to be touching) on the sofa together. Rising to his feet, defense counsel Horne objected to the relevancy of the testimony. Taking issue with Commonwealth Attorney Ward's assertion that the slumbering teenagers demonstrated lack of remorse, Horne stated that "there is nothing

. . . which has been a good law in Virginia since the 1920's, where the Commonwealth can appeal to the emotion and prejudice of the jury or refer to the lack of remorse, or the allegedly lack of remorse, by our client."[143] Accordingly, Horne demanded a mistrial.

The objection, however, was baseless and the motion denied. In overruling the motion for a mistrial, Judge Folkes pointed out that Virginia case law[144] undeniably permitted the introduction of evidence regarding a defendant's lack of remorse to establish future dangerousness. After issuing his ruling, however, he admonished the commonwealth attorney for his protracted presentation of evidence. "I wish we'd move along, Mr. Ward. I think we could speed this up a bit and get the — the standards are rather narrow. Let's move along."[145] Judge Folkes's continued push to try the case is inexplicable. Not only are the "standards" for sentencing broadly and ambiguously drawn, but the life of a young man hung in the balance.

His direct examination completed, Commonwealth Attorney Ward passed the witness. Stunningly, the defense attorneys had no questions for the man who had just testified that Chris Thomas was so lacking in basic human emotion that he took a nap with his lover in the hours after the murders. The failure to cross-examine, however, lay not in defense counsel's inability to appreciate the significance of the testimony, but likely in defense counsel's failure to thoroughly investigate the case and gather mitigation evidence. As argued by Chris's appellate lawyers in his state habeas petition, "[b]ecause defense counsel had failed to interview the appropriate witnesses . . . it was never brought out that the reason Chris and Jessica were asleep was that they had been given and had taken valium shortly before."[146] Nor was evidence ever introduced that Chris had barely slept in the previous forty-eight hours and had consumed alcohol prior to the murders. The combination of valium, alcohol, and sleep deprivation would easily provide an alternative explanation for Chris's actions.

To this point in the trial, the commonwealth attorney had followed a pattern of introducing straightforward evidence in support of the charge of capital murder as well as in support of the sentencing hearing's aggravating factors. In other words, Jimmy Ward had not sought to use questionable testimony to build his case against Chris. This methodical approach suddenly evaporated, however, as the prosecutor sought to introduce evidence that Chris Thomas had taken part in an escape attempt while in the local jail. While the Virginia Supreme Court has held that escape attempts are admissible to show future dangerousness,[147] the evidence offered by Ward was so weak that the trial court should have deemed it inadmissible. Judge Folkes, however, did not.[148]

The commonwealth began building its case of a purported jailbreak with the testimony of Lieutenant Ernest J. Robinson, a staff member at the Middle Peninsula Regional Security Center in Saluda, Virginia. After receiving an incident report, on July 9, 1991, Robinson instigated a search for contraband materials in one of the dormitory "blocks" where Chris Thomas and fifteen other prisoners were incarcerated. "We found a block on the far wall [of the dormitory]," testified Robinson. "It looked like it was tampered with, it was scraped. It looked like it was — someone had tried to remove the block."[149] Robinson added that in the mattress of one of the prisoners (not Chris Thomas), he found metal instruments "shaped to where it was used to chip the putty thing around the block."[150] During cross-examination, Robinson conceded that he did not know either when the scraping had commenced or how many prisoners had rotated through the dormitory since the alleged escape attempted had commenced.

Undeterred, Ward next introduced the testimony of Middle Peninsula Regional Security Center staff member Julia Graham. She testified that on the evening of July 8, 1991, she heard "banging" coming from the inside of the aforementioned dormitory. Ms. Graham was followed by a series of prisoners from the security center. While the prisoners had apparently given formal signed statements regarding the incident (the statements are not part of the official court record, and we do not know what they said), they refused to testify in the sentencing hearing and were held in contempt of court. After Judge Folkes announced that the commonwealth's efforts to elicit testimony from the prisoners was "an exercise in futility," Ward abandoned his efforts to link Chris Thomas to any escape attempt.

How damaging was the evidence that Chris Thomas had tried to escape from jail and the related inference that he might try again? While Horne strenuously objected to the relevance of the testimony, Chris's state habeas lawyers later contended that the limited evidence introduced by the commonwealth "nonetheless prejudiced Chris Thomas because it associated him with a nebulous escape attempt, and suggested that he was dangerous, even though in the end he was never connected to the alleged plot to escape."[151] The appellate lawyers further suggested that had the defense attorneys interviewed the proper witnesses before trial, they would have been aware that the prosecutor could not link Chris to the escape attempt and could have filed a pretrial motion to exclude the evidence in its entirety—thus protecting their client from the deadly inference created by the limited testimony about late-night jail breaks.

Commonwealth Attorney Ward introduced the jury to the prosecution's last, and most important, witness: clinical psychologist Henry O. Gwaltney, Jr., of the Central State Hospital in Petersburg, Virginia. Objecting to neither Dr. Gwaltney's credentials nor his testimony, the defense team silently listened to Dr. Gwaltney opine that (1) Chris Thomas "was not acting under extreme mental or emotional disturbance" [at the time of the murders],[152] and (2) he "appreciated the criminality of his conduct and had the capacity to conform his acts to the requirement of the law."[153] Finally, Dr. Gwaltney testified that he could not say that Chris Thomas would not commit future crimes.

> Q: You can't say, with all your experience, that when juveniles face capital murder charges that this [sic], you can't say that this defendant will not commit this crime again, can you?
> A: No, I can't say that he would not. I also can't say that he will.[154]

Once again, under Virginia law the prosecution has the burden of proving beyond a reasonable doubt "that there is a probability that the defendant would commit criminal acts of violence that would constitute a continuing serious threat to society."[155] This is one of the aggravating circumstances that makes a defendant eligible for the death penalty. By phrasing the question in terms of whether Dr. Gwaltney "could not" say, the prosecution—either inadvertently or purposefully—twisted the controlling legal principles and shifted the burden of proof to the defendants to provide evidence that Chris was not a future danger.

Turning to the issue of Chris's alleged lack of remorse, Ward asked Dr. Gwaltney if Chris Thomas ever expressed any remorse to him. While Dr. Gwaltney testified that Chris had not, he struggled to place his answer in context. Explaining that adolescents who kill "don't necessarily appreciate the finality of that decision and . . . [the] irreversible consequences of their behavior,"[156] Dr. Gwaltney stated that "he never admitted to me or said to me that he felt grief for Kathy and J. B. or their families. In all fairness, I never asked him, though."[157] Dr. Gwaltney quickly added, however, that Chris was suicidal the day after Jessica's trial. Dr. Gwaltney testified that he subsequently met with Chris, and concluded that "it had finally hit him as to what he'd done . . . the terrible nature of the killing."[158] Concluded Dr. Gwaltney: "Whether that is remorse . . . I don't know."[159] Displeased with the tone of Dr. Gwaltney's testimony, Ward quickly pointed out that the meeting between the doctor and Chris occurred after Jessica Wiseman's conviction and Chris's growing realization that he faced the death penalty. "And his remorse, if any, could be the fact that he was in trouble,"[160] suggested Ward. "Certainly could be," answered Dr. Gwaltney.[161]

It was the defense team's turn to question Dr. Gwaltney, but it would be inaccurate to state that the expert witness was cross-examined. Dr. Gwaltney was now in the peculiar situation of testifying as a mental health expert for both the prosecution and defense, a tactic that appellate counsel would later characterize as using Dr. Gwaltney "in effect, to rebut himself, which constituted the single most unsatisfactory way of putting on the defense's case in mitigation that one could possibly imagine."[162] In examining Dr. Gwaltney, Horne managed to elicit only a few favorable points. Characterizing the murders as a "conflict homicide," Dr. Gwaltney testified that "individuals who commit conflict related homicides or killings, are . . . less likely, to kill again than individuals who commit crime related homicides."[163] Yet Horne blundered badly when—in an attempt to undercut a hypothetical question posed during direct examination—he mockingly asked Dr. Gwaltney if he had ever known any death row inmates to "get out of jail and get young girlfriends again." The derisive question only opened the door for Dr. Gwaltney to respond, "I was well acquainted with a number of individuals who escaped death row in Mecklenburg. I haven't asked them whether they had girlfriends . . . [but], I wasn't very comfortable with them being out." By referring to the escape of six death row inmates from Mecklenburg in 1984, Dr. Gwaltney damaged Horne's efforts to downplay the future dangerousness of inmates serving life sentences.

As Dr. Gwaltney left the stand and the jurors were excused for lunch, Judge Folkes again questioned whether the attorneys were making efficient use of their time. "I wonder if we could speed this up a little bit," the judge asked. "I'd like to move it along. We're not making the progress I think that we should make."[164] The sentencing hearing was only three hours old, and Judge Folkes's impatience was baffling. The commonwealth rested its case after lunch, but as the defense called its first witness the court interrupted and again complained about the slow pace of the sentencing hearing. "I'm going to ask you to move this along. I don't want you to spend a lot of time."[165] Defense counsel took Judge Folkes's admonition to heart. They would call five lay (or nonexpert) witnesses to the stand, each averaging a scant ten minutes of testimony. The defendant's sole expert witness, Dr. Gwaltney, would testify for approximately fifteen minutes. In all, the mitigation defense raised by attorneys Horne and Ward took sixty-six minutes to present.

Margaret Thomas was the first witness called by the defense. Her presence at Chris's sentencing hearing was crucial, yet she testified for only some twelve minutes.[166] Given her limited time on the stand, Margaret Thomas could provide only the most perfunctory testimony. She was divorced from Chris's father. Chris never met his father, and she did not know where he lived. Chris lived with his grandparents until their deaths from cancer. Chris missed his grandparents. Chris and Margaret had typical mother-son disagreements. Chris did not like living in Chesterfield County because he could not hunt. After moving to Chesterfield County, his schoolwork suffered. Chris had a learning disability and was placed in special education classes. Margaret took Chris to see a therapist. Even the main source of Chris's anger and confusion toward his mother—her homosexuality—was dealt with in a superficial, perfunctory, and incomplete manner. When asked to explain her "different lifestyle," Margaret Thomas stated, "I'm gay."[167] At last, defense counsel had arguably reached the lodestar of Chris Thomas's young life and his relationship with his mother, but the issue of Margaret's homosexuality was barely explored. When asked how homosexuality had impacted her son, Margaret tersely replied that "he did not have a father-figure"[168] and claimed to be unaware of Chris's reaction upon discovering his mother's sexual preference. No further questions were asked about the subject.

To borrow a phrase from defense counsel, Margaret's testimony was a "sanitized" and one-dimensional story of Chris's life, summarized in short, one-sentence responses from a witness who later complained that she had not been properly prepared to testify by defense counsel. A private woman, it must have been terribly painful for her to discuss in open court her homosexuality and her estrangement from her son. Nevertheless, no other witness could have provided so much information and insight into Chris's young life. It was a tragically missed opportunity to humanize Chris. According to defense counsel, they recognized the importance of Margaret Thomas as a witness but were stymied in their efforts to present her story to the jury. "In both my telephone interview with her and her time on the stand (if you can't garner sympathy from your client's mother, [from whom] . . . can you get sympathy?) she appeared, by all who observed, sullen, morose, resentful and even reluctant to help," states Horne. "As far as witnesses go, she was the one that upset me the most."

Defense counsel next called a trio of teachers and staff members from Chris's former high school in Chesterfield County. First to testify was Laura Anderson, who explained to the jury that she first met Chris Thomas when he was a special education student at Clover Hill High School in Richmond, Virginia. Chris had been classified as an emotionally disturbed student, and Laura recalled that he was an impulsive teenager who lacked both self-control and self-esteem and was "very easily swayed" by his peers and his girlfriend.[169] Laura testified about the academic and social progress that Chris evidenced as her student, including improved grades, better judgment, and higher self-esteem. Laura stated that she never observed Chris behaving violently, nor felt threatened by her young pupil. "I did see Chris as a very, very frustrated, angry kid,"[170] she added. During a relatively brief cross-examination, Commonwealth Attorney Ward tried to elicit testimony to show that Chris Thomas's story was not that dissimilar from Laura Anderson's other special education students. While Laura conceded that sixteen-year-old children are generally vulnerable to peer pressure, she insisted that Chris differed from his fellow students in both the number of problems that he faced as well as the intensity of said problems.

Laura was followed by Bonnie Reed, the Clover Hill school psychologist who examined Chris. She testified that the death of Chris's grandparents had left him significantly depressed, impacting his grades and leading to his placement in the school's program for emotionally disturbed teenagers. Reed, like Laura, stated that she never observed Chris behaving violently, and she added that his behavior and grades improved. Commonwealth Attorney Ward followed a similar tactic when he cross-examined Reed, struggling unsuccessfully to get her to agree that "[t]here were a lot of other children that had similar problems"[171] in the emotionally disturbed program.

Former Clover Hill High School assistant principal Jackie Wilson was the third witness to testify about Chris's time in high school. Chris was referred to Wilson because he was skipping school and not following teachers' instructions; she testified that Chris told her that the cause of his behavior was unhappiness stemming from the fact that "people didn't care about him."[172] Echoing the testimony of both Laura Anderson and Bonnie Reed, Wilson stated that "Chris was the kind of child who was depressed and was easily swayed by others."[173] She never recalled seeing Chris act violently.

At the end of his direct examination of Jackie Wilson, the following exchange took place between Horne and his witness:

> Q: I'm going to ask you a question which I want you to answer honestly, and I know you will. Now, you said that Chris was easily swayed by others; is that correct?
>
> A: That's right.
>
> Q: Have I ever talked to you prior to this occasion —
>
> A: No.
>
> Q: With the exception of telling you to come to Court?
>
> A: No. No.[174]

In his closing argument, Horne reminded the jury of the above testimony. In doing so, he inadvertently confirmed what many had suspected: that defense counsel had failed to adequately prepare for the sentencing hearing. Horne stated: "They say never ask a question in law school that you don't know the answer to. I asked a question today I do not know the answer to. I asked the principal, had Chris ever been violent? And she said, no. We had never spoken to her. These are independent, unvarnished observations of the people who know him best. Not recycled through his attorneys."[175] For a lawyer in a capital murder trial to proudly announce to a jury that he has not interviewed his witnesses is not evidence of virtuous behavior. It is a damnable indictment of the attorney's skill and preparation.

Finished with Chris's former teachers, Horne called Wanda (Margaret Thomas's partner) to the stand. Having lived with Margaret for the last several years, one would have predicted that Wanda would provide valuable testimony regarding Chris's descent into addiction, truancy, petty crime, and depression. The direct and cross-examination of Wanda, however, took approximately three minutes. Her sole testimony was that while she had had arguments with Chris, he had never been violent toward her.

The defense's final witness was Dr. Gwaltney, who had previously testified as the prosecution's mental health expert. Despite the fact that the sentencing hearing had lasted barely four hours, and that Dr. Gwaltney's earlier testimony had taken all of forty-two minutes, Judge Folkes again warned defense counsel to be succinct. "Dr. Gwaltney has already testified extensively," he warned, "and I trust you won't be plowing any new ground, I mean any old ground."[176] Reassured by Horne that defense counsel hoped to "enlighten the jury to entirely new matters," Judge Folkes reluctantly responded, "All right. I just—it's been a long and difficult matter."[177]

During Dr. Gwaltney's second appearance on the witness stand, he was asked by defense counsel to discuss the presence of mitigation factors in Chris Thomas's case. For Dr. Gwaltney, what struck him about Chris's case was how "rapidly his behavior deteriorated"[178] after the death of his grandparents—"his anchors in life"—and the move to Chesterfield County. The dropping grades. The sporadic school attendance. The drug and alcohol use. The classification of being "emotionally disturbed." The petty criminal offenses. "I think that his history . . . speaks for itself in terms of the trauma that he suffered and the reasons . . . he couldn't cope with this as successfully as most people,"[179] concluded Dr. Gwaltney. While others might have weathered the storm, Chris could not, resulting in a "relatively rapid deterioration into . . . really pathological behavior."[180]

As Horne asked questions that Dr. Gwaltney could not answer, his lack of familiarity with his own expert witness became apparent. To Horne's question as to the impact of his uncle's death on Chris, Dr. Gwaltney conceded, "I never questioned him in depth about that" and "I don't have any opinion on that."[181] When Horne tried to elicit testimony that Chris's early development had been hampered by the lack of a father figure, Dr. Gwaltney pointed out, "I think it would be reasonable to assume that his grandfather played that role with him."[182] In response to Horne's question, "What sort of effect does prolonged drug use . . . would that have on Chris' decision-making ability?" (here Horne confessed, "I haven't asked you [this] before and I don't know [the answer] myself"), Dr. Gwaltney stated: "I'm not sure it would . . . I don't know that it has been so extensive that it has actually affected his brain."[183]

Before ending his direct examination of Dr. Gwaltney, Horne asked if he had considered the role of Jessica Wiseman in his mitigation report. Replied Dr. Gwaltney: "I described these homicides, these killings as a conflict, I think earlier. And that the major conflict was not between Chris and his victims, but between Jessica and the victims. Chris, for whatever reason, in my opinion, I don't know why he made the decisions as he did, because I believe that it is very clear that the killings that he committed, he was acting as an agent of Jessica Wiseman."[184] Running out of steam, defense counsel concluded his direct examination by asking Dr. Gwaltney, "[A]re there any other mitigating factors that you found in age or anything of that nature?"[185]

Dr. Gwaltney's short response — "age itself is not necessarily a mitigating factor, but the characteristics of a chronological age may be . . . adolescents . . . do not control their impulses as some of us do who are more mature and chronologically older"[186] — touched upon complicated topics of socialization and cognitive science that should have been exhaustively explored by defense counsel.

Dr. Gwaltney had endeavored to help defense counsel, but in the final analysis the psychologist had neither the time nor the resources to complete a substantial mitigation review. In the years after Chris Thomas's conviction, the case continued to haunt Dr. Gwaltney and he called for clemency. During a 1994 interview about the case, Dr. Gwaltney stated that Jessica was "'probably one of the coldest [people] I've ever interviewed'" and exhibited no remorse over her parents' death: "'It's just totally unfair that she has to be released at 21 and Chris is sitting on death row.'"[187] Shortly before Chris's June 1999 execution date, Dr. Gwaltney called the Thomas case "'the worst defeat in my whole career.'"[188] "'I even told the jury, as I recalled, that Chris may have pulled the trigger, but [Jessica] was really the murderer. . . . The jury didn't believe a thing I said, I guess, because they really socked it to Chris.'"[189] While a supporter of the death penalty, Dr. Gwaltney reiterated that Chris's verdict was unjust: "'I'd hate to see this boy get executed and I'm not against executions. . . . I've assisted in putting a significant number of people in the electric chair and I think I've kept a few out.'"[190]

Chris did not testify at his sentencing, emphatically resisting the repeated pleas of his attorneys, Dr. Gwaltney, and Laura Anderson that he tell his story to the jury.[191] In a letter written to Chris before the sentencing hearing, Laura begged him to take the stand. "It [the sentencing hearing] will be an easier job and probably a much more effective one if you participate. Don't let them railroad you."[192] Those visiting with Chris on the morning of his sentence hearing concluded that Chris was crushed that Jessica Wiseman had refused to testify in his defense and resigned to his fate. "'The fact that Jessica wouldn't say anything on his behalf took all the spirit out of him,'"[193] Horne told a reporter. "'The jury needed to know why he did it,'" Horne explained. "'With no explanation, they were just faced with some cold, hard facts.'"[194] For Dr. Gwaltney, who had struggled to help Chris, the refusal to testify signaled that the young man had given up: "'He was pretty resigned,' Gwaltney said. 'He said that he was willing to let the people of Middlesex do what they had to do.'"[195]

Having listened to Judge Folkes instruct the jury as to the relevant law regarding sentencing, all that remained was closing argument. Commonwealth Attorney Ward told the jury that the evidence was sufficient to support either a finding that the crime was wantonly vile or that Chris Thomas posed a future risk of danger. Chris was a young man whose pattern of juvenile offenses, efforts to harm his surrogate parents (Brenda and Herbert Marshall), and lack of remorse signaled that he "has no sanctity for human life"[196] and warned of future criminal acts. He was not the agent of Jessica Wiseman, argued Ward, but a killer who carefully planned the murders, donned camouflage clothing, and methodically executed the Wisemans at point-blank range.

Returning to the testimony of Dr. Gwaltney, Ward reminded the jury that the psychologist would not and could not testify that Chris would not murder again. "I said [']Dr. Gwaltney in your last statements, that some might believe that following a lengthy period of incarceration, that there would be little chance that he would murder again. What was your response, Dr. Gwaltney?' This examiner is unwilling to reach such a conclusion."[197] Concluded Ward: "There's absolutely no evidence which would definitively state that he would not kill again."[198] While Ward was arguably misinterpreting the law and improperly placing the burden of showing no future dangerousness on the defendants, no objection came from defense counsel.

As for the crime itself, Ward argued that sufficient evidence supported a finding that the murder of Kathy Wiseman was "outrageously or wantonly vile, horrible or inhuman" because it involved "aggravated battery." "Now, what is the jury instruction about aggravated battery," asked Ward. "One of them is a killing inflicted by multiple gunshot wounds may constitute an . . . aggravated battery where there's an appreciable lapse of time between the first shot and the last and where death does not result instantaneously from the first. Sound like anything familiar? Sounds like this particular case."[199]

As his closing statement drew to a finish, Ward skillfully placed the jurors back in the Wiseman home in the early morning hours of November 10:

> Think of the terror that must have confronted this lady. She's lying in bed next to her husband. Shotgun blast rings out. Her husband is dead beside her. She's injured. What does she do? She struggled to her — struggles to her daughter's room. We don't know why she did, but you can assume that she was going there for one reason, to check on her daughter. What did she greet? Possibly the last words that lady heard during her natural

life. The last things that she heard before she was killed was her daughter, screaming, oh God, Chris, please shoot her. And what did he do? He stated to Special Agent Johnson, that's when I shot her.[200]

Ward ended by reminding the jury that during voir dire, the jurors stated that they believed that children were responsible for their behavior. "Let the punishment fit the crime," concluded Ward. "This man took it upon himself to illegally take the lives of two innocent human beings. And now, he must pay the exact same price for his transgressions."[201]

In keeping with the defense's pattern throughout the entire trial of maddeningly conceding too much, Horne began his closing statement by granting that "[a]ll murders are vile and inhuman."[202] As the commonwealth had the burden of providing that the murders were "outrageously or wantonly vile" or inhuman, one wonders how Horne's admission that the murders of Kathy and J. B. Wiseman were vile and inhuman helped their client. Horne continued, claiming that these particular murders were not vile and inhuman because (1) Chris did not torture his victims, and (2) the murders were terrible, but not committed with "depravity of mind." "Chris is not a Ted Bundy rape murderer. He is not a lurking Son of Sam night stalker. He is not a Dahmer cannibal. He is not a John Wayne Gacy predator of little boys."[203] Granted, the Virginia Supreme Court had defined "depravity of mind" as "a degree of moral turpitude and psychical debasement surpassing that inherent in the definition of ordinary legal malice and premeditation,"[204] but Horne cleverly elevated the standard to mean that pedophilia, rape, and/or cannibalism constituted the only relevant evidence of a depraved mind.

As for the commonwealth's argument that the vileness of the murders was established by aggravated battery, Horne argued: "Did the killing go beyond what was necessary to accomplish the act? Certainly, the answer is also, no. Two people were killed by three blasts from a semi-automatic shotgun. They were not shot multiple times; stabbed repeatedly; dismembered, burned or mutilated beyond what actually resulted from the fatal wounds. They were shot. And mercifully, the fatal wounds killed them instantly."[205] If the defense had had any credibility remaining in the eyes of the jury, the above statement exhausted it. Kathy Wiseman was shot multiple times. She did not die instantly.

"Chris Thomas is guilty of capital murder. But the acts he perpetrated did not require a fiend," Horne argued as he continued. "And fiends are the only category of capital murder which the State of Virginia will allow to be executed."[206] While Horne sought to dramatize the fact that only the most outrageous and vile of crimes merited the death penalty, arguably his insertion of new phrases like "fiend" simply confused the jury.

Turning to the commonwealth's assertion that Chris Thomas posed a future risk of dangerousness to society, Horne argued that prison, not Middlesex County, was the society in which Chris would live out his days. "Look at him," Horne directed the jury. "Everyone here knows what goes on in prison. Will Chris endanger anyone or will he be in danger?"[207] Only a strained reading of Virginia statutory law would lead to the conclusion that the term "society" meant prison society, and the Virginia Supreme Court later explicitly held that the death penalty laws regarding future dangerousness do not "limit this consideration to 'prison society' when a defendant is ineligible for parole, and we decline [the defendant's] . . . effective request that we rewrite the statute to restrict its scope."[208]

At last, there was nothing left but to ask for the compassion and mercy of the jury. There were no facts to argue because a proper mitigation review had not been done. By sentencing Chris to death, said Horne, "[w]e have determined that a boy, born without a father, and raised without a mother, should also be deprived of his life. We have decided that a boy orphaned at twelve and shunted from home to home, should have no salvation."[209] Imploring the jury to recall Dr. Gwaltney's words—"Chris was the agent of Jessica Wiseman"—Horne ended with soaring but empty rhetoric: "Ladies and Gentlemen, I thank God, and I'm sure you do too, for that happy day some day in the future, when the enormous wound of that statement will have atrophied but a small scar on the soul of Middlesex County."[210]

Of the sentencing hearing, Chris Thomas's appellate lawyers would later write that "[a] cursory reading of the sentencing phase transcript demonstrates that defense counsel did very little to prepare the case in mitigation for Chris Thomas. They failed to interview potential witnesses; failed to discover readily available evidence; and failed to spend any significant amount of time with Chris Thomas (thus failing to completely gain his confidence)."[211] Horne himself concedes this point, writing: "I do recall 'witness prep' being a difficult—and frustrating—issue. We never seemed to have either enough time, or the correct line-up. Remember that we didn't even have an investigator for this Capital Murder case . . . someone to track down witnesses, do interviews, schedule meetings."[212] Recall, also, however, that early in the case mitigation specialist Marie Deans had offered her services, and there is no evidence in the court record that Horne and West formally petitioned the court to appoint an investigator.

As an example of defense counsel's failure to locate "readily available evidence," the appellate lawyers highlighted the suicide threats made by Chris Thomas after Jessica Wiseman's trial:

> Defense counsel Horne could have discovered evidence of Chris Thomas's extreme remorse if they had examined their client's file from the Middle Peninsula Regional Security Center. While Chris Thomas was being held at this facility awaiting trial, he requested and received counseling from jail nurse, Terry Henderson. Ms. Henderson counseled Mr. Thomas on several occasions and in one instance had to return to work in the middle of the night to counsel Chris. On that occasion Chris spoke of his inability to eat or to sleep. He complained of recurrent nightmares in which his mind replayed the particulars of his involvement in the Wisemans' killings. He, at that time, expressed what Ms. Henderson perceived to be a sincere desire to take his own life. Ms. Henderson filed a report in this incident. She subsequently stated that in her opinion Chris was extremely remorseful. She would gladly have testified to this fact had she been contacted by defense counsel.[213]

Chris's suicidal ideation was no great secret and, in fact, had been mentioned by the defense's own expert witness. Defense counsel, however, did not introduce this evidence. "In truth, I can't tell you why we did not," writes Horne. "Perhaps because Chris had become so unreliable, so contradictory and so difficult to predict . . . a perfect enigma . . . as well as the fact that the attempts, in all candor, did not really seem to rise to the level of credible efforts."[214]

Finally, the length of the trial and sentencing transcript itself is a measure of counsel's failure. In short, the sentencing hearing "only took up 61 pages of transcript out of a four day trial which took up a total of 795 pages. Amazingly, only 7.7% of the time and effort at trial was spent on the single most important part of the case [mitigation] from a capital defendant's point of view."[215] For Chris's appellate lawyers, the bottom line was simple: trial counsel "failed, ultimately, to have any coherent theme in mitigation."[216]

And what do Chris Thomas's trial attorneys say to this critique? Almost eighteen years after the trial, Damian Horne provides the following assessment:

After 21 years of practice. After many other murder cases. After being the Director of Training for a Statewide Public Defender Department. After instructing at the Faubush Capital Murder Defense Program, it is clear to me that Chris did not have seasoned, experienced or confident capital murder counsel. But he could never have had a more devoted team . . . one that was absolutely devoted to saving his life. Today, I never go to trial . . . hell, I rarely go to work . . . that I don't think of that case. For better or for worse, that case made me the lawyer I am today. And I don't mean that in a self-congratulatory way. I am cautious to a fault, and I am always inclined to recommend a plea even when the case indicates an acquittal may result. Yes, Chris could certainly have had better counsel . . . but he had me. AND with me, he had an offer that would have saved his life. I recommended he take that offer. I begged him to take it. He did not. This convergence of circumstances resulted in his execution.[217]

At 11:00 P.M. on Monday, August 26, 1991, a tired and drawn-looking Douglas Christopher Thomas reentered the courtroom of the Middlesex County courthouse and took a seat next to his attorneys at counsel table. It had been a long day, and the strain showed in the faces of all assembled in the hushed courtroom. Despite the late hour, more than fifty spectators — mainly friends, family, and a few journalists — remained in the courtroom.

As the jury weighed Chris's fate, a small cluster of relatives tended to the weeping Margaret Thomas. Two knocks on the jury room door announced that the jury had reached a verdict, and the hollow wooden rapping echoed around the courtroom and silenced the assembled throng. The jury had deliberated for approximately five hours, a portentous sign to those court watchers who subscribed to the rule of thumb that short deliberations mean death. As they filed back from the small jury room located immediately behind the judge's bench, several of the jurors stared at the floor. Taking the bench, Judge Folkes addressed the courtroom. "I will reiterate what I said last night," he said in stern tone. "I will not tolerate any outbursts or emotional expressions when this verdict is read, or you will be sanctioned for contempt." After receiving the jury verdict form, Judge Folkes glanced over it and handed it back to deputy clerk Peggy Walton. Chris Thomas was directed to rise, and he stared with vacant eyes as Walton read the verdict.

We the jury on the issue in joint, have found the defendant guilty of the willful, deliberate and pre-mediated murder of James Baxter Wiseman and

FIGURE 12. *Friends and family members console each other as Chris Thomas leaves the Middlesex County Courthouse after receiving a death sentence. Photograph courtesy of the* Daily Press *(Newport News, Virginia).*

Kathy Wiseman as part of the same transaction and that his conduct in committing the offense is outrageously or wantonly vile, horrible or inhuman and that it involved torture, depravity of mind or aggravated battery to the victim and having completed the evidence in mitigation of the offense unanimously fix his punishment at death.

Despite Judge Folkes's previous warning, a gasp tore through the courtroom as Walton completed reading the verdict form and sobbing could be heard. Chris, however, remained stone-faced.[218] Commonwealth Attorney Ward himself later claimed that he did not believe that the jury would impose the death penalty. "'That was why it was such a hush in the courtroom after the verdict was read,' he said. 'When you hear a verdict such as that it's going to cause you to stop a moment.'"[219]

A supportive circle of family members helped a crying Margaret Thomas leave the courtroom, and a small group of Chris Thomas's friends wept and hugged as they watched Chris be led away (fig. 12). Defense attorneys Damian Horne and Sydney West remained at counsel table, drained and unmoving. The solemnity of the moment was not lost on the relatives of Kathy and J. B. Wiseman. "'Nobody wins,'" remarked Edward Jones, the brother of Kathy Wiseman, as he walked out of the courtroom with his mother, Arvazine Thomas.[220] Jones told a second reporter that "he and his family have had a hard time dealing with the deaths of the Wisemans, and subsequent loss of his niece, Jessica Wiseman, to a state detention home. 'I don't know when I'll let it go, if ever,' said Jones."[221] "'There will be a lot more to come,'" Jones concluded. "'I'm afraid it's not the end. I'm sure they will appeal it to whatever extent they can go.'"[222] And Jones was correct: Chris Thomas would remain on death row for some eight years.

5

Life on the Row

It's the unending, uninterrupted immersion in death that wears on you so much. It's the parade of friends and acquaintances who leave for the death house and never come back, while your own desperate and lonely time drains away. It's the boring routine of claustrophobic confinement, punctuated by eye-opening dates with death that you helplessly hope will be averted. It's watching yourself die over the years in the eyes of family and friends, who, with every lost appeal, add to the emotional scar tissue that protects them, long before you're gone, from your death.

WILLIE LLOYD TURNER

Douglas Christopher Thomas arrived at the Mecklenburg Correctional Center in Boydton, Virginia on November 22, 1991. He remained on Mecklenburg's death row until August 3, 1998, when the death row moved to its new home at the Sussex I State Prison in Waverly, Virginia. With the exception of a few days in June 1999, Chris was imprisoned at Sussex I State Prison until January 6, 2000. Entombed for eight years, Chris spent his days and nights struggling with depression, boredom, and regret.

Thirty-five states at present have the death penalty, and their respective death rows vary in major and minor ways. In his book *Death Work*, Dr. Robert Johnson writes that there are in general two types of death row: "reformed" and "unreformed."

The unreformed regime offers unadorned long-term solitary or near-solitary confinement. The condemned prisoner spends the bulk of each

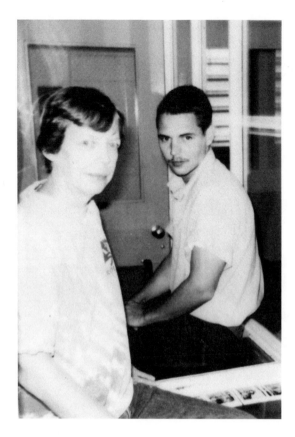

day alone in his cell. When out of the cell, he is alone or in small groups
and is heavily restrained and closely guarded. . . . The reformed model of
death row offers the condemned prison greater time out of the cell. This
time is generally spent in the dayroom appended to the cell block. There,
the prisoner engages in such diversions as ping-pong, chess, and cards. (In
some instances, the prisoner of a reformed death row is allowed to work
for a portion of the day.) The dayrooms that capture much of the prisoner's
out-of-cell time are, in essence, congregate or group cells that are removed
from the larger prison community.[1]

According to Johnson, the majority of America's modern death rows are
unreformed. Mecklenburg was a reformed death row, which allowed the inmates some freedom of movement and interaction. Virginia's current death
row at Sussex I State Prison, however, is an unreformed one, where the in-

FIGURE 14. *Marie Deans in her office at the Virginia Coalition on Jails and Prisons. Considered to be one of the nation's leading mitigation specialists, Deans's offer to help was ignored by Chris's original trial counsel. Photograph courtesy of the Virginian-Pilot.*

mates are locked down in their cells twenty-three hours a day and have no contact with one another.

While this chapter focuses on Virginia's two death rows, much of the information discussed below is representative of the death row experiences of inmates across the country. As death penalty opponent and mitigation expert Marie Deans writes, reformed or unreformed, America's death rows share one essential trait: "Death row, wherever it exists, is purgatory. . . . It is where the people we condemn to death suffer and where some expiate their sins. It is where human beings exist in a state of anticipation of their own predetermined deaths. No matter the conditions, whether relatively good, bad, or indifferent, death row is not and cannot be less than physical torture."[2] Whether we consider death row in Virginia, Texas, Oklahoma, or California, the fundamental institutional goal of these facilities is the same — what Johnson refers to as "human storage." He writes, "This goal dictates that condemned prisoners be treated essentially as bodies kept alive to be killed,"[3] adding, "the cumulative confinement experience of condemned prisoners —

from death row to the deathwatch and, finally, to the death chamber—is profoundly dehumanizing, resulting in nothing less than the literal moral death of the person, who is reduced to a compliant object of execution."[4] In short, a dead man walking.

Before we discuss the specifics of death row, a brief aside: the authors have spent countless hours talking with college students about prisoners' rights and the conditions of confinement on death row. In these conversations, we have encountered a wide range of opinions as to what prisoners "deserve." At one extreme is the position best articulated by Sister Helen Prejean: no matter the offense, prisoners retain their basic humanity and are better than their worst acts. This does not mean that we ignore or excuse the terrible crimes committed by these men and woman, but that we appreciate that even the worst offenders merit humane treatment.

At the other extreme is an attitude expressed by many college students: if an individual commits a crime, be it first-degree murder, involuntary manslaughter, sexual assault, or embezzlement, then the prison conditions that accompany the term of incarceration are part of the punishment. As one of my senior seminar students once explained, the risks inherent in incarceration—mediocre medical care, substandard food, harsh living conditions, a lack of vocational and educational training, and sexual or physical violence perpetrated by other inmates and guards—are the price one pays for committing a criminal act. That prison conditions vary by prison and by state, and that such variation may result in the same criminal acts subjected to vastly different punishments, did not trouble this young man. Concluded the student: "if you don't want to be raped in prison, then don't break the law."

Of course, many young adults struggle to form their own political, religious, and moral viewpoints and find it easier to fall back on the simplistic "law and order" rhetoric of politicians than to think deeply about complex issues. Sitting in a comfortable classroom and talking about men and women who have committed heinous acts, students find it easy to consign unknown criminals to an abstract punishment. Yet youth alone cannot explain this lack of empathy. The argument that death row inmates deserve whatever nightmarish conditions that faceless, unaccountable, state bureaucrats dole out rests upon the basic principle that some criminals are inhuman and disposable, thus deserving of inhumane conditions.

It is important for the reader to pause and evaluate his or her own views on prisoners and their basic human rights; such beliefs will color much of the following chapters. Chris Thomas was guilty of murder. Because of his acts, and his sentence of death, did he deserve humane conditions of confinement? And, if so, did he receive humane treatment? In answering these questions, one must first decide what fundamental rights are held by all prisoners — regardless of their crimes. Should a death row inmate be allowed to attend religious services and meet with a minister of his choice? Should an inmate be given healthy and nutritious food? Be allowed to have a television? A mattress? Have contact visits with family members? Conjugal visits with a spouse? Receive competent medical care? Be allowed to have a prison job? Be protected from violence by other prisoners? Have the opportunity to pursue a college degree? Have the right to receive pornographic magazines? Be permitted to exercise? In short, what fundamental rights are the "worst of the worst" owed regardless of their crimes, and how does the treatment of the most hardened criminals reflect the basic values of our society?

The Mecklenburg Correctional Center

Russian author Fyodor Dostoyevsky once wrote, "The degree of civilization in a society is revealed by entering its prisons." Perhaps some politicians and bureaucrats recognize the truth of Dostoyevsky's observation; in Virginia, it is impossible for its citizens to enter death row. It is a world hidden from society. During our research for this book, we quickly discovered the futility of trying to obtain information regarding death row from the Virginia Department of Corrections. Our requests for a tour of the facilities that housed Virginia's former and current death rows were abruptly rejected, and document requests filed under the Virginia Freedom of Information Act were summarily denied. Under Virginia law, prison officials have the absolute discretion to decide whether to release prison records. Virginia Department of Corrections officials repeatedly refused to exercise this discretion regarding the multiple requests that we filed.[5] When pushed to explain the lack of cooperation, we were flatly told that concerns about institutional security and safety prevented the Department of Corrections from providing any information about death row. Given that our document requests focused on a death row that no longer existed (the former death row at the Mecklenburg Correctional Center) and an inmate who was executed, the explanation for the blanket denial of our requests rang hollow.

The Virginia Department of Corrections's reticence is more likely a reaction to past criticism regarding its death row operations, include statewide ridicule after a successful escape of six death row inmates from Mecklenburg's death row on May 13, 1984. After gaining access to the cell block's control room, the inmates used homemade weapons to take twelve guards and two nurses hostage. They subsequently dressed themselves in their hostages' uniforms, seized a prison van, and bluffed their way out of the prison — claiming to be evacuating a bomb from death row. It would take a month to recapture the prisoners, and the manhunt stretched as far north as Canada.[6] To say, however, that the escape was an embarrassment for the Virginia Department of Corrections is an understatement; since the successful prison break, the Department of Corrections has been remarkably closed-mouthed about the operations of its facilities. The infamous death row prison break was not the first or last time, however, that Mecklenburg had been thrust into the public spotlight, for the notorious facility often drew the ire of death penalty activists and prison reformers. In the 1970s and 1980s, Marie Deans found death row at Mecklenburg to be a hellish place, where weapons and drugs flowed through the cells, beatings by guards occurred daily, and prisoners were isolated from their attorneys and families, and she was constantly trying to draw attention to these abuses.

In order to provide an accurate description of Virginia's death row in the early 1990s, we contacted former death row inmate Joseph Giarratano. Sentenced to death for his alleged role in the 1979 murders of a mother and her daughter, Giarratano spent ten years on Mecklenburg's death row — and was three days from execution — until concerns about his innocence and an international groundswell of public support led to a conditional pardon from then Governor Douglas Wilder. During his years in prison, Giarratano became an adept "jailhouse lawyer," whose work on behalf of other inmates directly and indirectly led to improved prison conditions and the exoneration of Virginia death row inmate Earl Washington, Jr. Giarratano's lawsuits regarding prisoners' rights so infuriated Virginia prison officials that they transferred Giarratano to prisons in Utah and Illinois, until his hunger strike forced his return to Virginia. In the years since his conditional pardon, Giarratano has become an accomplished author and the organizer of a prisoner group dedicated to studying alternatives to violence. "Joe is not Superman, and he's not Einstein, nor is he Gandhi," observes actor and death activist Mike Farrell. "But he is an exceptional human being."[7]

In Giarratano's opinion, it is virtually impossible for an individual who has not been condemned to death to fully comprehend and appreciate life — or "existence" — on death row. In explaining why those on the outside cannot understand the grim reality of death row, Giarratano recounted an interview that he once gave shortly before his scheduled execution date in the death house at the old Virginia State Penitentiary. At the end of the interview, the reporter asked to be locked into one of the death house cells — no doubt to provide the readers with a breathless, eye witness account of life behind bars. Writes Giarratano: "I remember saying to myself, 'What?' There is no freaking way you can get a feel for what the death row experience is like. What an idiot."[8] Giarratano believes that the experience of being on death row is "very personal" and "different for each individual who has been condemned to it."

Giarratano is not the first death row inmate to argue that outsiders lack the ability to truly understand the surreal atmosphere of death row. A Texas death row inmate once observed: "Many, many books have been written about prison life, but there is no way that you can ever know what this place is like unless you have been in this cage. You cannot describe the misery and despair in a place like this — one has to feel it."[9] Another unidentified death row inmate writes that he felt "like a ghost" on death row, an "'ill at rest'" phantom "caught between the world of the living and the dead" and entombed in a mausoleum. Other inmates challenge the basic assumption that "life" is possible on death row. "No one really 'lives' in here," concludes a death row inmate. "[W]e just do our best to survive."[10]

At the Mecklenburg Correctional Center, death row was located in Building 1. The death row was divided into sections or pods, with a portion of the inmates in three pods (A, B, and C pods). Each pod was further divided into two 12-cell units. The inmates were only permitted to interact and recreate with prisoners from their own pod. Each pod area was supervised by a control room that overlooked the day room and the cells. The control room was staffed by a corrections officer twenty-four hours a day, and from this control room the officer operated all the cell doors as well as the entry "gates" to the pod area. When the inmates were in their cells, additional guards patrolled the pod and peered into the cells for periodic security checks.

We don't know what Chris Thomas thought when he first entered Mecklenburg's death row, but undoubtedly thoughts of survival — and whether he would be able to survive — were foremost in his mind. After a ten-day period of segregation, Chris joined the men on death row. His cell in the B Pod was tiny: exactly 6 feet, 10 inches wide by 7 feet, 6 inches long. As a security precaution the inmates were rotated among cells; during his first year in B Pod

Chris occupied seven different cells. A steel bunk was welded to the wall, a bed, as former Virginia death row inmate Dennis Stockton wrote, "[that] has five rows of holes, each about the size of a silver dollar. There are 18 holes to a row, 90 in all. My mattress is 1½ inches thick. It is so thin that when I lie down, I can feel the holes underneath."[11] Chris suffered from back problems, and he eventually obtained a second mattress for his cell. It didn't help much. A metal box served as both a desk and a storage area, and a stainless steel unit held both a sink (hot and cold water) and a toilet. If the inmate wanted, he could purchase a metal plate to be attached to the wall and serve as a mirror. Finally, the inmate was given a single plastic chair.

Each death row cell at Mecklenburg had a window that the inmate could open with a crank handle, although the view was obscured by both security bars and metal mesh. For a young man who lived for the beauty of the changing seasons, watching the leaves turn or the approach of spring through a narrow slit in an concrete wall was a bitter privilege for Chris. Each death row inmate was permitted a thirteen-inch television, a cassette tape player, radio, clock, a lamp, and a typewriter—but they had to pay for the items out of their own pockets. Other items allowed in the cell included personal photographs, legal papers, letters, and a limited range of magazines, which the inmate could store on one of two shelves. The walls of the cells, at least in the early 1990s, were painted off-white (Stockton referred to the color as "nicotine white"[12]) and the floor was painted gray. There were no old-fashioned cell doors with steel bars at Mecklenburg's death row. The inmate lived behind a solid-steel door that had a small, 3-inch by 36-inch window and a food tray slot.

The inmates had no constitutional privacy rights; at any time correctional officers could enter the cells and search them—a process called a "shakedown" by the inmates. For the first four years Chris was housed at Mecklenburg, there were no procedural rules dictating how these searches were conducted. While admittedly the need for institutional security justified the careful search of an inmate's cell for contraband, searches were also used to intimidate and punish the inmates. In February 1995, Mecklenburg guards discovered that a piece of metal had been removed from a death row inmate's desk. Fearing that the metal would be fashioned into a weapon, the correctional officers started searching all cells in the pod. By the time the search ended, eight cells had been completed stripped of all personal items, mattresses, and bedding, and the eight occupants left clothed in only their underwear. The nearly naked inmates remained in the bare cells for three days, and they were banned from contacting their attorneys by telephone. Chris was one of those eight inmates, and he would be named as a plaintiff in a subsequent lawsuit filed by the American Civil Liberties Union against the Virginia Department of Corrections. A settlement was later reached in the lawsuit, and the Department of Corrections agreed to the adoption of regulations governing the searches of prison cells.[13]

Mecklenburg was not air-conditioned, but the inmates were allowed to purchase fans—although on several occasions prison officials confiscated the fans because they believed that the inmates were tearing the machinery apart and making weapons and escape tools.[14] The prison officials were likely overreacting to the ghosts of the 1984 Mecklenburg prison escape, and the temporary removal of the fans only caused tension to rise in the prison. "'Hot weather is the worst time on death row,' Dennis Stockton observed. 'The air is moist and hard to breathe. That's when I am pestered by flies. Can you imagine trying to type with flies buzzing around you and your work? I used to swat them with an old rolled-up newspaper, but then I got hold of a little money and was able to purchase a 39-cent genuine plastic fly swatter from the canteen.'"[15] Much of the heat was due to lack of ventilation on death row. "'The ventilation is so poor even the air is deadly still," writes Marie Deans. "It looks and feels like a sensory deprivation chamber. In the summer it is like a combination sensory deprivation chamber and oven."[16]

The daily schedule of the modern death row revolves around meal time, showers, and recreation period. At Mecklenburg, the meals were delivered to the death row pod areas and passed through the bars of the entry gate to the pod. Under normal circumstances, the inmates ate their meals together in the dayroom. Giarratano characterized the food as "institutional, some days were better than others,"[17] but Dennis Stockton was not so charitable. "It's the kind where you don't ask for seconds. The meal I look forward to most is on Saturday, when we get two toasted cheese sandwiches and pinto beans."[18] Marie Deans occasionally received a tray of food during her long visits at Mecklenburg, and she does not have fond memories of the fare. "It was absolutely awful. They would bring me a dinner and I always had to ask what it was." The guards were only able to answer Marie's question and identify the mysterious, meatlike patty on the tray by consulting a cafeteria schedule. From the prison commissary, inmates could supplement their meals by purchasing food (such as chips and cookies) and coffee. The commissary was also the source of cigarettes, stamps, and writing materials.[19]

Typically the inmates took their three meals in the common area. During lockdowns, however, the inmates ate in their cells. The inmates were permitted to spend additional time in the dayrooms, which contained three metal tables (each attached to the floor) and chairs, a color television set, and a modest collection of board games. Showers were located at the end of each tier of cells. The curtains hanging in the showers were shortened after the 1987 suicide of death row inmate John J. LeVasseur, who used a sheet to hang himself from a showerhead while inmates and guards were only yards away from the stall.[20]

Writing about the struggle to fill one's days on death row, Georgia death row inmate Victor Roberts states that the row "is a place of endless routines . . . where time itself is a dreadful task."[21] Author David Von Drehle echoes Roberts's observation, writing that on Florida's death row the "staggering task that is every man's burden on death row" is "filling the hours until he can sleep again," adding that "[s]leep — 'downy sleep, Death's counterfeit,' as Shakespeare put it — is the best way to pass time on death row."[22] The other limited options included in-cell calisthenics, talking through the air vents to other prisoners, cleaning their cells, reading, drawing, and "comb[ing] personal ads in magazines and newspapers, looking for likely marks. A popular diversion is to strike up pen-pal relationships with lonely homosexuals, then get on the bars [talk to the other prisoners] and scornfully read the letters they receive."[23] "And still all of these activities don't begin to fill the time — not when there are 364 identical days of the year and the years pile up one on the next."[24] Of course, the great "[e]lectronic tranquilizers" are the television sets on death row. Of Florida's death row, Von Drehle writes:

> Some dim bulbs on death row watch cartoons all day long. (One man heard about his last-minute stay of execution while watching *The Flintstones.*) Some men are devoted to soap operas. Whole tiers get on the bars every night and race one another for the answers during *Jeopardy!* Some watch the cop shows and cheer for the bad guys. At noon, and again at six in the evening, most prisoners watch the news — and they all watch the same station so they can have something in common to talk about. Sensational murder trials are followed with acute interest, and if the defendant gets something less than the death penalty, the men on the row get on the bars to decry the sentence.[25]

The otherworld qualities of any death row extend to the smells and sounds of the row. Every sound on death row reverberates through the bones of guard and inmate alike. The buzz of a television. The crackle of a walkie-talkie. The dull thud of closing doors. The moans of sleeping inmates. Mixed into the cacophony of noise are the bitter smells of the men. Writes Texas death row inmate Jonathan Wayne Nobles: "Smell is one of the first things you notice about prison. In the real world you often smell the love and joy of someone's home. Spices in the kitchens, sachet in the linens, pipe tobacco in the den, wood smoke from the fire, and the leather of a favorite chair. There is no polite way to describe the aroma of prison. Fear, anger, rancid sweat, blood, stale urine, and wasted seamen [sic]."[26]

In a typical day on the row, Chris was locked down in his cell for ninteen hours a day. He slept, watched television, and played cards in the dayroom. In the first years on death row, his podmates included Herman C. Barnes, Wayne "Buffalo" DeLong, Coleman Wayne Gray, Mario Benjamin Murphy, Larry Allen Stout, George Adrian Quesinberry, Jr., and Ronald Watkins.[27] Chris did not have any close friends among the inmates and kept to himself. His reticence in forming friendships likely stemmed from the fact that Chris was scared and intimated by his podmates. And with good reason. Herman Barnes was on death row for the murder of a Hampton, Virginia, supermarket owner and one of his employees. Wayne DeLong had been convicted of capital murder for the shooting of a police detective, a killing that occurred while DeLong was on probation for an earlier murder conviction. While on death row, DeLong was involved in the beating and crippling of another death row inmate. Larry Stout was on death row for the murder of Jacqueline Kooshian, whom he stabbed through the throat after robbing her dry cleaning store of approximately nine hundred dollars. Coleman Gray was convicted of putting six bullets in the back of the head of a convenience store manager in Portsmith, Virginia. Ronald Watkins had slashed the throat of a former employer to prevent him from identifying Watkins as the robber of his store. George Quesinberry had shot an owner of an electric supply company in the back and then killed him with a blow to the head, ultimately making off with two hundred dollars. Mario Murphy was a professional hit man who had used a steel pipe to beat to death the husband of a woman who wanted to be free of her marriage.

Two guardian angels were looking over Chris's shoulder, however, and working to ensure his safety. Shortly after his sentencing, Laura Anderson called Marie Deans and asked for her help. As noted in the preface, Marie became involved in death penalty work after the murder of her mother-in-law by an escaped convict. Surprising many involved in the murder investigation and subsequent trial, Marie spoke out against imposing the death penalty and subsequently formed a murder victims' reconciliation group. In 1982, the Reverend Joseph Ingle, then head of the Southern Coalition of Jails and Prisons, learned firsthand about prison conditions in Virginia when he traveled to the state and tried to convince death row inmate Frank Coppola to pursue his appeals. Shaken by what he saw in the Virginia State Penitentiary, Ingle immediately called Marie and urged her to move to Virginia and help fight for death row prisoners' rights.

When she moved to Virginia in early 1983, Marie founded the Virginia Coalition on Jails and Prisons, a nonprofit organization dedicated to securing the rights of death row inmates and attacking their convictions; she later started the Virginia Mitigation Project. The coalition helped lawyers and inmates with a number of different aspects of capital defense work, including investigations in capital murder cases, the gathering of mitigation evidence for trials and appeals, obtaining appellate lawyers for inmates, and pursuing clemency.[28] Through the 1980s and 1990s, Marie was a familiar presence on Virginia's death row. Her main responsibility was trying to save the inmates from the death chamber, and she worked long hours to gather mitigation evidence to be used either during trial or on appeal.

Marie was happy to get the phone call from Laura Anderson. She had a son who was approximately the same age as Chris, and—despite the fact that Chris's original trial counsel did not accept her offer to help—she felt a connection with Chris Thomas and his case. Marie immediately called the warden at the Mecklenburg Correctional Center and asked him to protect Chris. Marie knew from bitter experience, however, that the Virginia Department of Corrections alone could not protect its inmates, and she contacted Wayne "Buffalo" DeLong and ordered him to watch out for Chris. "They had a lot of trouble with rapes on Mecklenburg's death row," recalled Marie. "I knew who was doing the raping, and I knew who was not doing the raping, and I wanted to make sure that the people who were doing the raping didn't get anywhere near him."[29] Added Marie, "If I said 'nothing should happen to this kid,' then Buffalo would not let anybody come near him—and Buffalo would not come near him, either."

This was not the first time that Marie used her informal network of veteran inmates to protect the row's newest members. "I assigned people on death row that I trusted to take people like that [Chris] under their wing, watch them, make sure nothing happened to them. I also was able to talk to some of the guards and said 'If anything happens to this kid, you're gonna hear from me.'" As one of the only resources that the men on death row had, Marie knew that her instructions would be followed. "I'm not trying to sound important here, but I mean these guys depended on me," explains Marie. "There was no resource center, there was nothing else. If I said 'you touch that kid, then you've got me all over you,' then they're not going to mess with me." It is remarkable that as late as 1991, Virginia's death row security was sufficiently inadequate that a prison reformer like Marie Deans had to turn to the death row inmates themselves to maintain order.

Marie also called upon a few trusted inmates to "train up" Chris Thomas. When asked what she meant by "training him up," Marie explained:

> Teach him how to take care of himself. He didn't know how to take care of himself, and I really was deeply concerned. I had a client who was raped and committed suicide on death row. It is a very hard world. You cannot show your emotions. That is a very dangerous thing to do—to show your emotions. So, he [Chris] couldn't do that. He couldn't be the little kid who wanted to be outside and he couldn't be the smartass. Both of which he had in him. He could be quite a smartass, and it was part of his coping. I thought of him more as a child that needed to be taken care of and make sure that he was taken care of.[30]

Recognizing Chris's fragile self-confidence, Marie never told Chris of her efforts to protect him. "The idea was to let Chris think of himself as being a man on the row," explained Marie. "He was dealing with serious stuff and he didn't need to think that somebody was treating him like a child."

Robert Deans, the son of Marie Deans, was in high school when Chris arrived on death row, and he occasionally talked to Chris on the telephone. He distinctly recalls this transition period, when a nervous Chris Thomas was "trying to find his 'place' on the row." "[E]very inmate goes through an adjustment period where they 'become' a death row inmate—less in the sense of how to work the system, but how to survive on the row," explains Deans. "Usually it involves just figuring out everyone in your pod and who you have to be careful around [and] who you could count on to have your back. However, if you are 17 and haven't had a normal teen-aged life, and your first major offense lands you on the worst level of incarceration, that adjustment time takes a lot longer."[31] Deans adds that as Chris struggled to "become" a death row inmate, he sometimes overcompensated. "Chris tried to act tougher than he needed, almost to the point of getting into trouble." This fact is reflected in the limited death row records that we have, which list the multiple but petty infractions with which Chris was charged in the early to mid-1990s.

In December 1991, Laura wrote Chris and told him of her successful efforts to elicit the aid of Marie Deans. In his reply letter, Chris discusses his change of heart regarding fighting for his life: "I should have started fighting way before now, but like I told you it wouldn't have made a difference. Maybe now that the case is out of Middlesex Cty. I'll stand a better chance. And believe me, this time I refuse to give up."[32] Chris also speaks of his emerging faith on death row. "Even if it comes down to me going to the electric chair, at least God will be with me. He's helped me out very much in the past months. I just wish I could have went to him before these events took place."[33] In the remaining months of his life, Laura and Chris would return to the topic of faith and religion as they sat together in Virginia's death house.

In an unpublished 1999 Amnesty International interview, Chris explained what life was like on Mecklenburg's death row:

> We were in the pods together. And you usually don't have a lot of the stealing and the fighting. Anywhere you are going to have fighting because it is a close environment and you are dealing with the same people every day and usually people get frustrated, but a lot of the things that go on in prison usually don't happen in death row because we are all facing the same thing. I think, in our situation, it is the only time you will see everyone on neutral ground. We are all trying to achieve the same thing and that is to avoid death. We all understand what each other is going through . . .[34]

As for other services and privileges, former Virginia death row inmate Edward Fitzgerald explains, "The things you take for granted I don't even dream of getting: hot food, medical services, education, sunlight, fresh air, clean bed, clean room and many other normal things. All I get is threatened by a riot squad if I take more than eight minutes in the shower."[35]

Approximately three times a week, inmates were permitted to have recreation time. Giarratano describes the recreational yard as a "small, heavily fenced in area" with "a small patch of grass and dirt; a small asphalt court with a basketball hoop at one end; and a small weight rack bolted to the wall." Before the inmates could move from the cells to the recreation area, however, an elaborate set of procedures was followed:

Each inmate will pass the clothes that he will be wearing to the recreation yard through the food slot [in the cell door] to the officer for inspection Each inmate will be handcuffed through the food slot. . . . [T]he inmate will come out of his cell in his shorts. Under the supervision of two correctional officers, the handcuffs will be removed, and the inmate will be allowed to dress. The inmate will be recuffed with his hands behind him and ordered to the dayroom where he will be supervised by the lieutenant or sergeant.[36]

Chris spent his recreational time lifting weights and playing basketball with the other death row inmates. Razor wire covered the fence surrounding the recreation area, and the inmates exercised within view of the guard towers. Giarratano recalls that general population inmates exercised in similar yards, and it was possible to shout between the yards. "The conversations were usually short and strained. What does one talk about with those on death row, men set aside and slated to be killed?"[37]

Complicated procedures were followed when an inmate was moved to other areas of the prison as well. "We were fully stripped, searched, handcuffed, placed in waist chains, and our legs placed in shackles," writes Giarratano. "We were always escorted by two or more guards from the special 'tactical' team."[38] Giarratano recalls that the special tactical team wore different uniforms (black rather than the light blue of the regular correctional officers) and had SWAT (special weapons and tactics) team training. Before the shackled and handcuffed prisoner left the pod area, the control room officer would use his walkie-talkie to notify all officers in the facility that a death row inmate was moving. With this announcement, Giarratano writes that a charge went through the already tense atmosphere of the prison.

The tenor of the usual prison routine would change. The shift, though subtle, was palpable. You knew that all eyes were on you. All other prisoner movement in the area would cease, guards would stare, prisoners on the rec. yards would stop to look/watch as you shuffled by. Other staff would look and hurriedly glance away. None would hold or maintain eye contact. Guards would talk about you, or make references to you, as if you were not there.[39]

"It is as if they [the inmates] drag the death row regime behind them," writes Johnson of the security rules on Virginia's death row, "shackled to it by the chains that bind their hands and feet during these excursions."[40] For death row inmate Fitzgerald, the attention paid to the death row inmates stemmed from the basic fact that "for many we are zoo animals, for others we are monsters right out of fairy tales."[41]

Despite the extraordinary security measures of Virginia's death row, illegal narcotics were smuggled onto the row.[42] "You could still get drugs," recalled Marie Deans. "And you could get weapons." In fact, during Chris's time at Mecklenburg two different inmates overdosed on street drugs injected with syringes. Joseph Savino almost died in June 1994 from an overdose of heroin, while Wayne Kenneth DeLong died in June 1993 after he overdosed on alcohol and cocaine and then strangled himself.[43] At the time of Savino's drug overdose, a veteran administrator from Mecklenburg confidentially told a newspaper reporter that the facility had "a hell of a drug problem" that prison officials appeared powerless to stop.[44] Death row prisoners have claimed that the guards themselves often served as the drug smugglers, charges that are almost impossible to substantiate.

A second source of drugs on Mecklenburg's death row was the prison's psychiatric staff. Obtaining enough prescription medication to achieve a chemical high was "as simple as just asking for it," remarks Giarratano. His comments are echoed by former Virginia death row inmate Walter Correll, who added, "I have seen the drugs that are given to guys who are having problems. One guy I knew before he was executed was taking so many [prescription] drugs that he would walk around all day not knowing what he was doing."[45] State-sanctioned drug abuse was a familiar problem to Mecklenburg's death row. Marie Deans recalls that in the 1980s, "[m]any of the men were kept on dangerously high doses of psychotropic drugs." She adds, "If the men tried to refuse the drugs, they were beaten, chained down to their bunks, and the drugs were administered by force."[46] The use and abuse of prescription drugs continued when death row was moved to Sussex I State Prison; in 2001 death row inmate David Overto, Jr., was found dead in his cell from an overdose of antidepressants prescribed to him by the prison medical staff.[47]

The abuse of illegal and prescription drugs by death row inmates is not a phenomenon unique to Virginia. Facing the looming specter of death, inmates in death rows across the country have devised countless ways to obtain narcotics and temporarily—or permanently—escape from the depression and madness of their existence. Many of these inmates find a willing supplier in the prison staff, who view prescription drugs as another tool through which to maintain a serene and happy death row. More troubling are instances of forced medication, where inmates are medicated against their will to control their behavior or to make them competent to be executed.[48] Whether voluntarily or not, the legal drugging of death row inmates is an accepted practice, evidenced by the "Thorazine shuffle" of the men on death row. The readiness to use drugs to maintain a quiet and compliant inmate is no less evident in the death house, where prison officials across the country urge condemned prisoners to avail themselves of sedatives and anti-anxiety drugs during their final hours of life. "'A great deal of effort goes into preparing the condemned felon mentally for what he's about to face,'" explained the prison administrator in charge of Ohio's death house. "'Our goal is to get them to walk peacefully into that chamber.'"[49]

In the late 1980s and early 1990s, alcohol was the drug of choice for many on Virginia's death row. "Homemade hootch was much more frequent [than narcotics]. At times we would even cook it off, distill it from mash to clear," writes Giarratano. That the inmates were brewing "mash" must have been obvious to the corrections officers, as was the fact that the death row inmates were visibly intoxicated. Recalls Walter Correll in a letter to a pen pal:

I started drinking again. We made our own stuff. I knew I should have learned from the past, but with everything that had happened I needed some help to get by. . . . One Christmas everyone was drinking and someone turned a radio on and everyone started dancing. You have never seen anything as funny as a bunch of drunk men trying to dance. I was laughing so hard I couldn't catch my breath. This was one of the times that nothing happened, but to be honest there has never been a night when the guys weren't drinking. It gives them a chance to forget about where they are and what they are facing.[50]

Chris drank while at Mecklenburg, sometimes to excess, and in letters between Jessica Wiseman and Chris she repeatedly chides him for his alcohol consumption. In a January 1, 1992, letter, Jessica guesses that Chris "probably got drunk" to celebrate the New Year; two months later, she warns Chris, "you have no idea what they could be putting in that stuff your drinking."[51] The very next letter returns to the topic of Chris's drinking: "Seriously, though you better not get fat, and you better not get a beer belly," Jessica writes. "I'm serious Chris. I think you're drinking too much. Every time you write me a letter you're drinking."[52]

On death row, the most intimate relationships are between the correctional staff and the inmates. Locked together in prison, guards themselves often refer to their jobs as serving time, and the pressures of the row produce a variety of different relationships between the guards and the guarded. In the 1980s and 1990s, internal operating procedures in place on Virginia's death row discouraged any emotional bonds between inmate and guard:

All staff assigned to work in the Death Row Unit(s) . . . shall avoid any personal discussions. Employees must not be too familiar or discuss personal items of interest with the inmates. Employees must conduct business and activities on a professional basis and be observant at all times and be knowledgeable of all duties.[53]

"There is no such thing as small talk here" [on Virginia's death row], writes Johnson. "The death row commander warns his staff to 'speak cautiously, and always ask yourself "why" when someone is talking to you—what is he really after?'"[54] It is the death row guards, who have been trained to hold the inmates at a distance and treat them with constant suspicion, who have the prisoners at their mercy. Most death row guards are decent, caring individuals who treat the inmates as human beings. Yet the potential for the abuse of power is very real—especially for underpaid, overworked, and poorly trained guards who view their charges as less than human. In short, corrections officers on death row are not trained, paid, or encouraged to care about the inmates.[55]

In Giarratano's experience, relationships between prisoners and guards were "cordial." "Some guards were professional, some were on power trips, some were pleasant, some were real idiots. Some would apologize when they strip-searched you, cuffed you, shackled you, loaded you onto the van for transport to the death house and handed you over to their co-workers for killing."[56] Giarratano concludes, however, that even the most merciful guard never strayed from duty. "But whether apologetic or jerks, for you, the outcome was the same: the cuffs and the shackles bit into your flesh, your head was still shaved, the electrodes still affixed to your body."[57]

On death row, contacts with the outside world are fragile. Even if friends and family want to visit a death row inmate, institutional regulations make such visits difficult and time-consuming for inmate and family members alike. Johnson makes the important point that visits are a privilege, not a right, for death row inmates, and that prison administrators have the unfettered discretion to take away the privilege. Moreover, Johnson writes that the myriad rules regarding visits (such as how to get onto a visiting list, what days visits occur, and how long visits can last) have the effect—intended or unintended—of discouraging families and friends from coming to death row to see their loved ones. The inmates themselves typically are subjected to a strip search after contact and noncontact visits, a degrading procedure that further discourages the inmate from seeking visits. "You go down and you sit down for an hour . . . and you get your mind away from this place," explains a death row inmate. "And just as soon as you come in after having enjoyed yourself for a little bit . . . they strip you, look up your asshole and in your mouth . . . and handcuff you behind your back and drag you back up that hall. Well . . . they just broke your whole fucking visit. You would have been better off . . . if you'd just stayed in your cell."[58] The practical effect of these rules is that visits lessen and then stop—and the death row inmate becomes further isolated, alone, and estranged.

Although Mecklenburg qualified as a "reformed" death row, it was still highly restrictive compared to other reformed death rows:

> There is a feeling among many of the men on Virginia's death row that already they are not quite alive. For 19 hours a day, they are locked alone in their cells, allowed out for an hour each morning, an hour at noon and three hours in the evening. They are able to associate only with the 11 other men in their cellblock. In North Carolina, in contrast, death-row inmates are freed from their cells from 7 a.m. to 11 p.m. In Maryland, most of the state's 14 death-row inmates are permitted even more freedom, living among the general prisoners and serving on work details.[59]

For critics of Mecklenburg's death row, the forced isolation and limited access to other inmates, to jobs, to the touch of a loved one, and to the sunshine of the outside world were designed to further punish the inmates and to slowly kill their spirit long before the electric chair ended their physical lives. A Georgia death row inmate summarized this sense of total isolation: "I can easily stand criticism, correction, incarceration, even punishment. But the silence, the isolation, the unforgivingness [sic] from society—even from the churches, the pastors, the Christians—is terrifying and debilitating. Does anyone care?"[60]

As for the men of Virginia's death row, many were exceedingly vulnerable to the pressures produced by the isolation. Writes Giarratano:

Some were clearly mentally ill. Some mentally retarded. All of us, to one degree or another, had identifiable psychological difficulties shaped by troubled pasts. Most sought to escape the reality of their situation in any way they possibly could. Some struggled hard to deal with the reality that they were faced with. All were human beings, living, breathing, sentient creatures. All had parents, siblings, some had children, all had friends, grandparents, etc. All had histories. Each one of them, like each of us, had a story.

In short, at Mecklenburg's death row, depression, isolation, despair, and mental illness mixed together and hovered over the row like toxic thunderheads. Former Virginia death row inmate Joseph Patrick Payne, Sr., who faced execution until his death sentence was commuted, wrote a pen pal, "There are times when I feel so apart from life that reading, watching TV, listening to the radio or conversating [sic] seems useless, meaningless and at times irritating. ... The only way I know how to explain it is that life does not have the same joy and interest when death seems to overwhelm one and one so clearly feels ... or knows that he isn't really a part of life, and the small way he is will soon be deliberately ended."[61] "[E]very day you feel at least a moment of depression over something," adds Giarratano. "It could be the smell of the morning air, looking out the window and seeing the barbed wire, getting handcuffs put on, having to ask for a meal through a set of bars, or the memory of what once was and of those you've hurt just by being here."[62]

Throughout his time on death row, Chris, like other inmates, battled depression. Undoubtedly, one contributing factor to his despair was the ebb and flow of his legal appeals and the attendant struggle against false hope of a judicial reprieve. In Virginia (like other death penalty states), death row inmates have three rounds of appeals. While the procedural nuances may differ by state, the fundamental process is the same. After the circuit court imposes final judgment, state law dictates that the Virginia Supreme Court must review the death sentence. This is known as a "direct appeal." A complete copy of the court record and all exhibits are forwarded to the Virginia Supreme Court, and, after reviewing the evidence and the briefs of the two parties, the court considers whether (1) errors were committed by the trial court; (2) "the sentence of death was imposed under the influence of passion, prejudice, or any other arbitrary factor"; and (3) "the sentence of death is excessive or disproportionate to the penalty imposed in similar cases, considering both the crime and the defendant."[63] Under Virginia law, the state supreme court can affirm the death sentence, commute the sentence from death to life imprisonment, or remand the case back to the circuit court for a new sentencing hearing.

Although the purpose of this mandatory direct appeal is both "to assure the fair and proper application of the death penalty statutes in this Commonwealth and to instill public confidence in the administration of justice,"[64] there are limits to the direct appeal that arguably disadvantage a defendant. For example, if defense counsel does not make a timely objection to a perceived error by the trial court, then that objection is deemed waived and cannot be argued before the Virginia Supreme Court during the direct review. Making a timely objection before the circuit court, however, is not sufficient to have an alleged error reviewed by the Supreme Court; trial counsel must also formally submit a written "assignment of errors" to the Virginia Supreme Court and adequately explain said errors in the written brief prepared for the court. Moreover, such issues as ineffective assistance of counsel and prosecutorial misconduct cannot be raised on direct appeal. These issues must be raised during the second and third rounds of appeal, namely, habeas corpus actions filed in state and federal court. Finally, on appeal the Virginia Supreme Court considers the evidence introduced at trial in a light most favorable to the prosecution. If there are any factual ambiguities in the trial court record, they will be resolved in favor of the commonwealth.[65]

If the Virginia Supreme Court affirms the sentence of death, then a defendant has a limited amount of time in which to file a writ of habeas corpus with the Virginia Supreme Court. Other states refer to this as "postconviction review" or "collateral attack." Whether filed in state or federal court, a writ of habeas corpus is different from a direct appeal. The relevant question is not whether a defendant is guilty or innocent or whether the trial court committed errors. The sole issue raised by a writ of habeas corpus is whether or not a defendant is being detained in violation of his constitutional rights;[66] a court will not consider any claims in a habeas petition except those that, if found to be valid, would result in the immediate release of the defendant from incarceration.[67] In other words, "the truth-seeking function of the trial process yields to a focus on the legality of a petitioner's detention and whether the petitioner presently is detained in violation of any constitutional rights."[68]

In many instances a team of new attorneys work on a death row inmate's state habeas petition, but they do not operate off a clean slate: any errors made by trial counsel that were not properly preserved (objected to at trial), formally assigned as errors during the appeal, and adequately briefed to the Virginia Supreme Court during the direct appeal are deemed defaulted and cannot be raised in a state habeas petition. Finally, a defendant cannot file an endless string of state habeas corpus petitions. As in other states, a defendant is barred from filing subsequent habeas corpus petitions if said petitions raise claims that the defendant could have raised in previous petitions.[69]

Almost as a matter of course, a defendant will raise an ineffective assistance of counsel claim in a state habeas petition. As discussed in chapter 3, under the Sixth Amendment to the United States Constitution a defendant has a constitutional right to a reasonably competent attorney. In order to convince a court that the trial attorney's performance did not pass constitutional muster, a defendant has a heavy burden: not only must he show that his attorney's performance was not reasonable given the standards of the profession, but that there is a reasonable likelihood that a different result would have been reached at the trial but for the attorney's ineffective and unreasonable performance.[70] Specific examples of ineffective assistance of counsel claims in death penalty cases might include claims that the attorney improperly advised the defendant to enter a guilty plea, did not conduct a proper pretrial investigation, or did not properly present mitigation evidence at a sentencing hearing.

If a death row inmate does not prevail in his state habeas corpus petition, he has the option of filing a new habeas corpus petition in federal court. Once again, the scope of the federal habeas corpus petition is limited to whether the inmate is being held in violation of his constitutional rights.[71] Additional restrictions and requirements are placed upon the death row inmate who files a habeas corpus petition. For example, federal courts will not consider a habeas corpus petition if an inmate held in state custody has not first exhausted all his possible legal remedies in state court;[72] further, federal courts will not hear claims that were deemed procedurally barred under state law. Finally, even if the alleged errors that were not preserved involved issues of federal, not state, law, they are procedurally defaulted and cannot be raised during the defendant's third and last type of appeal, namely, a writ of habeas corpus filed in federal court.

The likelihood of a defendant overturning his conviction or sentence on appeal is made that much more difficult by the fact that a well-trained team of lawyers are opposing his efforts. In 1995, the Virginia Attorney General's

Office formed the Capital Litigation Unit. Nicknamed the "death squad"[73] by its critics, the unit was originally composed of five lawyers and was created to help the AG's office defend death penalty appeals in a more efficient, competent, and speedy manner. "[They] work doggedly to speed the convicted to their deaths. They have been successful: In the 13 years before the capital unit came into being, Virginia executed 26 people. In the 18 months the unit has worked exclusively on death-penalty cases, the state has put to death 12 people." For at least one lawyer on the team, their success rate and enthusiasm for their work stems partially from the fact that they are "'always on the good side, always on the right side.'"[74] For members of the Capital Litigation Unit, their skill and hard work alone do not account for the increased number of executions in Virginia. The team members also believe that they benefit from being on the "right side" of justice. "'It's fascinating and rewarding to be always on the good side, always on the right side,'" attorney Katherine Baldwin stated in a newspaper interview. "'It's a privilege to be able to do this. There's just no doubt about the justice involved. The jury has already decided what the truth is. The doubts are resolved. We're working in a system based on hundreds of eons of justice. How could that be wrong?'"[75] Moreover, the team members also hold a common attitude toward the prisoners who are bringing the appeals. "'I think of them as bad people,'" litigation unit leader Donald R. Curry remarked. "'I think of them as people who have done unimaginable things. ... I generally don't buy into the principle that because you were brought up in a less-than-great home and didn't go to college and had a mother who was an alcoholic—I don't think that means you can put a gun to someone's head and shoot them.'"[76] The Capital Litigation Unit has not focused its energies solely on pending death penalty appeals, but has waded into deeper political waters. For example, when members of the Virginia General Assembly proposed that a legislative committee scrutinize Virginia's appellate review of capital murder convictions, the aforementioned Mr. Curry faxed commonwealth attorneys and asked them to oppose the resolution on the ground that it might lead to a suspension of the death penalty in Virginia.[77]

While the litigation team members deny that they use highly technical rules and procedures to deny inmates a fair hearing on their allegations of substantive due process violations, there are examples to the contrary. Critics of the Capital Litigation Unit point to the case of Joseph O'Dell, a Virginia death row inmate whose petition for writ of habeas corpus was rejected because the attorney general's office successfully argued that the petition had the incorrect title. Another example can be found in the appeal of Virginia death row prisoner Coleman Wayne Gray, which the litigation team asserted (again successfully) should be denied because it was filed one day past the Virginia Supreme Court's formal deadline. In the opinion of former Washington and Lee law professor William Geimer, such technical arguments are "'the daily bread of the attorney general's office. . . . It's death by technicality.'"[78] While Geimer grudgingly admits that the Capital Litigation team is "'good at doing their jobs'" he adds, "'people ought to know it has little or nothing to do with justice.'" Virginia defense attorney Steven Rosenfield is less charitable. "'They're overly zealous, and that interferes with their advocacy judgments. . . . I don't understand their crazed aggressiveness. I don't mean to equate them to totalitarian governments, but there is a certain parallel. There's no way to really soften this — their exuberance to kill people can only be equated to [that of] totalitarian governments.'"[79]

Chris Thomas's direct appeal to the Virginia Supreme Court was handled by former trial counsel Damian Horne and Sydney West. They remained Chris's attorneys despite the fact that on March 19, 1992, Chris filed a handwritten motion in the Circuit Court of Middlesex County, asking that Horne and West be removed from his case. In the motion, Chris wrote:

> I feel that they . . . are useing [sic] my case to gain publicity for themselves. They also seem prejudice[d] in trying to help me. I have arranged to have another attorney take over my case, but I need to withdraw my present attorneys. If this is not done, I will not be able to have a "fair" chance when the Va. Supreme Court argues my appeal.

The motion appears to have been sparked by Damian Horne's plans to appear on a tabloid talk show that was devoting an entire episode to the case. The allegation that Chris's defense attorneys were selfishly seeking the public spotlight upsets Horne to this day. "This is another notion against which I can't help but recoil," he writes. "I did not seek out any of the Sally Jesse Raphael publicity, but when it came, I thought it would be an opportunity to garner a ground swell [sic] of public opinion against Chris's execution . . . precisely what I had represented to him." Moreover, Horne claims that he had Chris's permission to appear on the show. "I did indeed discuss Sally Jesse with Chris. . . . I told him that this would be the first step in trying to generate a Public Outcry against his execution. I even recall speaking with Chris while in New York right before the show. They wanted him to go on the air and, once again, Chris's peculiar . . . what was it? Shyness? Reticence? whatever prevented him from taking the opportunity of saying ANYTHING he wished."[80] There is no evidence that the motion was granted a hearing or reviewed by the court.

In the appeal filed before the Virginia Supreme Court, Horne and West argued that Judge Folkes made the following errors: (1) denying defense counsel's motion to remand the proceedings back to juvenile court for a transfer hearing; (2) denying the motion to dismiss the charges regarding the murder of Kathy Wiseman on double jeopardy grounds; (3) denying the change of venue motion; (4) forcing Chris to give up his attorney of choice (Benton Pollok) by denying defense counsel's motion to continue the trial date; (5) denying the motion to suppress Chris's confession; (6) denying the motion to dismiss due to the destruction of evidence; (7) failing to disqualify veniremen who knew Commonwealth Attorney Ward; and (8) denying the motion to suppress the photographs of the murder victims. Moreover, the appeals claimed that (a) the evidence did not support the jury's finding that the crime was vile (a sentencing aggravator); and (b) the death sentence was influenced by the passion and prejudice of the jury. Chris's state habeas lawyers were later dismissive of the brief filed by Horne and West. "Defense counsel's brief on appeal violates the first rule of appellate advocacy; it is replete with misspellings, and miscitations." On June 5, 1992, the Virginia Supreme Court unanimously affirmed Chris's capital murder conviction and his death sentence.[81]

Attorneys James C. Breeden and Alan W. Clarke were appointed to represent Chris on his state habeas corpus claim. They were assisted by Rob Lee, an attorney at the nonprofit Capital Representation Resource Center in Charlottesville, Virginia. A veteran group of lawyers, they immediately requested that the court authorize funds for a proper mitigation review—including the hiring of Marie Deans to conduct the mitigation investigation. On June 26, 1993, Chris's lawyers filed his habeas corpus petition. The main argument contained in the petition was that Chris Thomas received ineffective assistance of counsel. Specifically, the petition alleged that Chris's trial counsel failed to prepare a mitigation defense (including conducting a proper mitigation evaluation and obtaining a psychologist to testify at sentencing), failed to investigate whether Chris fired the third shot, and failed to have a rational basis for taking the case to trial. The petition also argued that the execution of juvenile offenders violated the Eighth Amendment of the United States

Constitution (it would be another decade before the Supreme Court accepted such an argument about the constitutionality of the juvenile death penalty). The Virginia Supreme Court dismissed his state habeas corpus petition on June 17, 1996, and on March 16, 1999, the United States Court of Appeals for the Fourth Circuit dismissed his federal habeas corpus appeal.[82]

The fact that Chris did not prevail on his appeals should not be surprising to anyone familiar with the appellate track record of Virginia's death row inmates. "Because the entire process takes time and can involve dozens of different judges," state the authors of a recent ACLU report, "it is assumed to constitute a guarantee that every capital defendant in Virginia receives a fair and high-quality trial. But this has not been the case."[83] The fundamental problem, argues the report, is that specific legal doctrines—such as the doctrine of procedural default—bar appellate courts from weighing the substantive nature of a defendant's appeal. Regarding the doctrine of procedural default, which applies to claims on direct appeal as well as state and federal habeas proceedings, "a defendant's lawyers must renew every one of their client's complaints in every step of the appeals process. If the lawyers fail to do so, any violation or error they missed is forever barred from consideration by any court."[84]

Moreover, the report argues that it is almost impossible for a death row inmate to demonstrate that he received ineffective assistance of counsel. "The U.S. Constitution entitles an indigent defendant to an attorney, but it does not entitle him to a good attorney . . . it entitles him to no more than a minimally competent one."[85] A defendant can only prevail on a claim of ineffective assistance of counsel if he or she demonstrates that the attorney's performance was unreasonable and that a different result in the trial or sentencing was caused by that unreasonableness. The doctrinal test, however, contains an additional element that can make a ineffective assistance of counsel claim even more difficult to successfully raise: if an attorney claims that the challenged performance was the product of a deliberate strategy, then courts are loath to find that the attorney behaved ineffectively.

The practical result of these doctrinal tests and procedural rules is that by the year 2000, the Virginia Supreme Court "had the lowest reversal rate on direct appeal in death cases in the country."[86] Combine this with the fact that during the same time period the United States Court of Appeals for the Fourth Circuit had only reversed 4 percent of the death penalty cases brought before it via federal habeas petitions, and the practical result is that defendants in capital murder cases are effectively dead men walking upon the imposition of their sentence by the circuit court.

Another cause of death row inmates' depression comes from watching inmate after inmate—some friends, some not—exhaust their appeals and be taken to the death house for execution. During Chris's time on death row, sixty men were taken from death row and executed. Another inmate—Wayne DeLong—committed suicide. As these men exited Mecklenburg's death row for their final journey to the death house, they often paused before the cells of friends, reached through the steel doors' food slots, and clasped hands in a final goodbye.[87]

> On nights when there's an execution in Virginia, and those are coming now with increasing frequency, there is a lonely silence among the men who live on death row. Whether they want to or not, they usually imagine themselves in that cell at the death house, getting their heads shaved too, eating the silly last meal that only the reporters care about, being strapped into the oak and leather chair with the death mask slipped over their eyes.[88]

On these days the men find no respite from the reality of their own impending death. "For the 49 men sentenced to death in Virginia—for such crimes as beating a college student to death with a rock; killing a man for money, then severing his hands; smothering a neighbor with a pillow—there is a new, darker mood of pessimism. It is no longer possible for them to pretend that they will not be killed, or to deny the increasing departures of other inmates."[89] In the pit of their stomachs, the men are keenly aware that they are the living dead. As the executions race forward, Virginia's death row inmates turn inward. "[T]he social reality is one of growing isolation," reported Johnson. "Prisoners keep to themselves more, talk to others less, trust no one. They are driven inward, away from each other, into their cells, which serve as cold, concrete havens of last resort."[90]

Not surprisingly, the combination of depression, isolation, drug abuse, tension, and mental illness ripens into self-destructive impulses and suicidal ideation. Longtime Mecklenburg death row chaplain Russ Ford observes, "[E]very man I've worked with has considered suicide."[91] An anonymous Virginia death row inmate writes: "Not a day passes that I do not fight just to get out of bed. And in the late hours of the night, it takes much strength just to keep a grip on my sanity. I have spent many hours at my window, standing on my toilet at the air vent, pleading with men who were considering suicide. ... I have been on that very edge myself."[92] An inmate contemplating suicide, however, is faced with one of the strangest paradoxes on death row: the state will not knowingly allow an inmate to kill himself.

In reporting on an unsuccessful suicide pact between two death row inmates, an incident in which the prisoners cut their wrists with weapons fashioned from razor blades and toothbrushes, the Newport News *Daily Press* touched upon the paradox that "Virginia spends hundreds of thousands of dollars to get death-row inmates ready for their executions, but the state has an obligation to keep them alive until the appointed time." Noting that Virginia's death row guards receive special training designed to help them spot suicidal inmates, the article reiterated the official position of the Department of Corrections, namely, that "suicides run counter to a prison's mission of providing a safe environment for inmates." "'Besides,' concluded a Department of Corrections spokesperson without a trace of irony, 'we wouldn't stand by and watch someone die.'"[93]

Joe Giarratano is right when he argues that the entire death row experience is, in a word, "insane." Inmates must be prevented from killing themselves until the state determines that they must die. It is a system that values only the safe delivery of the body to the death house; any attention placed on human rights and dignity is secondary and often the result of a mandatory court order. The Virginia Department of Corrections will not stand by and watch the inmate die at his own hand—for that would be a violation of the responsibility given to it by the citizens of Virginia—but it will itself kill the inmate at a predesignated time and location. Writes Robert Johnson: "This concern for preserving the body without regard for the quality of life reaches an extreme in suicide prevention efforts that amount to treating the person like a piece of meat." Perhaps philosopher Albert Camus is right when he observes, "The Greeks, after all, were more humane with their hemlock. They left their condemned a relative freedom, the possibility of putting off or hastening the hour of his death. They gave him a choice between suicide and execution."[94]

Given the realities of the modern death row listed above, is it any wonder that the "enforced isolation and extreme security measures of death row result in a dehumanizing, laboratory-like environment" filled with an "atmosphere of total despair and hopelessness"?[95] Given the fact that this "'unending, uninterrupted immersion in death' can continue for years while the appellate process plays out," should we be surprised to learn that studies of death row inmates have concluded that "prolonged death row incarceration undermines a prisoner's sanity and contributes to the total devastation of the inmate's personality"?[96] And should we care that "death row prisoners suffer extreme psychological anguish in anticipation of death [and] the onset of insanity while awaiting execution is not uncommon"?[97]

Thus was the world that Chris was thrust into in November 1991, when he arrived at Mecklenburg Correctional Center's death row. From the beginning of his incarceration, Chris had two constant visitors: his mother, Margaret Thomas, and Marie Deans. Although Marie had not been used as a mitigation expert at Chris's trial, she had been retained by Chris's appellate lawyers to gather mitigation evidence for his state habeas appeal.

Marie first met and interviewed Chris in the spring of 1993, meeting with him in an 8 × 10 glassed-in conference room that was located below Mecklenburg's death row. From the start she found him to be more child than adult. "My impression is that Chris (now age twenty) generally operates emotionally at about the level of a 15 or 16 year old and sometimes at a younger age level," Deans wrote in a subsequent mitigation report. "He has picked up and imitates a convict demeanor and attitude and has a thin macho veneer, but I feel he is terrified and cannot understand what he did, what has happened or what will happen to him." Moreover, in her conversations Marie soon picked up on the unspoken tension between Chris and his mother. "He seemed very pleased that I was working on his case," Marie reported. "However, when I began questioning him about his mother he became agitated and angry. He appeared to be feeling trapped."[98]

While Chris was "trained up" to hide his feelings from the other inmates, he learned that he could drop his emotional barriers during his private mitigation interviews with Marie. "When he was with me, he knew he had permission to cry and he cried a lot with me," remembers Marie. "He would giggle and play with me too, like a kid. He knew me enough to get very expressive with me. He could really tell me how he felt."[99] Marie quickly came to like the quiet young man. "I did feel motherly toward Chris. People think I feel motherly towards all the men [on the row] and that's not true. Some of those men I didn't really like, much less want to be their mother. I did feel motherly to him. I couldn't help that with Chris. He was my son's age. He was just a kid."

As Chris opened up to Marie, she began doubting Chris's claims that he fired the third shot that killed Kathy Wiseman. Her doubts were confirmed during an mitigation interview when Marie "tricked" Chris into telling the truth. She recalls:

> I always ask my client to recreate the crime for me. . . . I make them get up in the room and show it to me. And I keep stopping them—they'll move one hand and I'll stop them and say what were feeling then and just the whole thing. Chris got really into this. He was like a typical kid. He was recreating this crime as much as he probably could and he got into it and he goofed . . . he starts sort of fumbling around trying to show me how he killed mom and he finally comes up with this idea . . . he gets down on the floor on the other side of the bed and he somehow manages to kill mom from this distance. I've seen the forensic reports, and so I said something like "so did the bullet go up through the mattress?" He looked—he realized he's been caught . . . so he tries to finagle around that question, and he doesn't, and so finally he started crying. And he got up in his chair and he said, "You did that to me." And I said, "Yes, I did. I did do that to you. It's really time you told somebody the truth."

Marie was not the first person to believe that Chris had lied about firing the third and final shot. As mentioned earlier, Benton Pollok—Chris's first trial counsel—believed that Jessica Wiseman fired the third shot, as did the psychologist who examined Chris before the trial.

As a mitigation specialist, Marie's primary responsibility was to meet with the death row inmates and collect evidence for the mitigation portion of their appeals. Marie, however, also struggled to give her clients a reason to live. Marie sensed the helplessness and remorse that had haunted Chris since the murders, and she worked to convince Chris not to abandon the appeals. For Marie, it was a delicate balancing act. "You have to give them a reason not to give up," explained Marie. "At the same time I wasn't going to lie and promise that I could get them off the row. Lawyers would tell them that. 'You're going to walk home free.' It just pissed me off every time I heard a lawyer do that." As with all the men on death row, Marie told Chris that there was one fundamental reason for him to fight to live as long as possible: to achieve inner knowledge and peace. "The reason I gave Chris is the reason I gave all of them. You don't even know who you are. You're a kid. If they kill you at least know who the hell you are when they do it. Give yourself that much time to figure out who you are."

The feelings that Chris shared with Deans in the dingy interviewing room underneath death row included his growing awareness that he had been, and continued to be, manipulated by Jessica Wiseman so he would not point the finger at her. In the first two years of his incarceration on death row, the steady flow of letters from Jessica Wiseman continued unabated. While the Bon Air Learning Center forbade its residents from receiving letters from convicted felons, Chris and Jessica circumvented the rule by using Jessica's grandparents—Denby and Arvazine Thomas—as a conduit. Both Chris and Jessica mailed their letters to the grandparents, who subsequently hand-delivered Chris's letters to Jessica during their Sunday visits while remailing Jessica's letters to Chris in a new envelope bearing Arvazine's handwriting. The grandparents' willingness to help facilitate the exchange of letters is only one surprise in their relationship with Chris. On several occasions the grandparents visited Chris on death row, and Chris appears to have called Arvazine Thomas frequently.

Marie was troubled that Chris continued to write Jessica Wiseman. Specifically, Marie worried that Jessica would give the letters to the Virginia attorney general's Office, which in turn would find a way to use the letters against Chris—either in court or in future clemency hearings. She voiced her concerns to Chris, who gave her permission to read the letters and to use them in any way Marie deemed appropriate. As Marie pored over the letters, she recalls feeling "disgusted"—not by the sexual content of the letters, but by the transparent and clumsy attempts by Jessica to manipulate Chris. "I had not considered her quite as manipulative until I read those letters. And I thought she was just using and abusing him all over the place," recalled Marie. "She wanted to make sure she got out."

Like the letters mailed to Chris in the months immediately following the murders, the letters sent to death row contained flowery proclamations of Jessica's love—"[y]ou are everything to me! I will sacrifice everything for you, and for our everlasting love!"[100]—and hopelessly romantic predictions of a future filled with freedom, marriage, and endless sex. In a letter sent to Chris only four days after his arrival on death row, Jessica writes, "I keep on dreaming that we got to go home and Nanny and PawPaw took us to Jamaica and then they left us up or down there and we got married. . . . I can't wait until we get out so we can go home, pack our stuff, and get the hell out of Middlesex County."[101]

The fantasy that Chris and Jessica would be whisked away to a tropic paradise by the relatives of their murder victims may seem bizarre, but it is in keeping with Jessica's claims that her grandmother—the woman who gave birth to Kathy Wiseman—simply loved Chris. Arvazine Thomas's alleged affection and concern for Chris is a theme that appears again and again in Jessica's letters:

> Nanny was talking about you today, and she started crying. She said that she was so worried about you, because your [sic] always so upset and your mom treats you wrong, and she said she hopes you know how much she cares about you. She wants us to come home and be together and happy so bad. She said she wants to talk to you a lot more and get closer to you, but she doesn't know how to go about doing it, because she is afraid of saying the wrong thing. She also said she doesn't really know how you feel about her. I mean basically she wants you to know that she doesn't have any hard feelings or anything.[102]

In a subsequent letter, Jessica reassured Chris that Arvazine Thomas "loves you dearly" and "talks about you all the time."[103] While Jessica's pronouncements about her grandmother's affection for Chris must be taken with a grain of salt, before Chris's murder trial Arvazine Thomas herself told a newspaper reporter, "'I don't hate Chris, I feel sorry for him.'"[104] In the same newspaper article Arvazine Thomas tearfully observed, "'I feel like Jessica is the only piece of Kathy that I've got left.'"[105] One wonders if the distraught woman felt that she had to accept Chris into her life out of fear of losing Jessica.

The letters also reflect Jessica's continuing inability to comprehend either the enormity of their crimes or the stark reality of Chris's death sentence. As with the letters sent to Chris immediately after the murders, Jessica never mentions Kathy and J. B. Wiseman and only alludes to the horrific events of November 10, 1990. There are no confessions of remorse or contrition, no expressions of an anguished conscience, and no signs of mourning. In fact, there is little evidence that the murders emotionally impacted Jessica in any discernible manner. While the letters contain such passages as "I can't sleep in the dark anymore [sic] either. . . . I haven't been able to sleep in the dark ever since we first got locked up,"[106] it is impossible to know if the darkness evoked the bloody images of that fateful night or the fear of violence from other girls in the detention center.

What is constant in the letters is Jessica's repeated claim that she and Chris had been wrongfully or excessively punished. "I wish they would just let us go home," Jessica writes to Chris. "I think that we've suffered enough 'for no reason.'"[107] Echoing letters written shortly after the murders, Jessica again makes cryptic comments to the fact that she and Chris are "the only ones with the truth."[108] Whatever the "truth" is, however, it is not revealed in the correspondence. Rather than acknowledging the role that she played in the events leading to her own incarceration, Jessica instead complains bitterly about "all these lawyers, judges[,] courts and the good for nothing commonwealth,"[109] wishes out loud for "something that could be said or done to get us out and all of this stuff wiped off our records"[110] and wonders "is there anyone on this earth that can help us?"[111]

In keeping with her pronouncements of victimization, Jessica bemoans her treatment at the Bon Air Learning Center as well as her contempt for the administrators and counselors at the facility. It does not appear to have crossed her mind that death row inmates had their own share of pain and deprivations. "Death Row is just a name and it doesn't mean a thing," Jessica breezily reminds Chris. As for her conditions of confinement, Jessica angrily writes that she is treated "like a black person in a room full of K.K.K. people" and is singled out for special abuse. "I'm serious they treat me completely different from everyone, even the other serious offenders. . . . I have to be walked to EVERY class in school by one of the staff in my cottage. Ain't that some shit? Plus when I got to the dining hall or just outside period, I have to have 3 staff with me! So instead of the handcuffs, 3 people are stuck up my ass when I walk!!!!!"[112] The specific rules and restrictions that governed Jessica's life were dictated by her status as a "Serious Offender," a categorization that infuriated Jessica. "I can't stand to be put in a category like a damn Serious Offender. I'm not like all the rest of these hateful ass girls," Jessica whined to Chris. "I'm the nicest girl on this campus but if they keep on pissing me off, I'm gonna [sic] show them a damn Serious Offender!"[113] For the young girl who once drove around her subdivision in a golf cart, the perceived indignities of her incarceration included needless physical exertion. "I have to walk to the dining hall, school, and gym everyday. Rain hail, sleet or snow," Jessica complains. "As long as I've been here they should give me a car!"[114] Concludes Jessica: "I'm literally going through hell, in this place."[115]

Despite the allegedly hellish conditions of Bon Air, and her perceived persecution at the hands of uncaring adults, Jessica brags to Chris about the power she allegedly wields over the staff. "I tried to tell these people not to mess with me," she writes about a confrontation with staff members. "I swear if they keep on I'm gonna [sic] have to talk to the media, and I promised them that, already. . . . Their [*sic*] scared of me and I'm enjoying every minute of it."[116] The staff's fear of Jessica and her powers seemingly dissolved into love; only six months later Jessica brags to Chris, "as long as I've been here there isn't one staff [member] that doesn't love me to death and when ever [*sic*] somebody [another juvenile] says something to me [about the murder of her parents] they [the staff] get more offended than I do."[117]

Throughout the letters, Jessica continues to demand all of Chris's attention—often mocking Chris for not finding the time to write during his hours of isolation. In one letter, she angrily writes: "And write me 'more'!! And you can't say that your [*sic*] busy, because you ain't got a damn thing in the world to do but 'think about me,' 'write me,' eat, sleep and go to the bathroom!"[118] In another letter she wonders if Chris is "just to [*sic*] busy" to write and dramatically concludes, "I guess I just don't come first in your life anymore [*sic*]. . . . Why don't you love me anymore?"[119] Jessica's craving for Chris's undivided attention was so great that she repeatedly demands that he cut himself off from the rest of the world. In a letter written approximately one week after his arrival on death row, Jessica writes:

Chris this is really important so please don't forget it. Whatever you do please do not let anyone know where you are. I mean you know how Glenda wrote you a letter about me & you wrote her back explaining that you don't want anybody, but me? Well my point is (don't take this the wrong way) but please don't let her or anybody else know what your address is, because I don't trust Glenda she will give your address to everybody in Middlesex County!! So please promise me, okay. I'm so sick and tired of everybody like her thinking they can write to you at any time they want. And I hope and pray that Brenda doesn't know where your [*sic*] at NOW, because knowing her she will give it to Tracy [a former girlfriend]. Chris, would you tell me if she was writing to you or not? I asked you that, because you might not tell me if she was or not, because I worry so much! Please don't get mad at me for asking. Okay. Just promise me whatever happens mail wise, just don't let them have your private jail number only your mom, me and Nanny & PawPaw should have it![120]

Her paranoia over losing Chris's affection remained unabated, and in a subsequent letter Jessica asks Chris, "if you fell in love with someone else would you tell me, and if a girl was writing to you and you were writing her back, would you tell me, or just say you decided to write one of your old girlfriends would you tell me?"[121] In short, the isolated and lonely boy on death row had to prove his love by cutting himself off from any outside contacts not first approved by his jealous girlfriend.

Additionally, Jessica continued to worry that her letters might fall into the hands of others. She writes: "What ever happened to those letters that your first lawyer or one of them lawyers took and was suppose to give back? Please, tell me you have them or you can get them back. I swear if they don't give you those letters back if they haven't already then they will be sooooooooo very sorry. Because I'll personally get them back as soon as I get the hell out of this place. I'm really pissed now!"[122] It is impossible to know whether Jessica's focus on her letters merely reflected her desire for privacy, or whether she feared that a third party might see her transparent and clumsy efforts at manipulation and control and start asking Chris dangerous questions about the murders.

By the fall of 1992, Jessica's letters began reflecting the fault lines that were emerging in their relationship. While some of the correspondence contained the same syrupy language and romantic promises, more and more the letters demonstrated the tension between Chris and Jessica. Time was passing, and Jessica and Chris were traveling down very different roads. Writes Jessica:

> Look, I really don't know what else to do. I mean you complain if I don't write and then when I do it's not enough. I'm running out of stuff to talk about, but if you just want a piece of paper saying Hello, I love you, take care, and that's it, then fine. I'm glad that you can seem to handle being locked up, but I can't my nerves keep me "sick" all the time. I haven't seen my future husband in 2 years. I haven't been in the real world in two years. I'm sorry, I'm really trying hard, and you're just going to have to bare [sic] with me that is if you want to. I can't make you. . . . I go to school everyday and I have lot more things to do then [sic] I did in a locked cottage. Then all I did was sit around and watch T.V. So please try to understand. I just finished telling Nanny and Paw Paw the same thing I'm tell you because they wanted to know why I wasn't writing to them as much too. As for making Bon Air listen to me. That's impossible, they are gonna [sic] treat me any kind of way they want until I leave and it's getting worse everyday. So do you feel better now that I've explained to you? I hope so.[123]

By the spring of 1993 the romance between Jessica Wiseman and Chris Thomas abruptly ended. The details regarding their breakup are fuzzy, but

Chris's dawning awareness that he was being used was the catalyst. Despite her "disgust" over the letters, Marie Deans wanted Chris to arrive at this understanding on his own. "I never told him 'Jessica used you.' I never said anything like that," Marie explains. "But I asked him a lot of questions that made him come up with the answers himself and realize it himself." Chris and Jessica never communicated again, and in June 1999 the young woman who had repeatedly sworn that she would die for Chris issued a press release and publically disavowed any role in the murder of her parents.

Laura did not visit Chris on death row at the Mecklenburg Correctional Center. Laura and Chris exchanged regular telephone calls and letters, but she never journeyed into the prison itself. She was paralyzed by the fear of seeing the hell in which Chris had been plunged. When Laura talked to Chris, she could hear loud, rough voices in the background. Chris would try to cover the noise by talking louder, but he couldn't always mask the sounds of yelling and cursing men. In her mind's eye, Laura tried to imagine the world in which Chris lived: a world of concrete and steel, where sunlight and beauty were absent, a world of men who had committed unspeakable acts of violence. And Chris, still a teenager, growing up in such a place. These images overwhelmed Laura, and she often sobbed after hanging up the telephone.

At some point, however, Chris did ask Laura to visit him. Chris told Laura that he had only a handful of visitors — his mother, an aunt, and his former girlfriend, Dawn — and that he desperately wanted to see his former teacher turned friend and confidante. Laura scheduled a visit to the prison in January 1995, but at the last second she backed out. Writing to Chris, Laura tried to articulate the reasons for her canceling the visit. "Please forgive me for not visiting you. Part of me really wants to see you and part is scared to see you on death row. Chris you are so important in my life. You have always been very special to me . . . but I don't think I can see you behind bars. To just talk to you through a plate of glass would be very difficult."[124] Laura was scared. She was scared that the sight of Chris behind bars would forever erase the happy memories she had of the younger boy. Chris reassured Laura that he had not changed, but Laura could not get beyond her fear. She decided that — no matter how much she missed him — that she would not travel to death row. The canceled visit deeply upset Chris, and it would be several months before he wrote or called Laura.

The grief and uncertainty that Laura felt over Chris's sentence of death grew as the years passed, and Laura found herself dreading what the future held. Chris was a death row inmate. He would be executed. His death was inevitable. Nothing that Laura could do would stop her former student from being killed. The helplessness gnawed at her. One evening Laura did not accept Chris's collect call from death row. After hanging up the telephone, she turned to her husband, Ross. "I am feeling overwhelmed with guilt, but I've decided that I'm not going to take any more of Chris's phone calls," Laura said, in a despairing and tired voice. "And I'm going to stop writing him. Eventually he will stop calling, forget about me, and go on with whatever life he has left. I just can't keep pretending that Chris can beat this."

Ross's surprise showed in his face. "Why would you want to do that, Laura?" Laura paused. She knew the answer, but she was ashamed of her feelings. She was ashamed that she felt too weak to survive the death of her former student and friend. "I can't bear the pain any more. I can't stand thinking of him on death row. And I am utterly terrified of the day that Chris will die in the electric chair and the new pain it will cause me."

Laura began to cry, but continued through the tears. "So I am going to distance myself now." Ross held Laura as she wept. "You can try to kick him out of your life," he said. "But I don't think it will be that easy." Laura agreed. "No, it won't. But this is what I have to do." Laura took a deep breath before she continued. "If Chris calls, just hang up. Don't accept the charges. And please don't even tell me that he called." "Okay," said Ross, disbelievingly. He knew that Laura could not walk away from Chris so easily, but he would honor her wishes.

A few days later, Ross and Laura were sitting at home when the telephone rang. Ross answered it and immediately turned to Laura. "It's Chris," Ross said as he looked at his wife. "Do you want to take the call?" Laura reached for the phone, her anticipation of hearing Chris's voice outweighing her fear. She had not turned her back on Chris on that first meeting at Clover Hill High School, and she realized now that she couldn't turn away from Chris now. Relief flooded through her as she took the telephone. Toward the end of the conversation, a computerized operator broke in and announced that only ten seconds remained in the call. As the final seconds ticked down, Laura did something that she had wanted to do for years — she told Chris that she loved him. Before he could respond, the phone call was disconnected with a loud click. As Laura hung up the receiver, she knew in her heart that she would be at Chris's side until the bitter end. Sitting back in her chair, she closed her eyes and said a silent prayer, "*Thank you God, for keeping Chris in my life and for giving me the strength to not walk away.*" Of course, Laura had no idea that her journey with Chris would end in what she would later describe as the pits of Hell: Virginia's death house.

Sussex I State Prison

On the morning of August 3, 1998, Chris Thomas and the other forty-six death row inmates were loaded onto nine prison vans and moved to their new home at Sussex I State Prison in Waverly, Virginia. Escorted down the highway by a police escort, a K-9 unit, and a state police helicopter hovering overhead, Chris stared out the window and for the first time in more than six years saw the Virginia countryside that he loved so much.[125] During the two-hour drive, it must have crossed many of the inmates' minds they would not have a similar ride until their final journey to the death house.

The death row inmates were joining general population inmates at a brand new prison, a 700-bed facility that boasted the latest in correctional technology, including a fully computerized security system and an electronic fence perimeter detection system. New to Virginia was a building design used in western prisons: gun ports were installed in the control rooms overlooking the prison pod areas. Various guns could be used in the ports, with the weapon of choice being short-barreled shotguns that used shells that incapacitated only. "'It gives you a better weapon to protect inmates and staff from the occasional assaultive inmate,' explained a Department of Corrections administrator. 'It's impossible for a single unarmed officer to break up a fight between shank-wielding inmates.'"[126]

Perhaps in anticipation of an increase in capital murder convictions, Sussex I State Prison set aside eighty-eight of its 9-foot by 8-foot cells for death row inmates—an increase of twenty-eight cells over the sixty death row cells at the Mecklenburg Correctional Center. Death row comprises two groups of forty-four cells, with the cells arranged in two levels around a common pod area that the death row inmates cannot use. As with Mecklenburg, the inmates were sealed in their cells behind a solid steel door that had a two-foot square window used for observation and a slot through which food trays, mail, and medication was passed. A single control room, manned by two correctional officers, monitors all eighty-eight cells.

In an unpublished Amnesty International interview, Chris described his sterile new environment. For the inmates of the new death row, the biggest shock was increased isolation. No longer would inmates share meals and card games in a common dayroom or play pickup basketball games in the recreational area. The inmates remained separated in their cells, with two hours a week for individual showers and individual recreation time three times a week in 150 square foot areas that the inmates quickly nicknamed "dog kennels." The inmates were never placed together in the recreation areas, and they were not provided with exercise or athletic equipment. Not a basketball to bounce or a dumbbell to lift.

As with Mecklenburg, the death row inmates were permitted to purchase and have personal items in their cells, including a small television set, a radio, and a cassette player and headphones. The inmates were permitted to have books and photographs, although both were strictly limited in number. Inmates could select and purchase undergarments from the commissary, but all outer garments were provided by the prison. All meals were eaten in the cell, fare that was served at 6:00 A.M., noon, and 6:00 P.M. and that Chris called consistently "lousy": "Like this morning it was boiled eggs, potatoes, coffee cup of cereal, two slices of bread, milk, and coffee or I want to say coffee, colored water . . . chicken is always baked. You hardly ever get condiments with anything. Food is either undercooked or overcooked. You never get full."[127] The inmates could supplement their fare by ordering junk food and tobacco from the commissary, but orders were taken but once a week.

As for a "typical day," Chris stated that he "got up about seven, eat breakfast. On Friday, we go outside for two hours or two and a half hours. We come back in and usually watch TV or go to sleep until lunchtime. After lunch, kick back, watch TV, exercise. That is pretty much the whole day. Just watch TV and read."[128] Chris's favorite shows included *Married with Children*, *Martin*, and *Baywatch*. The monotony was at least partially broken by the privilege of making daily phone calls (the telephone was delivered to the cell), family visits on the weekends, and nonfamily visits (typically lawyers) during the week. As for any benefits of the new death row, at least the cells were slightly larger (72 square feet instead of 52 square feet) and air-conditioned, and the inmates could see the outside world with a 2-foot by 2-foot window.

After eight years on the row, Chris had a weary and jaundiced view of the men and women who ran death row. While Chris characterized some of the guards as "fairly lenient," others "think they have to go above and beyond the call of duty" by mouthing off to the inmates, writing up charges for nonexistent infractions, and "shaking down" (inspecting) the cells to demonstrate their power. To Chris, much of the show of power was useless:

"[T]hey just keep pressing you about standing up for count. Which it is part of procedure, but some of them need to realize that this is death row. We don't have parole. Charges won't hurt us. So . . . if you are going to write the charge, write the charge and go on about your business." In Chris's eyes, any guard who worked on death row was a supporter of capital punishment: "[I]f they weren't in favor of it, why would they be over here?" He conceded, however, that some viewed death row as a plum assignment. "You hear a lot of them say that they want to work over here because it is the quietest building in the compound," Chris explained. "[Y]ou don't do anything over here except pass the food out, pass the clothes out, pass the phone. So I can see where they get less work and the same amount of money."

While Laura Anderson continued to call and write Chris, she still did not visit. Laura prayed for the strength to visit Chris, and she asked God to still her fears and to give her the courage to step into the crypt that Chris called home. In the intervening years, Laura had volunteered at a juvenile prison, and the job eased her concerns about stepping into prison.

In the fall of 1998, Laura called Chris and excitedly told him that she would visit on the coming Saturday. On a bright Saturday morning, Laura left her home outside of Charlottesville, Virginia and began the long drive to Waverly, Virginia. Confidence filled her heart as she drove through the Saturday morning traffic, but she felt the old fears returning as she approached Sussex I. All she could see was razor wire, stretching in all directions. It draped the drab concrete fortress like icing on a sagging, dismal cake. As Laura came closer, she saw the tiny windows cut in the concrete — slits through which the inmates saw tiny fragments of the world. Laura parked and sat in her car for a few minutes, praying for the courage she so needed.

Laura exited her car and cautiously walked through the front doors of the visitation center. She saw that she was not alone. An elderly woman sat with two young children, and a number of younger women — wives or girlfriends, Laura imagined — slumped in nearby chairs. Laura couldn't help staring at the children, wondering whether they were frequent visitors to the prison. She walked to the security counter. "I am Laura Anderson," she said in a shaking voice, "and I'm here to see Chris. I mean Douglas Christopher Thomas." As she struggled to get the words out, Laura extended her hand with a driver's license tightly gripped between her fingers. She struggled to regain her composure. "*I don't want to look scared*," she thought. "*They might not let me visit if I look scared.*"

The corrections officer behind the counter gave Laura a blank stare. "You can have a seat." As Laura turned to the row of chairs, the officer continued. "Who are you here to see?" *"He is wondering why I'm here,"* thought Laura. *"Maybe I don't look like I belong."* Turning back and facing the officer, she repeated "Douglas Christopher Thomas." Then Laura added, in a low voice "on death row." Laura watched as the officer looked through an official visitor's list, his eyes occasionally looking up from the sheets of paper and scanning Laura's face. As the minutes passed, Laura started to feel a cold panic in the pit of her stomach: *"Do they always have these problems for visitors of death row inmates?"* She wondered if family members experienced this trouble as well, remembering that Margaret had mentioned something like this.

As corrections officers escorted family members through metal detectors, Laura felt as if all the eyes in the waiting room focused on her face and her cheeks burned. The officer concluded scanning the papers. "Ma'am, you are not on the list to visit inmate Thomas." Laura was stunned, and her words were jumbled when she spoke. "No, I am. I received something in the mail from the warden giving me clearance. Is this the same list as Mecklenburg?" The officer indicated that it was, flipping back through the pages as if Laura's name might magically appear. "My name has to be there," Laura continued, in a panicked voice. "I drove a long way, and Chris is waiting for me." The officer was not persuaded.

As Laura turned from the counter, she willed herself not to cry. *"He's waiting for me,"* she thought. *"Chris is alone and waiting for me."* Laura returned to the counter. "Can you at least get a message to Chris and let him know that I'm not coming?" The officer stared at Laura, as if she has asked him to release Chris into her custody. Finally, the officer spoke, "Well, I don't know." Feeling desperate, Laura continued. "Chris will be worried. He is expecting me and will think I've had an accident." The thought occured to Laura that she was more afraid that Chris would think that she backed out of the visit. With a sigh, the officer nodded and told Laura in a tired voice that he would pass along the message. He never did.

As Laura walked back into the bright sunshine, she shielded her eyes and scanned the prison. She could see the narrow windows cut in the face of the prison walls, and she wondered if the cells in death row had windows. *"Maybe Chris has a window,"* she thought. *"Maybe he can see me and know that I came."* She stood next to her car for a new minutes, hoping and praying that Chris knew she was there. In the next few months, Laura tried to get onto the visitors' list, but she was unsuccessful. Ironically, it would be the fact that Laura did not visit Chris on death row that would lead to a dramatic new chapter in their relationship in the last months of Chris's life.

As the years passed, Chris maintained a thin lifeline to the outside world. His mother still faithfully visited, and a small group of family members and friends continued to write and call. Sadly, Marie Deans was no longer a constant presence in Chris's life. The Virginia Coalition on Jails and Prisons closed its doors in 1993, the victim of a lack of funds.[129] While Marie continued to work as a mitigation specialist, she was exhausted and broke after having devoted her life to hundreds of death penalty trials and appeals. Marie could no longer afford to spend thousands of dollars a month accepting collect calls from prison inmates, and as the 1990s drew to a close, she was no longer traveling to Virginia's death row.

In the last two years on death row, however, a new woman came into Chris's life. Shortly after his move to the new death row at Sussex I, Chris was visited by Glenda Corbin. Despite Jessica Wiseman's demand that Chris isolate himself and not write or call other women, Chris and Glenda had regularly corresponded over the years. On a few occasions Glenda visited Chris at Mecklenburg, and on August 28, 1998, Glenda and Brenda Marshall came to see Chris Thomas at his new home at Sussex I. During the emotional visit, Chris proposed marriage. Glenda immediately accepted the proposal, later explaining, "All of my life, I wanted to be with him." Glenda began making weekly visits to death row, and on February 17, 1999, Glenda and Chris were married during a 15-minute contact visit in which the bride and groom were permitted to hold hands, take pictures, and kiss for the first time. There were neither presents nor wedding cake during the short ceremony, and the guests—their respective mothers—were outnumbered by the five correctional officers present.

In the hours before his June 1999 execution date, Chris wrote to Glenda and expressed his love and appreciation for his new life. Referring to her as "my light, my life, my one sliver of hope and happiness in this otherwise cruel and cold world I live in behind these walls," Chris wrote that before their relationship he had "all but given up on ever feeling love again":

> There are so many things I must thank you for, but I hardly know where to begin. I must thank you for listening to me patiently, with love and compassion. Encouraging me when I was depressed—as only you could

in your own special lil [*sic*] way! Laughing with me when I was happy, correcting me when I was wrong, praising me on the very few occasions I was right. Smile! Your gentle soothing voice, filled with compassion, will forever ring in my heart and ears. You could always wash away any feelings of anger and frustration for you, *Only you*, had that power. I guess my point is, you reminded me of my humanity and brought it out in me. You taught *me* to see beauty where there was none. To cherish tender moments and hold onto them in the bad times. In a sense honey, you *were* and *are* my salvation!

Indirectly acknowledging his pending execution, Chris promised Glenda that death would not end the love that he felt for his new wife. "If I pass from this earth, the love I feel for you will NEVER END but rather grow stronger with each passing day. As hard as this may be, don't cry for me if I die sweetheart, for you must know that I will NEVER leave you." Finally, Chris added that, in death, he would continue to watch over Glenda: "[W]hen you're alone and depressed or in need of comfort, be sure that I'll be there. You may be alone in a room and merely feel my presence, whatever the case may be, I'll watch over you as you have watched over me."

On one level, Chris's "goodbye" letter to Glenda contains echoes of the overheated, immature, and dramatic correspondence that had passed between Chris and Jessica. One cannot deny, however, that real emotion shines through the purple prose. As curious as it may seem, the practice of death row males romancing and sometimes marrying non-inmate females is not uncommon in Virginia. Five years before, Virginia Department of Corrections officials were red-faced when death row psychologist Caroline Schloss became romantically linked with notorious death row inmate Willie Lloyd Turner[130] (they couldn't get married because Lloyd had married another woman while in prison), and in 1997 Virginia death row inmate Joseph O'Dell married Lori Urs, a volunteer working on his appeals, on the day of his execution.[131] The wedding ceremony was attended by Sister Helen Prejean, who was in Virginia and frantically working to stop O'Dell's execution. In fact, the other juvenile offender on death row with Chris Thomas — Steven Roach — also got married to a pen pal three months after Chris's marriage to Glenda.[132]

Nor is the phenomenon of love blooming on death row unique to Virginia.[133] One of the most startling examples of this practice can be found in the case of California serial killer Richard Ramirez, (aka the "Night Stalker"), a man convicted of thirteen murders who wooed multiple women after his conviction, eventually marrying a journalist.[134] One of Ramirez's fellow death row inmates is Scott Peterson, the California fertilizer salesman convicted of murdering his wife, Laci Peterson, and their unborn child while simultaneously wooing a massage therapist. On the first day of Peterson's arrival on death row, "three dozen phone calls came into the warden's office . . . women were pleading for his mailing address, and one smitten 18-year-old said she wanted to marry him."[135] In short, California prison officials estimate that each year approximately five of their death row inmates tie the knot.[136]

Why would a rational woman be romantically attracted to a man who will never leave prison? Certainly some women are sincerely touched by an inmate's claims of innocence and develop true feelings of love despite the death row inmate's past crimes and looming execution, but these emotions do not explain the high number of prison romances. Fascinated by the phenomenon of death row inmates and "lifers" who woo and marry women on the outside, author Sheila Isenberg interviewed countless women who, in her words, "love men who kill." From these in-depth conversations, Isenberg found that many—albeit not all—of the women possessed similar characteristics. Referring to the women as "little girls lost," Isenberg writes that the majority of her interviewees came from "dysfunctional families where they were victims of abuse [emotional, physical, and/or sexual] at the hands of harsh, dictatorial fathers aided by passive mothers."[137] Having made the mistake of being drawn to men on the outside that shared their fathers' destructive traits and abusive behavior, Isenberg suggests that these women are attracted to killers, who, because of their incarcerated status, are "safe" companions. Locked away in prison, these men cannot demand a physical relationship (contact visits are limited and closely monitored) and remain obsessively devoted to the women who are their sole connections to the outside world. The relationships also fulfill the need that many of these women have for drama, for the dangers of prison and the taboo nature of the relationship provide endless excitement.

Isenberg believes that many of the women she interviewed are searching for the loving and devoted father that they never had. That is, they create an elaborate image of the perfect father figure, and then graft it onto their incarcerated Romeos: "The men they love are not real; they are fantasies created by the women's psychological and emotional needs."[138] The women pick incarcerated felons as the object of their fantasies not only because of the control they have over the men, but because of their own low self-esteem. "Women who love convicted killers are partly attracted to these men because, subconsciously, they want to remain victims. The women are aware, on some deep level, that they are being used . . . [but] these women are so convinced they should remain victims because they don't deserve anything better that they maintain the fiction that they are happy."[139] The women must deny that the men are unrepentant killers in order to make the fantasy work, and Isenberg finds that the interviewees often create elaborate stories to explain away or justify the men's criminal behavior. Many of the cons are skilled manipulators and are often eager to play along with the game in order to maintain a modicum of control.

We are *not* suggesting that Glenda fit this profile. Unlike the majority of the women interviewed by Sheila Isenberg, Glenda knew Chris prior to the murders and his incarceration and by all accounts felt genuine affection for him. Whatever Glenda Corbin Thomas's motivations for marrying Chris, however, she must have known in her heart that the most likely outcome was widowhood.

The year 1999 marked Chris's last full year on death row, and the pace of executions continued to accelerate. During that year, Chris watched a record number of Virginia inmates be executed. Mark Sheppard on January 20, 1999. Tony Fry on February 2, 1999. George Quesinberry on March 9, 1999. *David Lee Fisher* on March 25, 1999. Carl Chichester on April 13, 1999. Arthur Jenkins on April 20, 1999. Eric Payne on April 28, 1999. Ronald Yeatts on April 29, 1999. Thomas Strickler on July 21, 1999. Marlon Williams on August 17, 1999. Everett Mueller on September 16, 1999. Jason Joseph on October 19, 1999. Thomas Royal, Jr. on November 9, 1999. Andre Graham on December 9, 1999. In all, during Chris's eight years on death row the Commonwealth of Virginia executed approximately sixty inmates. Granted, Chris knew only a small portion of these men. Nevertheless, the emotional and psychological toll of watching the men on the row steadily march toward their executions—knowing that the number of men before him was dwindling—aged and hardened Chris.

6

Prelude to an Execution

As a general rule, a man is undone by waiting for capital punishment well before he dies. Two deaths are inflicted on him, the first being worse than the second, whereas he killed but once. Compared to such torture, the penalty of retaliation seems like a civilized law.

ALBERT CAMUS

For eight years, Chris Thomas sat in his death row cell and contemplated his crimes and his future execution. The bloody and jagged images of the Wiseman home were forever seared into his memory, and at night they came to Chris in his dreams. As Chris struggled to survive on death row, remorse and depression were familiar companions. Hope is a rare and elusive commodity on death row, and Chris's fragile optimism faded as the months passed and his legal appeals failed. Faced with the grim and unchanging face of death row, and haunted by the looming specter of death, Chris again turned to drugs and alcohol to deaden his pain. At times the reality of his situation became too much to bear, and Chris erupted in childish and foolish acts of vandalism and juvenile behavior—refusing an order to return to his cell or burning his mattress. The episodes ended with Chris in isolation, no phone or commissary privileges, thrown deeper into a world of quiet desperation and his own personal hell.

FIGURE 15.
An older Chris Thomas on death row. Photograph courtesy of the Associated Press.

Jessica Wiseman and her steady stream of letters were no longer part of his life, and as the years rolled by, Chris's contact with the outside world narrowed to a few family members and friends. With his transfer to Virginia's new death row at Sussex I in August 1998, Chris found himself even more isolated. Gone were meals in the common pod area, card games with fellow inmates, basketball games, and homemade wine. To the young man who loved the outdoors, being locked down in his small cell twenty-three hours a day felt like being buried alive. As he stared at the walls of the 6-foot by 9-foot cell, speculation as to the time, place, and method of his death was Chris's constant but unwelcome companion. The inescapable fact of his death was constantly reinforced by the whispered stories of botched executions, the steady turnover of the death row population, and the loss of inmates whom Chris now considered to be friends. As Chris prepared for his journey to the death house in June 1999, thoughts of his pending execution became an all-consuming nightmare. What would he find in the death house? Would he be able to walk to his death with dignity and strength? Did he want to die by "the needle" or by "the chair"? Would it hurt? And what waited beyond death?

FIGURE 16. *Chris Thomas with his father, his father's wife, and his mother in the visiting room of the death house at the Greensville Correction Center, June 1999. Photograph courtesy of the Thomas family.*

As in many other death penalty states, the preferred method of execution in the Commonwealth of Virginia in the eighteenth and nineteenth century was hanging. Until the early twentieth century, the responsibility for meting out this punishment lay with the sheriff in the city or county in which the offense took place. The location of the execution varied by locality and was left to the discretion of the sheriff:

> In Richmond [Virginia], hangings were frequent enough to result in the use of a "usual place of execution. This was a small clearing, surrounded by pines and undergrowth, just north of the intersection of today's Fifteenth and Broad streets." An early map of the city shows the gallows sharing this site with the "negroes' burial ground," an indication of the race of most subjects of this penalty.[1]

Many executions were highly publicized — if not festive — events attended by hundreds of people. "To convey that message of terror to the greatest number required careful management of the process by which criminals were put to death," writes historian Stuart Banner. "Most clearly, an execution had to be a public event, open to anyone wishing to attend. . . . By locating executions in open spaces affording views to large numbers of people, and by scheduling them in the daytime to maximize visibility and convenience for spectators, officials sought to broadcast terror as widely as possible."[2]

In 1908 the Virginia General Assembly decided to transfer the authority to execute inmates to the Virginia Department of Corrections, which meant that inmates would be housed and executed in a single location. At the time, it was hoped that the transfer of executions to the state penitentiary "would free the various communities of the excitement, the morbid curiosity and the maudlin sentiment connected therewith."[3] What is unclear is whether Virginia's public servants had concluded that public executions no longer had a deterrent effect, or that the "morbid curiosity" and "maudlin sentiment" evidenced by those citizens who delighted in public executions turned the stomach of even the staunchest "law and order" politician. Hiding death away, thus denying citizens the chance to hear the snap of the neck and to see the macabre dance of the dying man at the end of the noose, may have also had the effect of making state-sanctioned executions easier for the general population to support. John D. Bessler, however, points to an editorial in a contemporary issue of the *Richmond Times-Dispatch* to support his argument that racism also placed a part in the decision to eliminate public executions:

> The *Times-Dispatch* had long contended that the publicity, the excitement and the general hurrah-and-holiday air attending the old-time hanging were a positive allurement to the negro. His strong theatrical sense reveled in a final melodrama in which he was the conspicuous central figure. The electric execution wholly does away with that. The time set for turning on the death current is unannounced, the public is rigorously eluded, and the whole affair is conducted with secrecy and mystery, well calculated to inspire terror in the heart of the superstitious African.[4]

Not everybody liked the change. "[A] few state senators opposed Virginia's private execution law because 'local hangings served to impress the negroes'" and deter crime.[5]

A more grim and forbidding location for the death house could not have been selected. Since 1797, the Commonwealth of Virginia incarcerated its prisoners at a multibuilding complex formally named the Virginia State Penitentiary, but nicknamed "the Walls" by the inmates. The original penitentiary occupied a three-story, horseshoe-shaped building with arched colonnades designed by architect Benjamin Latrobe, whose other design credits include the United States Capitol. At the time of its construction, Virginia politicians, such as Thomas Jefferson, and reformers alike lauded the new penitentiary as the crown jewel of a new, progressive penal system that would replace Virginia's "bloody code" of executions and physical beatings. Their praise, however, was premature, and the penitentiary soon became known for its whippings, disease, filth, and violence. Additional buildings were added to the site as Virginia's demands for human warehouses grew. Well into the twentieth century the dungeons that lay hidden under Benjamin Latrobe's graceful architecture were used for solitary confinement, where inmates suffered both the lash and a diet of bread and water.[6]

Latrobe's original creation was demolished in 1928, and by the middle of the twentieth century the penitentiary stretched across sixteen acres in downtown Richmond and was composed of three massive, aging cellblocks, a prison library, an industry building (in which inmates made license plates), guard towers, and a power plant topped with a 150-foot tower. Virginia continued to use the site to house its worst offenders until 1990, when the sheer age of the buildings, combined with lawsuits over conditions of confinement, dictated that it be abandoned. Newspaper editorials universally hailed the closing of the penitentiary, which they described as "a vestigial beast from another age,"[7] a "living museum of society's most humane and most cruel notions about how to treat lawbreakers,"[8] "a colossus of peeling paint, rusted metal and pigeon dung,"[9] and a "'dinosaur with gangrene.'"[10] "That 190-year-old horror should have been put out of its misery decades ago," observed the *Roanoke Times*. "Inmates who remain—674 of them—are locked in their cells 22 hours a day (the locks, say prison officials, are so old that frequent locking and unlocking might break them). Prisoners allegedly have been denied rags and buckets to clean their filthy cells, [or] roach traps to kill the teeming bugs."[11]

In 1908, however, the penitentiary was the cornerstone of Virginia's growing prison system, and the new death house was placed in the basement of what was designated as the "A-building." Built in 1905, A-building was once hailed as a modern wonder that boasted both running water and electricity as well as graceful cupolas along its roofline. Although the building was only three years old when it became the new home of the death house, A-building aged as poorly as its prisoners; the overcrowded, inadequately maintained building was described as "a gulag of closet-sized cells, rusting steel bars, crumbling masonry and cracked paint."[12] The death house remained in the basement of A-building at the aging state penitentiary until 1991, a year after the penitentiary itself was finally closed.

As the authority to carry out executions was transferred to the Department of Corrections, the hangman's gallows was replaced with a brand-new, state-of-the-art electric chair. Considered to be a more modern and humane method of execution, Virginia became the first southern state to purchase an electric chair. The electrical system for the sturdy oak chair was designed and manufactured by the Adams Electric Company at a cost of $7,000, and the company made the following promise in its promotional materials: "All appliances used in the construction of this Electrocuting Plant have been designed with the utmost care, and the makers guarantee absolute reliability. The workmanship is of the best, and the entire outfit presents an elegant appearance notwithstanding the fact that it is to be used to despatch [sic] condemned murderers into eternity."[13] Legend has it that the oak chair itself was built by Virginia prisoners. Corrections officials hoped that the chair would replace the inexact science of the hangman's noose—a practice that more often slowly and painfully strangled its victims than cleanly and painlessly dispatched them.

The state wasted no time installing the electric chair in the basement of the A-building and testing its new killing machine. At 7:32 A.M. on October 13, 1908, twenty-two-year-old Henry Smith, a black man convicted of raping a seventy-six-year-old white woman, became the first Virginia prisoner to be executed in the electric chair. Newspaper accounts reported that the execution "was a success in every way," and Virginia penitentiary doctor Dr. Charles V. Carrington lauded the new electric chair as "a swift, sure, solemn and awe-inspiring mode of punishment, and to my mind is infinitely more humane than hanging."[14] The Virginia penal system embraced its new killing machine, and over the next fifty-four years 247 people (208 of them black) were executed in Virginia's electric chair. At least twenty-four of those executions were "double executions"; that is, executions taking place on the same day;[15] on February 2, 1951, Virginia set a record by electrocuting five men in a single day.[16]

Virginia's last execution in the "premodern" death penalty era was on March 2, 1962, when Carroll L. Garland was executed for the murder of a gas station employee. The electric chair sat silent and brooding in its underground lair for the next twenty years, as the federal and state courts struggled with lawsuits challenging the constitutionality of the death penalty. With the United States Supreme Court's decision in *Gregg v. Georgia* in 1976,[17] states resumed executions. Virginia, however, faced a problem: the electric chair had fallen into disrepair and no current members of the Department of Corrections had ever conducted an execution. Undaunted, the warden of the Virginia State Penitentiary researched the execution protocols of other states; he gussied up the old electric chair with new leather straps and a copper headpiece; replaced the old, artificial sponges used to conduct the electrical current through the body with natural sea sponges to reduce the possibility of fire;[18] purchased a new transformer; and drilled his volunteer team of executioners.

While the details of execution protocols are rarely shared with the public, in 1992 a lawsuit challenging the constitutionality of the electric chair was filed in federal court in Virginia. The pleadings provided a detailed description of the procedures followed by the Virginia Department of Corrections in the early 1990s, including the following:

> Virginia procedures call for a condemned man to be strapped to the chair at his arms, legs and chest. A mask is placed over his face and he is made to wear a diaper. His head is shaved, and a sponge soaked in salt water to improve conductivity is placed between the electrode and his head. A second sponge and electrode is connected to his leg. According to the suit, ". . . the avowed objective of the [state] is to pass sufficient current through the body and brain of the condemned person to render him brain dead or at least unconscious without unduly disfiguring the body." "However, no one knows the amount of voltage needed to render the condemned person instantaneously unconscious and the law leaves it up" to the department of corrections to decide. The amount of voltage used—and purpose of the mask, diaper and other equipment—is "to kill him without causing his body to explode and without allowing the witnesses to see indicia of suffering on his part," the suit alleges.[19]

Supporters of the electric chair claimed that the first jolt of electricity passed through the brain, causing unconsciousness and instantaneous brain death. The lawyers challenging electrocution believed differently. "Modern evidence, however, shows that electrical current seeks the path of least resistance and most of the current passes through his skin—not the skull or brain—on the way to the leg. . . . The effect is to burn the condemned person's skin at extreme temperature while he is awake and conscious for an indeterminate period," the suit alleged.[20] The plaintiffs, however, failed to convince the court that the electric chair violated the Eighth Amendment's prohibition against cruel and unusual punishment, and Virginia continued to use the electric chair well into the twenty-first century.

After a twenty-year hiatus, the electric chair roared to life again on August 10, 1982, when former Portsmouth police officer Frank J. Coppola was executed for the brutal murder of a forty-five-year-old woman. Given the long duration between executions, Coppola's final words to the execution team were macabre but arguably fitting: "fire it up." An attorney later gave the following account of what happened as the executioners administered the second planned jolt of electricity:

> I observed smoke rising to the ceiling in sufficient amounts to fill the entire death chamber with a smoky haze. . . . Although I was in an isolated booth with other witnesses separated from the death chamber by glass and wall, I could smell an acrid odor that I assume was the smell of burning flesh. During the second application of current, a sizzling sound could be heard that sounded like cooking flesh.[21]

No members of the media were allowed to witness Coppola's execution, and the facts surrounding his electrocution were not generally known by the public.

With Coppola's "successful" execution, Virginia ushered in another new change: executing prisoners at 11:00 P.M. rather than at dawn. Explained the warden of the state penitentiary, "'To do it in the morning, it made it look like you couldn't wait to get the guy executed.'"[22] Of course, executing prisoners in the dead of night also limited the number of protestors outside of "the Walls."

Although the Virginia penitentiary itself closed in the fall of 1990, the electric chair remained at the penitentiary, and in operation, until the following spring. With the prisoners removed from the penitentiary, and the security risk to visitors negligible, local school officials somehow convinced both themselves and parents that giving eighth graders tours of Virginia's death house constituted an educational and entertaining field trip. The trip by twenty-nine eighth graders was sponsored by a local Kiwanis Club. The students were shown the mask, helmet, and leg brace used to electrocute the inmates, and were allowed to peek into the death chamber and see the electric chair. "'This is not a scared-straight program,' said Andre Terrangi, administrative assistant to the warden. 'This is a reality program.'"[23]

The children who toured Virginia's death house in the winter of 1991 were not visiting a museum, but a fully operational facility; the death house had not been formally retired, and officials were carefully preparing for the February 22, 1991, execution of Joe Giarratano. At the time Giarratano was one of the highest-profile death row inmates in the country, and Giarratano had the surreal experience of being the only prisoner in the hulking state penitentiary as he sat in the death house and prayed for clemency. Social activist Mike Farrell recalls visiting Giarratano in the death house, sitting around a battered table with Giarratano, Marie Deans, and attorney Richard Burr:

> As we gathered our stuff, Dick asked Joe to tell me about the table. "Oh, this?" Joe asked, pointing down at the table around which we had been sitting. Dick nodded, and Joe said, "This is the cooling table." After being electrocuted, his [Joe's] body would be too hot to touch. Guards with asbestos gloves would quickly lift him out of the chair and lay him on this very table until he was cool enough to be moved.[24]

What Giarratano failed to mention: when the body of the executed prisoner was first laid on the table, the guards used sandbags to break the fused joints in the decedent's arms and legs. Scholars talk about the isolating nature of the death house, but it's difficult to imagine the feelings of loneliness that Giarratano felt as he sat around the cooling table as the last remaining prisoner in the rusting hulk of the state penitentiary. Governor Douglas Wilder subsequently pardoned Giarratano, thus giving Buddy Earl Justus the dubious distinction of being the last prisoner to be executed in the vacant penitentiary at 11:06 P.M. on December 13, 1990. By the time the electric chair was finally packed up and moved to a new home in the spring of 1991, it had executed 246 men (some juveniles) and one juvenile female.

As part of a statewide prison building boom, a new, state-of-the-art "megaprison," named the Greensville Correctional Center, was built in Jarratt, Virginia, in 1990. Designed to hold approximately two thousand inmates, prison officials publicly stated that the concrete structure was deliberately fashioned to look "somewhat hard and somewhat stark." Such a design was in keeping with a new attitude of Virginia correctional officers that the conditions of incarceration were as much a part of an inmate's punishment as the term of incarceration itself. A newspaper described the facility as follows:

The Greensville complex will be laid out in a giant hexagon with each side measuring 1,200 feet. The perimeter will be surrounded by two walls, 12 feet high and 30 feet apart. The outer wall will be covered with razor wire; the inner wall will contain electronic sensors that detect certain types of movement. Such sensors are already in place at the prison in Brunswick County. At each corner of the hexagon, just outside the outer wall, will stand a 52-foot guard tower. The location of the towers affords the guards lines of unimpeded vision throughout the complex. . . . The Greensville complex will be essentially three independent prisons, each containing about 500 prisoners and its own day rooms, classrooms, shop facilities and gym. There will also be a maximum security unit that can hold 200.[25]

Like many of Virginia's prisons, the Greensville Correctional Center was built in a remote area of southeastern Virginia. The facility is located in Jarratt, Virginia, a tiny town whose population hovers around five hundred people. At one time the town's economy was dependent upon a large Johns-Manville manufacturing plant, but today many of its residents rely, directly or indirectly, upon the tax dollars spent to operate the massive correctional complex. Some of the residents are ambivalent about having the death house in their community, and a few community members claimed that the town was "duped" by the Department of Corrections. When the plans for the new prison were announced, many hoped that the new facility would bring needed jobs and revenue to the economically depressed town. It was not until well into the construction process, however, that the citizens of Jarratt learned that their town would also be the new home for the state's electric chair. "We were sold a bill of goods," commented a local businessman. "Anytime anybody asked them about the death house, they said, 'We don't have any plans to move it here at this time.' Course, after that last brick was laid, that all changed."[26]

The plans for the Greensville Correctional Center placed the death house next to the prison's maximum security unit. The death house is a single-story, 4,000-square-foot building that contains three cells, a witness room, visitation areas for contact and noncontact visits, and the death chamber. A television is mounted on the wall opposite the three cells. Inside the death house, the predominant color is a depressing gray—including the cells and the walls of the death chamber—and the floors are covered with functional but cold tile.[27] One suspects that the color scheme was purposefully selected to help

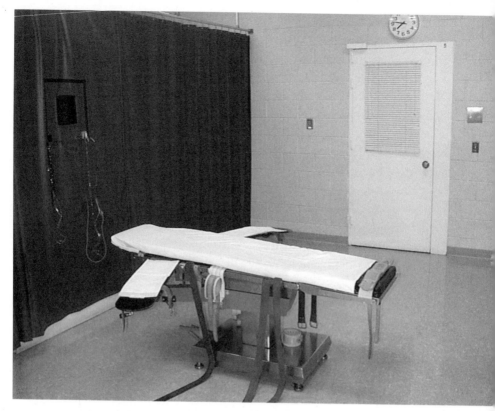

FIGURE 17. *The death house at the Greensville Correction Center in Jarratt, Virginia. Photograph courtesy of the Associated Press.*

subdue, not uplift the spirits of its temporary residents. "'This is the gloomiest place I've ever been in my life,'" remarked inmate Derick Peterson during a telephone interview from the death house. "'This place is a hellhole — sitting down here waiting to die. Everything is gray — the paint, the bars, the walls. It's like it's raining every day in this [expletive].'"²⁸ Outside, a fence topped with razor wire encircles the death house in order to separate it from the general population of the prison.

In the spring of 1991, the state's solid oak electric chair quietly traveled from the hulking ruins of the state penitentiary to the Greensville Correctional Center. The electric chair had been rewired prior to its trip, and Virginia corrections officials adopted a new procedure for administering the killing current. Abandoning the older practice of administering two 55-second surges of 2,500 volts of electricity seconds apart, the Department of Corrections decided to use a ten-second, 1,725-volt surge of electricity (to cause brain death) followed by a two-minute, 240-volt surge (to stop the heart).[29] At the time, corrections officials explained that one benefit of the new practice was that the lower voltage was less likely to burn the inmate's body.[30] At 11:00 P.M. on July 24, child rapist and murderer Albert Jay Clozza became the first inmate to be executed in the electric chair's new home in the death chamber at the Greensville Correctional Center. Witnesses to the execution reported that the newly rewired and refurbished electric chair efficiently dispatched Clozza. "'It was all very peaceful almost,'" commented a local television reporter. "'It wasn't violent at all.'"[31] There were no reports of smoke, flames, or the smell of burning flesh.

One of the witnesses observing the execution on that hot July evening was Phillip Hamilton, a member of Virginia's General Assembly. Earlier in the year Hamilton had introduced a bill to make lethal injection the state's method of execution. Hamilton proposed the legislation after the electrocution of Virginia inmate Wilbert Lee Evans in October 1990, an electrocution that caused Evans to excessively bleed from his nose. After the "botched" execution of Evans, Hamilton told newspaper reporters. "'The electric chair has been in Virginia since 1908. . . . In carrying out this state function . . . we can do it in a more modern and what I perceive is a less torturous way.'"[32] Hamilton's reform efforts were defeated, and he decided to attend Clozza's execution as a fact-finding mission.

Although the debate over lethal injection was not revived with the seemingly painless execution of Clozza, it was immediately renewed when the next inmate to sit in Virginia's electric chair, Derick Lynn Peterson, required two cycles of electricity before being pronounced dead. After the first jolt of 1,750 volts of electricity and the subsequent second jolt of 250 volts were administered through his body, a prison doctor found that Peterson had a pulse. After five minutes, the doctor reported that Peterson was still alive. A newspaper reporter wrote that witnesses gasped at the news, and a Virginia Department of Corrections official reassured them that "'the brain is dead— the doctor is listening to the heart.'" Adds the reporter: "the witnesses are not comforted."[33] The electric chair was fired up again, and the second cycle of electricity killed Peterson.

Concern was immediately expressed that the electric chair had not functioned properly, although defensive prison officials quickly claimed that

Peterson had suffered instantaneous brain death and was not in physical pain. "'We're dealing with brand new equipment,'" Virginia Department of Corrections Edward Murray said. "'I think you have to make adjustments as you use the equipment.'"[34] To death penalty opponents, the execution of Derick Peterson was called a "horrible and inhumane" act. "'It's like stabbing someone in the heart and, if they don't die, stabbing them again to make sure they're dead,'" a local politician commented. Delegate Phillip Hamilton stated, "'I've never heard of having to lethally inject someone twice'" and announced that he would likely reintroduce the lethal injection legislation.[35] Questions surrounding the effectiveness of the electric chair, and tales of electrocutions gone awry, are not unique to Virginia. Florida alone witnessed three "botched" electrocutions in the 1990s, two in which flames shot from the masks worn by the inmates.[36]

In retrospect, the execution of Derick Peterson triggered a change in the political winds in Virginia regarding lethal injection. By January 1992, an informal poll taken by the *Richmond Times-Dispatch* revealed that a majority of the members of the General Assembly who responded to the survey favored lethal injection over execution;[37] on January 16, 1992, new legislation was introduced to give inmates the option of either electrocution or lethal injection. This newest bill died in committee, but bills proposing the adoption of lethal injection continued to be submitted by Phillip Hamilton in subsequent sessions. Additionally, lawsuits arguing against the constitutionality of the electric chair were filed against the Virginia Department of Corrections. It would not be until February 1994, however, that the Virginia General Assembly passed legislation giving inmates a choice between lethal injection or electrocution.

On January 24, 1995, Dana Ray Edmonds became the first Virginia inmate executed by lethal injection. Edmonds was killed in the Virginia death chamber with a fatal cocktail of three drugs: sodium thiopental, pancuronium bromide, and potassium chloride. Proponents of lethal injection claim that the barbiturate sodium thiopental, if administered properly, renders the inmate completely unconscious before the pancuronium bromide paralyzes him and the potassium chloride stops his heart. The drugs are administered intravenously through the inmate's arm, with a backup IV in the second arm in case the first IV malfunctions. The flow of chemicals is triggered by two Department of Corrections officials, who stand in the Virginia death house behind a second blue curtain so as to remain anonymous. Also hidden behind the curtain is the electric chair. While no flashing light or buzzer signals the start of the process, witnesses report that the IV tube wiggles and moves slightly as the liquid passes through it. A heart monitor attached to the inmate's chest tells the execution team when he has expired. The sight of the inmate, with his arms spread out, uncomfortably reminds many witnesses of a crucifixion.

To the official witnesses of Virginia's first lethal injection, Edmonds appeared to die peacefully. The witnesses watched Edmonds walk to the steel gurney that served as his deathbed. Clad in a blue shirt, blue denim pants, white socks and flip-flop shower slippers, he was secured to the gurney with sturdy brown leather straps. A dark blue curtain was pulled to shield the witnesses from the sight of the IV lines being inserted; when the curtain was pulled back, Edmonds lay motionless. "When the chemicals were administered, Edmonds' mouth moved slightly as he twitched his feet. His chest heaved up and down for a few moments but then there was little movement except slight breathing for about 10 minutes."[38]

The success of lethal injection was trumpeted in an editorial in the Newport News *Daily Press*: "There was no blood, no smell of burned flesh, no indication he felt anything more than a flicker of pain from the injection itself. Edmonds surely felt less pain than did his victim, a Danville grocer whose skull was bashed with a brick and whose throat was cut in 1983." As for the argument that Edmonds had suffered from his years on death row, the editorial writer dismissed it: "Capital punishment is not intended to torment the condemned; its purpose is punishment of the guilty and deterrence of others. What is cruel and inhumane about it is not the execution itself but the waiting. However, if that is what is bothering the condemned man, he can shorten the appeals process himself."[39] In short, if an inmate does not care for life on death row, then he can forfeit his legal right to appellate review—despite whatever legitimate claims he may have—and end his pain. Chris Thomas had been on death row with Edmonds for four years, and he undoubtedly followed the newspaper stories about the older man's death and this new method of execution. And he began a long internal debate as to how he wanted to be put to death.

Opponents of lethal injection argue that the drug used to render the inmate unconscious (sodium thiopental) does not always sufficiently anesthetize the inmate, and that the paralyzing effects of the second drug (pancuronium bromide) masks any pain that the inmate endures from the fatal heart attack caused by the potassium chlorate. In short, an inmate might be outwardly peaceful but inwardly conscious and fully capable of feeling pain while the heart convulses and stops. Moreover, critics of lethal injection question whether the execution teams have the medical expertise to properly insert the IV lines and administer the correct dosages of medication. While a temporary halt to execution by lethal injection occurred in late 2007 when the Supreme Court agreed to review the lethal injection protocols followed by Kentucky, in April 2008 the Court held that the procedure, if administered correctly, did not raise a substantial risk of harm and, therefore, did not violate the Eighth Amendment's ban of cruel and unusual punishment.[40] While Virginia's procedures differed slightly from Kentucky's—Virginia uses one gram fewer of sodium thiopental and uses a "rapid flow" method that prevents the execution teams from verifying that the inmate is unconscious before administering the second and third drugs—federal courts have held that these differences are insignificant.[41]

While lethal injection has survived constitutional challenge, some medical experts argue that the three-drug cocktail is inferior to what veterinarians administer every day to injured and dying pets: a single dose of a barbiturate. This distinction was recently highlighted in a speech given by Supreme Court Justice John Paul Stevens, who observed that in Kentucky it was illegal to euthanize racehorses with the same drugs used to execute Kentucky's prisoners owing to concerns about causing the animals unnecessary pain.[42]

More changes were to come to the execution process. Edmonds became the first Virginia inmate since the reinstitution of the death penalty to be executed at 9:00 P.M. rather than the 11:00 P.M. killing time adopted in 1982. The change had practical as well as legal reasons. Not only would an earlier execution time save the state from paying overtime to its employees; it decreased the likelihood that a last-second delay would drag the execution into the next day—which would subsequently require a new court order setting a new execution date. The thirty-six states that have the death penalty vary in their time of execution. Texas, which leads all states in the number of executions in the "modern" death penalty era, executes its prisoners at 6:00 P.M. Mississippi also begins the execution at 6:00 P.M., while Pennsylvania waits one hour later. Several states schedule their executions in the middle of the night, including Indiana (midnight), Oregon (midnight), Tennessee (1:00 A.M.), and Connecticut (2:01 A.M.). Ohio, like Virginia, executes its inmates at 9:00 P.M. Most states, however, do not publicly release information on their execution protocols—including the time of the execution.[43]

Another change that took place shortly before Virginia adopted lethal injection involved who would be permitted to witness an execution. When the Greensville death house was originally built, it contained only a single witness room. The room was two-tiered, with three rows of white plastic chairs and a white and blue sign reminding witnesses that they are required to sit during the execution. When Virginia Governor George Allen changed state policy to allow family members of the victim to attend executions in March 1994, a second witness room was built. This private room for family members has smoked-glass windows, making it impossible for either the official witnesses or the condemned inmate to see which family members, if any, are present. The change in policy met with the approval of many Virginia legislators and citizens, and the *Virginian-Pilot* stated that the "decision is a commendable gesture of regard for the feelings of people the system tends to forget." Noting that Governor Allen ordered family members be shielded from media scrutiny in their own private observation room, the editorial concluded that "[the media] restriction will stand him in good stead with the public, and with family members who see in their presence at the execution not a callous desire for vengeance but fitting homage to loved ones cut down by another's callous disregard for life."[44] Some would argue, however, that watching a scared inmate being put down like an old dog hardly qualifies as a "fitting homage" to anybody nor demonstrates an appropriate regard for life.

What had not changed was the section of state law that permitted ordinary citizens to apply to the Department of Corrections to serve as official witnesses at an execution. While some might shudder at the idea of voluntarily attending a governmental ceremony in which an individual is ritualistically killed, the Virginia Department of Corrections has never lacked for volunteers; indeed, some citizens return again and again to the death house. While defenders of the state law argue that it serves the critical function of permitting oversight of democratic government by its citizens, others assert it is a ghoulish opportunity for voyeurs to see a life snuffed out.

The motivations to witness an execution are as varied as the individuals themselves. One frequent volunteer is an Emporia, Virginia, carpet salesman who has attended fourteen executions and cheerfully recounted the details to a reporter. " 'Sometimes, you can hear the chair go NNNNNNNNNNN. You know, hear it hum,' he said, grinning. 'And sometimes, you can smell it a little bit, too.' "[45] Other volunteers have included a budding novelist who wanted material for his book, a commonwealth attorney who thought it was his duty to watch an execution before he decided to charge a defendant with capital murder, and a computer operator who believed that executions were faked. "'I didn't think they were really being executed,' he said. 'I thought they maybe were being used as guinea pigs for drug experiments.'" After witnessing the electrocution of inmate Roger Coleman, the aforementioned computer operator "said he would have liked to see the autopsy as final proof, but he is now convinced that executions actually are carried out."[46] Thankfully, he was not granted his wish to attend the autopsy.

The presence of volunteer witnesses and their poorly hidden enthusiasm may explain convicted murderer Kevin DeWayne Cardwell's final words as he lay on the execution gurney and stared into the witness room: "'Why was all them sick people looking at me through that glass?'"[47] In fact, the presence of gawking voyeurs reminds some of the eerie photographs of flocks of white families smiling broadly as they watch lynchings, and this practice surely constitutes a final assault on any human being's dignity. We are not aware of any editorials in major Virginia newspapers that—as they did with the decision to permit family members witness executions—have celebrated the practice of letting curious bystanders, conspiracy theorists, and budding novelists witness an inmate's last seconds of life.

Thus were the procedures and practices in June 1999, when a frightened Chris Thomas arrived at the death house at the Greensville Correctional Center in Jarratt, Virginia. He would not, however, be there alone. Fear had kept Laura Anderson from visiting Chris on death row, but she was now determined to be with her former student. Shortly before his transfer to the death house, Chris asked Laura to be his spiritual advisor. Although Laura did not completely understand the role of a spiritual advisor, Chris explained that it would permit her to visit him in the death house during his final days and hours. Laura agreed to Chris's request, but then found herself momentarily stymied as to how to get official approval to serve in this capacity.

In May 1999, Laura was a consecrated diaconal minister, but not an ordained member of the clergy in the Methodist church. As a diaconal minister, Laura was charged with serving outside of the church in a public service capacity; in Laura's case, this requirement was satisfied by her work as a school administrator for the Virginia Department of Correctional Education. After talking to Chris, Laura contacted the assistant warden at Greensville Correctional Center and asked to serve as Chris's spiritual advisor. Laura was quizzed about her qualifications—the assistant warden was puzzled by the difference between a diaconal and ordained minister—and was questioned about her relationship with Chris. Ironically, the fact that Laura had not visited Chris—despite her guilt and her multiple aborted attempts to see her former student—may have been a deciding factor, as friends cannot serve as spiritual advisors.

The role of a spiritual advisor is not defined by state law, and opinions on the proper function of a spiritual advisor are as varied as the men and women who voluntarily walk into the death house. Most Americans were introduced to the concept of a spiritual advisor through Sister Helen Prejean, the author of the book *Dead Man Walking*. In the book, Sister Helen recounts her experiences ministering to two inmates on Louisiana's death row. The book was made into a critically acclaimed movie directed by Tim Robbins and starring Susan Sarandon and Sean Penn; since the movie's release, Sister Helen has barnstormed across America in a one-woman campaign to abolish the death penalty.

In Virginia, the role of spiritual advisor evolved from the combined efforts of two individuals: Russ Ford and Marie Deans. Russ Ford graduated from Southeastern Seminar in 1977 and soon thereafter took a job as a prison chaplain with Chaplain Service, the nonprofit organization that provides chaplains to Virginia's prisons. Ford soon became the head of chaplains at the Mecklenburg Correctional Center (the home of death row from 1979 to 1998), and from 1985 to 1994 he attended nineteen executions. Repeated clashes with the Virginia Department of Corrections and funding problems led to Ford's leaving Chaplain Service in 1994.

Described as a "charismatic, intense, emotional, intuitive . . . and dramatic" preacher,[48] Ford thought it critical that the spiritual advisor come to the death house without a personal agenda. "'You can't bring answers to death row. They've got to arrive at the answers themselves,'" Ford stated in a 1994 interview. "'You have to understand, most of these men never went to church unless Grandma took them on Easter. Jesus has been a curse word.'"[49] Ford has been called a "spiritual pragmatist" who is conversant with mainstream Christianity, Buddhism, and Eastern mysticism. His goal as a spiritual advisor and guide is to help the inmates face what Ford refers to as "the monster"; that is, to grapple with their inner demons and face their deaths with dignity and understanding of self. It took Ford himself time to understand his role in the process. As a young prison chaplain Ford learned that inmates, like the terminally ill, went through the familiar stages of denial, anger, fear, and acceptance. Ford knew that he could not alter that process, but he believed that, through the fear and trauma, he could help the inmate achieve a higher level of self-awareness. One essential part of the movement toward self-enlightenment involved confession. "'Confession is one of the thresholds dying people come to, because the body needs to purge itself,'" argued Ford. "'The damaged, suppressed areas need expression. They have to come out.'"[50] To help the inmate pass through the fear and pain, Ford had to first create a bond of trust—not an easy task in an environment like death row where openness and vulnerability are eagerly exploited by predators.

In articulating what he believed to be the proper role of a spiritual advisor, Ford candidly admitted that he did not possess all the answers.

> [He] likens it to the spiritual journey in Dante's Divine Comedy. Dante visits souls in hell and purgatory on his way to heaven. Fellow poet Virgil is his guide. "I see myself as Virgil, a spiritual guide.... Virgil doesn't know all the routes and back roads to heaven, but he has traveled enough to know some of the signposts. I help the men on 'row' on their journeys. I can't show them the way. They have to find it for themselves. But I can help."[51]

As he helped the inmates along this proverbial road, Ford also fought to prevent the inmates from becoming walking dead men. "'The death is the punishment, not the journey to the chair,'" Ford explained. "'I tell them to walk alive to the death house, to stay alive, to be alive. To not die before your time. And be alive as you're walking to the chair. Be alive as you're sitting in the chair.'"[52]

As a spiritual guide, Ford did not shy away from brutal honesty and hard truths. If asked, he told the inmates exactly what awaited them in the death house. The ride from death row to the death house. The personnel who watched over the prisoner. The configuration of the building. The components of the electric chair. Ford called it "'demythologizing the death house.'"[53] One aspect of the demythologizing process, however, changed over time. When frightened prisoners asked Ford if electrocution was painful, Ford used to say that it was fast and painless. Ford used this stock answer until the night of the execution of Roger Coleman, who bristled at Ford's traditional response, "That's easy for you to say, Russ. Nobody knows. Nobody comes back, so we really just don't know."[54] After Coleman's execution, Ford no longer claimed to know whether the execution was painless. Instead, he simply quoted Roger Coleman.

Ford's techniques did not earn him many supporters among the administrators and corrections officers on Virginia's death row. "'There's a school of thought within the Department of Corrections that part of the punishment is us not doing this, that these men should die unaided,'" Ford observed. "'They teach them down at Greensville that we are the enemy.'"[55] Such criticism did not trouble Ford, who earnestly believed that he was following the teachings of the "first death row chaplain," Jesus Christ. Ford once explained to a reporter that Christ ministered to convicted thieves as he himself hung on the cross, sentenced to death by the state, and Ford went to death row to follow Christ's command to work with the outcast members of society. When asked why he spent his time ministering to the lowest of the low, Ford responded, "love thy enemy."

At Ford's side in the death house for many of the nineteen executions was Marie Deans. While Marie's first responsibility was gathering mitigation evidence to be used for inmates' appeals, more than thirty condemned men asked her to sit with them in the death house during the final hours of their lives. For Marie, the requests were impossible to decline. "Deans sees herself as a crutch for men facing execution; she hugs them, cajoles them, soothes them, trying to keep up their strength and hope and to give them a sense of worth. Some have given up filing appeals; Deans tries to whip the fight back into them."[56] Moreover, like Ford, Deans urged prisoners to confront their internal demons: "I want them to take responsibility, to know what they have done. . . . They can't change until they take responsibility. A lot of them will say to me, 'Tell me what I've done. I have no idea what I've done to the family of who I've killed.'"[57]

Both Ford and Deans spent countless hours in the death house, doing what they referred to as their "death work." "It involves spending the last few minutes of life with a man who can't quite believe he isn't going to be saved; listening to him talk about his wife, his mother, his victims; promising him they will tell his friends on the row that he faced death with dignity and courage. It means spending time in a place called the death house."[58] It is difficult to fathom the physical and emotional toll such work inflicts, which is perhaps why Deans once observed that one has to be a "courageous fool" to do what she and Ford did.

In trying to accurately summarize the extraordinary work that Deans performed on behalf of Virginia's inmates, a newspaper reporter spoke to Willie Leroy Jones—a man convicted of double murder and the fifteenth inmate that Deans would accompany to the death house.

"Without Marie Deans, there'd be no me, right?" said Jones over the telephone Monday afternoon. "They been trying to execute me the last eight years, right? She's the reason I hung on. She's been a friend to me. She's been the person I could call and talk to any time of day. I could always pick up the phone and call Marie, no matter how big or small the problem was." But Deans is no pushover, he said. "She won't tolerate no nonsense. 'You got to get in the books. Get in that law library, Willie. You got to get your act together, Willie.' She'd just sit down and use common sense," he said. "When someone does that, that's what means a lot to me, you know?"[59]

On the night before the scheduled date of Jones's execution, Deans spent five hours in the death house with him. She returned the next day. When Jones's final meal arrived, he told Marie that he had ordered the dinner for her. It was widely known both inside and outside of death row that Marie largely subsisted on coffee and Marlboro cigarettes, and Jones insisted that she eat:

He ordered steak, baked potato and salad, and he said, "I want you to eat. I'm going to sit here and watch you eat," Deans said. Stunned, Deans tried to honor his wishes. "The potato was huge. I said, 'I can't eat that.' So I broke it like you break bread and we all ate," she said. "It was like a communion."[60]

Deans and Ford did not pass through the death house unscathed. They both suffered from symptoms that they attributed to post-traumatic stress disorder, including insomnia, nightmares of executions, and crying fits.[61] Deans often found herself hurdled into future, not past memories: "'[P]eople have flashbacks — I began to have flash-forwards. When I'd be working with a prisoner, I'd see him sitting in the electric chair. A psychiatrist friend wanted me to back off from going to the death house for my own good.'"[62] Ultimately, it would be a lack of funds, not "flash-forwards" or extreme stress, that drove Deans from her death work.

What is important to appreciate is that not all spiritual advisors follow the approach of a Russ Ford or Marie Deans. The Department of Corrections would prefer that the chaplain or spiritual advisor help keep the inmate calm and compliant during the final hours in the death house. Idle chit-chat and superficial conversation that make the hands of the clock quickly spin are the order of the evening; introspection and deep feeling on the part of the inmate are not encouraged. Self-examination leads to emotion and unpredictable behavior, which run counter to the administration's wishes for a "clean" and efficient execution. Thus the spiritual advisor can wittingly or unwittingly become an extension of the execution team.

Moreover, some who voluntarily journey to the death house become blinded by their own religious beliefs and confuse what they believe is best — salvation through a particular religious path — with what the inmate truly wants or needs. This is not to say that spiritual growth and personal salvation are not legitimate goals, but rather that advisors must be cognizant that they are literally preaching to a captive audience. Finally, a few unfortunate souls seek out the position for the limelight that comes with ministering to the damned. One longtime spiritual advisor refers to these publicity seekers as "Bible notchers." Whether sincerely or cravenly motivated, both types of spiritual advisors bring their own agendas to the death house.

On Sunday, June 13, 1999, Laura and her husband, Ross, drove from their home outside of Charlottesville, Virginia, to the Greensville Correctional Center. The last time Laura had seen Chris, he was sitting in a courtroom as Laura testified at his sentencing hearing and tried to save his life. Now Chris was a twenty-six-year-old convicted murderer who had literally grown up on death row. To Laura, her relationship with Chris had evolved from a student-teacher association to a friendship in which Laura, as spiritual advisor, hoped to provide emotional support to Chris and, if he wanted, to share with him a religious message of hope and salvation.

Although Laura herself worked as an educational administrator in several different state prisons, she was still startled by the size of the Greensville Correctional Center and its elaborate security measures. Metal detectors. Concrete and razor wire. Rifles in the guard towers. Patdowns. A search of her Bible. Multiple logbooks. Repeated demands for her identification. The clanging of heavy metal doors. Laura was too distracted to count, but other visitors to the Greensville Correctional Center report that three different logbooks are signed, and eight different gates or locked doors are passed through, before a visitor arrives into the interior of the death house. After Laura passed through the first security checkpoint, she was driven in a prison van across a large compound to a small, one-story cinderblock building surrounded by a fence. In an odd way, Laura found herself surprised by the unassuming appearance of the death house. As she stared at the building, she thought, *"shouldn't a building in which the ultimate punishment is imposed look a little more imposing?"*

As the metal door to the death house slowly swung open, guided by some invisible hand or mechanism, and Laura crossed the threshold, her pulse quickened and she scanned the room for Chris. All she saw were more unsmiling correctional officers. A voice ordered Laura to empty her pockets, place her Bible on the table in front of her, and sign the visitor log. Another female officer appeared, and both Laura and her Bible were again searched for weapons and contraband. As Laura bent over and signed the log book, she froze. Directly above her own name was the name of Chris's mother, Margaret. Laura did not know why she was taken aback. *"Of course Margaret came today,"* she thought. *"She is Chris's mother."*

Another officer arrived and again asked Laura to explain the reason for her visit. As Laura told him, an interior metal door clanged open and the officer motioned for Laura to enter. In later years, Laura described it as passing through the gates of Hell. Laura stepped through the door and walked down a dark hallway painted in battleship gray. As Laura came to the end of the hallway and began to turn left, she could see the front of a cell to her right and the distant hum of a television. The strong smell of indistinguishable food filled the air. With a pounding heart and beads of sweat forming on her forehead, Laura completed the turn to her left and saw a very large correctional officer sitting at a table and talking on a telephone. Across from the officer was a cell, the middle of three cells that occupied the long hallway. Directly in front of the cell was a green plastic chair, and inside the gloomy interior of the cell she saw a flash of an orange jumpsuit. Tears welled in Laura's eyes. It was Chris.

> I reached my hands through the bars and stroked his face. "It is so good to see you," I said as tears streamed down my face. I sat in the plastic chair that had been placed in front of Chris' cell. Keeping one hand tightly on my Bible, the other on Chris, I was overwhelmed with joy as I looked into his blue eyes. I had almost forgotten how beautiful they were. I was shocked at his appearance. It had been eight years since I last saw him. He looked pale. Not the ghostly white that he looked at his trial, but the look of someone who had not seen sunlight in a few years. "It is good to see you too," Chris said in a very low voice. I took his hands in mine—his skin cool to the touch, mine sweaty, clammy and shaking. I squeezed his hands very tightly, and Chris returned the squeeze. I knew then and there I never wanted to let go.

Seeing Chris sitting in the cell, so at ease behind steel bars, was troubling to Laura. In her countless telephone conversations with Chris over the last eight years, she had never imagined him behind bars. And his voice. The voice that Laura had heard so many times in her classroom seemed terribly out of place in the cold, gray cell. Overwhelmed and at a loss for words, Laura touched Chris's head and commented on his shaved head. She thought silently that the closely cut hair made Chris look like a convict. Chris put his own hand to his head, felt the stubble, and tried to put Laura at ease by making a joke. "Well, this is easier to manage," he said with a chuckle. The humor reminded Laura of the laughing, misbehaving young teenager she once knew and it helped her get her bearings.

"Hey Chris, here comes your friend," called out the corrections officer at the desk. Laura turned, expecting to see someone coming down the hallway. "You might want to pick up your feet," Chris said, laughing. "We have a pet mouse." As Laura lifted up her feet and propped them on the cell's bars, Chris added: "Sometimes I keep him in the cell with me. He lives in the bottom of my trash can at night." "Really?" Laura responded in a confused voice. "Everybody needs a pet," Chris explained. Finally understanding that the mouse was Chris's companion, Laura responded. "That makes sense, Chris. I also have a number of pets. But my pets would eat your pet." Laura, Chris, and the corrections officer laughed. Frightened by the sound, the mouse darted past Laura's feet and disappeared. "I wonder if he can get in there" said Chris, motioning with his head to a white door at the end of the hall. Laura suddenly felt a chill and did not ask what was behind the door. At that point, she did not want to know.

After an awkward silence, Laura reached for her Bible and read aloud a few verses that she had been drawn to earlier in the day. Chris seemed unsure what to say or do, not very interested yet not wanting to appear rude. Chris asked for the Bible, telling Laura that he had a favorite Scripture. Leafing through the Bible for a few minutes, Chris finally located the verse and passed the Bible back to Laura through the food tray slot in the cell door. It was First Corinthians 13, and Laura began to read it aloud:

And now I will show you the most excellent way. If I speak in the tongues of men and of angels, but have not love, I am only a resounding gong or a clanging cymbal. If I have the gift of prophecy and can fathom all mysteries and all knowledge, and if I have a faith that can move mountains, but have not love, I am nothing. If I give all I possess to the poor and surrender my body to the flames, but have not love, I gain nothing.

"That part is okay," Chris interrupted, "but the next part is what makes it my favorite." Laura continued:

Love is patient, love is kind. It does not boast, it is not proud. It is not rude, it is not self-seeking, it is not easily angered, it keeps no record of wrongs. Love does not delight in evil but rejoices with the truth. It always protects, always trusts, always hopes, always perseveres. Love never fails.

There was a long silence. "That is the most important part," said Chris. "Love never fails." As Chris talked, Laura thought to herself, *"but how often has love failed you, Chris? Love is what got you into this situation. Not a healthy love but a juvenile, immature love."* "I have come to learn what love really is," Chris added. "I never knew before." Laura found herself again blinking back tears.

Throughout Laura's visit, the corrections officer remained at the table. He was soon joined by a second officer, and they began playing cards. It goes without saying that an inmate in the death house is closely monitored during his final three days. Every time the inmate uses the bathroom, receives a phone call, eats a meal, or smokes a cigarette, his activities are recorded in a logbook.[63] We requested a copy of Chris's death log from the Virginia Department of Corrections, but, once again, our request was denied. To death row inmates like Derick Peterson, the bitter irony is that the inmate the state is actively preparing to kill is on a suicide watch designed to prevent that inmate from first killing himself: "They keep you safe and make sure you don't hurt yourself so they can do it. Pretty sick. It's the system. They're like, 'No, let us do it.'"[64]

At about 7:00 P.M.—an hour into the visit—Laura and Chris both turned at the sound of a lock clicking open in a door down the hallway. A tall man, with sandy brown hair and cowboy boots, walked toward Laura and Chris. His name was Peter,[65] and he was the chaplain assigned to death row and the death house by Chaplain Service. Laura felt her muscles tense. She had spoken with Peter several days ago, as she struggled to get approval to serve as Chris's spiritual advisor. Peter was curt during the call, telling Laura that he doubted that she would be permitted to serve as an advisor. Laura thought that Peter seemed overaggressive during their conversation, as if he was guarding "his turf" from outside invaders. An assistant warden later told Laura that

Peter would be displeased to hear of her appointment as Chris's spiritual advisor.

As Peter walked to the cell, Laura tried to put the previous encounter out of her mind. "Well, you got in," was Peter's only response to Laura's greeting, as he pulled up another plastic chair and sat down. "How did you do it?" Laura paused before answering. Peter was angry and defensive, and Laura did not want to make the situation worse. "I made a few phone calls," Laura carefully replied, "and God opened the door for me to be with Chris." Laura's efforts to break the tension failed. "You must know some people in high places, don't you," snorted Peter. When Laura mentioned the head of Chaplain Service, Peter glared and snapped back, "Oh, yes. High places." Laura noticed that Peter did not carry a Bible.

Trying a different tack, Laura showed Peter the Scripture that she had been reading to Chris. Her attempt at finding a common ground failed. Rocking on the back legs of his chair, Peter began quizzing Laura about her religious training. Laura fought the urge to flip him over in the chair, instead answering his questions in a slow, steady voice. When Laura inquired about Peter's own education, he suddenly found the topic unpalatable and turned back to Chris. He started spinning tales of the different death row inmates who had previously journeyed to the death house. Chris visibly perked up, interested to hear the stories about the men who had walked this same road before him. They were men with odd prison nicknames, inmates Laura had only heard about on the nightly news. Chris and Peter never discussed the men's crimes, but exchanged stories of the men's personalities and antics as well as the curious bonds of friendship that formed in the pressure cooker of death row. And they talked about how each man faced the death chamber in his own unique way. Perhaps they talked about Carl Chicester, who walked into the death chamber while muttering obscenities under his breath. Mark Sheppard, the Richmond drug dealer who pronounced his innocence to the bitter end. Douglas M. Buchanan, Jr., who murdered four family members and smilingly told the execution team, "get the ride started. I'm ready to go." Mario Benjamin Murphy, a contract killer who announced that "today is a good day to die" and laughed as the killing chemicals began flowing through the IV. Joseph O'Dell, who got married the day of his execution. Lem Tuggle, a former death row escapee whose arm bore a "born to die" tattoo and who wished his executioners a "Merry Christmas." Dennis Stockton, the former drug addict who jokingly asked the guards to fill the IV with methamphetamine. Willie

Lloyd Turner, the fifteen-year "dean" of death row who left behind a prison typewriter containing a .32 caliber handgun, twelve bullets, and a note that said "smile." Willie Leroy Jones, who kissed the electric chair before sitting in it. And Timothy Dale Bunch, the former marine who fought unsuccessfully to have his execution videotaped and who argued against wearing a hood over his face, telling the assembled witnesses, "I wanted a more dignified way. You would have had to look me in the face."

Laura felt chilled, overwhelmed by the sudden understanding that Chris's role models and parental figures had been rapists and murders. And yet he had still survived, and he had found redeeming qualities in the broken men of the row. Yet one thought kept haunting her, *"Why couldn't I have saved Chris from this life?"*

As the conversation meandered, Peter and Chris turned to the subject of homemade prison wine or "mash." As Chris cheerfully ticked off the ingredients for his favorite type of mash, Laura groped for ways to turn the focus back to Chris. As a spiritual advisor, she felt compelled to talk about weightier issues. "You know," Peter said, "the electric chair is down there." He motioned to his left, to a white door with a window covered by a Venetian blind on the other side. Laura stared at the door, as if it were drawing her closer. Pulling her eyes away, she turned back to Chris. "What is that?" Laura asked. Even though she knew the answer, she hoped that she was wrong. "That's the room," Chris said simply. All Laura managed to utter was "oh." Chris wanted to see the room. He wanted to know what it looked like, what to expect. While Laura was initially confused by his inquisitiveness, it struck her that Chris did not want any surprises in the last minutes of his life. "Go try and look in the window," Chris said. Laura couldn't. No matter how curious she was. In the coming days, Laura prayed that she would never see the inside of that room at the end of the hallway. She started to cry again, but angrily wiped away her hot tears. She did not want to cry in front of Peter.

The subject mercifully changed. Chris had met his biological father for the first time earlier in the day, an experience he described as looking into the face of a stranger. Chris later recounted the meeting:

He said that he knew that he hasn't been a good father. He knows he wasn't there for me and he is here now and hopefully if everything works out, he will be there for me in the future. He said, that he feels if he had been there, you know, living up to his fatherly duties, you know, maybe this would not have happened. Which I told him, I mean, because you weren't there, it wasn't like I wasn't taken care of. Because, I mean, my grandparents gave me what I needed.

That topic exhausted, Peter and Chris returned to the subject of former inmates. Inmates who were executed. Inmates who received temporary stays. Inmates who received executive clemency and forever escaped the specter of the death house. Again silence, as Laura held Chris's hand. Then Chris spoke in a hushed voice. "J. B. and Kathy did not have the opportunity to say good-bye to their family. I wish I didn't, either — it isn't fair." "Don't be thinking about those things," Peter said sharply. Before he could continue, Laura interrupted. "No, Chris needs to speak about what he is feeling." Chris was expressing true and deeply felt remorse, and Laura did not want to let Peter control Chris's thoughts and feelings. Chris continued, "They should come in unannounced and execute me. Give me the same as I gave them." Laura gave up fighting the tears. They flowed down her face, spilling onto her arm and soaking the front of her dress. As Peter continued to tell Chris that he needed to "stop talking like that," Laura vowed to find a way to help Chris talk through his emotions, his guilt, and his fear.

The visit was over. As Laura exited the death house into the cold night air, she raised her eyes to the sky and searched for a star. Any star. She wondered if Chris could see the night sky, suddenly unable to remember if there was a window in his cell or a skylight in the death house. The thought that Chris might never again see the glow of starlight struck Laura like a fist, and she wept as she climbed into the prison van. Laura and Peter rode in silence as the van crossed the compound and pulled up to the prison's main building. They exchanged goodbyes, and Laura sat exhausted in the car as her husband drove home through the darkness. As the prison lights faded into the blackness, Laura blew Chris a kiss and silently thought, *"Three more days until the execution."* Then she prayed.

Despite Peter's admonition to avoid dwelling on the past, Chris was speaking out and expressing his remorse to others. In an interview that same week with Amnesty International, Chris spoke of the crime, his co-conspirator, and his victims. In the interview, Chris referred to the murders as a "senseless mistake" and that he was deeply troubled by the fact that, unlike himself, Kathy and J. B. Wiseman and their families did not have the opportunity to say goodbye. "The victims' family was never given that chance. I think about that. I feel guilty that they didn't know when they were going to die and I do. I am afforded the chance to visit with my family and they never were." Chris revealed that he had sent a letter to Kathy Wiseman's family, asking for their forgiveness. "I know they will never forget, but maybe they can find it in their heart to forgive." Returning to the subject of last visits, Chris discussed his own struggles to support his grieving family during his final days. "Mostly I have just been trying to comfort my mother, my wife, and my aunt, and my friend who has been through it all with me. I mean, no parent wants to bury their child, under any circumstances. I try my best to let them see me happy, smiling, laughing."

As for Jessica, Chris stated:

> I don't harbor any evil feelings towards her because I still had the choice to make that decision. I made the wrong decision, even with her influence, I still had the power to choose. If she didn't pursue the issue, I don't think it would have happened. But sitting from where I am sitting, sitting from where I have sat, in Mecklenburg, Sussex, the death house, I don't hate her, I don't love her, I don't care for her. She did her time, or the time that the law said for her to do, she got out. Hopefully, she is able to move on with her life.

Chris was not the same angry, lost teenager who pulled the trigger on that fateful November night. In an interview given to a local newspaper the day before his first execution date, Chris reiterated that he had changed: "'[J]udge me as who I am now, someone who has matured, who feels sorry for what's happened. Someone who is compassionate, respectful, not as naive as I used to be.'"[66] In sum, Chris had grown, he had matured, he was remorseful and empathic, and he had learned from his mistakes—sincere and real changes that supporters of the death penalty claimed were not possible for the damned who occupied death row.

Aware of these public sentiments about death row inmates, in interviews Chris tried to debunk the myth that the men who occupied Virginia's death row were inhuman and disposable: "'They classify death row [inmates] as monsters. We are human beings like everyone else. We just made wrong decisions in our lives. We still have feelings. We still have emotions. Some of us cry, some of us deal with our time in other ways. All of us are sorry for what we did. I say this for myself, I am sorry for what I did.'" Finally, throughout the interview and his final days Chris expressed his wish for the impossible: to "'go back and redo it . . . just have a chance to relive that second over.'"

On the evening of Monday, June 14, Laura went back to the death house, much to the surprise of the corrections officers who had assumed that one night would be enough for a woman. Laura returned, determined to help Chris express his feelings and find peace. As she walked down the short hallway and turned to Chris's cell, Laura felt less nervous. The surroundings weren't new any more. Considering that Chris had two days before his execution, Laura found him to be remarkably composed and focused. After discussing his day, Laura shared more biblical passages with Chris. "I am really sorry for last night," Chris said in a very quiet voice. "Peter made it very difficult for us. I am going to tell him not to come. I don't need him attacking you, and, besides, you are the one I want here anyway." Laura was touched by the way that Chris, facing his own death, was more concerned with defending her honor. She reassured Chris that she could handle Peter.

Laura felt the pressure of precious time slipping away, and she wanted to talk to Chris, really talk, before a confrontation with Peter. As Laura broached the subject of baptism with Chris, a loud "click" echoed through the hallway and Laura's heart sank as the same pair of cowboy boots appeared around the corner. Peter did not address Laura, but pulled up a chair and greeted Chris. "Hey, dude," Peter said, "How are you doing?" Laura braced for a fight and asked Chris about today's family visits. "The morning visit was really tough," Chris replied. "Everyone seemed on edge and kept crying. My aunt is having a very difficult time. She just keeps crying and crying." "She needs to be told to stop being emotional or don't come back," Peter snapped. Laura was shocked by his response. "Isn't it expected that she would be upset, Chris? Has she visited you before?" "No, she hasn't," said Chris, "and I can't handle her being so emotional." Peter repeats that Chris needs to tell her not to come back.

Laura was appalled. In the last days of his life, Chris should be embracing his family and sharing their grief. She searched her mind, trying to find the right words to explain why his aunt was distraught and why it was important for Chris to understand her grief. "I can't deal with her crying. It makes it stressful for everyone," Chris said. "The last thing you guys need in that room is an emotional woman," Peter agreed. Laura couldn't respond. *What is his purpose here?* she thought to herself.

"What were you talking about tonight," said Peter. Laura noticed that the chaplain had again come to the death house without a Bible. "Baptism," Laura replied in a strong voice. Peter's response was short. "Why?" "Because I wondered if Chris had been baptized and, if not, if he wanted to be." Laura continued, feeling defensive. "It is important that Chris think about these things," she finally added. "No," Peter replied in a firm voice. "Chris doesn't need to be thinking at all. He should just be talking about stuff, not thinking about anything." The pieces clicked in place for Laura. Peter's role was to help facilitate a clean execution. He was there to help create a nonthinking, unemotional inmate. Chris couldn't be allowed to think. To question. To regret. To mourn. The more that Chris thought, the more emotional he might become. And an emotional inmate could pose problems for the execution team.

Laura felt a wave of nausea come over her, and she fell mute as Chris and Peter resumed their gossipy stories about other inmates. Thoughts raced through Laura's mind: *"How can I address Chris's spiritual needs if Peter is here, blocking my every effort? How can I simply be alone with Chris? How can I help Chris before Wednesday? And what would happen on Wednesday?"*

Laura interrupted. "Chris, do you know what Wednesday will be like?" Chris shook his head and looked to Peter. In a causal tone, Peter explained how "simple" the day would be. Two visits with the family, in the morning and afternoon. Chris could decide which of the two visits would be a contact visit. "You should keep the visits light, don't talk about what is going to happen," instructed Peter. "Just talk about things that make you happy." Laura felt her anger rising. "Don't you think that you should tell your family how you feel about them, and let them tell you the same?" "No," Peter shot back, before Laura could respond. "That will just cause problems." "I don't want anyone upset," Chris agreed with Peter. "Just light talk." *"I've got to get rid of this guy,"* Laura thought. Her job seemed more and more impossible every minute.

"You will say goodbye to your family at 3:00 P.M.," Peter continued. "At that time, your attorneys and spiritual advisor can visit with you. I will be with you, or, if you want, Laura can." Chris looked up. "Laura will be with me." "That's up to you, Chris," said Peter. "Your last meal will come around 4:00 P.M., and either Laura or I can stay with you until 6:00 P.M. Then we will be asked to leave so they can prepare you." Laura's grip on Chris's hand tightened. "At that point, you will have a shower and shave. You will change clothes. They will fingerprint you for identification purposes and give you a shot of Valium. After that, your spiritual advisor can come back." Chris protested. "I'm not going to take the shot." For once, Laura and Peter agreed as they both urged Chris to take the medication.

"A few minutes before 9:00 P.M., the largest men you have ever seen will come to the cell," said Peter. "The warden will read your death warrant, and they will escort you down the hall. You can have me walk with you, if you want." "I want Laura with me," Chris said, more of a request than a statement, as he looked directly into Laura's eyes. Laura was surprised, as it occurred to her for the first time that she might be walking through that white door at the end of the hallway. "Yes, Chris," she replied. "I will go if they let me." At the thought of passing into the death chamber, Laura started to shake, and she reached again for Chris's hand. "I don't think they will let you," Peter retorted, "but I didn't think they were going to break the rules and let you in at all, either."

"At that point, whoever is there with you will either go into the witness box or leave the building completely," Peter said. "The execution begins with the first injection, which will put you to sleep. That's the end." Laura noticed that Chris was studying her face, watching her reaction. Laura struggled to keep a neutral face as her mind screamed out questions: *Can I do it? Do I have the strength? Please, God, give me the strength."*

Laura and Chris both jumped as the phone rang at the officer's desk. After speaking into the receiver, he hung up and announced, "five more minutes." Laura prayed silently for a few moments alone with Chris, and she received her wish when Peter stood up, walked over to the door leading to the death chamber, and tried to peer through the glass. Laura spoke quickly. "Are you all right?" Chris said that he was. "I love you, Chris," Laura said as she started crying again. "I love you, too," Chris replied in a solemn voice. "I hope that the visit with your family goes well tomorrow. Try to understand your aunt's feelings." Chris nodded. "I will do the best that I can." As the officer announced that the visit was over, Laura rose and walked to the bend in the hall. She turned and smiled one last time at Chris. Conflicting emotions churned in Laura's heart as she walked away. She did not want to leave Chris in that gloomy place, but she couldn't wait to walk into the open air.

Laura decided not to return to the death house on Tuesday, June 15. Exhausted by the tension of the visits and her struggles with Peter, she decided that it would be best not to subject Chris to an emotional and spiritual tug-of-war between his two spiritual advisors. Laura called Chris's mother, Margaret, and asked her to tell Chris that she had been called back to work and couldn't make the trip to Greensville but to please call her at home that night. Having to return to work was a lie, but Laura didn't want to burden Chris with the truth. That evening Chris called Laura. Guilty, she confessed the real reason that she didn't visit and was horrified to discover that Chris had not received a visit from Peter. Laura could have visited alone with Chris after all. The two tried to make up for the irrecoverable loss of time by talking about Chris's day. The mental anguish of the final days in the death house was clear, as Chris talked about the last goodbye that he had with his distraught aunt on Tuesday (only immediate family were allowed to visit on Wednesday, the day of the execution).

Laura shifted gears. Chris had told her that he did not want to be executed while wearing his wedding ring. He wanted to be buried with the wedding ring, and Chris was convinced that, if the Department of Corrections took possession of the ring after his execution, it would be lost or stolen. Therefore, they had to devise a way that Chris could slip her the ring prior to his walk to the death chamber. Chris was confident that he could make the exchange while under the constant supervision of the death watch team, but Laura was dubious. She pressed on. "Chris, I don't think that they will let me be with you in the death chamber." "If they won't let you be with me, then I want you in the witness room." Laura paused for a moment, unsure if she could watch Chris die. She collected her thoughts and answered him, "I will do it if you want me to." "I do," said Chris. "I want you to be in the very front. I want your face to be the last face that I see." All Laura could do was choke out, "okay."

Laura and Chris spent the remainder of the phone call discussing Chris's spiritual life. Laura shared with Chris the fact that her entire church congregation was praying for Chris, and she urged him to pray for strength and guidance in the coming hours. Not days now, but hours. Laura felt that a higher power had been guiding her over the last weeks and months, and she struggled to share that message with Chris. Sitting on her back deck as she spoke, Laura stared at the bright stars stretching over her country home and spoke with Chris about her belief in God, in salvation, and in eternal life.

As Chris's execution date drew near, his appellate lawyers were working frantically to save his life. They proceeded along two fronts. First, they filed a petition with the Virginia Supreme Court arguing that Chris's conviction was void and he warranted a new trial because both of his biological parents were not notified of his original juvenile court proceedings. They simultaneously filed a similar motion in Middlesex County Circuit Court. Under Virginia law at the time, the parents of a minor must be notified that their child has been charged with a crime. While the law was widely interpreted to mean that notification must be given to one of the parents, on the Friday before Chris's execution the Virginia Supreme Court held in an unrelated case that the law meant that, at a minimum, an effort must be made to notify both parents. Because Chris's biological father, Bobby Thomas, had not been notified, Chris's lawyers quickly filed a petition arguing that Chris must be given a new trial.

On Friday, June 11, the second prong of the plan to save Chris swung into action as his lawyers filed a ten-page petition seeking clemency from the Virginia governor. As in all death penalty states, clemency is the last avenue through which a death row inmate can seek to have his sentence reduced to life in prison. In many states a governor receives a binding or nonbinding recommendation from a board prior to granting clemency, but Virginia is one of fourteen states that vests the power of commutation solely in the hands of its governor. The clemency petition was sent to the office of Virginia Governor James Gilmore. A native of Richmond, Virginia, Gilmore was an attorney who had previously served as Henrico County commonwealth attorney and state attorney general; as a Republican, he had touted his crime-fighting credentials during his gubernatorial campaign. Based on Gilmore's professional record and his self-professed conservative roots, Chris's lawyers knew that clemency was a long shot.

The clemency petition presented what should have been introduced at Chris's original sentencing hearing: evidence of the repeated losses suffered by a young Chris Thomas and his resulting emotional and psychological tailspin. Moreover, the lawyers highlighted the vastly disparate sentences given to Chris and Jessica. The petition concluded:

> The true nature of clemency is both mercy and an opportunity to prevent injustice. It would be an injustice to put Chris to death when the person who planned the crime and convinced Chris to participate in it goes free. . . . Chris does not contend nor has he ever contended that he should not be punished severely for his acts, but putting him to death is simply too severe of a sanction when his involvement and sentence is compared to co-defendant Jessica Wiseman.

The petition asserted that many of the individuals associated with Chris's trial believed that the death sentence was inappropriate. "No one who was involved in this case—not the trial judge, the commonwealth's attorney, the state's mental health expert, the court-appointed mental health expert, or even the surviving victim's family members—believe that the Commonwealth should go forward with Chris' execution." Chris's former state habeas attorney, James Breeden, echoed the statements contained in the petition, publicly announcing that his close friend, the late trial court judge John Folkes, was troubled by the jury's decision to give Thomas death. "'He expressed to me many times in the years after this conviction that he was very disturbed by the outcome. He said he did everything he could to suggest to the lawyers representing Thomas that if he pleaded guilty, he wouldn't have sentenced him to death.'"[67] Jimmy Ward, the commonwealth attorney who prosecuted Chris, immediately took issue with the clemency petition, however, reassuring a newspaper reporter, and presumably the Middlesex County voters that put him into office, "'The jury rendered the decision for the death penalty, and I always support the jury's verdict.'"[68]

Even Chris's trial counsel spoke up. Now running for the position of Gloucester County commonwealth's attorney (a race that he would lose) Damian Horne dismissed what he referred to as the "routine" allegations of ineffective assistance of trial counsel raised by Chris's appellate lawyers. "[Horne] said he even advised Thomas at the end of the trial that the lawyers representing him in the appeal process would tell him his trial lawyers had been ineffective," reported the Newport News *Daily Press*, "and that Thomas needed to pursue that avenue and exhaust all his post-conviction remedies."[69] As for Horne's assessment of his performance at trial, he stated, "'I don't lose any sleep over the job I did. . . . I know the effort that Sydney and I put in. I've had many reflective moments about whether I should have done something different. Do I feel guilty? No. But I do feel an enormous sense of sadness.'"[70]

Chris's lawyers were not the only people pleading for clemency. Governor Gilmore's office reported that by the Monday before his execution date, the governor had received more than fifty phone calls against the execution, an Amnesty International petition, and a letter from the president of the American Bar Association. In the letter written by ABA President Philip S. Anderson, he informed the governor that the ABA "opposes the imposition of capital punishment upon any person for an offense committed while under the age of eighteen." Pointing out that the "vast disparity in sentences between these two juvenile co-defendants . . . is particularly troubling," Anderson concluded that the death of Chris Thomas "serves no principled purpose and only demeans our system of justice."[71]

Feeling powerless but desperate to do anything, Laura herself wrote to Governor Gilmore shortly before she first stepped into the death house. In the letter, she stated:

I am writing to ask for you to save a life. A young man is going to die on June 16, 1999 and he should live. I am not asking for Douglas Christopher Thomas to walk free, for he is guilty of a crime, but I am asking for this case to receive serious consideration. Chris Thomas is not a danger to society. And Chris Thomas DID NOT have a fair trial, for I was there and witnessed the travesty.

Chris Thomas was a 17-year-old emotionally disturbed boy who believed the only person he loved in the world was going to be taken away from him. He and his girlfriend made a very bad decision, but how is it truly different from a crime of passion? Chris killed one parent and Jessica killed the other. That is a fact that may not have come out during the trial. Chris believed very strongly that he did not have a chance with the Middlesex jury. His mom is gay and he believed he would be punished by the sins of his mother.

Governor Gilmore, I was Chris Thomas' teacher for two years prior to the crime. He was a confused young man who was manipulated by his girlfriend. I saw it! Please look into the transcripts of the trial. His attorney did not know what he was doing. It was his first capital murder trial and he has lost other capital murder trials since Chris'. I called his attorney, Damien [sic] Horne for many weeks prior to the trial and each time Mr. Horne or his co-worker stated that all was going very well. They stated that Chris was participating in his defense and they were making progress. Why then did Mr. Horne call me the night before the trial began and ask me to come to Chris' jail cell the next morning to convince him to take the stand in his own defense? Why then after the loss did Mr. Horn[e] state that Chris had not participated in his own defense?

All I have ever wanted for Chris was a chance. He was in shock after the trial. He was Romeo trying to protect his Juliet. Governor Gilmore, I know that you look very seriously at every situation of each death row inmate. I am asking that you look carefully at this young man's life. He has not received justice from the beginning, as his attorney was not competent, to his rights being violated as a juvenile when his father was not contacted.

I pray daily for God's intervention to save Chris' life. And now I am asking for your mercy on the life of a young man who does not deserve to die.

On Monday, June 14, the appeal for clemency gained momentum when a young woman stepped forward and claimed that Jessica Wiseman shot her mother. The young woman, simply referred to as "Nicolle," had been in the Richmond Detention Center with Jessica, and she stated in an affidavit that Jessica had told several young girls that she, not Chris, shot her mother. Specifically, in the affidavit she attested that Chris did not want to shoot Jessica's parents, preferring to run away together, but that Jessica had other plans. "'I wanted to make my parents feel the pain that they had caused me,'" said Jessica. Furthermore, she admitted that she shot Kathy Wiseman after Chris froze.[72]

Several months before Nicolle came forward, Laura herself had written Jessica Wiseman and begged her to do something, anything, to help Chris. "Jessica are you willing to do SOMETHING to save his life? I know you loved him at one time and that is the tragedy of this whole thing," Laura wrote. "Can you or will you attempt to help?" Explaining to Jessica that she could reach out to the media or state politicians, Laura pointed out that a few words from Jessica could have a dramatic impact on the clemency process. "Your voice is louder than anyone's since you were with Chris and convicted of the murder. Please find it in your heart to do something. We only have a few months left."[73] We don't know if Jessica received the letter, but Laura never got a response. But the pressure on Jessica Wiseman to speak out was growing.

A second woman filed a similar affidavit the morning after Nicolle's announcement, stating that Jessica made the same claim while the two girls were at the Bon Air Juvenile Center. In the affidavit, the woman, identified only as "J," stated: "She told me she went into the bedroom and saw her mother sitting on the side of the bed or something like that. She shot her once and then . . . [her mother] started coming toward her, saying, 'Jessica, why? Jessica, why?' She said she just looked at her, said 'F— you, b—, die,' and she shot her again." The article concludes: "the morning after Jessica bragged about the murder, J. asked to be transferred out of the room. 'I said that I would rather sleep in the hallway than in a room with Jessica Wiseman,' J. said in the affidavit to Gilmore."[74]

While the claims that Chris did not fire the third shot arguably affected his capital murder conviction—if the third shot was the fatal shot, and if Jessica had fired the third shot, then Chris could not be convicted of capital murder because he had not killed two people in a single transaction as required by Virginia law—any new evidence that Jessica killed her mother was considered to be *legally* irrelevant. Under Virginia law, any and all evidence of factual innocence of a crime had to be presented to a court within twenty-one days of a defendant's conviction—a harsh and often criticized rule unique to Virginia's judicial system (the law has subsequently been amended). Instead, Chris's lawyers hoped that the new evidence would convince the governor to grant clemency because the evidence showed that Chris was not as morally culpable as first believed.

After eight years of silence, Jessica Wiseman finally spoke. If, however, Chris's attorneys had any hope that she might confess to firing the third and final shot, it was quickly dashed. In a statement released by an attorney, Jessica flatly denied the allegations.

> After hearing what the media has to say, it is obvious that their only goal, after all these years, is still to sell a paper. That's very sad if you think about it. This is why I feel the need to make a statement as to the extent of my involvement. In a sense, "to set the record straight." I am fully aware that my silence has been perceived as guilt by some. In fact, I was instructed from the very beginning by my legal counsel to never speak in my own defense. I was told it would make matters worse and that was the last thing I wanted to do. The "truth" that everyone is searching for has never come close to being told, but it will. I do not deny my involvement, but I fully disagree with what the media is saying. I've never killed anyone nor have I manipulated anyone to do it for me! As for the fact that people are now coming forward with statements, I've never spoken to anyone except my immediate family, my clinical psychologist, or my legal counsel concerning the details of what occurred that evening. No one, neither the media nor anyone else, seem to understand that the remorse I feel over the loss of my parents is my own personal affair. It is between God and myself.

At least one member of the media lashed back at Jessica Wiseman. Calling her "self-absorbed and clueless as ever," longtime Newport News *Daily Press* columnist Jim Spencer wrote that "Her [Jessica's] chosen role of victim plays as credibly as Roseanne [Barr] cast as Heidi. She has not served a single day of truly hard time for two of the most grisly, senseless murders this area has ever seen." Ticking off Wiseman's role in the murder of her parents, Spencer concluded, "even if Wiseman didn't shoot her mother and won't testify that she did, her posturing this week should make any judge or juror think twice about sentencing Thomas to die."[75] As for "the truth" that Jessica claimed "has never come close to being told, but it will," to date it still remains to be revealed, despite repeated efforts by the authors to get Jessica and her immediate relatives to divulge it.

On Wednesday afternoon, Chris spent what he believed to be his last contact visit with his mother, his father, and his wife, Glenda. It was an emotional meeting, and during the contact visit Chris touched and hugged his father for the first time. Chris later talked about that final visit and his efforts to maintain a happy face in the face of his pending death.

> [We talked] pretty much about the past. I mean, I didn't want to sit there and dwell on what was about to happen. In a sense you would have to go into the unit to understand it. The room we are sitting in is three feet away from the execution chamber. I mean . . . it has got three windows with the blinds pulled down. If you put the blinds up, you can see the electric chair and the gurney . . . everything is right there. So I tried, pretty much to just keep their mind off what was about to happen.

Chris was distracted by the presence of his father at the final contact meeting. "I knew he wouldn't have the emotional ties to me that my mom and my wife would so I pretty much concentrated all my attention on them to try to keep their spirits up."[76]

It is absurd to think that anybody could put an execution out of his mind under such circumstances, and Chris's family was devastated when they said their final goodbyes at 3:00 P.M. that afternoon. "'They were a wreck when they were leaving,'" recalled one of Chris's lawyers present at the death house. "'They were just as low as someone could possibly be.'"[77] As for Chris, throughout the day he struggled to comprehend the frightening reality of his pending execution. "It was just weird," Chris stated later. "The thought in the back of your mind was, 'this is the last thing I am ever going to eat.' Just like that morning I was taking a shower, 'this is going to be my last shower, this is going to be my last visit' . . . everything was just 'last.'"[78]

The families of the condemned have been called the forgotten victims of the death penalty. "[T]he death penalty is unrelieved agony for this group," writes Professor Margaret Vandiver. "Innocent of any offense, they pay a crushing price. If the death penalty benefits other families of homicide victims, it does so at the expense of these innocent people."[79] Author Rachel King, who has written about the families of murder victims as well as the families of the condemned, observes that "we ignore the fact that he [the condemned man] has a mother, father, sister, brother, daughter, son, and others who will be permanently harmed by the execution."[80] For King, the execution of an inmate creates "new victims. . . . Each execution ripples out through the generations, shredding families and destroying lives."[81] Moreover, King writes, the two groups of family members — relatives of the murdered and the condemned — have remarkably similar experiences:

> Death row family members shared many common experiences with each other and with the murder victims' family members. Dealing with a homicide or a possible execution took all of the family's financial and emotional resources. When families looked to the government for help, it was usually not there. Victims' services are woefully inadequate in most jurisdictions, and any assistance that might be available for counseling, medical expenses, or funeral expenses is not available to death row family members, who are not legally considered victims.[82]

King adds that the family members of death row inmates not only see their bank accounts wiped out, but can face ridicule from their community and harassment from the media. Of course, the fact that a defendant charged with capital murder has a family is irrelevant from a legal perspective; guilt or innocence of an accused man does not turn on his familial status. From a moral perspective, however, should we consider the impact of the death penalty on these hidden and forgotten victims?

As Laura Anderson drove to the Greensville Correctional Center, Chris returned to his cell and met with his lawyers. At 4:00 P.M., attorney Rob Lee, who worked for the Capital Defense Resource Center and was assisting on Chris's appeals, called and told Chris that the Virginia Supreme Court had issued a stay of execution. At first Chris did not know if the stay would be a temporary reprieve of a few hours. When his appellate attorneys — Lisa O'Donnell and Lawrence Woodward, Jr. — explained that he would not be executed that night, Chris started to weep. "He just kind of bowed his head and said, 'Thank God,'" Woodward recalled. "The first thing he wanted to do was call his wife and mother."[83] Margaret Thomas was in the parking lot outside the prison, and when Chris told her about the stay she shouted "Thank God" and burst into tears. As Chris tried to absorb the news, a corrections officer delivered Chris's final meal. The dinner of fried chicken, French fries, and apple pie remained uneaten.

One would think that a stay of execution would be an unambiguously joyous event for a condemned prisoner, but Chris's internal emotions were decidedly mixed on that late Wednesday afternoon. "I was kind of relieved for my family, but personally I was disappointed because the one thing that I have been looking for nine years I haven't got, and that is finality," Chris explained in an interview shortly after the stay. "Whether it would have been life or death, at least it would have been some closure. Instead of just sitting around wondering what is going to happen. You know, after nine years I think that is long enough."[84]

To Laura, the news of a stay of execution was the miracle for which she had so fervently prayed. After learning of the stay, she collapsed in the arms of Lisa O'Donnell, simultaneously crying and asking the attorneys to explain what the stay meant. Composing herself, Laura cleared the first checkpoint and boarded the prison van for the ride to the death house. As she passed corrections officers, she was surprised to see their smiling faces and hear their congratulations. *They are as relieved as we are,* Laura thought.

She found Chris in his cell, holding the fried chicken dinner in his lap and staring into space. Laura thought that Chris would be elated, but he looked in shock. "Chris," Laura cried out. "Why aren't you jumping for joy?" Slowly looking up into Laura's eyes, Chris responded in a shaking voice, "After we talked last night, I got down on my knees here in the cell and I prayed." Laura started weeping. "Chris, God loves you so much. He intervened. He saved your life. I believe that completely." Chris could only slowly shake his head, bewildered by what he and Laura considered to be divine intervention.

Their visit was short, for Chris would be immediately transported back to Sussex I. As Laura kissed Chris's hand goodbye she promised him that they would never meet again in such a terrible place. She was wrong.

7

The Death of Douglas Christopher Thomas

I had learned as a child from my Catholic catechism that some sacraments like baptism leave an "indelible" mark on the soul, a mark that can never be erased. Does witnessing an execution also leave an "indelible mark?"

SISTER HELEN PREJEAN

On June 16, 1999, Chris Thomas sat in his cell, his final meal cooling on the tray in his lap, trying to absorb the astonishing developments of the day. He would not die at 9:00 P.M. The Virginia Supreme Court had stayed his execution. He would see his family again. A new trial might be in his future. And another journey to the death house might also await him.

While Chris had momentarily escaped the executioner's gurney, his excitement was tempered by the realization that he would be quickly returned to a small cell on death row at the Sussex I State Prison. There he would return to the familiar routine of isolation and tedium. But at least it was life. To Laura, in the subsequent months Chris seemed changed, reborn and at peace. During their telephone conversations, his voice brimmed with humor, optimism, and joy. In an interview with Jordan Reynolds for Amnesty International, Chris discussed the changes in his life: "This is more hope than I have had in the past nine years. And I think this is more hope than my family has had. I feel a sense of relief because they are happy because I am still here. And when they are happy, I am happy." Laura and Chris spoke on the telephone several times a week, their conversations lasting hours. Chris had found a new meaning to his world, as well as a deeper understanding of himself, and he was eager to share this news with Laura.

One thing that Laura did not do was visit Chris on death row. While Laura was confident that Chris would receive a new trial, a little voice inside urged her to be pragmatic. Chris might return to the death house. And if Chris did return to that cold and sterile place, Laura was determined to be at his side. One of the keys to being appointed Chris's spiritual advisor was that Laura had not visited him on death row. Now Laura feared that visiting Chris would jeopardize her future status as spiritual advisor, and she and Chris decided that, at least for the moment, she should not come to see him. Instead, in the months following the execution Laura wrote as many friends, neighbors, parishioners, ministers, and legislators as possible, telling Chris's story, asking for their prayers of support, and encouraging them to write Governor Gilmore and ask that he spare Chris's life.

On November 5, 1999, the hope that Chris and his family felt was dashed: the Virginia Supreme Court denied Chris's petition for writ of habeas corpus.[1] As discussed earlier, at the time of Chris's arrest, Virginia law stated that a juvenile's "parents, guardian, legal custodian or other person standing in loco parentis" be notified of future court proceedings. To fail to do so invalidated any and all subsequent judicial proceedings, including trials. Because Bobby Thomas had not been notified of Chris's juvenile court proceedings, Chris's lawyers argued that the subsequent transfer hearing, at which Chris waived his right to a hearing to determine whether he be tried as a juvenile or an adult, was illegitimate and his trial a legal nullity.

In principle, the Supreme Court agreed that, under Virginia law, an effort must be made to notify *both* biological parents of the initiation of juvenile proceedings, and that if such notification is not made then the subsequent transfer of the juvenile to circuit court to be tried as an adult is ineffectual and any subsequent conviction is void. The sole exception to this requirement is when the trial court certifies that the identity of one of the biological parents is not reasonably ascertainable, a certification that the court did not make in Chris's case. The court, however, found that when Chris was adopted by his grandparents, his biological parents were divested of all legal rights — including the right to be notified of juvenile court proceedings. Chris's aunt and uncle, Herbert and Brenda Marshall, were notified of the juvenile proceedings, which satisfied the statute's notification requirements. Chris would not get a new trial.

When Laura learned that the Virginia Supreme Court had denied Chris's writ, she felt the same shock as the day she learned of Chris's death sentence. Chris tried to console Laura, telling her that he hadn't gotten his hopes up for a new trial. But Laura had, and she now felt that God had let her down: *"Wasn't the stay of execution the miracle we sought? Hadn't God answered our prayers for mercy?"* Laura immediately fired off a second round of letters to state politicians, religious leaders, and journalists, trying to draw attention to the injustice and inequity of Chris's looming execution. Laura directed her letters to anybody who might listen and intervene. Sister Helen Prejean. Social activist Susan Sarandon. State Senator Emily Couric. Congressman Jesse Jackson, Jr.

In a form-letter response to Laura's plea for mercy, Virginia Governor James Gilmore ignored the fundamental question raised by Laura — whether he would stay the executioner's hand — and ponderously lectured her on the tough choices he faced as a servant of the people:

> While I was a prosecutor in Virginia's courts, I found that making the choice of whether or not to seek the death penalty was among the most difficult decisions I ever had to make. However, it was also my responsibility to protect the safety of our citizens and to assure the public that proper punishment was imposed in especially vile crimes. As Governor, I now have a greater duty to protect law-abiding Virginians from criminal predators.[2]

With the denial of the writ of habeas corpus, the wheels of justice began to grind again. On November 17, 1999, Middlesex County Circuit Court Judge William Shaw III signed Chris's execution order:

> Pursuant to Section 53.1–232.1 of the Code of Virginia, having determined that the Supreme Court of Virginia has denied habeas corpus relief to the defendant, this Court hereby ORDERS that the death sentence of Douglas Christopher Thomas be carried out on the 10th day of January, 2000, at such a time of day as the Director of the Department of Corrections shall fix. It is further ORDERED that at least ten (10) days before January 10, 2000, the Director shall cause a copy of this Order to be delivered to the

defendant and, if the defendant is unable to read it, cause it to be explained to him.

Typically the original trial court judge signs the execution order, but Judge John Folkes was dead. The order was duly delivered to Chris at 2:25 P.M. on December 13, 1999, at the Sussex I State Prison by prison operations officer Heidi P. Clark. Chris called Laura later that day, solemnly informing her of the new execution date. After tears were shed, Chris tried to lighten the mood: "At least I get to see the year 2000."

Until the day that he was transferred back to the Greensville Correctional Center, Chris and Laura talked on a daily basis. The telephone calls took on a new sense of urgency, as the two realized that their time together would soon be over. They could not waste a single minute. Laura felt that Chris was now part of her family, and she was now comfortable expressing her love for him. It was not a romantic love, nor was it the love felt between siblings. It was the love of two people who had joined hands and together faced down death. Laura felt as if their hearts were now bonded together. Despite all the pain from the relationship, she found herself thanking God for bringing Chris into her life.

In the months after Chris's stay of execution, the relationship between Chris and Glenda, however, became strained. By the summer of 1999, Chris grew tired of the tension. "[W]ith all the arguments and all the problems, it seemed like me being on death row still facing execution was overlooked," Chris angrily remarked during an unpublished Amnesty International interview. "Somehow my life being in the court's hands next month was overlooked." Chris was further distressed that Glenda was spending time with Brenda Marshall, who Chris believed had betrayed him during his criminal trial and was untrustworthy. Although Chris issued an ultimatum, telling Glenda, "I will talk to my attorneys Monday and we will resolve this because I don't have time to deal with these issues," the couple did not divorce. The relationship had been fatally damaged, however, and the couple was not in close contact in the weeks leading up to Chris's execution.

Chris Thomas celebrated his last Christmas on death row on December 25, 1999. It was a difficult day, and Chris tried to remain upbeat as Christmas carols played over his tiny radio. This time of year always reminded him of his grandparents and days gone by. He spoke with his mother, and Chris later admitted that the conversation was forced: "We both knew this . . . probably will be my last Christmas. . . . We tried to think of past memories, of good thoughts. We tried to avoid the topic of the 10th."[3] When he spoke with Laura, she reminded him of the tremendous gift his family had received—a stay of execution, more time together, and hope. "You are the greatest Christmas present I have ever received," Laura told him. "We thought you would be gone, but you are still here with us."

Laura Anderson returned to the death house, which she had once vowed never to see again, at 6:00 P.M. on Saturday, January 8, 2000. Nothing had changed. The television blared, a stern-looking correctional officer sat at the desk across from Chris's cell, and the green plastic chair awaited Laura. For a moment, Laura and Chris simply stared at each other. Then Chris chuckled. "I remember the last time I saw you sitting in that chair," he said. "We were celebrating." "Yes, we were," replied Laura, not knowing what else to say. "It's so different this time," Chris said thoughtfully. Laura was surprised. "Really? How?" "I am not afraid this time," Chris answered confidently. "Chris, that is the peace that God gives you," said Laura with a catch in her voice. "God will take very good care of you. He loves you so very much."

Taking her Bible, Laura opened to a Scripture passage that she felt directed to share with Chris and handed the open book to Chris. It was Philippians 4:6–7: "Do not be anxious about anything, but in everything, by prayer and petition, with thanksgiving, present your requests to God. And the peace of God, which transcends all understanding, will guard your hearts and your minds in Christ Jesus." As Chris read and reread the passage, Laura watched his face and prayed that it would give Chris the peace he needed in the final forty-eight hours of his life.

That would be the last time that Chris and Laura were alone in the death house. When Laura returned the next night, she was surprised to see that another cell was occupied by death row inmate Steve Roach. Another juvenile offender, at age seventeen, Roach had shot and killed an elderly woman who had befriended him. Thomas and Roach considered themselves friends, and Roach, like Thomas, had recently gotten married while on death row. Now twenty-three years old, Roach's execution was scheduled for January 13. Virginia law requires that a death row inmate be transported to the death house four days before his execution, so Roach would watch Chris walk through into the death chamber and be executed before taking the same walk three days later.

The death house had held multiple inmates before. In December 1996, death row inmate Lem Tuggle, a murderer and rapist who briefly escaped from death row in 1984, wept as he watched fellow death row inmate Larry Stout enter the death chamber. According to Marie Deans, the burly, 300-pound Tuggle cried because he wanted to be executed before his friend: "'It comes across as if someone has thought of a new form of torture, a kind of psychological torture. . . . It makes no sense.'"[4] Father Jim Griffin, then one of the Mecklenburg death row chaplains, was equally appalled: "'It just seems unsavory to me. . . . There needs to be a little humanity in the whole thing. It just doesn't seem like humans would treat humans like this. I'm not even as angry as I am disappointed that they would not just move them out of there.'"[5]

Two more death row inmates — Joseph O'Dell and Ronald Lee Hoke, Sr. — were subsequently moved to the death house after Stout's execution, and they both watched the execution team escort Tuggle into the execution chamber. Marie Deans visited with O'Dell and Hoke after Tuggle's execution, and she described the two inmates as deeply shaken. "'I've seen shock and I've been in shock and it's what they look like,'" Deans said. "'They just were sitting there, kind of staring, and they weren't having very coherent conversation.'"[6] Prison officials were not sympathetic, citing institutional security as their first and foremost concern. "'We aren't going to jeopardize that [security] because an inmate may feel traumatized that he's about to be executed,' said a Department of Corrections spokesman. 'That's why there are three cells in the death house.'"[7]

As Laura sat down in the chair, she could tell that Chris was agitated by the presence of a fellow death row inmate. "I'm not happy about Steve being here," Chris said quietly. Laura was surprised. She thought that Chris would have welcomed the company. "I don't want to have to be strong for him," Chris explained. "I have always been like a big brother to Steve, and I don't want to have to be strong for him. I would rather do this alone." Laura did not know what to say. "Chris, he doesn't expect anything from you. Just be yourself. The two of you can lean on each other now." "No," Chris replied emphatically. "I have to be the strong one." It was not, however, simply about being strong for Steve Roach. Chris had been conditioned to hide his emotions from the men of the row. He had been "trained up." As he once explained to a reporter:

You are still around people [on death row] that if you open yourself up to will try to capitalize on, so you always have to keep a wall up. You only tell people what you want them to know, so I mean, I talk to them. I get along with everyone in here, you know. There is no one person I think, I can, you know, just tell them, "I am having a depressed day, I just feel like crying."[8]

Having built an emotional wall between himself and the other inmates, in his final days of life Chris did not want Steve to witness his sadness, fear, and grief. To Laura, it was another reminder of the bizarre world in which Chris had grown up. An upside-down world in which love, compassion, and altruism were punished while anger, intimidation, and selfishness were rewarded.

For a couple of minutes Laura and Chris idly watched a football game on the television mounted on the wall across from Chris's cell. The Miami Dolphins were trailing the Seattle Seahawks. "Chris," Laura finally spoke. "Driving down to the prison tonight, I had a wonderful daydream. I dreamed that the governor had pardoned you after attending church, and you were waiting for me in front of the prison." Chris listened intently. "You know, if I had pulled up and found you waiting for me, free to go, you would have to drive because I would be in no shape to." Chris laughed. "Well, I don't have a license any more so I better not drive. I don't want to get arrested. We will just walk to Richmond, okay?" Laura felt her chest tighten. The thought of walking anywhere with Chris, free from his shackles and handcuffs, was suddenly overwhelming to her.

Over the weekend, Chris was interviewed by several different news organizations. In the interviews, the degree to which Chris had grown and changed was evident: "'I can't blame the United States; I can't blame Virginia. . . . In a sense, I put myself here. It was a childish decision. I was a child. I'm not a victim of my environment, I'm not a victim of drugs. In the US we live under a democracy with freedom of speech, freedom of choice. Unfortunately, I made a bad choice.'"[9] During the interview, Chris again repeated that Jessica fired the third and final shot: "'I should have said it during my trial. I told her I would take full responsibility.'" Chris, added, however, that he did not feel any hostility toward Jessica: "'At 17 I was impulsive. I was gullible, I was still searching for my identity, I was being who everyone wanted me to be. Now I've grown up. I've changed.'"[10]

Chris was aware of the public campaign to save his life, and during an interview with the Newport News *Daily Press* he explained that he was touched by the fact "'[t]hat even though how horrific the circumstances are, there are people still thinking about me, that people still consider me a human being, instead of a cold-blooded killer.'"[11] As for the daily letters of support that Chris received, he added, "'It brightens my day to know that someone who I don't even know took the time to think about me.'"[12] Chris's faith was evident as he discussed the future: "'I think Monday will be a glorious day, whatever way it goes. . . . If it's commuted, I get some sort of life back. If it's not commuted, then I move on to another life. I believe death is only the beginning.'"[13]

In the early morning hours of January 10, Chris Thomas sat in his cell and in a clear, strong hand wrote farewell letters to his family members. One of the letters was to his aunt, Barbara Ann.

Dear Cox — If you are reading these words, then I have moved onto the next life, where I will be free from this cruel, harsh world. I want you to know I will be okay for I'll be in God's hands. Cox, thank you for being such a special person to me. You have *always* been there for me in every imaginable way. We have so many special memories over the years. Nothing — not man, not this state will *ever* take them away from me. All Virginia will get is my body. My heart, my soul will *forever* live on.

There are so many things I can write, but you know what I'm saying. I want you to know this is not good-bye!! This is only I'll see you later, for I do believe we will see one another again. We again will all be the happy family.

So, I will cut this short and say I will see you later. Please take comfort in knowing I am okay as I will in knowing y'all will be okay. I love you very much! And as my Momma told you, when you walked out that visiting room today you walked out with a piece of my heart. I love you always and take care of yourself. Until we see one another again — I love you.

Love Eternally, Chris."

P.S. I will miss you. Thank you for being a *Mom*. You did a great job because I am who I am today because of you; My Momma, Wanda, Laura and we can never forgot Winfrey, Nonna, Gogga — you have been my angels.

Sleep also eluded Laura, and by 5:00 A.M. she threw back the covers and crawled out of bed. After fixing a strong cup of coffee, she slipped on a Pittsburgh Steelers jacket, called to her border collie, Tippy, and walked out into the cold morning air. Laura and Ross lived in the country, and the lack of city lights meant that the stars stretched across the sky like clear, bright diamonds. Falling to her knees, Laura prayed. It was a familiar prayer that she had prayed hundreds of times before, but this time it was spoken with a raw, desperate urgency. "Please, God, hear my prayer," Laura called out. "Please spare Chris's life. Touch the governor's heart. Don't let them kill him." Laura knelt forward, her forehead touching the frosty hard ground, tears falling down her cheeks. Then a feeling of peace passed over her. A warm, familiar feeling that Laura still did not always understand but welcomed. Rising to her feet, Laura walked back to the house.

As Chris prepared himself to say goodbye to his family, faint hope still remained. His attorneys had filed a petition for a stay of execution with the United States Supreme Court as well as a petition for writ of certiorari, arguing that an international treaty signed by the United States forbid juvenile executions. The same argument had been made the week earlier before the Virginia Supreme Court, which rejected the claim. They had also again petitioned Governor Gilmore for clemency. Building on the argument that the different sentences that Chris and Jessica received were unjust, Chris's attorneys pointed to a third affidavit recently executed by another young woman who lived in the detention home with Jessica Wiseman. The allegations contained in the affidavit of a woman identified only as "Carli" mirrored the statements of the two affidavits executed by "J" and "Nicolle" the previous June: that Jessica had told Carli that "she had killed her own mother but that Chris had taken the rap for it because he loved her so much."[14] To Thomas's attorneys, the new evidence that Jessica Wiseman fired the third shot underscored the argument that Chris should never have been tried for capital murder. Unlike the previous summer, Jessica Wiseman remained silent.

The appeal for clemency was echoed by the American Bar Association, Amnesty International, the European Union, the National Mental Health Association, and a local Catholic diocese. In a guest column appearing in local newspapers, American Bar Association President William G. Paul urged Virginians to recognize the juvenile death penalty for what it was—a thirst for vengeance.

Why is it necessary to use the death penalty for those who were juveniles when they committed the crime? We know that adolescents lack a full appreciation of the consequences of their actions, and that juveniles sometimes make rash and terrible decisions because they are young and haven't developed the judgment we expect of adults. For this reason, juveniles cannot vote or serve as jurors. Experts confirm that capital punishment has little or no deterrent value for adolescents. With no deterrent benefit, the only other possible rationale to execute those who killed when they were juveniles is to satisfy our need for vengeance. Many of the young men on death row have crippling mental or behavioral disorders, or have suffered horribly from physical, psychological and sexual abuse. It reflects more upon us as a society than it does on the offender that we would seek legal vengeance through execution for the crimes of a child.[15]

Tellingly, few voices were raised in favor of the execution. A newspaper reporter managed to interview Denby Thomas, the stepgrandfather of Jessica Wiseman. "'We just want it to be over,'" Thomas was quoted as saying. As the *Daily Press* reported, "Whether the young man is executed or granted clemency, either would be a resolution. . . . But the family doesn't want endless stays of execution, only to have the case back in the news again. . . . That just keeps bringing back the bad memories."[16] One of the few public statements supporting the execution came, once again, from the commonwealth attorney who had prosecuted the original case, Jimmy Ward. Echoing comments that he made prior to Chris's first execution date, Ward deferred to the jury system. "'I'm not without a conscience,' Ward said. 'But I have an obligation to the citizens of this county. Once the jury made its decision, I have felt it is incumbent on me to enforce that decision.'"[17] Mr. Ward did not say, however, if the original jury members still supported the verdict, and no jurors have ever spoken out.

Neither the United States Supreme Court nor Virginia Governor Gilmore stayed the executioner's hand. The Supreme Court denied the application for a stay of execution at approximately 5:00 P.M. on January 10, and shortly thereafter Governor Gilmore announced that he would not grant clemency. Despite some 1,400 phone calls to the governor's office, the affidavits from the three young women, and the imbalance in the sentences imposed upon Chris and Jessica, Governor Gilmore concluded, "Thomas' responsibility under the law wasn't any less because of the protections afforded his younger accomplice. Indeed, in a society where the incidence of youth violence has increased, we must continue to demand complete accountability for such terrible crimes."[18] Thus, in Governor Gilmore's eyes a minor was as morally and legally accountable as an adult for the crime of first-degree murder.

As Laura and her husband, Ross, drove to Greensville on that final afternoon, Laura was struck by the beauty of the sunny day. Fluffy white clouds drifted across the blue sky, and the sun warmed her face. She stared at the traffic, at the people racing to meet their own deadlines, and wondered if they knew—or cared—that a young man's execution was scheduled for that evening.

Laura looked at her watch. Chris would be having his final visit with his mother. *"How do you say good-bye to your child?"* Laura thought. Closing her eyes, she returned to silent prayer. She prayed that Margaret and Chris would have the strength to make it through their final goodbyes. She prayed for the courage to enter the death chamber. She prayed that God's mercy would spare Chris from death. And she prayed that she would find the final words of peace and love to share with Chris, and that her words would not be lost among her tears of grief. Despite Ross's reassurance that God would help her find the appropriate words to speak, Laura remained fearful that the dark killing energy of the death chamber would strike her mute. Laura opened her Bible to a blank page and began to write down the words she would need to baptize Chris. Again, tears.

The drive, which usually seemed so long, passed by too quickly. As the truck exited the highway, Laura felt sweat forming on her brow. She was only minutes away. When Laura returned to the death house, she found that Chris had been moved to the cell closest to the door of the death chamber. The mood in the death house was strikingly different. The television volume was lower, and the officers sitting at the table across from Chris's cell were no longer playing cards. As Laura walked to Chris's cell, she couldn't help trying to look through the window of the death chamber's door. "They practice, you know," Chris said quietly. "They have been practicing all day—actually for the last few days. They go through every step to make sure it's done perfectly." The inhumanity of it all struck Laura like a fist. *"My God,"* she thought, *"practicing within earshot of Chris. This is utter torture."*

Laura knew how precious these last few hours would be, and she did not want to waste them with idle banter. Chris told Laura of his final visit with his mother, and how they had cried together. A female corrections officer in the visiting room had actually helped Chris and Margaret through the final visit. "I don't think we could have done it without her help," Chris said. "I am so thankful she was there for you," Laura replied. "I am sure it was the hardest thing you all have ever done." Chris's final meal, the second "final" meal he had been served in the death house in the last year, sat untouched on his bed. Nearby, Laura and Chris heard his appellate lawyers talking in hushed tones. Chris was chain-smoking, and he kept apologizing to Laura for the stale cigarette smoke that hung in the air.

At approximately 6:30 P.M., Laura and the attorneys were informed that they would be escorted back to the prison's main waiting area while Chris was prepared for his execution. Laura asked to stay — worried that if she left, the prison might not let her return for the execution — and the officer brusquely told her that there was no exception to the policy for spiritual advisors. After Laura squeezed Chris's hand and promised to return, she stopped briefly at Steve Roach's cell and whispered some words of encouragement. The sight of the two men together in the death house, barely looking old enough to shave, struck Laura like a slap across the face. *"It's really going to happen,"* Laura thought as she left the building. *"They are going to kill these two young men."*

The van ride from the death house to the front lobby of the prison was deathly silent. It was if there were no more words to describe the sense of doom that they all felt. When they reached the lobby, Larry Woodward immediately called his office to see if Governor Gilmore had decided to intervene. No word from the governor's office. Laura sat in the lobby, staring at the floor. She felt utterly powerless, as if she were a tiny ship caught in a terrible storm. The lobby phone rang, and Laura froze, afraid of what the telephone call signified. A correctional officer called for Woodward, who took the phone. Silence for a moment, and then Woodward spoke in an angry, tense tone and put down the receiver. "The governor denied the request," he said in a voice hoarse with emotion. "They are proceeding with the execution." There was nothing for the small group to do but cry and hug each other. As Laura again wiped her eyes, she felt as if she had cried a lifetime of tears in the last two days.

It was time to return to the death house. Laura hugged Ross tightly, drawing strength from her husband before reentering the van for her last ride to the place she called hell. As she walked to Chris's cell, the ever-present cigarette hung from his mouth as he talked to his aunt on the telephone. No longer dressed in the orange jumpsuit of prior visits, Chris was clothed in a blue denim shirt with slits cut in the sides and denim pants.

When Chris ended the phone call, Laura glanced at the clock. 8:30 P.M. Only thirty minutes left. "Chris," Laura quickly said. "Do you want to be baptized?" "Yes, I do. Will you baptize me now?" Knowing that Laura needed water for the ritual, Chris called to a female correctional officer—the same who had previously comforted Chris and his mother during their last visit—and asked for a glass of water. Laura added "without ice," but a Styrofoam cup appeared moments later filled to the brim with water and ice. Laura stuck her finger in the water, smiled, and they both managed to laugh when Chris said, "COLD!"

Laura's Bible had been confiscated when she returned to the death house, and she did not have her book of worship and the baptism text, but she remembered the words that she had written on the Bible's back page. "Chris," she said in a strong voice. "You are a blessing in my life, and I thank God for you! Your life has touched my life in a wonderful way, teaching me love, compassion, trust, and friendship. The time is upon you to rest in the loving arms of Christ. Do you desire to be baptized into Christ's holy church?" "Yes," said Chris in a voice thick with emotion. Laura dipped her fingers into the cold water and reached through the bars of the cell, placing her hand on Chris's hot, moist head. "Chris, I baptize you in the name of the Father, the Son, and the Holy Spirit." "Amen," Chris replied. "God forgives you all your sins, and you have been set free from the sins that brought you to this place," Laura concluded. "You are a new life in Christ."

Both Chris and Laura cried tears of joy, holding hands and letting the moment wash over them. "You know," Laura said with a smile, "I am a little envious. In a few minutes you will be in heaven, walking with Christ. You will be free. No more shackles, no more chains, no more bars. Pure freedom." Chris smiled back at Laura. "Yes, I will be." In her heart, Laura believed that Chris was at peace. In the months between his first and second execution date, Laura felt that a power had worked through her and had led Chris to accept Christ. Chris would die knowing that he had been saved by grace.

A squeak of metal hinges, and Chris strained to look down the hallway. Another guard had entered. Chris's face briefly sagged. *"Not his time yet,"* she thought. Laura and Chris, teacher and student, continued to stare into each other's eyes, holding hands, and waiting. Everything they wanted and needed to say had been said. All they could do was wait.

The phone on the wall rang. Chris and Laura jerked back, and Laura looked at the clock on the wall: 8:53 P.M. They both knew what the ringing telephone meant—a signal to the execution team that it was time. "We are ready, Chris. We can do this," Laura said and she squeezed his hand tightly. "Absolutely," Chris said in a strained voice. They were both shaking, but Laura felt the presence of God. The hallway was silent as the execution team moved into position. Laura's thoughts flashed to Margaret: *"How must it feel for a mother to know that in a matter of minutes her only child will be killed?"*

It was 8:55 P.M. The doorway at the end of the hallway opened, and around the corner walked a large number of grim-faced men. The warden was coming to read Chris the death warrant. Laura's heart began to race. A prison administrator touched Laura on the shoulder. "It is time," he said. "Please step over here." He motioned for Laura to move across the hallway to the wall. Laura stood, and Chris, still holding her hands, tenderly kissed each hand three times. Laura pulled her hands from Chris's grip, and she stepped back. She felt helpless to stop the nightmare unfolding before her eyes. Laura put her hands to her face and tried to maintain her composure. Chris rose from his green plastic chair and, trembling, looked the warden straight in the eye. The warden read the death warrant. The words washed over Laura's uncomprehending ears. The warden finished and asked Chris if he understood. Chris said that he did. "Do you have any questions," the warden asked. Chris could barely speak. "No," he rasped. The warden stepped back from the cell door.

The death squad, dressed in their starched blue uniforms, stepped into place. They had arrived in the death house earlier in the day, staying in a special room where they ate their meals, watched television, and slept. Laura noticed that their uniforms bore no name tags. Like the executioner, the corrections officers who took Chris to his death bed remained forever anonymous. One of the no-name members of the execution team stepped forward, reached through the bars of the cell, and handcuffed Chris. The cell door was smoothly opened, and the execution team surrounded Chris and wrapped their arms around him. Wearing the state-issued blue denim pants and blue shirt with the sides cut out, Chris shuffled forward in his rubber flip-flops. Surrounded by the execution team, he appeared to be more floating than walking. As Chris moved down the hallway, he turned his head and called to Steve Roach, watching in a nearby cell. "I love you, Roach," Chris said. "Be strong."[19] Roach sank to his knees and prayed for God to spare Chris.

The warden stepped to Laura's side, leaned down to her ear, and asked if she was Chris's spiritual advisor and would she be accompanying him. Her throat dry with fear, Laura managed to gasp out yes, and the warden motioned for her to walk behind the officers. "The team will assist him onto the table and secure him," the warden said. "You will then be allowed to have fifteen seconds with him." *"Fifteen seconds,"* Laura thought. *"All that is left is fifteen seconds? Twelve years of friendship and now fifteen seconds to say goodbye?"* Laura followed the officers and silently prayed that Chris would die quickly.

As Chris Thomas walked into the death chamber, a small group of friends and family members held a candlelight vigil in a field outside the walls of the Greensville Correctional Center. It was a windy night, and the candles held by Margaret Thomas, Bobby Thomas, and Glenda Corbin Thomas kept flickering. A small shrine was erected, and family members placed pictures and one of Chris's childhood toys on it. Earlier in the evening Margaret Thomas had watched the setting sun and announced that she felt as if Chris's life would be spared, but her hopes must have been waning as darkness fell. "'There ain't no more hope,'" Bobby Thomas told a reporter shortly before the execution. "He's my son . . . what he did is wrong but I'll still hold up for him.'"[20] Nearby, Glenda Corbin Thomas sobbed at the news that the United States Supreme Court refused to grant a stay of execution.[21]

Laura entered the death chamber. She was shocked at how small and ordinary it was. And she was startled to see that the witness room was almost directly at the foot of the gurney. There would be no privacy, no intimacy in the final moments of Chris's life. Chris looked small and frail, as if he had shrunk in size in the short walk from the cell to the execution chamber. The execution team swiftly and effortlessly lifted Chris onto the gurney and moved him into position. Fear now showed on Chris's face. The blank-faced officers quickly secured the thick leather straps into place. Chris watched each strap being fastened. When the officers tightened the strap across Chris's chest, he gasped and struggled to take a deep breath. "It's too tight," he called out. "I can't breathe." The officers remained stone-faced, acting as if they had not heard him.

The warden leaned in close again. "You have fifteen seconds." On trembling legs Laura walked the five feet to the gurney and leaned her face next to Chris's. She did not want her words to be overheard by the guards, by the warden, or by the witnesses. The words were only meant to be heard by Chris and by God. As Laura began speaking, time seemed to stop. The room felt silent. Even the breathing of the others in the death chamber faded away. Laura had been afraid that she wouldn't find the words to comfort Chris, but in that still quiet place the words of comfort and love spilled out. Chris nodded and spoke. The warden touched Laura on the shoulder, and the reality of the death chamber came crashing back over Laura. She ached at the thought of leaving the scared young man alone, but Laura kissed Chris softly on the cheek and moved away.

A female corrections officer gestured for Laura to walk to the witness room. Laura wanted to scream, but she turned and slowly walked toward the door. As she moved away, a voice called out. "I love you," said Chris for the last time. Those would be his final words. Laura wanted to walk back to the gurney, but she couldn't. She had to be strong now. Laura turned her head back to Chris. "I love you, too." Then she walked out of the death chamber.

As Laura stepped into the witness room, the door behind her closed and an officer directed Laura to the back row. Looking up, Laura was alarmed by the unfamiliar faces staring at her. Sitting in the back row were Chris's lawyers and a prison chaplain. Laura hugged them and sat down. The clock on the wall said 9:00 P.M. *"The Department of Corrections continues to be prompt,"* Laura thought grimly. *"All the practicing paid off."* A blue curtain covered the window to the death chamber. Behind it, the execution team was inserting intravenous lines into both arms. Chris had told Laura that this was the part that scared him the most — being alone in the execution chamber.

> The blue curtain opened, and all I could see was Chris's beautiful, precious face. The heads of the people sitting in front of me blocked my view, and I was saved from seeing his arms outstretched or the IVs in his arms. I watched his face and prayed. I prayed for God to come and take him quickly. Do I watch Chris die? I don't want to watch him die. But I wanted to be able to tell Margaret that Chris died peacefully. I watched until I could no longer see him breathing. I turned my head away and prayed. At 9:03 my dear sweet, loving friend was pronounced dead. My head dropped into my hands, and I sobbed. The curtain pulled shut. We could no longer see Chris. I could feel my heart breaking in two.

Douglas Christopher Thomas was dead. He was, however, still the property of the Commonwealth of Virginia. As the witnesses filed out of the death house, the body of Chris Thomas was placed into a body bag and loaded into a blue state van. Its destination was the medical examiner's office in Richmond, Virginia. Despite the fact that Department of Corrections officials deliberately and methodically killed Chris pursuant to a carefully orchestrated and refined execution protocol, state law still required that the state medical examiner certify the cause of death. At 9:15 P.M., the van pulled away from the death house. Chris's family and friends broke their vigil and, sobbing, watched the van carrying Chris's body slowly pass through the gates of the Greensville Correctional Center.

All death penalty states require a postexecution autopsy in order to protect against allegations that an inmate died as the result of torture at the hands of the state. "'It's no more bizarre than when someone is shot and is in critical condition in the hospital, and are [sic] expected to die,'" explained a physician in the Virginia medical examiner's office. "'We have quite a few cases we know about from the newspaper before the person dies.'"[22] One might reply, however, that seldom does the government itself kill the citizen and then cut him open to see its handiwork. Upon his arrival at the state medical examiner's office in Virginia, Chris's body was unloaded and placed in a walk-in refrigerator in the morgue. The body of the boy who once feared the shadows and darkness outside his boyhood home would remain all night alone in the dark and silent padlocked refrigerator, his corpse chilled to 36 degrees and a body tag dangling from his toe.

At 7:30 A.M. on January 11, 2000, Chris's autopsy was performed. In a newspaper article describing the autopsy of executed Virginia inmate Willie Leroy Jones, a reporter painted the scene: "the dissection instruments were ready: knives with 14-, 9- and 5½-inch blades; six syringes; four pairs of scissors; two huge pairs of tweezers; and a probe. Scales for weighing organs swing over each of the room's three stainless-steel autopsy tables. Four ion generators purge the air of the smell of formaldehyde."[23]

According to Chris Thomas's autopsy report, Chris suffered a "violent or unnatural" death caused by the "[l]ethal injection of drugs due to judicial execution." The time of death was listed at 9:12 P.M. At death, Chris was 68 inches tall and 173 pounds. After a remarkably thorough autopsy—an examination that included photographing the body, testing for drugs and disease, weighing Chris' heart (429 grams), lungs, liver, spleen, kidneys, and brain, and examining the contents of Chris's stomach and bladder—the report also concluded that Chris suffered from "no significant medical diseases." In other words, Chris Thomas was a perfectly healthy young man who died a violent death at the hands of the Commonwealth of Virginia.

Having been pumped full of poison, dissected, and photographed, Chris was finally released from state custody. His body was sent to the Bristow-Faulkner Funeral Home in Saluda, Virginia, located two blocks from the jail in which he sat during his trial as well as the courthouse in which he was convicted. As his body was prepared for its viewing, the funeral home workers dressed Chris in the dark blue suit that he had worn to his trial and his sentencing hearing.

At the behest of Chris, Laura would perform yet another "first" in her brief career as a minister; she would preside over Chris's funeral service. Laura had slept little in the days since the execution, and she found herself adrift in grief. When she and Ross arrived at the funeral home on a clear and cold Saturday, Laura slowly walked to Chris's open casket and stared down at the pale, lifeless face that she had held in her hands only days before. The casket itself was covered with a blanket of red roses, and the sickly smell of the flowers, the warmth of the room, and her fatigue made Laura's head spin.

Laura reached down and placed in Chris's cold hands a wooden cross that she had bought in Israel. Others had placed a small toy skateboard and a Beanie Baby into the casket. Margaret Thomas stood nearby, and she called to Laura to join her in a small side room. There she pressed a small, gift-wrapped box in Laura's hand, telling her it was from Chris. Laura started to cry again. "Oh, no," Laura said through her tears. "Don't do this to me now." Inside the box were a pair of aquamarine earrings—Laura's birthstone. She put the earrings on and hugged Margaret Thomas tightly.

It was time for the service. Laura went to Chris's casket and touched his still hand one more time, saying goodbye before the funeral director carefully closed the casket's lid. As the music started playing, Laura scanned the room for familiar faces. Margaret wanted to reserve time in the service for family and friends to share their memories of Chris, and Laura was frankly nervous. *"Will someone from the community come to disrupt the service? After all these years, would Chris's friends come to mourn his death?"* Putting aside her fears, Laura stood up, took a slow breath, and walked to the front of the room.

The Scripture readings and the songs had been carefully selected. Listening to the opening verses of Psalm 91, Laura prayed that Chris had found shelter in the loving arms of God.

> He who dwells in the shelter of the Most High will rest in the shadow of the Almighty. I will say of the LORD, "He is my refuge and my fortress, my God, in whom I trust." Surely he will save you from the fowler's snare and from the deadly pestilence. He will cover you with his feathers, and under his wings you will find refuge; his faithfulness will be your shield and rampart. You will not fear the terror of night, nor the arrow that flies

by day, nor the pestilence that stalks in the darkness, nor the plague that destroys at midday. A thousand may fall at your side, ten thousand at your right hand, but it will not come near you. You will only observe with your eyes and see the punishment of the wicked. If you make the Most High your dwelling—even the LORD, who is my refuge—then no harm will befall you, no disaster will come near your tent. For he will command his angels concerning you to guard you in all your ways; they will lift you up in their hands, so that you will not strike your foot against a stone.

Psalm 91 was followed by Chris's favorite Scripture passage, 1 Corinthians 13:1–13, and after the beautiful melody of "On Eagle's Wings" friends and family members rose, one by one, and shared stories of Chris's antics as a child and young teenager. Laura felt her fears of a disruption fading away, until she saw an elderly man stand up and shuffle slowly to the front of the room. "Oh, no," she thought. "Not on this day." She felt the tension drain from her body as the man began to speak. In a thin and wavering voice, the man did not hurl words of hatred or recrimination. He spoke of the pain that the community had endured and called for a time of forgiveness and healing.

The assembled mourners recited the Lord's Prayer, listened to a soloist sing "Morning Has Broken," and the service was over. All that remained was the journey to the graveyard. The wind picked up, and the air grew colder as a small group of family and friends gathered at Chris's gravesite. Joining hands, they sang "Amazing Grace" and said goodbye to the young boy whose life was marked with so much pain and tragedy, redemption and joy. As she walked across the frozen ground to her car, Laura prayed that the healing had begun. She knew, however, that she would be indelibly marked by the life and execution of her student and friend, Douglas Christopher Thomas.

Concluding Thoughts

For years now, the lawyers have controlled the conversation about legal homicide, marginalizing other voices. Now we need to reverse this. I mean no disrespect to traditional legal scholars. All I mean is that doctrinal analysis isn't what we need now. What we need are poets and historians and anthropologists and criminologists and sociologists and philosophers. In short, storytellers with experience.

MICHAEL A. MELLO

Today we speak of the execution of juvenile offenders in the past tense. This development is not due to a change in state law, but a fundamental shift in constitutional law. In 2005, a slim majority of Supreme Court justices held in *Roper v. Simmons*[1] that the execution of juvenile offenders (those who committed crimes while under the age of eighteen) violated the Eighth Amendment's ban against cruel and unusual punishment. After observing that the prohibition contained in the Eighth Amendment is grounded on the basic premise that a punishment meted out by the state must be proportionate to the crime, and that whether a punishment is proportionate must be interpreted by "the evolving standards of decency that mark the progress of a maturing society," Justice Anthony Kennedy first looked to state legislatures for evidence of an emerging national consensus against juvenile executions. Concluded Justice Kennedy: "[T]he objective indicia of consensus in this case—the rejection of the juvenile death penalty in the majority of States; the infrequency of its use even where it remains on the books; and the consistency in the trend toward abolition of the practice — provide sufficient evidence that today our society views juveniles . . . as 'categorically less culpable than the average criminal.'"[2]

Next, Justice Kennedy explained the rationale underlying the movement away from the juvenile death penalty. Juvenile offenders are considered to be less morally culpable than their adult counterparts because juveniles are less mature, more susceptible to peer pressure, and less likely to have a fully formed sense of identity than their adult counterparts. "Their own vulnerability and comparative lack of control over their immediate surroundings mean juveniles have a greater claim than adults to be forgiven for failing to escape negative influences in their whole environment," he writes. "The reality that juveniles still struggle to define their identity means it is less supportable to conclude that even a heinous crime committed by a juvenile is evidence of irretrievably depraved character . . . for a greater possibility exists that a minor's character deficiencies will be reformed."[3] In conclusion, juveniles "cannot with reliability be classified among the worst offenders."[4] If juveniles cannot be categorized as the most morally culpable criminals, then the Eighth Amendment forbids the imposition of the most severe punishment available to the state: death.

Having defined the basic characteristics of juvenile offenders, Justice Kennedy turns to the main justifications for the death penalty, to wit, retribution and deterrence. Philosopher John Rawls writes that the theory of retributive justice maintains "that punishment is justified on the grounds that wrongdoing merits punishment. It is morally fitting that a person who does wrong should suffer in proportion to his guilt, and the severity of the appropriate punishment depends on the depravity of his act."[5] In the context of the death penalty, proponents of retributive justice believe that "[t]hose who commit the most premeditated or heinous murders should be executed simply on the grounds that they deserve it."[6]

Death penalty scholars Michael L. Radelet and Marian J. Borg add, "Retributive arguments are often made in the name of families of homicide victims, who are depicted as 'needing' or otherwise benefiting from the retributive satisfaction that the death penalty promises."[7] By satisfying this need, the state minimizes the chances that the family members of a murder victim will seek their own revenge. For supporters of retributive justice, the key distinction is between revenge and retribution. Some argue that revenge is "'a private act between one person or group and another' and may or may not be justified," while retribution is "the formal act of a community against one of its members, and is carried out in the manner and for the reasons that are justified under the political constitution of the community."[8] Others assert that revenge or vengeance "signifies inflicting harm on the offender out of anger because of what he has done," while retribution is "not based on hatred for the criminal" but rather on the belief "that the criminal *deserves* to be punished and deserves to be punished in proportion to the gravity of his or her crime, whether or not the victim or anyone else desires it."[9] To those who argue that the state is committing the same act for which it is punishing the condemned, the response is that the condemned took an innocent life and the state a guilty one.[10]

Alternatively, deterrence theory suggests that citizens are less likely to commit criminal acts such as murder if they see that fellow citizens are severely punished for committing such acts. Thus the death penalty has the general deterrent effect of decreasing murder rates in the population, while simultaneously having a specific deterrent effect as to the condemned criminal; simply put, dead men neither tell tales nor commit future crimes. Why might the death penalty not deter? For critics of "deterrence theory," the inherent flaw in the argument lies in the assumption that individuals are rational and capable of weighing the costs and benefits of their actions. Writes Professor Robert M. Bohm:

> Most murderers, especially capital murderers, probably do not rationally calculate the consequences of their actions before they engage in them. ... Any who may have calculated the consequences of their actions before engaging in their crimes probably did not consider that the punishment might be death. And even if would-be killers knew that execution was the possible penalty for their actions, it likely would not deter them anyway ... [since] [t]he chances of being executed for criminal homicide is very remote.[11]

Deterrence theory also assumes that murderers will consider the death penalty a worse penalty than life in prison — another assumption that criminologists challenge.[12] Finally, some death penalty scholars argue that executions actually increase, not decrease, crime because they send the message that the killing of human beings is justified.[13]

Given these basic definitions of retributive justice and deterrence theory, Justice Kennedy challenges their applicability to juvenile offenders:

Whether viewed as an attempt to express the community's moral outrage or as an attempt to right the balance for the wrong to the victim, the case for retribution is not as strong with a minor as with an adult. Retribution is not proportional if the law's most severe penalty is imposed on one whose culpability or blameworthiness is diminished, to a substantial degree, by reason of youth and immaturity. . . . As for deterrence, it is unclear whether the death penalty has a significant or even measurable deterrent effect on juveniles. . . . [and] the absence of evidence of deterrent effect is of special concern because the same characteristics that render juveniles less culpable than adults suggest as well that juveniles will be less susceptible to deterrence.[14]

Because of a juvenile's diminished moral culpability, and the impulsiveness and lack of maturity that accompanies youth, the standard justifications for the death penalty no longer warranted the imposition of the state's most severe sanction. Concludes Justice Kennedy: "When a juvenile offender commits a heinous crime, the State can exact forfeiture of some of the most basic liberties, but the State cannot extinguish his life and his potential to attain a mature understanding of his own humanity."[15]

If one strips away the facts of the *Roper* case, Justice Kennedy could easily be writing about Chris Thomas rather than Chris Simmons. A teenager who was more "vulnerable or susceptible to negative influences and outside pressures, including peer pressure"[16] from a vocal girlfriend who wanted to be free from her parents. A juvenile whose personality was "more transitory, less fixed" in the teenage years after his grandparents' deaths and his eventual return to Middlesex County. A teenager whose lack of maturity resulted in "impetuous and ill-considered actions,"[17] including petty crime, drug use, and promiscuity. And as to whether Chris Thomas weighed the consequences of his actions on that fateful morning in November 1990, "[t]he likelihood that . . . [he] has made the kind of cost-benefit analysis that attaches any weight to the possibility of execution is so remote as to be virtually nonexistent."[18] Chris did not consider the death penalty. Chris was so naïve that he did not consider that he might be arrested, charged with capital murder, convicted, and executed—and he likely would not have been deterred even if such thoughts had crossed his mind.

Unfortunately for Chris, the words penned by Justice Anthony Kennedy came fifteen years after his indictment on charges of capital murder and five years after his execution. And the Supreme Court's determination that society has evolved to the point where juvenile executions are cruel and unusual came much too late for the other juveniles executed by the Commonwealth of Virginia. The children and teenagers who died at the hands of Virginia's executioners include Clem, a slave convicted of two murders and hanged on May 11, 1787, at the age of twelve. William, a slave convicted of arson and hanged on September 16, 1796, at the age of thirteen. Isaac, a slave convicted of attempted rape and hanged on October 21, 1825, at the age of sixteen. Arthur, a slave convicted of the attempted murder of a white female and hanged on October 23, 1857, at the age of seventeen. Charles William Beaver, a black male convicted of the rape of a ten-year-old white female and hanged on March 30, 1883, at the age of sixteen. Gabriel Battaile, a black male convicted of the rape of a white female and hanged on June 8, 1906, at the age of sixteen. Winston Green, a black male convicted of the attempted rape of a white female and electrocuted on October 30, 1908, at the age of seventeen. Aurelius Christian, a black male convicted of the rape and murder of a white female and electrocuted on March 22, 1909, at the age of seventeen. John Eccles, a black male convicted of the murder of a black male and electrocuted on November 11, 1910, at the age of seventeen. Harry Sitlington, a black male convicted of the murder of an elderly white female and electrocuted on December 16, 1910, at the age of seventeen. Virginia Christian, a black female convicted of robbery and murder of her white employer and electrocuted on August 16, 1912, at the age of seventeen. Alfred Wright, a black male convicted of rape and electrocuted on May 16, 1913, at the age of sixteen. Percy Ellis, a black male convicted of murder and electrocuted on March 15, 1916, at the age of sixteen. Tolson Bailey, a black male convicted of robbery and murder of a white male and electrocuted on July 2, 1918, at the age of seventeen. Fritz Lewis, a black male convicted of robbery and murder of a white male and electrocuted on September 12, 1924, at the age of seventeen.[19] Dwayne Allen Wright, a black male convicted of murdering an Ethiopian immigrant when he was seventeen years old and executed via lethal injection on October 14, 1998, at the age of twenty-six. Steve Roach, a white male convicted murdering an elderly white female when he was seventeen and executed via lethal injection on January 13, 2000, at age twenty-three.[20] These are the children and teenagers executed by the Commonwealth of Virginia in its four hundred–year history.[21]

What lessons about the death penalty can we draw from the story of Douglas Christopher Thomas? A young, immature, depressed, and lonely teenager,

Chris Thomas made a terrible decision and participated in the murder of two innocent people. Having been abandoned repeatedly throughout his adolescence, Chris decided that he would kill rather than lose the one person that he believed truly loved him. Whether that decision was made in a cold and premeditated fashion or in the single instant that Chris stepped across the hallway from Jessica's bedroom and aimed his shotgun at the sleeping forms of Kathy and J. B. Wiseman, Chris's actions clearly undermine one of the central arguments made in support of the death penalty, namely, deterrence. No law or punishment would have stopped the lovesick boy who walked through the darkness of the Piankatank Shores subdivision on that fateful November morning, carrying his beloved grandfather's shotgun and drawing on a marijuana joint for artificial courage.

As for the second major justification for the death penalty — retribution — did Chris deserve to be killed? Should our system of justice be grounded upon the Old Testament principle of "an eye for an eye,"[22] and, if so, *was* proportionate justice meted out? J. B. Wiseman was instantly killed by a single blast to the head; Kathy Wiseman experienced the shock and terror of waking up to the roar of a shotgun, finding her slain husband, and dying moments later at the hands of either her own daughter or Chris Thomas. Neither victim had a chance to say goodbye to their family members or make peace with their God. Alternatively, Chris Thomas spent nine years locked in a small cell. Each day of those nine years provided the opportunity to contemplate his crimes and to dwell on his pending death. Deprived of all but the most basic human necessities, Chris struggled with his remorse and the crushing boredom of death row. Chris, unlike Kathy and J. B. Wiseman, got to say goodbye to his family and to make peace with his God. And unlike his victims, Chris experienced the full horror of his impending death as he was strapped down on a steel gurney, staring at unfamiliar faces and waiting for the chemicals to enter his veins. Albert Camus observed that the very nature of the death penalty means that the punishment imposed — death — is disproportionate to the crime itself :

> But where could not really be any justice unless the condemned, after making known his decision months in advance, had approached his victim, bound him firmly, informed him that he would be put to death in an hour, and had finally used that hour to set up the apparatus of death. What criminal ever reduced his victim to such a desperate and powerless condition?[23]

Did the execution of Douglas Christopher Thomas bring justice to his victims and peace to their families? Or did it produce more pain, more death, and more victims? And was Chris's intellectual and moral development during his nine years on death row evidence that he was a young man whose value could not be measured by his worst act?

Finally, what of the criminal justice system that tried, convicted, sentenced, and executed Chris Thomas? Was Chris Thomas denied his basic due process rights by a judge who wanted to try the criminal case quickly regardless of whether an entire county had been biased by pretrial publicity? Did Judge John M. Folkes select a fair and impartial jury of Chris's peers? Or did the "death-qualifying" process produce a jury eager to convict? Did the Commonwealth of Virginia satisfy its constitutional obligations to select qualified attorneys to represent Chris zealously and competently? Was Chris treated in a humane and civilized manner during his nine years on death row? And was justice achieved when one juvenile was executed and another juvenile was freed from state custody on her twenty-first birthday?

As of this writing, the majority of Americans remain committed to keeping the death penalty. Even the most ardent supporters of the death penalty, however, must agree with the essential premise underlying the Eighth Amendment of the United States Constitution: "[c]apital punishment must be limited to those offenders who commit 'a narrow category of the most serious crimes' and whose extreme culpability makes them 'the most deserving of execution.'"[24] There is compelling evidence, however, that this is not the system that we have. Writing more than twenty years ago, law professor Jack Greenberg wrote:

> Since at least 1967, the death penalty has been inflicted only rarely, erratically, and often upon the least odious killers, while many of the most heinous criminals have escaped execution. Moreover, it has been employed almost exclusively in a few formerly slave-holding states, and there it has been used almost exclusively against killers of whites, not blacks, and never against white killers of blacks.[25]

Professor Greenberg's comments echo Justice Potter Stewart's concurring opinion in *Furman v. Georgia*, in which the justice concludes that a death penalty regime in which the ultimate punishment is "so wantonly and so freakishly imposed"[26] violates the basic due process protections of the Constitution. While Justice Stewart passed on the question of whether the capricious imposition of the death sentence is due to racial animus, Professor Goldberg rails against the system on the grounds that it cannot either fashion rules for imposing the death penalty on the worst offenders or protect defendants from society's lingering biases and prejudices.

So how does Virginia's capital punishment regime measure up? Consider the facts of Chris Thomas's crime, which resulted in his execution. Now compare those facts to the following recent cases in which defendants who were charged with capital murder by Virginia prosecutors did not receive the death penalty.

1. Marcus Garrett shot five people and killed three of them (including the mother of his daughter). He was sentenced to life in prison after pleading guilty to capital murder charges.[27]
2. Thomas Manuel Page, Jr., murdered two women and shot two other individuals. He was sentenced to two life sentences in prison pursuant to a plea agreement.[28]
3. William T. Wallace, Jr., was convicted of two counts of capital murder for the execution-style killings of two grocery store employees. He escaped death when prosecutors agreed not to seek the death penalty because Wallace had waived his right to a jury trial.[29]
4. Charles Cobler was convicted of capital murder for the beating death of a female minister during a futile robbery attempt. He was sentenced to life in prison in exchange for his guilty plea to capital murder.[30]
5. Irvin "Jack" Fountain, a twenty-eight-year-old married man, was convicted of capital murder and sentenced to life in prison for the shotgun slaying of his eight-month pregnant girlfriend, who wouldn't get the abortion that Fountain demanded. Prosecutors declined to seek the death penalty in the case.[31]
6. Gary Wayne Huffman was sentenced to two life sentences after pleading guilty for the shooting deaths of his former girlfriend and her husband. Huffman killed his former girlfriend to prevent her from testifying against him in a rape trial. Huffman shot each victim seven times with a rifle.[32]
7. Talion Hawkins killed his grandparents after they threw him out of their house because of his drug use. He pled guilty to capital murder charges and was sentenced to two life terms.[33]
8. Dale Crawford was sentenced to life in prison by a jury for the rape

and murder of his estranged wife. The evidence at trial showed that Crawford kidnapped his wife, shot her, drove her to a hotel, and later raped her as she was dead or dying.[34]

9. Jason Andrew James was found guilty of capital murder during a bench trial and sentenced to life in prison for a knife attack that left two family members dead and another two family members wounded.[35]

10. Kenneth Maurice Tinsley was sentenced to life in prison after pleading guilty to the rape and murder of Rebecca Lynn Williams, a nineteen-year-old mother of three young children. Former Virginia death row inmate Earl Washington was wrongfully convicted and almost executed for the crime.[36]

11. Donald R. Kaiser pled guilty to capital murder charges and was sentenced to life in prison for beating to death a seventy-three-year-old man with a hammer and robbing him.[37]

12. Michael Todd Hancock was convicted of the murder and robbery of two men over a two-day period, including shooting one man in the head five times. The killings were triggered by Hancock's need for rent money, and he got $150 from the two murders. Prosecutor agreed to a plea deal after the jury found Hancock guilty.[38]

13. William Shanklin was convicted of capital murder and child abuse for the death of a four-year-old boy and sentenced to life in prison by a jury.[39]

14. Michael A. Hetrick was convicted of cutting the throat of a twenty-year-old mother of an infant in exchange for $2,500.

15. Jameson James Wood was sentenced to life in prison after pleading guilty to beating his wife to death with a golf club and strangling his two children.[40]

Given the facts of the above cases and the sentences imposed, can we sincerely argue that Virginia reserves the death penalty for the worst offenders?

Chris Thomas lies in a grave in the edge of a small cemetery in Middlesex County, Virginia. Carved onto his headstone are the images of a cat and a bouquet of roses, two things that Chris loved. The grave is close to a large stand of trees, but the idyllic setting is marred by the buzz of traffic from a nearby highway. Even in death Chris is not reunited with his grandparents, who are buried several miles away. His aunt, Barbara Ann Williams, makes sure that his grave is marked with flowers, and for several years a small rose bush labored to produce a few blossoms.

Since his death, his mother, aunt, and Laura Anderson have made regular trips to the graveyard to lay flowers and tell stories about Chris. Sometimes they laugh, sometimes they cry, and sometimes they still get angry. We do not know if Jessica Wiseman has ever visited Chris's grave. She still lives in Virginia, having changed her name and seemingly escaped her past. Our sources indicate that she is both a wife and mother. Jessica declined our requests for an interview, so we do not know how the deaths of her parents and Chris Thomas have touched her life. Her grandparents have also repeatedly refused our interview requests, steadfastly maintaining that the "true story" has never been told.

Thus is the story of Douglas Christopher Thomas, who died at the hands of the Commonwealth of Virginia on January 10, 2000. His wish was that others might read his story and learn from his mistakes. To that, we add only that we hope that the readers of this story also weigh the mistakes that we have made in our long embrace of the death penalty.

Notes

Preface
1. *Roper v. Simmons*, 543 U.S. 551 (2005).
2. *Baze v. Rees*, 553 U.S. ___ (2008).
3. *Kennedy v. Louisiana*, 554 U.S. ___ (2008).

Chapter 1. The Seeds Are Sown
1. Larry J. Siegel, Brandon C. Welsh, and Joseph J. Senna, *Juvenile Delinquency: Theory, Practice, and Law*, 9th ed. (Belmont, Calif.: Thomson Wadsworth, 2005).
2. Ibid., 66.
3. Ibid.
4. Ibid., 108.
5. Ibid., 143–144.
6. Ibid., 122–123.
7. Ibid., 124.
8. Douglas Christopher Thomas's November 21, 1991, Presentence Investigation Report.
9. July 22, 1993, interview of Chris Thomas by Marie Deans.
10. Ibid.
11. Ibid.
12. Douglas Christopher Thomas's November 21, 1991, Presentence Investigation Report.
13. Not her real name.
14. State Habeas Corpus Petition of Douglas Christopher Thomas, p. 45.
15. Not her real name.
16. July 22, 1993, interview of Chris Thomas by Marie Deans.

Chapter 2. Love and Murder
1. Douglas Christopher Thomas's November 21, 1991, Presentence Investigation Report.
2. State Habeas Corpus Petition of Douglas Christopher Thomas, p. 47.
3. "Rumors Called 'Out of Control' — Neighbors, Officials Sort Murder Facts," *Daily Press* (Newport News, Va.), November 15, 1990.
4. Mark Felsenthal, "Behind Teens' Smiles, Dark Edges," *Daily Press* (Newport News, Va.), November 18, 1990.

5. Mark Felsenthal, "Middlesex Teen's Murder Trial to Begin Today," *Daily Press* (Newport News, Va.), February 27, 1991.

6. Mitigation interview.

7. Douglas Christopher Thomas's November 21 1991, Presentence Investigation Report.

8. Mark Felsenthal, "Did Teen Held in Murders Fall Through the Cracks?" *Daily Press* (Newport News, Va.), July 21, 1991.

9. Ibid.

10. Mel Oberg, "Accused Teens Were 'Desperate to Be Together,'" *Richmond Times-Dispatch*, November 18, 1990.

11. June 29, 1991, letter from Jessica Wiseman to Douglas Christopher Thomas.

12. "Teen Killer's Grandmom Stands by Her," *Virginian-Pilot*, March 15, 1992.

13. Felsenthal, "Rumors Called 'Out of Control.'"

14. Felsenthal, "Behind Teens' Smiles, Dark Edges."

15. Deborah Kelly, "A Teen's Road to Death Row—A Hopeless Childhood And A Romance Gone Wrong Ended In Double-Slaying," *Richmond Times-Dispatch*, October 9, 1994.

16. Ibid.

17. Ibid.

18. After the murders, however, Jessica's great-grandmother dismissed the notion that Chris and Jessica had tried to obtain a marriage license. "'Jessica's no fool,' she said. 'She knew she couldn't get married at her age.'" Ibid.

19. State Habeas Corpus Petition of Douglas Christopher Thomas, p. 48.

20. Amnesty International interview with Douglas Christopher Thomas.

21. "Teen Killer's Grandmom Stands by Her."

22. Amnesty International interview.

23. Ibid.

24. November 26, 1990, Virginia State Police Report (interview of Lainie Marie Creech).

25. Ibid.

26. Unpublished Amnesty International interview with Chris Thomas.

27. There is no concrete evidence, however, to back up this allegation. Kathy Wiseman's autopsy report states that she had two rings on her right hand (including her ring finger) and three rings on her left (including ring finger). In a letter to Chris, Jessica writes that "no matter what happens keep my wedding ring, PLEASE, and don't lose it, you don't have to wear it if you don't want to just keep it! Because I don't want anyone else to have it, but you." November 22, 1990, letter from Jessica Wiseman to Douglas Christopher Thomas.

28. Ibid.

29. Report of Middlesex County Deputy Sheriff Donald Rhea, contained in Douglas Christopher Thomas's November 21, 1991, Presentence Investigation Report.

30. Mel Oberg, "They Were Good Parents,' Friend of Couple Says," *Richmond Times-Dispatch*, November 13, 1990.

31. Amnesty International interview.

32. Oberg, "They Were Good Parents."

33. November 10, 1990, Virginia State Police Report.

34. Amnesty International interview.

35. Testimony of Larry Johnson, trial transcript of Douglas Christopher Thomas trial.

36. Amnesty International interview.

37. Authors' correspondence with Damian Horne.

Chapter 3. The Death Penalty in Virginia

1. Douglas Christopher Thomas's November 21, 1991, Presentence Investigation Report.

2. *Gideon v. Wainwright*, 372 U.S. 335 (1963). The right to court-appointed counsel in a capital case first recognized by the United States Supreme Court in *Powell v. Alabama*, 287 U.S. 45 (1932).

3. *Strickland v. Washington*, 466 U.S. 668 (1984). In the *Strickland* case, the United States Supreme Court held that to demonstrate ineffective assistance of counsel a defendant must prove (1) his attorney's performance was deficient, and (2) the deficiency resulted in prejudice; that is, the inadequate performance changed the outcome of the case.

4. James S. Liebman, "Opting for Real Death Penalty Reform," *Ohio State Law Journal* 63 (2002): 315–342; 323 (citation omitted).

5. Stephen B. Bright, "Counsel for the Poor: The Death Sentence Not for the Worst Crime, but for the Worst Lawyer," *Yale Law Journal* 103 (1994): 1835–1883; 1836.

6. Ibid., 1843–1844.

7. Ibid., 1842–1843.

8. Note to "The Eighth Amendment and Ineffective Assistance of Counsel in Capital Trials," *Harvard Law Review* 107 (June 1994): 1923–1940.

9. *Study of Representation in Capital Cases in Virginia: Final Report* (Spangenberg Group, 1988), 4. In the Thomas case, the bill submitted by Damian Horne and Sydney West was cut in half by Judge Folkes; ultimately each attorney received approximately nine thousand dollars. Prior to submitting the bill, Horne had consulted several death penalty experts and determined that the number of hours submitted by Horne and West fell within the range of hours typically submitted by capital defense attorneys. "I knew Judge Folkes habitually bragged about how much he used to do as Court Appointed Counsel in the early 1960s and how he did so much with so little. Against this backdrop, you can see I didn't want anyone—much less my Judge—to think we were ripping off the system. You can imagine my delight to discover that the time we put into the case fell almost precisely in the middle of what other attorneys had

historically billed. I wrote a long letter to Judge Folkes detailing all of this. The letter accompanied our billing. To no avail. He still cut our hours in half." Authors' correspondence with Horne.

10. Ibid., 27.

11. American Civil Liberties Union of Virginia, *Unequal, Unfair and Irreversible*, 12.

12. Authors' interview with Benton H. Pollok.

13. Ibid.

14. November 10, 1990, Virginia State Police Report (interview of Lainie Marie Creech).

15. November 12, 1990, Virginia State Police Report (interview of Lainie Marie Creech).

16. Ibid.

17. Ibid.

18. November 26, 1990, Virginia State Police Report (interview of Lainie Marie Creech).

19. Undoubtedly the media's interest in the case was partially due to a similar and sensational murder case in 1985, in which two University of Virginia honors students were convicted for the brutal slayings of the female student's parents. Like the Thomas trial, the case of former students Elizabeth Haysom and Jens Soering involved claims that a young woman manipulated her gullible teenage lover into murdering the parents that she despised. Haysom pled guilty to conspiring to kill her parents, while Soering was convicted of two counts of first-degree murder. Jay Conley, "Blood, Sweat and Convictions," *Roanoke Times*, April 3, 2005.

20. Mel Oberg, "Accused Teens Were 'Desperate to Be Together,'" *Richmond Times-Dispatch*, November 18, 1990.

21. Mel Oberg, "'They Were Good Parents,' Friend of Couple Says," *Richmond Times-Dispatch*, November 13, 1990.

22. Oberg, "Accused Teens."

23. Oberg, "They Were Good Parents."

24. Greg Schneider, "Young Love Led to Parents' Murder, Police Say," *Virginian-Pilot* (Norfolk, Va.), November 13, 1990.

25. Mark Felsenthal and Tina McCloud, "Teen May Have Tried to Kill Before," *Daily Press* (Newport News, Va.), November 14, 1990.

26. Ibid.

27. Ibid.

28. Frank Green, "Thomas' Execution Set for This Week," *Richmond Times-Dispatch*, June 14, 1999. Jones was also distributed by a comment that Chris Thomas made to him about the murders, namely, that "girlfriends always get me into trouble" (ibid.).

29. Mark Felsenthal, "Behind Teens' Smiles, Dark Edges," *Daily Press* (Newport News, Va.), November 18, 1990.

30. November 15, 1990, letter from Jessica Wiseman to Douglas Christopher Thomas.

31. Mark Felsenthal, "Teens' Murder Charges to Be Heard," *Daily Press* (Newport News, Va.), November 29, 1990.

32. Mark Felsenthal, "Teen's Trial Status to be Ruled in Public," *Daily Press* (Newport News, Va.), December 13, 1990; emphasis added.

33. Ibid.

34. Virginia Code 16.1-269(A).

35. Mark Felsenthal, "Alleged Murderer to be Tried as Adult," *Daily Press* (Newport News, Va.), January 24, 1991.

36. "Case Certified in Deaths of Girlfriend's Parents," *Richmond Times-Dispatch*, January 24, 1991.

37. Susan Friend, "RADAR," *Daily Press* (Newport News, Va.), January 29, 1991.

38. *Broken Justice: The Death Penalty in Virginia* (American Civil Liberties Union of Virginia, 2003): 8–16. See also, *Review of Virginia's System of Capital Punishment* (Joint Legislative Audit and Review Commission of the Virginia General Assembly, 2000).

39. "Candidates Vie for Constitutional Offices — Middlesex's Commonwealth Attorney," *Daily Press* (Newport News, Va.), October 23, 1991.

40. "In Middlesex County — Crittenden, Eley, Bray Friday Favored for Board," *Daily Press* (Newport News, Va.), October 22, 1991.

41. Legal scholars have argued that a host of extralegal factors affect prosecutorial discretion, such as electoral politics, race of either the prosecutor or the defendant, and region of the state. See, for example, Amanda S. Hitchcock, "Using the Adversarial Process to Limit Arbitrariness in Capital Charging Decisions," *North Carolina Law Review* 85 (2007): 931–973; Michael J. Songer and Isaac Unah, "The Effect of Race, Gender, and Location on Prosecutorial Decisions to Seek the Death Penalty in South Carolina," *South Carolina Law Review* 58 (2006): 161–206; Kenneth Bresler, "Seeking Justice, Seeking Election, and Seeking the Death Penalty: The Ethics of Prosecutorial Candidates' Campaigning on Capital Convictions," *Georgetown Journal of Legal Ethics* 7 (1994): 941–958; Jeffrey J. Pokorak, "Probing the Capital Prosecutor's Perspective: Race of the Discretionary Actors," *Cornell Law Review* 83 (1998): 1811–1820; James Vorenberg, "Decent Restraint of Prosecutorial Power," *Harvard Law Review* 94 (1981): 1521—1573.

42. Correspondence with authors.

43. Statistics of executions provided by the Death Penalty Information Center.

44. Robert M. Bohm, *Deathquest II: An Introduction to the Theory and Practice of Capital Punishment in the United States*, 2nd ed. (Cincinnati, Ohio: Anderson Publishing, 2003), 2.

45. David Thomas Konig, "Dale's Law and the Non-Common Law Origins of Criminal Justice in Virginia," *American Journal of Legal History* 26, no. 4 (October 1982): 354–375; 364.

46. "Virginia Has Sent 1,369 to Death," *Richmond Times-Dispatch*, August 8, 2004.

47. There is some inconsistency in the historical literature as to whether the execution occurred in late 1607 or early 1608, but 1607 appears to be the more accurate date. As for whether Kendall was a spy or a scapegoat, it depends on the source you consult. For example, see George Holbert Tucker, *Cavalier Saints and Sinners: Virginia History Through a Keyhole* (Norfolk, Va.: The Virginia Pilot and Ledger Star, 1990): 10–11. Tucker is much more confident of Kendall's duplicity and service to Spain.

48. "Digging for Answers About America's Oldest English Town," Scripps Howard News Service, August 14, 1997.

49. "Capital Punishment in Virginia," *Virginia Law Review* 58, no. 1 (January 1972): 97–142; 102 n. 35.

50. Bohm, *Deathquest II*, 2; M. Watt Espy Files, Death Penalty Information Center.

51. Ibid., 7.

52. Ibid., 9.

53. Ibid., 106.

54. Ibid., 105–109.

55. Espy Files, Death Penalty Information Center.

56. American Civil Liberties Union of Virginia, *Unequal, Unfair and Irreversible*, 38–43.

57. The Espy Files, Death Penalty Information Center; Victor L. Streib, *Death Penalty for Juveniles* (Bloomington: Indiana University Press, 1987), 75–76.

58. Frank Green, "The Execution Files — State's Death Penalty History Told in Personal Records of the Condemned," *Richmond Times-Dispatch*, December 5, 2004.

59. Streib, *Death Penalty for Juveniles*, 55.

60. Ibid., 90.

61. Ibid., 207.

62. Ibid., 79.

63. Mathew Paust, "Retired Circuit Court Judge John M. Folkes Dies," *Daily Press* (Newport News, Va.), June 18, 1998.

64. In a January 12, 1991, letter, Jessica writes: "I've been crying a lot today because my lawyer and 'another' doctor came to see me, and they took your letters from me. Don't worry I'm gonna [*sic*] get them back next week. My lawyer was the one that took them, he said he has to save a copy of every letter." January 12, 1991, letter from Jessica Wiseman to Chris Thomas.

65. November 22, 1990, letter from Jessica Wiseman to Douglas Christopher Thomas.

66. Ibid.

67. November 12, 1990, letter from Jessica Wiseman to Douglas Christopher Thomas.

68. December 27, 1990, letter from Jessica Wiseman to Douglas Christopher Thomas.

69. Ibid.

70. December 13, 1990, letter from Jessica Wiseman to Douglas Christopher Thomas.

71. December 12, 1990, letter from Jessica Wiseman to Douglas Christopher Thomas.

72. December 13, 1990, letter from Jessica Wiseman to Douglas Christopher Thomas.

73. December 3, 1990, letter from Jessica Wiseman to Douglas Christopher Thomas.

74. December 31, 1990, letter from Jessica Wiseman to Douglas Christopher Thomas.

75. January 10, 1990, letter from Jessica Wiseman to Douglas Christopher Thomas.

76. December 27, 1990, letter from Jessica Wiseman to Douglas Christopher Thomas.

77. December 13, 1990, letter from Jessica Wiseman to Douglas Christopher Thomas.

78. November 22, 1990, letter from Jessica Wiseman to Douglas Christopher Thomas.

79. December 6, 1990, letter from Jessica Wiseman to Douglas Christopher Thomas.

80. Ibid.

81. December 4, 1990, letter from Jessica Wiseman to Douglas Christopher Thomas.

82. November 29, 1990, letter from Jessica Wiseman to Douglas Christopher Thomas.

83. December 10, 1990, letter from Jessica Wiseman to Douglas Christopher Thomas.

84. December 17, 1990, letter from Jessica Wiseman to Douglas Christopher Thomas.

85. January 1, 1991, letter from Jessica Wiseman to Douglas Christopher Thomas.

86. January 10, 1991, letter from Jessica Wiseman to Douglas Christopher Thomas.

87. January 12, 1991, letter from Jessica Wiseman to Douglas Christopher Thomas.

88. Authors' correspondence with Damian Horne.

89. Ibid.

90. Ibid.

91. November 27, 1990, letter from Laura T. Anderson to Douglas Christopher Thomas.

92. February 6, 1991, letter from Douglas Christopher Thomas to Laura Anderson.

93. "The Eighth Amendment and Ineffective Assistance of Counsel in Capital Case," 1925 (citations omitted).

94. Ibid.

95. Transcript of January 28, 1991, Hearing Before Judge John M. Folkes, p. 12, lines 22–23.

96. Authors' correspondence with Damian Horne.

97. Pollok requested, and grudgingly received, an extension for filing motions.

98. A motion to deem the crime scene photographs inadmissible on the grounds that any relevance they had were outweighed by their inflammatory nature was also filed at approximately the same time and subsequently denied by the court.

99. Transcript of March 22, 1991, Hearing Before Judge John M. Folkes, p. 155, lines 16–18.

100. Ibid., p. 195, lines 11–14.

101. Ibid., p. 220, lines 19–22.

102. Transcript of April 16, 1991, Hearing Before Judge John M. Folkes, p. 3, lines 19–20.

103. Ibid., p. 3, line 22–p. 4, line 2.

104. Ibid., p. 4, lines 15–16.

105. Ibid., p. 13, lines 19–21.

106. Ibid., p. 14, lines 9–18. See also, "Judge Won't Postpone Thomas Murder Trial," *Daily Press* (Newport News, Va.), April 18, 1991.

107. Mark Felsenthal, "Lawyer Petitions to Stay on in Murder Trial," *Daily Press* (Newport News, Va.), May 7, 1991.

108. Kirk Saville, "RADAR," *Daily Press* (Newport News, Va.), September 24, 1992.

109. Virginia Code § 19.2-264.2; Bacigal, *Trial of Capital Murder Cases*, ¶ 5.101.

110. Virginia Code § 19.2-264.4(B) (emphasis added); Bacigal, *Trial of Capital Murder Cases*, ¶ 5.102.

111. Alan W. Clarke, "Virginia's Capital Murder Sentencing Proceeding: A Defense Perspective," *University of Richmond Law Review* Vol. 18 (1984): 341–359. Ibid. at 342.

112. Alan W. Clarke, "Procedural Labyrinths and the Injustice of Death: A Critique of Death Penalty Habeas Corpus" (Part One), *University of Richmond Law Review* 29 (December 1995): 1327–1388; 1372.

113. Gary Goodpaster, "The Trial for Life: Effective Assistance of Counsel in Death Penalty Cases," *New York University Law Review* 58 (May 1983): 299–362; 303.

114. Ibid., 1373 (quoting Marie Deans).

115. Under Virginia law, a defendant in a capital murder case can request that the court appoint a mental health expert (defined as a psychiatrist or a clinical psychologist) to "evaluate the defendant and to assist the defense in the preparation and presentation of information concerning the defendant's history, character, or mental condition, including (i) whether the defendant acted under extreme mental or emotional disturbance at the time of the offense; (ii) whether the capacity of the defendant to appreciate the criminality of his conduct or to conform his conduct to the requirements of the law was significantly impaired at the time of the offense; and (iii) whether there are any other factors in mitigation relating to the history or character of the defendant or the defendant's mental condition at the time of the offense." Virginia Code

§19.2-264.3:1. The examination conducted under this statute is different than examinations conducted to see if (1) the defendant was legally insane at the time of the offense, or (2) the defendant is competent to stand trial.

116. American Civil Liberties Union of Virginia, *Unequal, Unfair and Irreversible*, 17.

117. Clarke, "Virginia's Capital Murder Sentencing Proceeding," 341.

118. Damian Horne strongly denies receiving any offer of help from Marie Deans. One possible explanation is that the offer went to the original trial counsel, Benton Pollok.

119. May 7, 1993, affidavit of Henry O. Gwaltney, Jr.

120. Ibid., p. 6, ¶ 25.

121. Virginia Code § 19.2-168.

122. Virginia Code § 19.2-264.3:1(E).

123. Transcript of May 21, 1991, Hearing before Judge John E. DeHardit, p. 15, lines 13–14.

124. Transcript of May 21, 1991, Hearing before Judge John E. DeHardit, p. 16, lines 13–14.

125. Ibid., p. 17, lines 5–8 (emphasis added).

126. Ibid., p. 29, lines 11–20.

127. Transcript of May 21, 1991, Hearing before Judge John E. DeHardit, p. 18, lines 12–18.

128. Greg Schneider, "Saluda Teen Guilty of Murdering Parents," *Virginian-Pilot* (Newport News, Va.), June 27, 1991.

129. Mark Felsenthal, "Boy Facing Trial in Murders Hospitalized," *Daily Press* (Newport News, Va.), June 29, 1991.

130. Tom Chillemi, "Jessica Wiseman Found Guilty of Killing Parents," *Southside Sentinel*, June 27, 1991. The juvenile court file of Jessica Wiseman remains sealed, and we were never able to obtain a copy of a trial transcript.

131. Jim Spencer, "Child's Play: Murder Parents to Get Your Way," *Daily Press* (Newport News, Va.), June 28, 1991.

132. Chillemi, "Jessica Wiseman Found Guilty of Killing Parents."

133. Tom Chillemi, "Wiseman Murders Planned in Detail, Testimony Reveals," *Southside Sentinel*, July 3, 1991.

134. Schneider, "Saluda Teen Guilty of Murdering Parents."

135. Mark Felsenthal, "Teen Guilty of Killing Parents," *Daily Press* (Newport News, Va.), June 27, 1991.

136. Susan Friend, "Down Home Security," *Daily Press* (Newport News, Va.), July 2, 1991.

137. June 29, 1991, letter from Jessica Wiseman to Douglas Christopher Thomas.

138. "14-Year-Old Sentenced to State Supervision for Parents' Murders," *Virginian-Pilot*, August 1, 1991.

139. In the weeks before his trial, Chris's attorneys would seek a dismissal of the murder charges on the grounds that key evidence—namely, a bag of

marijuana allegedly laced with PCP from which Chris rolled and smoked a joint on the night of the murders—had been deliberately destroyed by the Middlesex County Sheriff's Office. A hearing was held on the motion to dismiss, and during that hearing Chris Thomas briefly took the witness stand for the first—and only—time during his trial. The allegations that Commonwealth Attorney Jimmy Ward had purposefully destroyed relevant evidence only inflamed tensions between Ward and defense counsel, with Ward stating in open court: "Except for the death of my parents, I don't think I've faced anything more devastating than to be accused, in the papers, of destroying evidence." Judge Folkes denied the dismissal motion, finding that the destruction of the evidence was not done in bad faith and did not impact Chris's ability to receive a fair trial. Mark Felsenthal, "Teen's Fair Trial Not at Risk, Judge Rules," *Daily Press* (Newport News, Va.), August 15, 1991.

Chapter 4. On Trial for His Life

1. Robert A. Carp, Ronald Stidham, and Kenneth L. Manning, *Judicial Process in America*, 7th ed. (Washington, D.C., CQ Press, 2007): 238–239.
2. *Witherspoon v. Illinois*, 391 U.S. 510 (1968). See also, *Wainwright v. Witt*, 469 U.S. 412 (1985); *Lockhart v. McCree*, 476 U.S. 162 (1986).
3. Scott E. Sundby, *A Life and Death Decision: A Jury Weighs the Death Penalty* (New York: Palgrave Macmillan, 2005), 22.
4. Ibid., 23.
5. The body of studies on the effects of death qualification are too voluminous to properly summarize. Examples include the following: Richard Salgado, "Tribunals Organized To Convict: Searching for a Lesser Evil in the Capital Juror Death-Qualification Process in United States v. Green," *Brigham Young University Law Review* (2005): 519–553; William J. Bowers and Wanda D. Foglia, "Still Singularly Agonizing: Law's Failure to Purge Arbitrariness from Capital Sentencing," *Criminal Law Bulletin* 30 (2003): 51; John H. Blume, Sheri Lynn Johnson, and A. Brian Threlkeld, "Probing 'Life Qualification' Through Expanded Voir Dire," *Hofstra Law Review* 29 (Summer 2001): 1209–1264; Rick Seltzer, Grace M. Lopes, Marshall Dayan, and Russell F. Canan, "The Effect of Death Qualification on the Propensity of Jurors to Convict: The Maryland Example," *Howard Law Journal* 29 (1986): 571–608; Craig Haney, "Examining Death Qualification: Further Analysis of the Process Effect," *Law and Human Behavior* 8 (1984): 133–151.
6. Carp, Stidham, and Manning, *Judicial Process*, 238.
7. *Batson v. Kentucky*, 476 U.S. 79 (1986); *J.E.B. v. Alabama ex rel T.B.*, 511 U.S. 127 (1994).
8. The Supreme Court has held that death penalty states that impose mandatory death sentences for those convicted of capital offenses are unconstitutional. *Woodson v. North Carolina*, 428 U.S. 280 (1976); *Roberts v. Louisiana*, 428 U.S. 325 (1976).

9. 428 U.S. 153 (1976). *Gregg v. Georgia* was one of several test cases that the Supreme Court heard regarding the death penalty. Two other cases considered by the Supreme Court at the same time were *Jurek v. Texas*, 428 U.S. 262 (1976); and *Profitt v. Florida*, 428 U.S. 242 (1976).

10. Sundby, *A Life and Death Decision*, 15.

11. Ibid.

12. Ibid.

13. Va. Code § 8.01–358.

14. Douglas Christopher Thomas Trial Transcript, 1:51, lines 14–15 (hereinafter Trial Transcript).

15. Given recent case law, preserving the objection for appeal may have been pointless. In 1997, the Virginia Court of Appeals held that — although state law clearly granted attorneys the right to ask questions during voir dire, and that the refusal of a trial court judge to permit attorneys to do so was an abuse of the court's discretion — that such an error was harmless because "it plainly appears from the record that this error did not affect the questions propounded to the prospective jurors, the selection or composition of the jury panel or its partiality." *Charity v. Commonwealth*, 24 Va. App. 258, 267 (1997) (en banc).

16. "Known as the contemporaneous objection rule, [Virginia Supreme Court] Rules 5:25, in pertinent part, provides that '[e]rror will not be sustained to any ruling of the trial court . . . before which the case was initially tried unless the objection was stated with reasonably certainty at the time of the ruling, except for good cause shown or to enable [the Supreme Court of Virginia] to attain the ends of justice.'" Michael A. Groot, "To Attain the Ends of Justice: Confronting Virginia's Default Rules in Capital Cases," *Capital Defense Digest* 6, no. 2 (Spring 1994): 44–48; 44.

17. Trial Transcript, 1:276, line 23.

18. Ibid., 1:37, lines 1–4.

19. Ibid., 1:47, lines 6–9.

20. Ibid., 1:52, lines 8–12.

21. Ibid., 1:47, lines 11–12.

22. Trial Transcript, 2:296, lines 17–22.

23. Ibid., 2:296, lines 23–25.

24. Ibid., 2:297, lines 1–4.

25. Ibid., 2:297, lines 8–13.

26. State Habeas Corpus Petition of Douglas Christopher Thomas, pp. 59–60.

27. Author's correspondence with Damian Horne.

28. Thomas A. Mauet, *Fundamentals of Trial Technique*, 3rd ed. (Boston: Little, Brown, 1992), 41.

29. Ibid., 43.

30. *United States v. Dinitz*, 424 U.S. 600, 612 (1976).

31. Mauet, *Fundamentals of Trial Technique*, 46.

32. August 22, 1991, Trial Transcript, 1:317.

33. Ibid., 1:318.

34. Tom Chillemi, "Jessica Wiseman Found Guilty of Killing Parents," *Southside Sentinel*, June 27, 1991.

35. August 22, 1991, Trial Transcript, 1:321.

36. Mauet, *Fundamentals of Trial Technique*, 47–48.

37. August 22, 1991, Trial Transcript, 1:323.

38. Ibid., 1:323–324.

39. Ibid., 1:324.

40. Ibid., 1:325.

41. Ibid.

42. Ibid., 1:331.

43. Authors' correspondence with Damian Horne. Horne writes: "In the many emotions I had after the sentence of death—shock, regret, anger . . . and mostly numbed exhaustion—I remember railing at Sydney that Chris's inability to 'defer gratification' had really put me out. By that, I mean Chris lived his life from second to second . . . if something wasn't instantly gratifying . . . or a course might provide him discomfort, he was unable to see any future benefits his efforts might obtain. That is often typical—in my experience—of defendants. They are willing to face the reality of a grim (sometimes deadly) future if, in their inaction, addictions or whatever, they don't have to take THE stand or A stand. It isn't easy to be in a witness box . . . but, in my opinion, that is what he had to do in order to have a chance of saving his life. Ultimately, Chris would not make that effort because it wasn't easy or immediately gratifying."

44. Authors' correspondence with Horne.

45. August 22, 1991, Trial Transcript, 1:331.

46. Ibid., 2:483.

47. Ibid., 2:488.

48. Ibid., 1:371.

49. Ibid., 2:403–404.

50. Ibid., 2:404.

51. Ibid., 2:410.

52. Ibid., 1:393.

53. Ibid., 1:394.

54. Ibid., 2:458.

55. Ibid., 2:464.

56. Ibid., 2:466.

57. Ibid., 2:426.

58. Ibid., 2:427.

59. Ibid., 2:427–428.

60. Ibid., 2:430.

61. Ibid., 2:431.

62. Ibid., 2:433.

63. Ibid.

64. Ibid., 2:434.

65. Mark Felsenthal, "18-Year-Old Convicted of Capital Murder," *Daily Press* (Newport News, Va.), August 24, 1991.

66. August 23, 1991, Trial Transcript, 1:524.

67. Ibid., 1:525.

68. Ibid., 1:536.

69. Authors' correspondence with Horne.

70. State Habeas Corpus Petition of Douglas Christopher Thomas, p. 50.

71. Ibid.

72. In civil and criminal cases, both sides have the opportunity to submit written jury instructions to the trial judge. At his discretion, the trial court judge may use those jury instructions or use his own set of instructions. Commonwealth Attorney Jimmy Ward submitted a proposed set of jury instructions to the court. While Chris's appellate lawyers later believed that defense counsel failed to submit jury instruction, Damian Horne maintains that he did. Horne explains that the defense team originally submitted "titled" jury instructions (as is the practice in federal court), but were then required to submit "clean" copies of the instructions to Judge Folkes.

73. August 23, 1991, Trial Transcript, 1:535.

74. Ibid., 1:536.

75. Ibid.

76. Ibid., 1:545.

77. Ibid., 1:555.

78. Ibid., 1:557.

79. Ibid., 1:562, lines 11–12.

80. Ibid., 1:562, lines 14–18.

81. Ibid., 1:562, line 19–563, line 2.

82. Ibid., p. 563, lines 3–15.

83. Bruce Nash and Allan Zullo, eds., *Lawyer's Wit and Wisdom: Quotations on the Legal Profession, in Brief* (Philadelphia: Running Press, 1995): 152.

84. August 23, 1991, Trial Transcript, 1:563, lines 15–18.

85. Ibid., 1:563, line 25–564, line 9.

86. Ibid.

87. Ibid., 1:564, line 19–565, line 1.

88. Ibid., 1:565, lines 12–16.

89. Ibid., 1:565, lines 17–24.

90. Ibid., 1:566, lines 18–21.

91. Ibid., 1:566, lines 4–6.

92. Ibid., 1:566, lines 7–16.

93. Ibid., 1:568, lines 5–8.

94. Mark Felsenthal, "18-Year-Old Convicted of Capital Murder," *Daily Press* (Newport News, Va.), August 24, 1991.

95. August 23, 1991, Trial Transcript, 1:570, line 22–571, line 4.

96. Ibid., 1:571, lines 12–14.

97. Ibid., 1:571, lines 15–21.

98. Ibid., 1:572, lines 1–2.

99. Ibid., 1:572, line 10–573, line 1.

100. Micah 6:8.

101. August 23, 1991, Trial Transcript, 1:573, lines 14–21.

102. Ibid., 1:574, lines 3–6.

103. Ibid., 1:575, lines 22–25.

104. Tom Chillemi, "Emotions Ran High During Four-Day Trial," *Southside Sentinel*, August 1991.

105. August 23, 1991, Trial Transcript, 1:582, lines 5–10.

106. Tom Chillemi, "Emotions Ran High."

107. Felsenthal, "18-Year-Old Convicted of Capital Murder."

108. Ibid.

109. Ibid.

110. Ibid.

111. Horne himself realized — albeit much too late — that it would be a disaster to put on the stand at the sentencing hearing the psychologist appointed to serve as an expert witness. "The mere specter of trial literally had him quivering. One of the most memorable things about the case was his taking me off to the side and saying (these are his exact words) 'Are they going to be mean to me?' I was stunned. More than stunned, I was in near panic mode. I had a Judge who wouldn't even appoint us our own investigator . . . or consider appointing us another psychologist . . . and who acted like every delay or request for assistance was a personal affront to the bench and his time schedule. Suddenly, I had an 'expert' the other side (Gwaltney included) indicated they were going to humiliate and prevent from even being qualified as an expert. [Our expert's] report, in my opinion, was absolutely worthless. He kept calling me up and asking me what he should say, how to say it . . . and, Lord . . . I can't even begin to describe the tragi-comedy of these conversations." Author's correspondence with Horne.

112. May 7, 1993, Affidavit of Henry O. Gwaltney, Jr., p. 7, ¶ 27.

113. August 26, 1991, Sentencing Hearing of Douglas Christopher Thomas, 1:592, lines 3–8.

114. Ibid., 1:592, lines 12–15.

115. Virginia Code § 19.2-264.2; Bacigal, *Trial of Capital Murder Cases*, ¶ 5.101.

116. *Smith v. Commonwealth*, 219 Va. 455, 478 (1978).

117. 229 Va. 469 (1985).

118. Ibid., 489–490.

119. Ibid., 490.

120. *Burns v. Commonwealth*, 261 Va. 307, 339 (2001).

121. Bacigal, *Trial of Capital Murder Cases in Virginia*, ¶ 5.202, pp. 234–235 (citations omitted and emphasis added).

122. *Roach v. Commonwealth of Virginia*, 251 Va. 324 (1996); *O'Dell v. Commonwealth of Virginia*, 234 Va. 672 1988).

123. *Roach v. Commonwealth of Virginia*, 251 Va. 324 (1996).

124. Virginia Code § 19.2-264.4(B) (emphasis added); Bacigal, *Trial of Capital Murder Cases*, ¶ 5.102.

125. Bacigal, *Trial of Capital Murder Cases*, ¶ 5.302, p. 244.

126. August 26, 1991, Sentencing Hearing of Douglas Christopher Thomas, 1:597, line 10.

127. Ibid., 1:597, lines 17–18, 23–25 to 598, line 1.

128. Ibid., 1:599, lines 5–7.

129. Ibid., 1:598, lines 11–16.

130. Ibid., 1:599, lines 15–18.

131. Ibid., 1:605, lines 15–23.

132. State Habeas Corpus Petition of Douglas Christopher Thomas, p. 13. A plea bargain was not some remote, fanciful idea that would not have been accepted by the court. Shortly before Chris's first execution date, Jim Breeden, one of Chris's appellate lawyers and a friend of Judge Folkes, stated that the judge "expressed to me many times in the years after this conviction that he was very disturbed by the outcome. He said he did everything he could to suggest to the lawyers representing Thomas that if he pleaded guilty, he wouldn't have sentenced him to death." Patti Rosenberg, "Many are Opposed to Man's Execution—Thomas Only Killed for Girlfriend, Love, They Say," *Daily Press* (Newport News, Va.), June 15, 1999.

133. August 26, 1991, Sentencing Hearing of Douglas Christopher Thomas, 1:606, lines 6–16.

134. Ibid., 1:606, lines 23–24.

135. Ibid., 1:606, line 22.

136. Ibid., 1:607, lines 2–7.

137. Ibid., 1:608, lines 17–20.

138. Ibid., 1:609, lines 9–10.

139. Ibid., 1:609, lines 12–14.

140. Ibid., 1:609, line 24–610, line 3.

141. Ibid., 1:611, lines 5–7.

142. Ibid., 1:610, line 23–611, line 2.

143. Ibid., 1:627, line 23–628, line 6.

144. *Clark v. Commonwealth*, 220 Va. 201, 210 (1979).

145. August 26, 1991, Sentencing Hearing of Douglas Christopher Thomas, 1:628, line 22–629, line 4.

146. State Habeas Corpus Petition of Douglas Christopher Thomas, p. 19.

147. *Frye v. Commonwealth*, 231 Va. 370 (1986).

148. Damian Horne recalls that Chris Thomas bragged to him about the alleged

escape attempt. "He even boasted to us about it . . . I'm not sure how successful it was, but he represented to us that he 'was almost there' [meaning outside the jail]. I have to doubt that . . . but that is what he said." Author's correspondence with Horne.

149. August 26, 1991, Sentencing Hearing of Douglas Christopher Thomas, 1:639, lines 3–5.

150. Ibid., 1:640, lines 7–8.

151. State Habeas Corpus Petition of Douglas Christopher Thomas, p. 20.

152. August 26, 1991, Sentencing Hearing of Douglas Christopher Thomas, 1:664, lines 14–16.

153. Ibid., 1:665, lines 1–4.

154. Ibid., 1:665, lines 16–21.

155. Virginia Code §§ 19.2–264.2; 19.2–264.4(C).

156. August 26, 1991, Sentencing Hearing of Douglas Christopher Thomas, 1:667, lines 21–24.

157. Ibid., 1:668, lines 9–12.

158. Ibid., 1:669, lines 7–9.

159. Ibid., 1:669, lines 18–19.

160. Ibid., 1:670, lines 19–20.

161. Ibid., line 21.

162. State Habeas Corpus Petition of Douglas Christopher Thomas, p. 32.

163. August 26, 1991, Sentencing Hearing of Douglas Christopher Thomas, 1:673, lines 5–8.

164. Ibid., 1:681, lines 8–11.

165. Ibid., 1:688, lines 10–12.

166. The trial transcript does not make note of the times that the witnesses took and left the stand, but notes taken by court personnel have memorialized the exact length of each witnesses' testimony during the sentencing hearing.

167. August 26, 1991, Sentencing Hearing of Douglas Christopher Thomas, 1:696, line 22.

168. Ibid., 1:696, line 25.

169. Ibid., 1:705, line 15.

170. Ibid., 1:708, lines 18–19.

171. Ibid., 1:725, lines 2–3.

172. Ibid., 1:731, lines 20–21.

173. Ibid., 1:732, lines 18–19.

174. Ibid., 1:732, line 23–733, line 8.

175. Ibid., 1:776, line 25–777, line 8.

176. Ibid., 1:739, lines 17–19.

177. Ibid., 1:740, lines 3–6.

178. Ibid., 1:742, line 12.

179. Ibid., 1:743, line 25–744, line 3.

180. Ibid., 1:746, lines 3–4.

181. Ibid., 1:746, lines 18–21.

182. Ibid., 1:747, lines 4–6.

183. Ibid., 1:747, lines 11–18.

184. Ibid., 1:748, lines 17–24.

185. Ibid., 1:748, line 25–749, line 2.

186. Ibid., 1:749, lines 3–9.

187. Deborah Kelly, "A Teen's Road to Death Row — A Hopeless Childhood And A Romance Gone Wrong Ended In Double-Slaying," *Richmond Times-Dispatch*, October 9, 1994.

188. Rosenberg, "Many are Opposed to Man's Execution."

189. Frank Green, "Thomas' Execution Set for This Week," *Richmond Times-Dispatch*, June 14, 1999.

190. Ibid.

191. Mark Felsenthal, "Teen Murderer Refused to Testify," *Daily Press* (Newport News, Va.), August 28, 1991.

192. August 27, 1991, letter from Laura T. Anderson to Douglas Christopher Thomas.

193. Ibid.

194. Ibid.

195. Felsenthal, "Teen Murderer Refused to Testify."

196. August 26, 1991, Sentencing Hearing of Douglas Christopher Thomas, 1:763, line 24.

197. Ibid., 1:765, lines 9–15.

198. Ibid., 1:765, line 24–766, line 1.

199. Ibid., 1:767, line 23–768, line 6.

200. Ibid., 1:770, line 21–771, line 8.

201. Ibid., 1:771, lines 19–23.

202. Ibid., 1:772, line 24.

203. Ibid., 1:773, lines 9–13.

204. *Smith v. Commonwealth*, 219 Va. 455 (1978).

205. August 26, 1991, Sentencing Hearing of Douglas Christopher Thomas, 1:773, lines 14–22.

206. Ibid., 1:774, lines 21–25.

207. Ibid., 1:775, lines 19–21.

208. *Lovitt v. Commonwealth*, 260 Va. 497, 517 (2000).

209. August 26, 1991, Sentencing Hearing of Douglas Christopher Thomas, 1:777, line 24–778, line 4.

210. Ibid., 1:778, line 22–779, line 1.

211. State Habeas Corpus Petition of Douglas Christopher Thomas, p. 39.

212. Authors' correspondence with Horne.

213. State Habeas Corpus Petition of Douglas Christopher Thomas, p. 55.

214. Authors' correspondence with Horne.

215. State Habeas Corpus Petition of Douglas Christopher Thomas, p. 24.

216. Ibid., 39.
217. Authors' correspondence with Damian Horne.
218. "Thomas Sentenced to Death For Capital Murder," *Southside Sentinel*, August 29, 1991; "Teen Murderer Sentenced to Electric Chair," *Daily Press* (Newport News, Va.), August 27, 1991.
219. Felsenthal, "Teen Murderer Refused to Testify."
220. Felsenthal, "Teen Murderer Sentenced to Electric Chair."
221. Tom Chillemi, "Emotions Ran High During Four-Day Trial," *Southside Sentinel*, August 1991.
222. Ibid.

Chapter 5. Life on the Row

1. Robert Johnson, *Death Work: A Study of the Modern Execution Process* (Belmont, Calif.: Thomson/Wadsworth, 2006), 84.
2. Marie Deans, "Working Against the Death Penalty," in *Writing for Their Lives: Death Row USA*, ed. Marie Mulvey-Roberts (Champaign: University of Illinois Press, 2007), 59.
3. Johnson, *Death Work*, 94.
4. Ibid., 64.
5. Under Virginia law, "all records of persons imprisoned in penal institutions in the Commonwealth provided such records relate to the imprisonment" are excluded from mandatory disclosure under the Freedom of Information Act. Virginia Code § 2.2–3706 (F)(6). The release of such records is left to the discretion of the custodian of records at the Virginia Department of Corrections. Of course, a refusal to *ever* exercise a grant of discretion granted to an agency by a state legislature seems an abuse of that very discretion.
6. "Death Row Breakout," *Virginian-Pilot*, May 31, 1994.
7. "Giarratano Discovers Life on Death Row While Hoping for a New Trial," *Roanoke Times*, September 9, 1993.
8. Correspondence with authors.
9. Jan Arriens, ed., *Welcome to Hell: Letters and Writings from Death Row* (Boston: Northeastern University Press, 1997), 45.
10. Ibid.
11. "In Stockton's Words," *Roanoke Times*, August 14, 1995.
12. Ibid.
13. "Settlement of Inmates' Suit Enacts New Cell Search Rules," *Richmond Times-Dispatch*, May 24, 1995; "ACLU Sues Virginia Over Prison Treatment," *Daily Press* (Newport News, Va.), March 6, 1995.
14. "Virginia Inmates' Fans Confiscated—Prisoners Feel the Heat," *Virginian-Pilot*, April 25, 1996.
15. "In Stockton's Words."
16. Deans, "Working Against the Death Penalty," 61.
17. Correspondence with authors.

18. "In Stockton's Words."

19. "A Teen's Road to Death Row," *Richmond Times-Dispatch,* October 9, 1994.

20. "LeVasseur Committed Suicide, Probe Finds," *Richmond Times-Dispatch*, April 22, 1987.

21. Arriens, *Welcome to Hell*, 58.

22. David Von Drehle, *Among the Lowest of the Dead: The Culture of Capital Punishment* (Ann Arbor: University of Michigan Press, 2005), 121–122.

23. Ibid., 124.

24. Ibid., 125.

25. Ibid., 126.

26. Arriens, *Welcome to Hell*, 90.

27. With the exception of Joseph Payne and Wayne DeLong, all inmates who sat on death row with Chris Thomas have been executed. Payne had his death sentence commuted, while DeLong committed suicide.

28. "Virginia Inmates on Death Row Lose Chief Ally," *Virginian-Pilot*, September 4, 1993.

29. Authors' interview with Marie Deans.

30. Ibid.

31. Authors' correspondence with Robert Deans.

32. December 3, 1991, letter from Douglas Christopher Thomas to Laura Anderson.

33. Ibid.

34. Amnesty International interview.

35. Arriens, *Welcome to Hell*, 46.

36. Johnson, *Death Work*, 78.

37. Correspondence with authors.

38. Ibid.

39. Ibid.

40. Johnson, *Death Work*, 77.

41. Arriens, *Welcome to Hell*, 60.

42. "Latest Chapter in Sad History of Prison War — State Now Fighting Death Row Drugs," *Richmond Times-Dispatch*, July 29, 1993.

43. "Death Row Inmate Took Heroin — Another Prisoner Found With Gun on Person," *Richmond Times-Dispatch*, June 3, 1994.

44. "Inmates Say Guards Didn't Supply Drugs," *Richmond Times-Dispatch*, June 14, 1994.

45. Arriens, *Welcome to Hell*, 117.

46. Deans, "Working Against the Death Penalty," 60.

47. "Overdose Killed Death Row Inmate," *Richmond Times-Dispatch*, May 15, 2001.

48. "Forced Medication Order — Judge Rules Death Row Inmate Must Take Anti-Psychotic Drugs," *Fort Worth Star-Telegram*, April 12, 2006; "Death-Row Inmate's Appeals About Force-Fed Drugs Run Out," *Orlando Sentinel*, November 5, 2003.

49. "Death Row Drugs," *Associated Press*, November 6, 2006.

50. Arriens, *Welcome to Hell*, 117–118.

51. March 21, 1992, letter from Jessica Wiseman to Douglas Christopher Thomas.

52. March 22, 1992, letter from Jessica Wiseman to Douglas Christopher Thomas.

53. Johnson, *Death Work*, 79.

54. Ibid.

55. Ibid., 98.

56. Correspondence with authors.

57. Ibid.

58. Johnson, *Death Work*, 99.

59. "Getting Ready to Die—Death-Row Inmates Wait in Line," *Daily Press* (Newport News, Va.), September 13, 1992.

60. Arriens, *Welcome to Hell*, 39.

61. Ibid., 62.

62. Ibid., 61.

63. Code of Virginia § 17.1–313 (2008).

64. *Akers v. Commonwealth*, 260 Va. 358, 364, 535 S.E.2d 674, 677 (2000).

65. For many death row inmates in the 1980s and 1990s, Virginia's notorious "21-Day Rule" presented another hurdle in seeking justice. Simply put, Virginia law held that a defendant had twenty-one days after sentencing to introduce evidence on innocence. Even if the evidence of innocence was overwhelming, after this twenty-one-day period Virginia courts were banned from granting the defendant a new trial and considering the evidence. The law has recently been modified to permit the introduction of new evidence in limited circumstances.

66. *Lovitt v. Warden*, 266 Va. 216, 585 S.E.2d 801 (2003).

67. *Virginia Parole Board v. Wilkins*, 255 Va. 419 (1998).

68. *Lovitt v. Warden, Sussex I State Prison*, 266 Va. 216, 240 (2003).

69. Code of Virginia § 8.01–654 (2008).

70. *Strickland v. Washington*, 466 U.S. 668 (1984).

71. 28 U.S.C. § 2241, et seq.

72. 28 U.S.C. § 2254(A).

73. In 1998, then Virginia Attorney General Mark Earley wrote an editorial criticizing the use of the phrase "death squad" by Washington and Lee law professor William Geimer. "The people in this office who represent the Commonwealth during the appeals of capital punishment cases are carrying out the sentence imposed by Virginia juries and Virginia judges," wrote Earley. "If there is a death squad in Virginia, it is composed of the murderous individuals being held on Death Row." Mark L. Earley, "Objections are Fine; Insults are Not," *Richmond-Times Dispatch*, April 10, 1998.

74. Greg Weatherford, "Team Strives to Quicken the Death Penalty's Pace," *Virginian-Pilot*, April 5, 1997.

75. Ibid.

76. Ibid.

77. Frank Green, "Official Fears Moratorium on Executions in State," *Richmond-Times Dispatch*, February 4, 2000.

78. Ibid.

79. Ibid.

80. Authors' correspondence with Horne.

81. *Thomas v. Commonwealth*, 244 Va. 1, 419 S.E.2d 606; *cert. denied*, 506 U.S. 958 (1992).

82. *Thomas v. Taylor*, 170 F.3d 466 (1999).

83. American Civil Liberties Union of Virginia, *Unequal, Unfair and Irreversible: The Death Penalty in Virginia* (2000), 24.

84. Ibid.

85. Ibid., 28.

86. Ibid., 31.

87. "Getting Ready to Die — Death Row Inmates Wait in Line," *Daily Press* (Newport News, Va.), September 13, 1992.

88. Ibid.

89. Ibid.

90. Johnson, *Death Work*, 79–80.

91. "Death Row Parish," *Roanoke Times*, July 11, 1993.

92. Johnson, *Death Work*, 79–80.

93. "State Required to Ensure Safety of Condemned," *Daily Press* (Newport News, Va.), April 8, 1995.

94. Albert Camus, *Resistance, Rebellion, and Death* (New York: Knopf, 1961), 202.

95. Kathleen M. Flynn, "The 'Agony of Suspense': How Protracted Death Row Confinement Gives Rise to an Eighth Amendment Claim of Cruel and Unusual," *Washington and Lee Law Review* 54 (Winter 1997): 291–333; 295–296.

96. Ibid., 296 (quoting former Virginia death row inmate Willie Lloyd Turner). Of course, some death penalty proponents submit that death row inmates can spare themselves such prolonged agony by waiving their appeals.

97. Ibid., 297.

98. June 7, 1993, Marie Deans mitigation interview of Chris Thomas.

99. Authors' interview with Marie Deans.

100. December 20, 1992, letter from Jessica Wiseman to Chris Thomas.

101. November 28, 1991, letter from Jessica Wiseman to Chris Thomas.

102. February 9, 1992, letter from Jessica Wiseman to Chris Thomas.

103. July 21, 1992, letter from Jessica Wiseman to Chris Thomas.

104. "Middlesex Teen's Murder Trial to Begin Today," *Daily Press* (Newport News, Va.), February 27, 1991.

105. Ibid.

106. March 10, 1992, letter from Jessica Wiseman to Chris Thomas.

107. April 4, 1992, letter from Jessica Wiseman to Chris Thomas.

108. June 3, 1992, letter from Jessica Wiseman to Chris Thomas.

109. December 5, 1991, letter from Jessica Wiseman to Chris Thomas.

110. January 3, 1992, letter from Jessica Wiseman to Chris Thomas.

111. Ibid.

112. March 31, 1992, letter from Jessica Wiseman to Chris Thomas.

113. July 1, 1992, letter from Jessica Wiseman to Chris Thomas.

114. March 21, 1992, letter from Jessica Wiseman to Chris Thomas.

115. March 31, 1992, letter from Jessica Wiseman to Chris Thomas.

116. January 30, 1992, letter from Jessica Wiseman to Chris Thomas.

117. August 19, 1992, letter from Jessica Wiseman to Chris Thomas.

118. February 29, 1992, letter from Jessica Wiseman to Chris Thomas.

119. February 23, 1992, letter from Jessica Wiseman to Chris Thomas.

120. November 28, 1992, letter from Jessica Wiseman to Chris Thomas.

121. June 11, 1992, letter from Jessica Wiseman to Chris Thomas.

122. June 28, 1992, letter from Jessica Wiseman to Chris Thomas.

123. October 12, 1992, letter from Jessica Wiseman to Chris Thomas.

124. February 12, 1995, letter from Laura Anderson to Douglas Christopher Thomas.

125. "47 Death Row Inmates Moved to Sussex I Prison," *Richmond Times-Dispatch*, August 4, 1998.

126. "New Home for Death Row Inmates—Sussex County Prison Heightens Security," *Daily Press* (Newport News, Va.), March 22, 1997.

127. Unpublished Amnesty International interview.

128. Ibid.

129. "Death-Row Coalition Loses Fight for Funds, Survival," *Daily Press* (Newport News, Va.), September 5, 1993.

130. "A Murderer's Twisted Creation—Killer, Psychologist Had Strange Bond," *Richmond Times-Dispatch*, December 31 1995.

131. "O'Dell, Friend Exchange Vows," *Richmond Times-Dispatch*, July 24, 1997.

132. "Death Row Inmate, Woman Wed at Prison," *Richmond Times-Dispatch*, May 23, 1999.

133. "It's Death-Row Mancing—Psycho Killers and Their Lovers," *New York Post*, August 24, 2008.

134. "Serial Killers Have Women Calling," *Inland Valley Daily Bulletin*, August 14, 2006.

135. "No Shortage of Women Who Dream of Sharing a Husband on Death Row," *San Francisco Chronicle*, March 27, 2005.

136. "Serial Killers Have Women Calling," *Inland Valley Daily Bulletin*, August 14, 2006.

137. Sheila Isenberg, *Women Who Love Men Who Kill* (BackinPrint.com, 2000), 223. Another interesting book on the same topic is *Dream Lovers: Women Who Marry Men Behind Bars* by Jacquelynne Willcox-Bailey (Wakefield Press, 1999).

138. Isenberg, *Women Who Love Men Who Kill*, 168.

139. Ibid., 181.

Chapter 6. Prelude to an Execution

1. Paul W. Keve, *The History of Corrections in Virginia* (Charlottesville: University Press of Virginia, 1986), 61.

2. Ibid., 10.

3. Frank Green, "VA. Readies Electric Chair — Killer has Requested Form of Execution Once Seen as More Humane but Now Rarely Used," *Richmond Times-Dispatch*, July 16, 2006 (quoting from a 1908 issue of the *Richmond Times-Dispatch*).

4. John D. Bessler, *Death in the Dark: Midnight Executions in America* (Boston: Northeastern University Press, 1998), 61.

5. Ibid.

6. Eric Sundquist, "The Last Days of the Pen," *Richmond Times-Dispatch*, July 29, 1990.

7. Ibid.

8. Ibid.

9. Jeff Gammage, "Virginia's Old Pen to Close Chapter of Human Suffering," *Philadelphia Inquirer*, November 13, 1990.

10. "Virginia Corrections: 'Wall' Gone But Not Ills," *Virginian-Pilot*, December 23, 1990.

11. "Virginia's Prisons: Bring in the New," *Roanoke Times*, September 18, 1990.

12. Bill Byrd, "Infamous Era Will Pass When Penitentiary Closes," *Virginian-Pilot*, November 26, 1990.

13. Jim Mason, "Prison Doomed, but Chair to be Spared," *Richmond Times-Dispatch*, October 12, 1990.

14. Ibid.

15. Tom Campbell, "Multiple Executions Could Happen Again," *Richmond Times-Dispatch*, August 8, 1994.

16. Frank Green, "Virginia Has Sent 1,369 to Death," *Richmond Times-Dispatch*, August 8, 2004.

17. 428 U.S. 153 (1976).

18. Laura LaFay, "Electrocution in Virginia — The Science, Ritual and History of Putting People to Death," *Virginian-Pilot*, September 5, 1993.

19. Frank Green, "Suit Describes Electric Chair as Torture Device," *Richmond Times-Dispatch*, January 17, 1993.

20. Ibid.

21. Deborah W. Denno, "Is Electrocution an Unconstitutional Method of Execution? The Engineering of Death Over the Century," *William and Mary Law Review* 35 (Winter 1994): 551–693; 665.

22. Laura LaFay, "Electrocution in Virginia — The Science, Ritual and History of Putting People to Death," *Virginian-Pilot*, September 5, 1993.

23. Wynne Woolley, "Penitentiary Tour Gives Reality Lessons," *Richmond Times-Dispatch*, February 1, 1991.

24. Mike Farrell, *Just Call Me Mike: A Journey to Actor and Activist* (New York: RDV Books, 2008), 254.

25. Bill Geroux, "Prison Designers Plan Spartan Complex," *Richmond Times-Dispatch*, February 19, 1989.

26. Matthew Dolan and Chris Grier, "State of Contrasts . . . While Town Pays Little Attention to Them," *Virginian-Pilot*, June 24, 2000.

27. Associated Press, "State to be Without Place for Executions for 2 Months," *Roanoke Times*, October 12, 1990; Bill Geroux, "Prison Designers Plan Spartan Complex," *Richmond Times-Dispatch*, February 19, 1989.

28. Mike Allen, "Death Diary: Pleas, Anger Fill Days Before Execution," *Richmond Times-Dispatch*, August 25, 1991.

29. "Electrical Shocks Will Double in Future Executions, Officials Say," *Daily Press* (Newport News, Va.), August 24, 1991.

30. Ibid.

31. Parker Holmes and Teresa Lemons, "Mixed Sentiments Mark First Execution in Greensville Chair," *Richmond Times-Dispatch*, July 25, 1991.

32. Michael Hardy, "Wilder Refuses to Block Execution Scheduled Tonight at Greensville," *Richmond Times-Dispatch*, July 24, 1991.

33. Mike Allen, "Death Diary: Pleas, Anger Fill Days Before Execution," *Richmond Times-Dispatch*, August 25, 1991.

34. Mike Allen and Nelson Schwartz, "Death Penalty Opponents Angry About Latest Execution," *Richmond Times-Dispatch*, August 24, 1991.

35. Ibid. Chris Thomas's capital murder trial started on the day of Peterson's execution, and it is likely that Chris knew of the execution — and the multiple rounds of electricity used to kill Peterson — well before the jury sentenced Chris to die in the same electric chair. The electric chair so frightened Chris that he couldn't refer to it by name, instead calling it the "E.C." in his correspondence.

36. Jenny Staletovich, "Electric Chair May Have Had Last Reprieve," *Palm Beach Post*, November 8, 1999.

37. Bruce Potter, "Many Support a Change to Execution by Injection," *Richmond Times-Dispatch*, January 1, 1992.

38. "Inmate is First to be Executed by Lethal Injection in Virginia," *Daily Press* (Newport News, Va.), January 25, 1995.

39. "Lethal Injection — Executions are Made a Little More Civilized," *Daily Press* (Newport News, Va.), January 27, 1995.

40. *Baze v. Rees*, 553 U.S. (2008).

41. Associated Press, "Court Panel: State's Method of Lethal Injection is Constitutional," *Virginian-Pilot*, July 11, 2008.

42. Associated Press, "Justice Stevens Contrasts Lethal Injection Methods," May 10, 2008.

43. Deborah W. Denno, "When Legislatures Delegate Death: The Troubling

Paradox Behind State Uses of Electrocution and Lethal Injection and What it Says About Us," *Ohio State Law Journal* 63 (2002): 63–98; table 16.

44. "The Governor Steps in on Executions Family as Witness," *Virginian-Pilot*, March 11, 1994.

45. Chris Grier, "Emporia Man Adds Watching Executions to List of Hobbies," *Roanoke Times*, July 5, 2000.

46. June Arney, "State's Electrocutions Always Play to Full House," *Roanoke Times*, December 16, 1993.

47. Associated Press, "Man Executed After Appeal Rejected," *Daily Press* (Newport News, Va.), December 4, 1998.

48. Lynn Waltz, "Death Walk," *Roanoke Times,* September 11, 1994.

49. Ibid.

50. Sebilla Connor, "Death Row Parish," *Roanoke Times*, July 11, 1993.

51. Erik Brady, "Bringing God to Death Row," *USA Today*, August 25, 1995.

52. Lynn Waltz, "Death Walk," *Roanoke Times,* September 11, 1994.

53. Ibid.

54. Ibid.

55. Sebilla Connor, "Death Row Parish," *Roanoke Times*, July 11, 1993.

56. Greg Schneider, "Looking for a Meaningful Life on Virginia's Death Row," *Roanoke Times*, September 20, 1992.

57. Doug Struck, "'Life Preserver' for Condemned Killers," *San Francisco Chronicle*, May 13, 1990.

58. Sue Ann Pressley, "Guiding the Trip Through the Darkness," *Washington Post*, September 2, 1992.

59. Schneider, "Looking for a Meaningful Life on Virginia's Death Row."

60. Ibid.

61. Pressley, "Guiding the Trip Through the Darkness."

62. Joe Jackson, "Virginia Inmates Lose Chief Ally," *Virginian-Pilot*, September 4, 1993.

63. LaFay, "Electrocution in Virginia."

64. Mike Allen, "Death Diary: Pleas, Anger Fills Days Before Execution," *Richmond Times-Dispatch*, August 25, 1991.

65. Not his real name.

66. Patti Rosenberg, "Judge Me as Who I Am," *Daily Press* (Newport News, Va.), June 16, 1999.

67. Patti Rosenberg, "Many are Opposed to Man's Execution — Thomas Only Killed for Girlfriend, Love, They Say," *Daily Press* (Newport News, Va.), June 15, 1999.

68. Patti Rosenberg, "Mercy Sought for Killer — Middlesex Man Faces Execution Wednesday," *Daily Press* (Newport News, Va.), June 12, 1999.

69. Ibid.

70. Ibid.

71. Rosenberg, "Judge Me as Who I Am."

72. Patti Rosenberg, "Woman's Affidavit Could Invalidate Thomas' Sentence," *Daily Press* (Newport News, Va.), June 15, 1999.

73. March 29, 1999, letter from Laura T. Anderson to Jessica Wiseman.

74. Frank Green and Carrie Johnson, "Wiseman Denies Killing Mother," *Richmond Times-Dispatch*, June 16, 1999.

75. Jim Spencer, "Jessica Wiseman Can't Erase Dark Event With Words," *Daily Press* (Newport News, Va.), June 18, 1999.

76. Amnesty International interview.

77. Patti Rosenberg, "Thomas is Granted Stay of Execution," *Daily Press* (Newport News, Va.), June 17, 1999.

78. Amnesty International interview.

79. Margaret Vandiver, "The Death Penalty and the Families of Victims: An Overview of Research Issues," in *Wounds That Do Not Bind: Victim-Based Perspectives on the Death Penalty*, ed. James R. Acker and David R. Karp (Durham, N.C.: Carolina Academic Press, 2006), 245. See also, Susan F. Sharp, *Hidden Victims: The Effects of the Death Penalty on the Families of the Accused* (New Brunswick, N.J.: Rutgers University Press, 2005).

80. Rachel King, *Capital Consequences: Families of the Condemned Tell Their Stories* (New Brunswick, N.J.: Rutgers University Press, 2005), 7.

81. Ibid., 8–9.

82. Ibid., 10.

83. Patti Rosenberg, "Thomas is Granted Stay of Execution," *Daily Press* (Newport News, Va.), June 17, 1999.

84. Amnesty International interview.

Chapter 7. The Death of Douglas Christopher Thomas

1. *Thomas v. Garraghty*, 258 Va. 530; 522 S.E.2d 865 (1999).

2. November 18, 1999, letter from James S. Gilmore III to Laura T. Anderson.

3. "Killer Holds Out Hope Amid Regrets," *Daily Press* (Newport News, Va.), January 9, 2000.

4. "Death House Cell Assignment Called Torture," *Richmond Times-Dispatch*, December 15, 1996.

5. Ibid.

6. Ibid.

7. Ibid.

8. Amnesty International interview.

9. "Last Supper For Boy Killer on Death Row," *Guardian*, January 10, 2000.

10. Ibid.

11. "Killer Holds Out Hope Amid Regrets."

12. Ibid.

13. "Last Supper For Boy Killer on Death Row."

14. Frank Green, "Thomas Executed for Death of Couple — He was 17 Years Old at Time of Slayings," *Richmond Times-Dispatch*, January 11, 2000.

15. "Too Young to Die?" *Daily Press* (Newport News, Va.), January 9, 2000.
16. "Thomas Execution Nearing—Juvenile Case Getting National Attention," *Daily Press* (Newport News, Va.), January 7, 2000.
17. "Two Virginia Death Penalty Cases Receive World Attention—Groups Speak Out for 2 Who Were Juveniles When They Killed," *Virginian-Pilot*, January 9, 2000.
18. "Man Executed for Murders Committed at 17—Gilmore, High Court Say No to Appeals," *Daily Press* (Newport News, Va.), January 11, 2000.
19. "'I Love You, Roach. Be Strong.'—Thomas' Last Words to Fellow Condemned Man," *Richmond Times-Dispatch*, January 12, 2000.
20. "Family's Hope Dies Too," *Daily Press* (Newport News, Va.), January 11, 2000.
21. "Friends, Relatives Hold Vigil at Prison," *Richmond Times-Dispatch*, January 11, 2000.
22. "Autopsy is Final Chapter in Executions—State's Policy Aims to Avoid Cover-Up Charge," *Richmond Times-Dispatch*, September 28, 1992.
23. Ibid.

Chapter 8. Concluding Thoughts

1. *Roper v. Simmons*, 543 U.S. 551 (2005).
2. Ibid., 567 (internal citations omitted).
3. Ibid., 570.
4. Ibid., 569.
5. John Rawls, "Two Concepts of Rules," *Philosophical Review* 1 (1955): 4–5.
6. Michael L. Radelet and Marian J. Borg, "The Changing Nature of Death Penalty Debates," *Annual Review of Sociology* 26 (Summer): 43–61; 52.
7. Ibid.
8. Robert M. Bohm, *Deathquest II: An Introduction to the Theory and Practice of Capital Punishment in the United States*, 2nd ed. (Cincinnati, Ohio: Anderson Publishing, 2003), 170.
9. Louis P. Pojman, "Why the Death Penalty is Morally Permissible," in *Debating the Death Penalty*, ed. Hugo Bedau and Paul Cassell (Oxford: Oxford University Press, 2004), 57.
10. Jeffrey H. Reiman, "Justice, Civilization, and the Death Penalty: Answering van de Hagg," *Philosophy and Public Affairs* 14, no. 2 (Spring 1985): 115–149; 116.
11. Bohm, *Deathquest*, 93.
12. Ibid.
13. William J. Bowers and Glen L. Pierce, "Deterrence or Brutalization: What is the Effect of Executions?" *Crime and Delinquency* 26, no. 4 (1980): 453–484; John J. Cochran, Mitchell B. Chamlin, and Mark Seth, "Deterrence or Brutalization? An Impact Assessment of Oklahoma's Return to Capital Punishment," *Criminology* 32, no. 1 (March 2006): 107–134.
14. *Roper*, 571.
15. Ibid., 573–574.

16. Ibid., 569.

17. Ibid.

18. Ibid., 572.

19. Of course, the historical record is incomplete, and it is very likely that more juvenile offenders were executed by the Commonwealth of Virginia. Professor Victor Streib believes that the following black males were either seventeen or eighteen at the time of their offenses and eighteen when executed by the Commonwealth of Virginia: Thurman Spinher (convicted of murder, executed on January 14, 1910), Byrd Jackson (executed on June 21, 1912), Sherman Stanfield (convicted of attempted rape and executed on September 7, 1915), Raleigh Haskins (convicted of the murder of a while male, executed on September 30, 1921), Calvin Groome (convicted of the rape of a white female, executed on June 26, 1931) and Sam Pannell (convicted of the rape of a white female, executed on May 20, 1932). Victor L. Streib, *Death Penalty for Juveniles* (Bloomington: Indiana University Press, 1987), 207.

20. This list is taken from the aforementioned *Death Penalty for Juveniles* as well as the Espy Files. The reader should note that there are discrepancies between the two works.

21. Death Penalty Information Center, Espy Files.

22. Exodus 21:23–21:27: "If any harm follows, then you shall give life for life, eye for eye, tooth for tooth, hand for hand, foot for foot, burn for burn, wound for wound, stripe for stripe. When a slave-owner strikes the eye of a male or female slave, destroying it, the owner shall let the slave go, a free person, to compensate for the eye. If the owner knocks out a tooth of a male or female slave, the slave shall be let go, a free person, to compensate for the tooth."

23. Camus, *Resistance, Rebellion and Death*, 202.

24. Justice Kennedy, *Roper v. Simmons*, 568.

25. Jack Greenberg, "Against the System of Capital Punishment," *Harvard Law Review* 99, no. 7 (May 1986): 1670–1680; 1670.

26. *Furman v. Georgia*, 408 U.S. 238, 310 (1972).

27. Duane Borne, "Life Sentence Given for Triple Slayings," *Virginian-Pilot* (Newport News, Va.), October 4, 2008.

28. Mike Allen, "Man Gets Life in '89 Killings," *Roanoke Times*, August 6, 2008.

29. Mark Bowes, "Man Convicted in Food Lion Killings," *Richmond Times-Dispatch*, February 6, 2008.

30. Mike Allen, "Man Admits Killing Pastor," *Roanoke Times*, November 22, 2007.

31. Rob Seal, "Death of Woman Brings Life Term," *Richmond Times-Dispatch*, November 21, 2007.

32. "Man Pleads Guilty, Gets Consecutive Life Terms," *Daily Press* (Newport News, Va.), July 13, 2007; "Man Gets Life in Double Slaying," *Richmond Times-Dispatch*, July 13, 2007.

33. John Hopkins, "Grandson, 19, Given Two Life Sentences," *Virginian-Pilot*, July 12, 2007.

34. Liesel Nowak, "Man Gets Two Life Sentences in Killing," *Daily Progress* (Charlottesville, Va.), May 4, 2007.

35. Bill McKelway, "Man Sentenced in Death of Uncle, Cousin," *Richmond Times-Dispatch*, April 24, 2007.

36. Frank Green, "Tinsley Pleads Guilty in '82 Death," *Richmond Times-Dispatch*, April 12, 2007.

37. Jamie C. Ruff, "Man Gets Life for 2005 Killing," *Richmond Times-Dispatch*, April 6, 2007.

38. James C. Ruff, "Man Gets Life Sentence in Nottaway Killings," *Richmond Times-Dispatch*, March 30, 2007.

39. Beverly N. Williams, "Judge Gives Child Killer Life With No Parole," *Daily Press* (Newport News, Va.), February 10, 2007.

40. Tom Campbell, "Man Gets Life for Killing Wife and Children," *Richmond Times-Dispatch*, July 13, 2006.

Bibliography

Allen, Mike. "Autopsy is Final Chapter in Executions — State's Policy Aims to Avoid Cover-Up Charge." *Richmond Times-Dispatch*, September 28, 1992.

——. "Death Diary: Pleas, Anger Fill Days Before Execution." *Richmond Times-Dispatch*, August 25, 1991.

——, and Nelson Schwartz. "Death Penalty Opponents Angry About Latest Execution." *Richmond Times-Dispatch*, August 24, 1991.

Allison, Wes, and Frank Green. "Inmates Say Guards Didn't Supply Drugs." *Richmond Times-Dispatch*, June 14, 1994.

American Civil Liberties Union of Virginia. *Broken Justice: The Death Penalty in Virginia*, 2003.

——. *Unequal, Unfair, and Irreversible: The Death Penalty in Virginia*, 2000.

Arney, June. "State's Electrocutions Always Play to Full House." *Roanoke Times*, December 16, 1993.

Arriens, Jan, ed. *Welcome to Hell: Letters and Writings from Death Row*. Boston: Northeastern University Press, 1997.

Associated Press. "ACLU Sues Virginia Over Prison Treatment." *Daily Press* (Newport News, Va.), March 6, 1995.

——. "Court Panel: State's Method of Lethal Injection is Constitutional." *Virginian-Pilot*, July 11, 2008.

——. "Death-Row Coalition Loses Fight for Funds, Survival." *Daily Press* (Newport News, Va.), September 5, 1993.

——. "Death Row Drugs." November 6, 2006.

——. "Death Row Inmate, Woman Wed at Prison." *Richmond Times-Dispatch*, May 23, 1999.

——. "Inmate is First to be Executed by Lethal Injection in Virginia." *Daily Press* (Newport News, Va.), January 25, 1995.

——. "Justice Stevens Contrasts Lethal Injection Methods." May 10, 2008.

——. "Man Executed After Appeal Rejected." *Daily Press* (Newport News, Va.), December 4, 1998.

——. "New Home for Death Row Inmates — Sussex County Prison Heightens Security." *Daily Press* (Newport News, Va.), March 22, 1997.

——. "State Required to Ensure Safety of Condemned." *Daily Press* (Newport News, Va.), April 8, 1995.

——. "State to be Without Place for Executions for 2 Months." *Roanoke Times*, October 12, 1990.

Bacigal, Ronald J. *Trial of Capital Murder Cases in Virginia*. 3rd ed. Richmond, Va.: Virginia CLE, Virginia Law Foundation, 2008.

Banner, Stuart. *The Death Penalty: An American History*. Cambridge, Mass.: Harvard University Press, 2002.

Bessler, John D. *Death in the Dark: Midnight Executions in America*. Boston: Northeastern University Press, 1998.

Blume, John H., Sheri Lynn Johnson, and A. Brian Threlkeld. "Probing 'Life Qualification' Through Expanded Voir Dire." *Hofstra Law Review* 29 (Summer 2001): 1209–1264.

Bohm, Robert M. *Deathquest II: An Introduction to the Theory and Practice of Capital Punishment in the United States*. 2nd ed. Cincinnati, Ohio: Anderson Publishing, 2003.

Bowers, William J., and Wanda D. Foglia. "Still Singularly Agonizing: Law's Failure to Purge Arbitrariness from Capital Sentencing." *Criminal Law Bulletin* 30 (2003): 51–86.

Brady, Erik. "Bringing God to Death Row." *USA Today*, August 25, 1995.

Bresler, Kenneth. "Seeking Justice, Seeking Election, and Seeking the Death Penalty: The Ethics of Prosecutorial Candidates' Campaigning on Capital Convictions." *Georgetown Journal of Legal Ethics* 7 (1994): 941–958.

Bright, Stephen B. "Counsel for the Poor: The Death Sentence Not for the Worst Crime, but for the Worst Lawyer." *Yale Law Journal* 103 (1994): 1835–1883.

Byrd, Bill. "Infamous Era Will Pass When Penitentiary Closes." *Virginian-Pilot*, November 26, 1990.

Campbell, Tom. "Multiple Executions Could Happen Again." *Richmond Times-Dispatch*, August 8, 1994.

Camus, Albert. *Resistance, Rebellion, and Death*. New York: Knopf, 1961.

"Candidates Vie for Constitutional Offices — Middlesex's Commonwealth Attorney." *Daily Press* (Newport News, Va.), October 23, 1991.

"Capital Punishment in Virginia." *Virginia Law Review* 58, no. 1 (January 1972): 97–142.

Carp, Robert A., Ronald Stidham, and Kenneth L. Manning. *Judicial Process in America*. 7th ed. Washington, D.C.: CQ Press, 2007.

"Case Certified in Deaths of Girlfriend's Parents." *Richmond Times-Dispatch*, January 24, 1991.

Chillemi, Tom. "Jessica Wiseman Found Guilty of Killing Parents." *Southside Sentinel*, June 27, 1991.

———. "Wiseman Murders Planned in Detail, Testimony Reveals." *Southside Sentinel*, July 3, 1991.

Clarke, Alan W. "Virginia's Capital Murder Sentencing Proceeding: A Defense Perspective." *University of Richmond Law Review* 18 (1984): 341–359.

Conley, Jay. "Blood, Sweat and Convictions." *Roanoke Times*, April 3, 2005.

Conner, Sebilla. "Death Row Parish." *Roanoke Times*, July 11, 1993.

Cosco, Joseph. "Death Row Breakout: 6 Men Made A Desperate Gamble 10 Years

Ago Today, Six Men Escaped From Virginia's Most Secure Prison." *Virginian-Pilot*, May 31, 1994.

Deans, Marie. "Working Against the Death Penalty." In *Writing for Their Lives: Death Row USA*, edited by Marie Mulvey-Roberts. Champaign: University of Illinois Press, 2007.

Denno, Deborah W. "Is Electrocution an Unconstitutional Method of Execution? The Engineering of Death Over the Century." *William and Mary Law Review* 35 (Winter 1994) 551–693.

———. "When Legislatures Delegate Death: The Troubling Paradox Behind State Uses of Electrocution and Lethal Injection and What it Says About Us." *Ohio State Law Journal* 63 (2002): 63–98.

"Digging for Answers About America's Oldest English Town." *Scripps Howard News Service*, August 14, 1997.

Dolan, Matthew, and Chris Grier. "State of Contrasts . . . While Town Pays Little Attention to Them." *Virginian-Pilot*, June 24, 2000.

Earley, Mark L. "Objections are Fine; Insults are Not." *Richmond-Times Dispatch*, April 10, 1998.

Edds, Margaret. *An Expendable Man: The Near-Execution of Earl Washington, Jr.* New York: New York University Press, 2003.

"Electrical Shocks Will Double in Future Executions, Officials Say." *Daily Press* (Newport News, Va.), August 24, 1991.

Farrell, Mike. *Just Call Me Mike: A Journey to Actor and Activist*. New York: RDV Books, 2008.

Felsenthal, Mark. "Behind Teens' Smiles, Dark Edges." *Daily Press* (Newport News, Va.), November 18, 1990.

———. "Boy Facing Trial in Murders Hospitalized." *Daily Press* (Newport News, Va.), June 29, 1991.

———. "County Find Judges Guilty of Asking Too Much." *Daily Press* (Newport News, Va.), September 6, 1990.

———. "Did Teen Held in Murders Fall Through the Cracks?" *Daily Press* (Newport News, Va.), July 21, 1991.

———. "Lawyer Petitions to Stay on in Murder Trial." *Daily Press* (Newport News, Va.), May 7, 1991.

———. "Middlesex Teen's Murder Trial to Begin Today." *Daily Press* (Newport News, Va.), February 27, 1991.

———. "New Evidence Delays Trial for Killing Parents." *Daily Press* (Newport News, Va.), February 28, 1991.

———. "Rumors Called 'Out of Control' — Neighbors, Officials Sort Murder Facts." *Daily Press* (Newport News, Va.), November 15, 1990.

———. "Teen's Fair Trial Not at Risk, Judge Rules." *Daily Press* (Newport News, Va.), August 15, 1991.

———. "Teen Guilty of Killing Parents." *Daily Press* (Newport News, Va.), June 27, 1991.

"Few Records of Historical Execution — Teenage Girl's Death Preserved in Papers."
Daily Press (Newport News, Va.), August 15, 1999.

Fimrite, Peter, and Michael Taylor. "No Shortage of Women Who Dream of Sharing
a Husband on Death Row." *San Francisco Chronicle*, March 27, 2005.

Flynn, Kathleen M. "The 'Agony of Suspense': How Protracted Death Row
Confinement Gives Rise to an Eighth Amendment Claim of Cruel and Unusual."
Washington and Lee Law Review 54 (Winter 1997): 291–333.

"47 Death Row Inmates Moved to Sussex Prison." *Richmond Times-Dispatch*, August
4, 1998.

Gammage, Jeff. "Virginia's Old Pen to Close Chapter of Human Suffering."
Philadelphia Inquirer, November 13, 1990.

Geroux, Bill. "Prison Designers Plan Spartan Complex." *Richmond Times-Dispatch*,
February 19, 1989.

"Giarranto Discovers Life on Death Row While Hoping for a New Trial." *Roanoke
Times*, September 9, 1993.

Glenn, Stacia. "Serial Killers Have Women Calling." *Inland Valley Daily Bulletin*,
August 14, 2006.

Goode, Randolph. "Settlement of Inmates' Suit Enacts New Cell Search Rules."
Richmond Times-Dispatch, May 24, 1995.

Goodpaster, Gary. "The Trial for Life: Effective Assistance of Counsel in Death
Penalty Cases." *New York University Law Review* 58 (May 1983): 299–362.

"The Governor Steps in on Executions Family as Witness." *Virginian-Pilot*, March 11,
1994.

Green, Frank. "Death House Cell Assignment Called Torture." *Richmond Times
Dispatch*, December 15, 1996.

———. "Death Row Inmate Took Heroin — Another Prisoner Found With Gun on
Person." *Richmond Times-Dispatch*, June 3, 1994.

———. "The Execution Files — State's Death Penalty History Told in Personal
Records of the Condemned." *Richmond Times-Dispatch*, December 5, 2004.

———. "'I Love You, Roach. Be Strong.' — Thomas' Last Words to Fellow
Condemned Man." *Richmond Times-Dispatch*, January 12, 2000.

———. "Latest Chapter in Sad History of Prison War — State Now Fighting Death
Row Drugs." *Richmond Times-Dispatch*, July 29, 1993.

———. "A Murderer's Twisted Creation — Killer, Psychologist Had Strange Bond."
Richmond Times-Dispatch, December 31, 1995.

———. "Overdose Killed Death Row Inmate — Took Two Prescription
Antidepressant Drugs." *Richmond Times-Dispatch*, May 15, 2001.

———. "Suit Describes Electric Chair as Torture Device." *Richmond Times-
Dispatch*, January 17, 1993.

———. "Thomas Executed for Death of Couple — He was 17 Years Old at Time of
Slayings." *Richmond Times-Dispatch*, January 11, 2000.

———. "Thomas' Execution Set for This Week." *Richmond Times-Dispatch*, June 14,
1999.

———. "VA. Readies Electric Chair—Killer has Requested Form of Execution Once Seen as More Humane but Now Rarely Used." *Richmond Times-Dispatch*, July 16, 2006.

———. "Virginia Has Sent 1,369 to Death." *Richmond Times-Dispatch*, August 8, 2004.

———, and Carrie Johnson. "Wiseman Denies Killing Mother—Ex-Boyfriend Scheduled to Die By Injection at 9." *Richmond Times-Dispatch*, June 16, 1999.

———, and Bob Piazza. "O'Dell, Friend Exchange Vows—'It Was a Spiritual Union,' Bride Says After Ritual." *Richmond Times-Dispatch*, July 24, 1997.

Grier, Chris. "Emporia Man Adds Watching Executions to List of Hobbies." *Roanoke Times*, July 5, 2000.

Groot, Michael A. "To Attain the Ends of Justice: Confronting Virginia's Default Rules in Capital Cases." *Capital Defense Digest* 6, no. 2 (Spring 1994): 44–48.

Haney, Craig. "Examining Death Qualification: Further Analysis of the Process Effect." *Law and Human Behavior* 8 (1984): 133–151.

Hardy, Michael. "LeVasseur Committed Suicide, Probe Finds." *Richmond Times-Dispatch*, April 22, 1987.

———. "Wilder Refuses to Block Execution Scheduled Tonight at Greensville." *Richmond Times-Dispatch*, July 24, 1991.

Hitchcock, Amanda S. "Using the Adversarial Process to Limit Arbitrariness in Capital Charging Decisions." *North Carolina Law Review* 85 (2007): 931–973.

Holmes, Parker, and Teresa Lemons. "Mixed Sentiments Mark First Execution in Greensville Chair." *Richmond Times-Dispatch*, July 25, 1991.

"In Middlesex County—Crittenden, Eley, Bray Friday Favored for Board." *Daily Press* (Newport News, Va.), October 22, 1991.

"In Stockton's Words." *Roanoke Times*, August 14, 1995.

Isenberg, Sheila. *Women Who Love Men Who Kill*. BackinPrint.com, 2000.

Jackson, Joe. "Va. Inmates on Death Row Lose Chief Ally." *Virginian-Pilot*, September 4, 1993.

Johnson, Robert. *Death Work: A Study of the Modern Execution Process*. Belmont, Calif.: Thomson/Wadworth, 2006.

"Judge Won't Postpone Thomas Murder Trial." *Daily Press* (Newport News, Va.), April 18, 1991.

Kelly, Deborah. "A Teen's Road to Death Row—A Hopeless Childhood And A Romance Gone Wrong Ended In Double-Slaying." *Richmond Times-Dispatch*, October 9, 1994.

Keve, Paul W. *The History of Corrections in Virginia*. Charlottesville: University Press of Virginia, 1986.

King, Rachel. *Capital Consequences: Families of the Condemned Tell Their Stories*. New Brunswick, N.J.: Rutgers University Press, 2005.

Konig, David Thomas. "Dale's Law and the Non-Common Law Origins of Criminal Justice in Virginia." *American Journal of Legal History* 26, no. 4 (October 1982): 354–375.

LaFay, Laura. "The Death of an Inmate Gives Birth to a Gun Mystery." *Virginian-Pilot*, May 28, 1995.

———. "Electrocution in Virginia—The Science, Ritual and History of Putting People to Death." *Virginian-Pilot*, September 5, 1993.

"Last Supper For Boy Killer on Death Row." *Guardian*, January 10, 2000.

"Lethal Injection—Executions are Made a Little More Civilized." *Daily Press* (Newport News, Va.), January 27, 1995.

Liebman, James S. "Opting for Real Death Penalty Reform." *Ohio State Law Journal* 63 (2002): 315–342.

Mason, Jim. "Prison Doomed, but Chair to be Spared." *Richmond Times-Dispatch*, October 12, 1990.

Mauet, Thomas A. *Fundamentals of Trial Technique.* 3rd ed. Boston: Little, Brown, 1992.

McAllister, Pam. *Death Defying: Dismantling the Execution Machinery in 21st Century U.S.A.* New York: Continuum, 2003.

McDonald, Melody. "Forced Medication Order—Judge Rules Death Row Inmate Must Take Anti-Psychotic Drugs." *Fort Worth Star-Telegram*, April 12, 2006.

McGlone, Tim. "Two Virginia Death Penalty Cases Receive World Attention—Groups Speak Out for 2 Who Were Juveniles When They Killed." *Virginian-Pilot*, January 9, 2000.

Mello, Michael A. *Dead Wrong: A Death Row Lawyer Speaks Out Against Capital Punishment.* Seattle: University of Washington Press, 1997.

Montefinise, Angela. "Its Death-Row Mancing—Psycho Killers and Their Lovers." *New York Post*, August 24, 2008.

Nash, Bruce, and Allan Zullo, eds. *Lawyer's Wit and Wisdom: Quotations on the Legal Profession, in Brief.* Compiled by Kathryn Zullo. Philadelphia: Running Press, 1995.

Note to "The Eighth Amendment and Ineffective Assistance of Counsel in Capital Case." *Harvard Law Review* 107 (June 1994): 1923–1940.

Oberg, Mel. "Accused Teens Were 'Desperate to Be Together.'" *Richmond Times-Dispatch*, November 18, 1990.

———. "'They Were Good Parents,' Friend of Couple Says." *Richmond Times-Dispatch*, November 13, 1990.

Paul, William G. "Too Young to Die?" *Daily Press* (Newport News, Va.), January 9, 2000.

Pojman, Louis P. "Why the Death Penalty is Morally Permissible." In *Debating the Death Penalty*, edited by Hugo Bedau and Paul Cassell. Oxford: Oxford University Press, 2004.

Pokorak, Jeffrey J. "Probing the Capital Prosecutor's Perspective: Race of the Discretionary Actors." *Cornell Law Review* 83 (1998): 1811–1820.

Potter, Bruce. "Many Support a Change to Execution by Injection." *Richmond Times-Dispatch*, January 1, 1992.

Pressley, Sue Ann. "Getting Ready to Die—Death-Row Inmates Wait in Line." *Daily Press* (Newport News, Va.), September 13, 1992.

———. "Guiding the Trip Through the Darkness." *Washington Post*, September 2, 1992.

Radelet, Michael L., and Marian J. Borg. "The Changing Nature of Death Penalty Debates." *Annual Review of Sociology* 26 (Summer): 43–61.

Reiman, Jeffrey H. "Justice, Civilization, and the Death Penalty: Answering van de Hagg." *Philosophy and Public Affairs* 14, no. 2 (Spring 1985): 115–149.

Review of Virginia's System of Capital Punishment. Joint Legislative Audit and Review Commission of the Virginia General Assembly, 2000.

Rise, Eric W. *The Martinsville Seven: Race, Rape and Capital Punishment.* Charlottesville: University Press of Virginia, 1995.

Rosenberg, Patti. "Judge Me as Who I Am—Killer Hopes for 11th-Hour Stay of Execution." *Daily Press* (Newport News, Va.), June 16, 1999.

———. "Killer Holds Out Hope Amid Regrets." *Daily Press* (Newport News, Va.), January 9, 2000.

———. "Man Executed for Murders Committed at 17—Gilmore, High Court Say No to Appeals." *Daily Press* (Newport News, Va.), January 11, 2000.

———. "Many are Opposed to Man's Execution—Thomas Only Killed for Girlfriend, Love, They Say." *Daily Press* (Newport News, Va.), June 15, 1999.

———. "Mercy Sought for Killer—Middlesex Man Faces Execution Wednesday." *Daily Press* (Newport News, Va.), June 12, 1999.

———. "Thomas Execution Nearing—Juvenile Case Getting National Attention." *Daily Press* (Newport News, Va.), January 7, 2000.

———. "Thomas is Granted Stay of Execution." *Daily Press* (Newport News, Va.), June 17, 1999.

———. "Woman's Affidavit Could Invalidate Thomas' Sentence." *Daily Press* (Newport News, Va.), June 15, 1999.

Ruff, Jamie. "Friends, Relatives Hold Vigil at Prison." *Richmond Times-Dispatch*, January 11, 2000.

Salgado, Richard. "Tribunals Organized To Convict: Searching for a Lesser Evil in the Capital Juror Death-Qualification Process in United States v. Green." *Brigham Young University Law Review* (2005): 519–553.

Saville, Kirk. "RADAR." *Daily Press* (Newport News, Va.), September 24, 1992.

Schneider, Greg. "Looking for a Meaningful Life on Virginia's Death Row." *Roanoke Times*, September 20, 1992.

———. "Saluda Teen Guilty of Murdering Parents." *Virginian-Pilot*, June 27, 1991.

Schwarz, Philip J. *Twice Condemned: Slaves and the Criminal Laws of Virginia, 1705–1865.* Baton Rouge: Louisiana State University Press, 1998.

Seltzer, Rick, Grace M. Lopes, Marshall Dayan, and Russell F. Canan. "The Effect of Death Qualification on the Propensity of Jurors to Convict: The Maryland Example." *Howard Law Journal* 29 (1986): 571–608.

Sharp, Susan F. *Hidden Victims: The Effects of the Death Penalty on the Families of the Accused.* New Brunswick, N.J.: Rutgers University Press, 2005.

Siegel, Larry J., Brandon C. Welsh, and Joseph J. Senna. *Juvenile Delinquency: Theory, Practice, and Law.* 9th ed. Belmont, Calif.: Thomson/Wadsworth, 2005.

Smith, Mark. "Smith is Executed for 1977 Slaying." *Richmond Times-Dispatch,* August 1, 1986.

Songer, Michael J., and Isaac Unah. "The Effect of Race, Gender, and Location on Prosecutorial Decisions to Seek the Death Penalty in South Carolina." *South Carolina Law Review* 58 (2006): 161–206.

Spencer, Jim. "Child's Play: Murder Parents to Get Your Way." *Daily Press* (Newport News, Va.), June 28, 1991.

———. "Jessica Wiseman Can't Erase Dark Event With Words." *Daily Press* (Newport News, Va.), June 18, 1999.

Staletovich, Jenny. "Electric Chair May Have Had Last Reprieve." *Palm Beach Post,* November 8, 1999.

Streib, Victor L. *Death Penalty for Juveniles.* Bloomington: Indiana University Press, 1987.

Struck, Doug. "'Life Preserver' for Condemned Killers—Her mother-in-law's murder hasn't squelched her zeal against executions." *San Francisco Chronicle,* May 13, 1990.

Study of Representation in Capital Cases in Virginia: Final Report. The Spangenberg Group, 1988.

Sundby, Scott E. *A Life and Death Decision: A Jury Weighs the Death Penalty.* New York: Palgrave Macmillan, 2005.

Sundquist, Eric. "The Last Days of the Pen." *Richmond Times-Dispatch,* July 29, 1990.

"Teen Killer's Grandmom Stands by Her." *Virginian-Pilot,* March 15, 1992.

Tucker, George Holbert. *Cavalier Saints and Sinners: Virginia History Through a Keyhole.* Norfolk, Va.: Virginia Pilot and Ledger Star, 1990.

Vandiver, Margaret. "The Death Penalty and the Families of Victims: An Overview of Research Issues." In *Wounds That Do Not Bind: Victim-Based Perspectives on the Death Penalty,* edited by James R. Acker and David R. Karp. Durham, N.C.: Carolina Academic Press, 2006.

Vick, Kara. "Family's Hope Dies Too." *Daily Press* (Newport News, Va.), January 11, 2000.

"Virginia Corrections: 'Wall' Gone But Not Ills," *Virginian-Pilot,* December 23, 1990.

"Virginia Inmates' Fans Confiscated—Prisoners Feel the Heat." *Virginian-Pilot,* April 25, 1996.

"Virginia's Prisons: Bring in the New." *Roanoke Times,* September 18, 1990.

Von Drehle, David. *Among the Lowest of the Dead: The Culture of Capital Punishment.* Ann Arbor: University of Michigan Press, 2005.

Vorenberg, James. "Decent Restraint of Prosecutorial Power." *Harvard Law Review* 94 (1981): 1521–1573.

Waltz, Lynn. "Death Walk." *Roanoke Times,* September 11, 1994.

Weatherford, Greg. "Team Strives to Quicken the Death Penalty's Pace." *Virginian-Pilot*, April 5, 1997.

Willcox-Bailey, Jacquelynne. *Dream Lovers: Women Who Marry Men Behind Bars.* Kent Town, S.A.: Wakefield Press, 1997.

Woolley, Wynne. "Penitentiary Tour Gives Reality Lessons." *Richmond Times-Dispatch*, February 1, 1991.

Young, William G. "Vanishing Trials, Vanishing Juries." *Suffolk University Law Review* 40, no. 1 (2006): 67–94.

Index

abandonment, 8, 10, 18, 21, 251
actual innocence defense, 110
Adams Electric Company, 191
Advice of Rights form, 50
affidavits: potential juror, 78–79;
    of Wiseman's guilt, jailhouse, 222,
    235
age, as mitigating factor, 133
aggravated battery, 81, 120, 134–35, 139
aggravating circumstances, 81–82, 120
Alexander, Dawne, 76
Allen, George, 201
American Bar Association, 220, 235
American Civil Liberties Union, 149
Amnesty International interviews with
    Thomas, xv, 38, 154, 178–79, 213–14,
    227–28, 230
Anderson, Laura: attempted visit at
    Sussex I, 180–82; attempt to convince
    Thomas to testify, 95–97; baptism of
    Thomas, 215–16, 239; correspondence
    with Thomas, 75–76; at death house,
    225–26, 231–33; enlisting Dean's aid,
    151, 154; execution day, xii, 237–42;
    fear of visiting Mecklenburg, 176–78;
    at funeral service, xii, 244–45; grave
    site visits, 255; last gift from Thomas,
    244; last prayers, 234–35, 237; letter
    to Gilmore re clemency, 221–22;
    phone conversations after stay of
    execution, 227–30; relationship with
    Thomas, overview, xiii–xiv; as special
    education teacher, 13–16; as spiritual
    advisor, 202–3, 207–13, 215–17, 231–33;
    stay of execution, 225–26; testimony

at trial, 130; on Thomas's return to
    Middlesex County, 19–20
Anderson, Philip S., 220
Anderson, Ross, 95, 177, 207, 234,
    236–38, 244
appeals process, death sentence,
    160–64, 166–67
"Articles, Lawes, and Orders Divine,
    Politique, and Martiall," 66
assignment of errors, 160–61
autopsies: Thomas, 243; Wiseman,
    James "J. B.," 103–4; Wiseman, Kathy,
    103–4

Bacigal, Ronald J., 121
Bailey, Tolson, 250
Baldwin, Katherine, 163
Banner, Stuart, 66
baptism, 215–16, 239
Barnes, Herman C., 151
Battaile, Gabriel, 250
battery, aggravated, 81, 120, 134–35, 139
Beaver, Charles William, 250
Belote, Ida Virginia, 69
Bessler, John D., 189
Bible, 208–9, 211, 215, 231, 237, 239
"Bible notchers," 207
bifurcated trial, 91–92
bill of indictment, 63
Bill of Rights, xiv
Bohm, Robert M., 248
Bon Air Juvenile Correctional Center,
    172–75, 222
Borg, Marian J., 247
Breeden, James C., 165, 220

Green, Winston, 250
Greenberg, Jack, 252–53
Greensville Correctional Center.
    See Thomas, Chris, at Greensville
    Correctional Center
Gregg v. Georgia, 92, 192
Griffin, Jim, 232
guided discretion statutes, 92
guns. *See* murder weapon
Gwaltney, Henry O.: as mitigation spe-
    cialist, 83–84, 118–19, 122; at Oyster
    Festival, 35; testimony at Thomas
    trial, 127–29, 131–33

habeas corpus petitions, 110, 122,
    125–26, 161–62, 165–66, 169, 228–29
Hamilton, Phillip, 197–98
Hancock, Michael Todd, 254
hanging, 188–89
Hanover Learning Center, 16–18
Hatch, Margaret, 66
Hawkins, Talion, 253
Henderson, Terry, 137
Hetrick, Michael A., 254
Hicks, Robert D., 70
Hoke, Ronald Lee, Sr., 232
Holmes, Oliver Wendell, Jr., 113
homosexuality of Margaret Thomas.
    See lesbianism of Margaret Thomas
Hopper, Roger G., 87
Horne, Damian: on capital murder
    indictment, 65; on clemency appeal,
    220; closing argument, sentencing
    hearing, 135–38; closing argument,
    trial, 112–16; continuance hearing,
    84–85; cross-examination, 108–9;
    demand for mistrial, 125; direct
    appeal, 164–65; failure to establish
    trust, 95–97; on Folkes's inexperi-
    ence, 77; inexperience, 80–81;
    mitigation defense, 131–33; motion
    to dismiss jury, 94; objections to voir

dire, 94; plea bargain, 75; request
    for removal by Thomas, 164–65;
    Wiseman trial, 87
Huffman, Gary Wayne, 253
hung jury, 91

indictment for capital murder, 63
indigent defendants, 54–56
individualized consideration, 92
ineffective assistance of counsel,
    166–67
Ingle, Joseph, 152
insanity defense, 84–85
Institute of Law, Psychiatry and Public
    Policy, 83
intent, defined, 105
Isenberg, Sheila, 184–85
isolation, 159–60, 167–68, 178–79, 187

Jackson, Jesse, Jr., 229
jailbird stigma, 19, 21
James, Jason Andrew, 254
Jefferson, Thomas, 190
Jenkins, Arthur, 185
Johnson, Larry A., Sr., 48–52, 57–59, 86,
    103–5, 108, 135
Johnson, Robert, 141–42, 155–56, 158–59,
    167, 168
Jones, Edward, 140
Jones, Lewis, III, 60, 87
Jones, Willie Leroy, 205–6, 212, 243
Joseph, Jason, 185
judicial reprieve, 160
jurors, contamination of, 77
jury nullification, 91
jury selection, 90–95
justice, proportionate, 76, 160, 246–49,
    251
Justus, Buddy Earl, 194
juvenile death penalty, xiv, 68–69, 127,
    165–66, 235–36, 246–55
juvenile delinquency, theories of, 1–4

quality of court-appointed counsel, xiv, 54–56, 68, 82–83, 162, 166, 221
Quesinberry, George Adrian, Jr., 151, 185

racism, death penalty and, 67, 188–89
Radelet, Michael L., 247
Ramirez, Richard, 183–84
Raphael, Sally Jesse, 164
Rappahannock Central Elementary School, 7
rational choice theory of juvenile delinquency, 3, 21
Rawls, John, 247
Read, James, 65
Reed, Bonnie, 130
reformed death rows, 141–42
Reid, Bonnie, 13, 25
remorse, lack of: Thomas, 46, 122, 124–25, 127–28, 134; Wiseman, 61, 71, 133, 172, 223
remorse, Thomas, 103, 137, 170, 186, 213–14, 251
retributive justice, 247–51. *See also* vengeance, death penalty as
revenge. *See* vengeance, death penalty as
Reynolds, Jordan, 227
Rhea, Donald, 45–46, 102
Richmond City Jail, 70
Roach, Steven, 183, 231, 238, 240, 250
Roberts, Victor, 150
Robinson, Ernest J., 126
Robitussin, 12
Roper v. Simmons, 246
Rosenfeld, Steven, 164
Royal, Thomas, Jr., 185

Sarandon, Susan, 229
Savino, Joseph, 156
Schloss, Caroline, 183
selection phase of sentencing hearing, 81–82, 121
Senna, Joseph J., 3–4
sentencing hearing, 81–85, 121

sentencing verdict, 138–40
shakedowns, 148
Shanklin, William, 254
Shaw, William, III, 229
Sheppard, Mark, 185, 211
shotguns. *See* murder weapon
Siegel, Larry J., 3–4
Simmons, Chris, 249
Simmons, Roper v., 246
Sitlington, Harry, 250
Sixth Amendment, U. S. Constitution, 54–55, 162
slave executions, juvenile, 250
Smith, Donald H., 78–79
Smith, Henry, 191
social conflict theories of juvenile delinquency, 3–4
social process theories of juvenile delinquency, 3
social reaction theories of juvenile delinquency, 3
Social Security, 4, 7, 32
social structure theories of juvenile delinquency, 3
sociological theories of juvenile delinquency, 3–4
sodium thiopental, 198–200
Southern Center for Human Rights, 54
Sowell, Robert J., 124
spiritual advisors, role of, 203–7
Stanek, Robert W., 50, 86
state habeas corpus petitions, 161–62
state-sanctioned drug abuse in prison, 156–57
stay of execution, 225–26
stay of execution petition, 235–36
Stevens, John Paul, 200
Stewart, Potter, 252
Stockton, Dennis, 148–49, 211
Stout, Larry Allen, 151, 232
Streib, Victor L., 69
Strickler, Thomas, 185

Thomas, Chris *(continued)*
    sexual activity, early, 14, 18, 20, 26–27;
    sexual assault of, 70; shoplifting, 16;
    suicidal ideation, 16–17, 70, 87, 127;
    suspension for trespassing at school,
    16; transfer hearing waiver, 61–63;
    truancy, 13, 25, 33; trust fund, 32;
    vandalism of uncle's car, 37–39, 57,
    60, 105, 107, 121; Wiseman trial, 85,
    87. *See also* murders of Kathy and
    J. B. Wiseman
Thomas, Chris, at Greensville
    Correctional Center: alcohol use,
    186; Anderson as spiritual advisor,
    202–3, 207–13, 215–17, 231–33; bap-
    tism, 215–16, 239; clemency petition,
    218–26; death row chaplain "Peter,"
    203–7, 210–13; drug use, 186; execu-
    tions at, 198–202; final feelings for
    Wiseman, 214; isolation, 187; meeting
    father, 212–13; other executions at,
    198–202; remorse, 213–14; return to
    after execution order, 230; stay of
    execution, 225–26. *See also* Thomas,
    Chris, execution of
Thomas, Chris, at Mecklenburg
    Correctional Center, 141–85; alcohol
    use in, 157; breakup with Wiseman,
    175–76; correspondence with
    Wiseman, 157, 171–75; daily life,
    described, 147–51, 154–60; Deans
    and, 151–54; direct appeal, 164–65;
    emerging faith, 154; execution of
    other inmates, 167; habeas corpus
    petitions, 110, 122, 125–26, 165–66,
    169, 228–29; mitigation defense at
    appeal, 169–71; request for removal
    of Horne and West as appeals
    attorneys, 164–65; "training up,"
    153, 169, 232. *See also* Mecklenburg
    Correctional Center
Thomas, Chris, at Sussex I State Prison:
    correspondence with Corbin, 182–83;

daily life, described, 178–80; execu-
    tion of other inmates, 185; isolation,
    178–79; marriage to Corbin, 182–83;
    relationships between prisoners and
    staff, 179–80; return to after stay of
    execution, 227–30
Thomas, Chris, execution of, 227–45;
    Anderson as spiritual advisor, 231–33;
    autopsy, 243; candlelight vigil, 241;
    clemency petition, 235–36, 238;
    death, 242; death log, 210; death
    warrant, 240; denial of writ of
    habeas corpus, 228–29; execution
    order, 229–30; final press interviews,
    233–34; final visit with mother,
    237; funeral service, 244–45; grave
    site, 254; last Christmas, 230–31;
    lessons learned from, 250–51; letter
    to Barbara Ann Childress, 234;
    phone conversations with Anderson,
    227–30; public campaign to save his
    life, 233–34; return to Sussex I State
    Prison, 227–30; stay of execution
    petition, 235–36; strained relation-
    ship with Corbin, 230; transfer to
    Greensville CC, 230
Thomas, Chris, trial of, 90–140; actual
    innocence defense, 110; Anderson's
    attempt to convince to testify,
    95–97; case-in-chief, 102–8; closing
    arguments, 111–16; closing argu-
    ments, sentencing hearing, 134–38;
    correspondence with Wiseman,
    118; crime scene photos, 102–4, 110,
    111–12, 115, 165; defense case, 109–10;
    defense counsel's cross-examination,
    108–9; failure to make timely objec-
    tions, 93; future dangerousness, 37,
    120–23, 125–28, 134, 136; jailbreak
    attempt, 125–26; jury deliberation,
    117; jury instructions, 110–11; jury
    selection, 90–95; lack of remorse, 46,
    122, 124–25, 127–28, 134; mitigation

Virginia State Penitentiary, 147, 152, 189–93
Virginia Supreme Court, 160–61
voir dire, 79, 90, 92–94, 135
volunteer witnesses at executions, 202
Von Drehle, David, 150

Wallace, William T., Jr., 253
Walton, Peggy, 138
Ward, James H. "Jimmy": affidavits of non-prejudice, 78–79; background, 64–65; capital murder indictment of Thomas, 64; case-in-chief, 102–8; closing argument, sentencing hearing, 134–35; closing argument, Thomas trial, 111–12; detention hearing and, 61; mitigation defense, 129–33; opening statement, sentencing hearing, 121–22; opening statement, trial, 97–98; plea bargain and, 75; rebuttal of defense closing argument, 116–17; refusal to reduce charges, 85; in support of execution, 236; transfer hearing waiver, 63; Wiseman trial, 86
Washington, Earl, Jr., 146, 254
Watkins, Ronald, 151
Watkins v. Commonwealth, 120
weapons. *See* murder weapon
wedding ring, 218
Welsh, Brandon C., 3–4
West, Sydney: appointment as defense counsel, 80; continuance hearing, 84–85; direct appeal, 164–65; failure to establish trust with Thomas, 95–97; inexperience, 80–81; motion to dismiss jury, 119; opening statement, sentencing hearing, 122–24; opening statement, trial, 98–102; request for removal by Thomas, 164–65; Wiseman trial, 87
Wiecking, David K., 104–5
Wilder, Douglas, 146, 194

Williams, Barbara Ann Childress. *See* Childress, Barbara Ann "Cox"
Williams, Earl, 85, 110
Williams, Marlon, 185
Williams, Rebecca Lynn, 254
Wilson, Jackie, 130–31
Wiseman, James "J. B.": autopsy, 103–4; death, 43; described, 28; funeral service, 60–61; reconciliation with Kathy Wiseman, 32–34; threat to kill Thomas, 38, 43, 51. *See also* murders of Kathy and J. B. Wiseman
Wiseman, Jean, 117–18
Wiseman, Jessica: accusation of Thomas as killer, 50–51; at Bon Air Juvenile CC, 172–75, 222; breakup with Thomas, 175–76; confession, 50–51, 58, 103; correspondence with Thomas, 70–74, 88, 118, 157, 171–75; described, 27–28; detention hearing, 61; discussion of sex with Brenda Marshall, 34; fear of pregnancy, 29, 33, 34, 60; Fifth Amendment rights, 109; final public statement, 223–24; initial involvement with Thomas, 27–29; interviews by Virginia State Police, 46–47, 48–50; jailhouse affidavits on her guilt, 222, 235; lack of remorse, 61, 71, 133, 172, 223; life after detention, 255; as manipulative, 27, 59; marriage attempt with Thomas, 35–36; Miranda rights, 49; murder trial, 85–88; as Oyster Festival Poppy Queen, 35; protected by Thomas, 51–52, 57, 75, 97, 118, 233; scheduling of trial, 61; schooling of, 28; sentencing, 88–89; separation from Thomas, 31–32; suicidal ideation, 31; testimony at Thomas trial, 109; third and final gunshot, 47–48, 51, 110, 165, 169–70, 223, 233, 235; of Thomas, 73, 86, 102, 171, 175, 221, 223. *See also* murders of Kathy and J. B. Wiseman